MW01625719

LIKE A LITTLE DOG

LIKE A LITTLE DOG

Andy Warhol's Queer Ecologies

Anthony E. Grudin

UNIVERSITY OF CALIFORNIA PRESS

University of California Press
Oakland, California

Cataloging-in-Publication Data is on file at the Library of Congress.

ISBN 978-0-520-38357-9 (cloth : alk. paper)

Printed in China

30 29 28 27 26 25 24 23 22 21
10 9 8 7 6 5 4 3 2 1

For Wright Cronin

CONTENTS

ACKNOWLEDGMENTS

I AM DEEPLY grateful to the friends, family, and colleagues whose kindness nurtured this book. Particular thanks are due to Binta Ayofemi, Lamia Balafrej, Jessica Beck, Susan Bielstein, Josh Bongard, Alan Braddock, Steve Budington, Penelope Cray, Keri Cronin, Wright Cronin, Whitney Davis, Natasha Eaton, Stephen Eisenman, Jonathan Flatley, Pamela Fraser, Blake Gopnik, Meredith Hoy, Monica Juneja, Riad Kherdeen, Nadine Little, Jessica Moll, Peter Parshall, Archna Patel, Ananda Pellerin, AnnMarie Perl, Sugata Ray, Jordan Rose, Robert Slifkin, Gus Stadler, Shivani Sud, Michael Sundue, Justin Underhill, Carl Walesa, and the anonymous readers at University of California Press, who responded to these arguments at crucial stages; to Leora Black, Jess Bongard, Krista Buckley, Bethanne Cellars, Jeff Cellars, Sona Desai, Kyle Ferguson, Michaela Grudin, Nick Grudin, Robert Grudin, Ted Grudin, Michael Hermann, Jacob Holzberg-Pill, Cristina Huezo, Matt Jacobs, Hilary Maslow, Nate Moreau, Grace Oedel, Bill Racolin, Julie Rubaud, Uli Schygulla, Jeff Tonn, Laurel Waters, Morgan Waters, Rebecca Weisman, and Alison Williams, for their generosity and encouragement; and to Clio, Daphne, Jasmine, and Joyce Cellars, for all their joyous love.

Support for this project was provided by the Andy Warhol Foundation and by the Humanities Center at the University of Vermont. Early versions of some of these arguments appeared in Anthony E. Grudin, "Warhol's Animal Life," in *Criticism: A Quarterly for Literature and the Arts* 56, no. 3. Copyright © 2014. Wayne State University Press.

A NOTE ON TERMINOLOGY

THROUGHOUT THIS BOOK, I have used the problematic terms "nonhuman animals," and occasionally "animal" and "animals," in their most expansive sense, to include not only mammals, but fish, birds, and invertebrates.[1] I use the term "plants" in a similarly informal way to refer to organisms that photosynthesize nutrients and absorb water through their roots. I use the term "animality" to refer to a creaturely quality that might be seen to be shared across species lines, linking humans with other sentient beings. And I use the term "vegetal" to refer to qualities that might seem to be shared among plants and other living things. I rely on these flawed terms not in order to posit unified groups of radically disparate beings but instead to describe cultural worldviews that Warhol and his collaborators inherited and explored, since, as Christoph Cox reminds us, "there are no essential divisions in nature," and all "such boundaries can only ever be pragmatic choices, never ontological givens."[2]

INTRODUCTION

Warhol's Nonhuman Life

FEW TWENTIETH-CENTURY ARTISTS are more closely associated with the anti-ecological categories of technology and profit than Andy Warhol. Didn't he insist that art was completely commercial—no more than a commodity, like a can of soup, a bottle of soda, or even a form of currency? Hadn't he called his studios "factories," and infamously declared that he "wanted to be a machine," that he "love[d] plastic" and "want[ed] to be plastic?"[1] Wasn't his greatest innovation fundamentally technological: attempting to collapse all distinctions between mechanical reproduction and fine art? What better artist than Warhol, "the Henry Ford of a new form of capitalist art," to emblematize an age in which human technology and the capital that underwrites it threaten to destroy all formerly viable ecosystems, since, as he proclaimed, "making money is art, and working is art and good business is the best art"?[2] It stands to reason that Andy Warhol, whose mechanized style "is a tribute to the machine and its takeover of natural occurrences," might be the anti-ecological artist par excellence.[3]

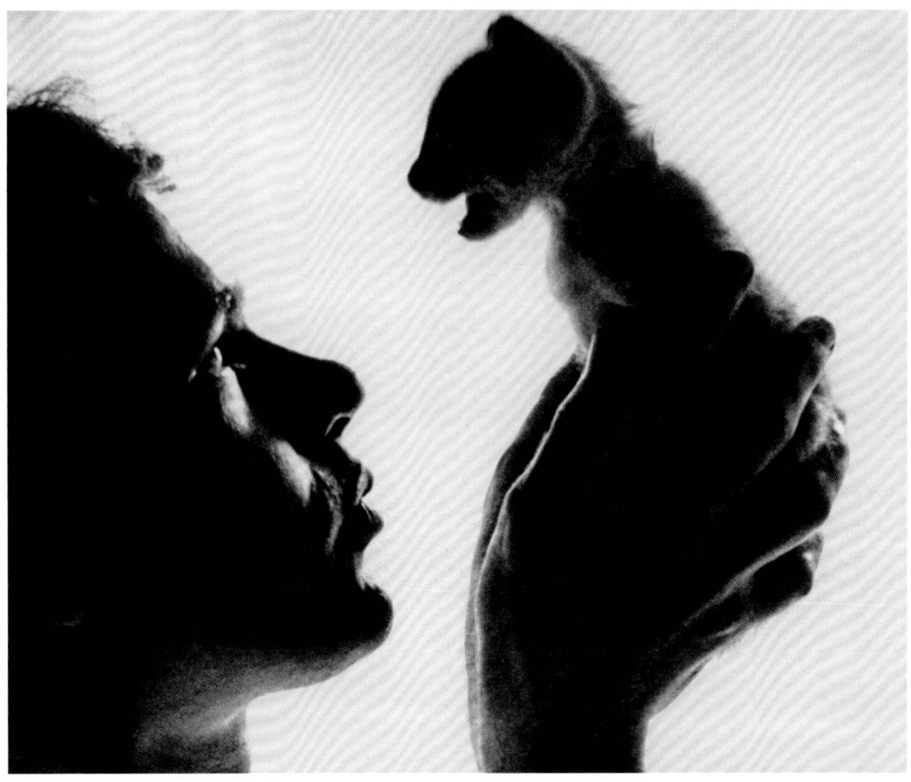

FIGURE 1
Edward Wallowitch, *Andy Warhol with Kitten,* c. 1957. Photo by Edward Wallowitch. ©2021 Paul Wallowitch. All Rights Reserved.

Against the grain of this common knowledge, this book argues that Warhol was a "biocentric" artist in Margot Norris's sense, fundamentally concerned with the related themes of anthropocentrism, animality, and nonhuman life.[4] (See figure 1.) These are central and persistent concerns in Warhol's work, problems that he examined from two main directions: questioning the prerogatives granted to humans over nonhuman life-forms, and exploring the expression of nonhuman spirits and perspectives.[5] In so doing, he disputed the traditional claim that culture distinguishes the human from the merely animal and vegetal, and anticipated the contemporary scientific consensus "that humans are not unique in possessing the neurological substrates that generate consciousness."[6] The preponderance of nonhuman life in Warhol's work is thus neither haphazard nor merely metaphorical; it is central to his redefinition of artistic theory and practice, and to his interests in technology and profitability. What's more, Warhol demonstrated a lifelong fascination with the erotic worlds of nonhuman life-forms, particularly as they related to queer forms of love and kinship and to the abject Other. For Warhol, the ultimate pornography would be animalistic or even vegetal: "If I had wanted to make a real sex movie

I would have filmed a flower giving birth to another flower. And the best love story is just two love-birds in a cage."[7]

None of this should be taken to mean, however, that Warhol ought to be celebrated as an ecological visionary, or a champion of anti-speciesism. Whereas he lived during an age of rapidly accelerating ecological devastation, and although he "seemed to care as much about animals . . . as about people," and could sometimes even empathize with the suffering of vegetal life, this book will demonstrate that Warhol's interactions with nonhuman life-forms were profoundly ambivalent and contradictory, imbued with all the tension and volatility conveyed by Nicole Shukin's concept of "animal capital."[8] This book will attempt to track the complexity of these interactions: the various and contradictory "rendering[s] of animal figures and animal flesh" that tend to characterize human-animal relations under capitalism, but also capitalism's increasing efforts to "economis[e] not only the striving of Homo sapiens but of other species as well."[9] Warhol's relationships with other life-forms were certainly marked by these tensions, vacillating between "'sympathetic' technologies of representation and 'pathological' technologies of control," among other ambivalent bonds and associations.[10] As we will see, this wild and unwieldy mélange is apparent from the beginning of Warhol's life, in the ways in which he was introduced to animals and their sexual and artistic reproduction, all the way to its end, when he came face to face with the possibility of extinction as a gay man living in the time of HIV/AIDS.

Along the way, this book will trace a variety of ways in which Warhol's artistic, personal, and imaginary interactions with nonhuman life-forms challenged "the discourse of the jungle": a popularized Darwinist-Freudian worldview that predominated in US culture during the early twentieth century.[11] This worldview imagined all life as being driven by narrowly evolutionary imperatives: "'naturally' violent in the name of survival, and heterosexual in the name of reproduction."[12] Warhol ought to be seen as a late addition to the list of cultural figures who resisted this imperialist version of biology—insisting in various ways that life cannot be reduced to this restrictive model. What's more, the scope of Warhol's investigations of an expanded vision of biology radically exceeded those of his predecessors, touching on strange and profound questions regarding a variety of behaviors that are difficult to reconcile with the evolutionary perspective, including the exuberant use and abuse of illicit drugs, sexuality that is not only nonprocreative but also physically hazardous, interspecies eroticism, and the production of shame.

There are at least three main layers, then, within Warhol's complex and contradictory relationship to nonhuman life-forms. First, a pervasive antihumanist effort to imagine art as an earthy and organic force: fundamentally interested rather than disinterested, imbued with appetite and desire at every node (artists, materials, themes, audiences), and thumbing its nose at almost every social and aesthetic convention.[13] Second, a recognition that the standard evolutionary understandings of appetite, with their emphasis on heterosexual reproduction and violence in the name of survival, would not accurately account for the complexity of organic life, desire, intoxication, and suffering, in all their various unpredictable and counterintuitive forms. And third, in great tension with these sympathetic moments, a propensity for the exploitation and domination of other life-forms in the service of profit and transgression. Despite his sympathy for and interest in nonhuman life, Warhol's interactions with other life-forms were in large part infected by the capitalist tendency to treat these lives as "natural resources," since capitalism is "profound[ly] contingent on nonhuman nature," and Warhol was (among many other things) a highly productive capitalist.[14]

The relationship between nonhuman life and the machine in Warhol's production is therefore far more complex than it would at first appear, and so is the interplay between sympathy and pathology. The first three chapters of this book trace the surprising ways in which Warhol's erotic and artistic interests in nonhuman life were cultivated by his mother, Julia Warhola; the force these interests exerted on the aberrant world of his Silver Factory; and the ways in which they stimulated his scandalous embrace of machinic, financial, and ecological processes in his artistic production. I argue that these unusual psychobiographical connections between mother, Factory, and nonhuman other—between shame, machine, and transgression—although rarely remarked by art historians, have long been visible, and that they deepen the relevance and complexity of Warhol's life and work. Drawing on a range of creative and theoretical precedents, the book's final two chapters investigate Warhol's two major late projects that explicitly advocated for animals facing extinction, demonstrating that this closer attention to precariousness and death in the time of the HIV/AIDS epidemic intensified many of the tensions explored in his earlier work.

Warhol's artistic production returned almost compulsively to the representation of nonhuman life-forms, to a degree that is unsurpassed among his contemporary peers. The work he produced during college, and afterward as an advertising illustrator, is laced with animal and vegetal figures—most prominently flowers, plants, cats, and dogs, but also birds, rabbits, fish, worms, butterflies, eels, snakes, and many others. Animal and vegetal figures remain prominent in his classic Pop paintings (lightly disguised as ingredients on the labels of many of the iconic soup cans), and they return with a vengeance in the *Cow Wallpaper* (1966) and the over ten thousand *Flowers* he produced over the course of his career. Animals appear frequently in his work on film—sometimes in cameos, sometimes in supporting roles, and sometimes as stars in their own right. The second reel of Warhol's 1965 film *Horse,* which predates Jannis Kounellis's *Untitled* (*12 Horses*) by four years and Marcel Broodthaers's *Interview with a Cat* by five, is composed of a thirty-three-minute long shot of a horse accompanied by its trainer, with a microphone raised to the horse's mouth. (See figure 2.)

But Warhol's interests in nonhuman life-forms extended well beyond these thematic boundaries. We learn from his diaries, interviews, and books that he was fasci-

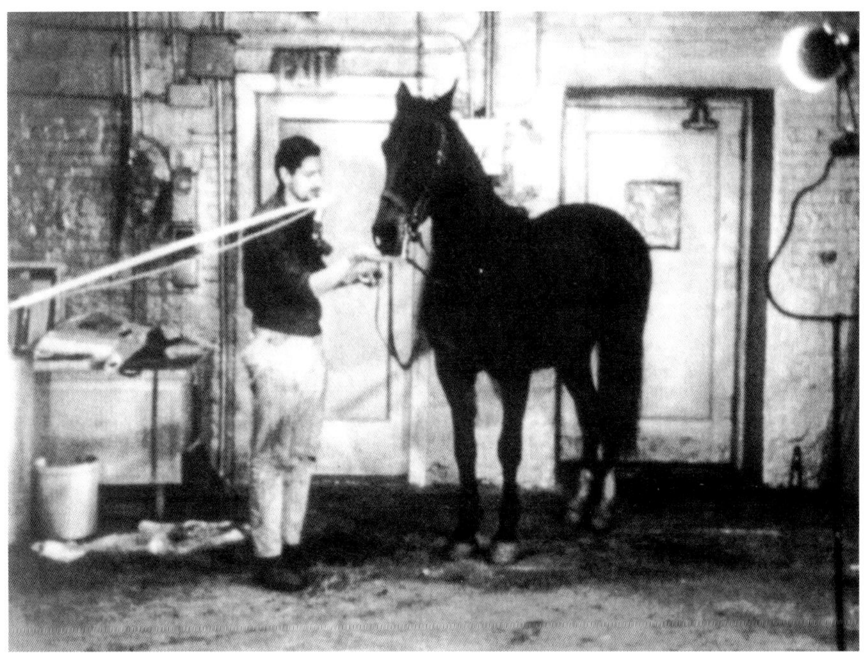

FIGURE 2
Still from *Horse* (Andy Warhol, 1965).

nated by the vulnerability of animal and vegetal life, and by the ways in which this vulnerability undermines anthropocentric hierarchies; by the queer possibilities posed by nonhuman and cross-species eroticism; by the collaborative, scavenging, amphetamine-fueled, sadistic, and masochistic swarm of energies gathered in the Silver Factory; by the regressive and animalistic pleasures of mimetically and indiscriminately "liking things"; and by the limitations and contradictions of aesthetic anthropocentrism—the idea that artistic creativity and receptivity distinguish human life from the animal- and vegetal-machines that grow from dirt and muck, and (supposedly) can only react and never truly respond. Warhol, of course, was constantly proclaiming his own inability to be anything more than reactive, anything more than a muckraking animal- or vegetal-machine making his way in a world ruled by humans, tracking and tracing the marks left by others.

From a humanistic perspective, there were also sinister overtones to Warhol's embrace of machinic production, and particularly to his enthusiasm for commodification and marketing. Humanism, as Achille Mbembe points out, had "understood that the human person (who the West mistook for the white man) was neither a thing nor an object . . . [nor] an animal or a machine."[15] With Warhol, we see the inklings of what Mbembe describes as a neoliberal worldview, in which "all these dikes collapse, one after the other. It is no longer certain that the human person is very distinct from the object, the animal, or the machine."[16] The intensity of Warhol's imaginative and artistic interactions with nonhuman life meant that both of these trajectories—the possibility of a new artistic biocentrism and the grim specter of a completely objectified and commodified world—could simultaneously be active in his work.

———

Warhol had an unusually vivid animal and vegetal life. He was preoccupied with the predicaments of nonhuman life-forms, and he often imagined his own life and art in creaturely or ecological terms. Others agreed. An early portrait by Roger Anliker, entitled *Mute Song,* depicted the young artist delicately holding a cheap toy bird—both figures in profile, beak to ear, as if Warhol were expecting the mechanical bird to sing to him. (See figure 3.) This would be among the first of many such cross-species portraits and self-portraits of the artist, including some in which the artist held flowers in front of his face, as if they could stand in for him. In 1962, Emile de Antonio described Warhol as "a super intelligent white rabbit."[17] Marcel Duchamp made a similar connection immediately upon meeting Warhol in 1966: "He looks like a Merino [sheep], a white rabbit with pink eyes."[18] David Bowie sensed a very different kind of creature: "I extended my hand and the guy retired, so I thought, 'The guy doesn't like flesh, obviously he's reptilian.'"[19] Kennedy Fraser thought he was a habitat unto itself: "His face was like a woodland creature's, under a stork's nest of hair."[20] Carol Blanchard apparently dubbed him "Warthole"; Valerie Solanas addressed him as "Toad."[21] Donald Newlove said that he had "the big, batting brown eyes of a querulous lemur," eyes that were "absolutely *strange*. . . . Almost never hav[ing] an emotion, only a gentleness."[22] Warhol's own passion for other life-forms was unequivocal: he worried repeatedly over the suffering of plants, and claimed to have "never met an animal I didn't like"; we'll see that there were exceptions, and that liking didn't always mean defending or cherishing, particularly when there was money to be made.[23]

———

In a previous book on Warhol's relationship to social class and egalitarianism, I traced the various purposes and implications of what Warhol's contemporaries called his "working-class" or "peasant mentality," which they associated with his alleged propensity to "[do] everything for money."[24] As Betty Asche Douglas, one of Warhol's only Black classmates at Carnegie Tech, argued, "There was an ambivalence of attitude at that particular moment in history, as to what degree one should celebrate rising above one's common lower-class background, and to what degree one should stay with it and celebrate it. Like Courbet . . . Andy wore his peasant heritage like a badge of honour. His use of the working-class vernacular was part of it."[25]

In many ways, my book could have been extrapolated from Douglas's insightful words: it argued that the "ambivalence" regarding class that she rightly sensed in their lifeworld necessarily infected the "peasant heritage" and "working-class vernacular" that Warhol deployed "like a badge of honour." As Douglas emphasized, Warhol

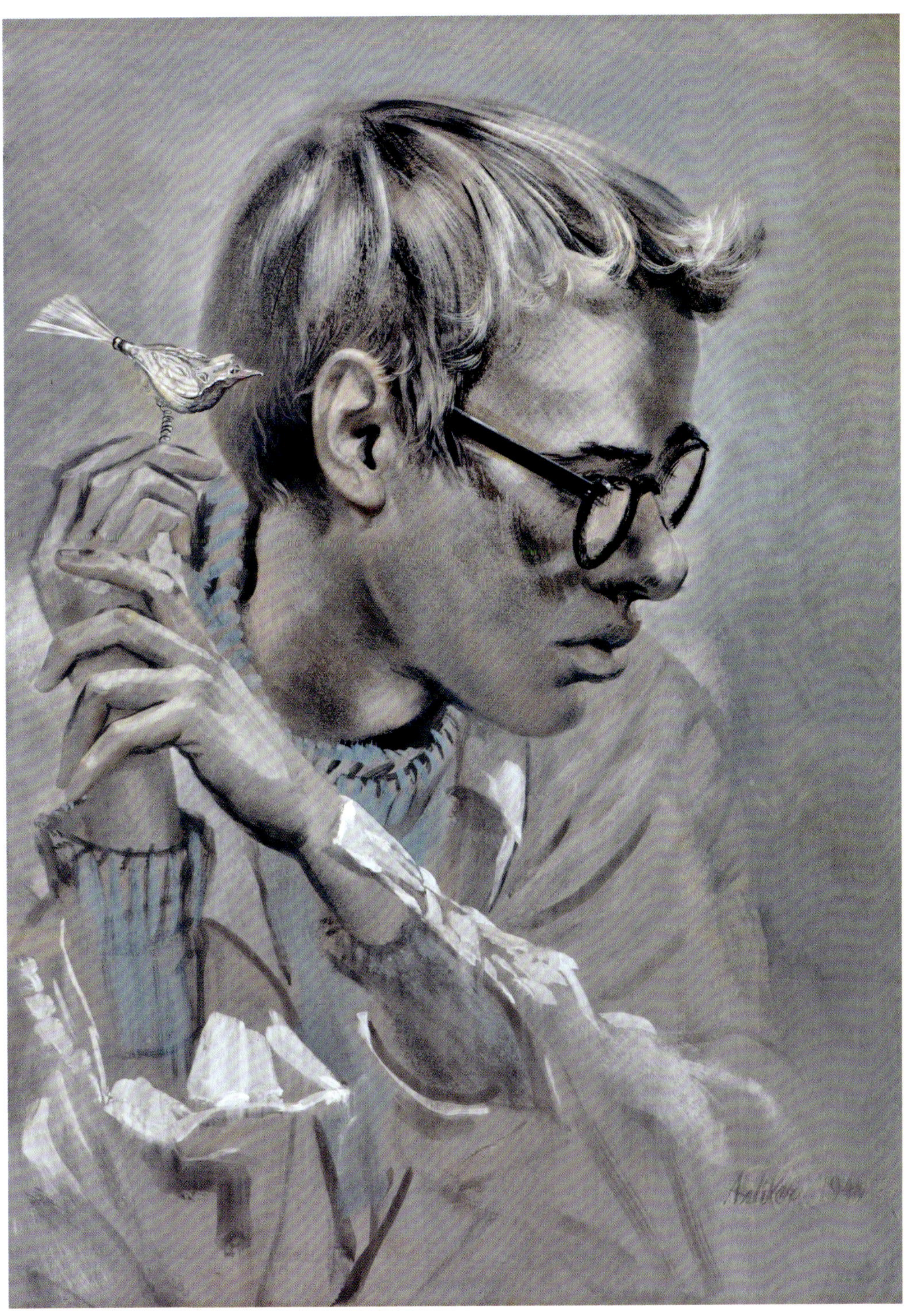

FIGURE 3

Roger Anliker, *Mute Song (Andy Warhola)*, 1949. Collection of Dale O. Roberts.

understood the power of these signs of class while also sensing that, in a society defined by economic deception and exploitation, this power would necessarily be strange and contradictory. A "working-class vernacular" could be simultaneously truthful and deceitful, for instance, since even as it recorded one person's class experience (which in Warhol's case changed drastically over time), it also marketed it to others who did not share it and who might hope to co-opt it in various ways. What's more, Warhol's "amateurish and vulgar" work hyperbolically embraced a stereotypically working-class interest in fame, success, and upward mobility that forms a red thread through his work.[26]

Working-class life was never a simple or heroic subject in Warhol's production, but it persisted throughout his career. In his final years, he was still searching for a way to address it: as he put it in a late book, "I wish somebody great would come along in public life and make it respectable to be poor again."[27]

Just as he was never a working-class activist, Warhol was by no means an exemplary environmentalist. If nonhuman life-forms have long been exploited by humans as a "zoo-proletariat," Warhol never managed to embrace revolution, or the "the emancipation of all instrumentalized living beings" that contemporary voices have championed.[28] Prior to the 1980s, the closest he came to environmental activism was agreeing to design a poster for the German Green Party in 1978, at Joseph Beuys's request. But crucially, in both contexts, Warhol explored some radically queer and egalitarian ideas that were practically unthinkable for most of his peers. In much the same way that his work records an unusual critical viewpoint on class and social inequity in America, it also provides novel and nuanced perspectives on the conceptually related problems of animal and vegetal life.

And yet, like his reflections on human egalitarianism, Warhol's imaginings of nonhuman life were typically expressed in a tragicomic tone, as if he understood them to be literally utopian—desirable but unattainable. This mood may be partly attributed to his own bodily limitations. Health problems rendered him especially vulnerable to the outdoors from an early age, a circumstance that Warhol and those around him recognized and ridiculed. When Beuys—a truly committed biocentric activist—convinced Warhol to endorse the Green Party, Bob Colacello teased him relentlessly for "turn[ing] purple" at the beach, losing his breath in the mountains, getting "itchy" in the woods.[29] Indeed, Warhol told an interviewer in 1980, "I think it's horrible to live."[30] The related problems of shame, death, transgression, desire, and advocacy in Warhol's investigations of nonhuman life are recurring themes in the chapters that follow.

Chapter 1, "'Like a Little Dog,'" tracks Warhol's animal and vegetal interests and interactions from his impoverished childhood in Pittsburgh, through the controversial work that he produced in college, to his extraordinarily successful first career as an advertising illustrator in New York. Warhol's life and work during these decades were densely populated with nonhuman life-forms: dogs, cats, plants, and chickens, but also mice, insects, worms, and various much more exotic living things. As his family struggled to bootstrap themselves out of a socioeconomic position that was widely viewed as bestial, Warhol chose to embrace animality—animal companions and animal desires—as an escape from the predicaments he encountered as a queer child with a problematic body, living in a homophobic world.[31] In the face of extreme economic, racial, sexual, and bodily insecurities, he turned to two main sources of solace: his mother, Julia, and the real and imaginary animals that were available to him. As it happens, these two refuges were closely linked: Julia administered Warhol's animals when they lived together, both during his childhood and during their decades of cohabitation in New York: drawing them, procuring them, feeding and cleaning up after them, breeding them, butchering and cooking them, disposing of them when they became inconvenient or profitable. In a variety of playful ways, Warhol and his mother experimented with the possibilities of overturning the hetropatriarchal hierarchies associated with anthropocentrism: hierarchies of abjection and propriety, of gender, of species, of creativity, authorship, and reproduction. In the process, they developed a fertile new approach to art and artistry, one that prioritized the traditionally animal and vegetal qualities of appetite and mechanicity over the humanistic priorities of disinterest and creativity. But they often did so under pressure, with Julia treating Andy as a surrogate daughter, husband, and animal whose transgressive productivity ultimately belonged to her. These early interests and interactions became central elements of Warhol's artistic self-fashioning, from which he would continue to draw over the course of his career.

Chapter 2, "Factory Badlands," investigates how animal and ecological themes, spirits, and figures remained central to Warhol's collaborative production as it transitioned into one of the most influential and iconic sites in postwar culture: the Silver Factory of the mid-1960s. While nonhuman life-forms remained active in Warhol's work during this period, they became less obviously central as his attention shifted to mass media and commodity forms. But Warhol's Silver Factory also encouraged another form of animality, only recently recognized by scientists as a nearly universal aspect of animal existence: intoxication, which Warhol and his collaborators imagined as a technique for becoming animal.[32] This drug-fueled experimentalism was embodied and chronicled by three of Warhol's most important Silver Factory collaborators: Billy Name, Mary Woronov, and Ronald Tavel. Name modeled intoxicated animality in a variety of ways: he was a consummate recycler (what Warhol called "a good trasher"), profoundly collaborative, and (fueled by ungodly quantities of methamphetamine) almost superhuman in his speed and endurance.[33] Woronov, in her remarkable memoirs, chronicled the Factory as a pharmaceutical menagerie, bestial in its sadistic and masochistic appetites and interactions—which were also directly explored in Tavel's screenplays and the films that resulted from them, like *Horse*. In all of these ways, the Silver Factory provided Warhol with a fascinating laboratory for ecological/

artistic production, a model that he could administer and admire but never fully embody. He would profit from the transgressive productivity of these factory animals, much as his mother did from him, even as the Factory's primary commodity—film (photographic and cinematic)—directly relied on the residue of animal slaughter: gelatin, what the Kodak corporation called its "Image Recorder."[34]

Chapter 3, "Machines, Animal and Vegetal," proposes that Warhol's signature commitment to all things machinic ought to be understood as deeply inflected by his interest in nonhuman life, and more specifically by the ways in which animals and plants have traditionally been demeaned in Western thought as fundamentally mechanical and subordinate. Western anthropocentrism defines these life-forms as subhuman, driven by instinct and appetite, unreflective and mechanistic. Where "the human" writes, speaks, and creates, "animals" and "plants" leave only traces. This longstanding prejudice forms a powerful component of various ideologies—including patriarchy, classism, racism, ageism, and homophobia—that rely upon invented hierarchies of species and type to justify themselves, with "the animal" always lurking near the bottom of each scale, and "the plant" even lower than that.[35] Warhol challenged this tradition from two directions. First, he persistently wondered over the capacity of other life-forms, both individually and in networks, to exceed the merely mechanical in their experiences of affection, desire, death, language, memory, and aesthetic production and reception. Second, with at least equal persistence and in a similar range of areas, he explored and emphasized his own animality, and even his own links to the vegetal—his inability as a "human" to transcend his earthly origins. Across a wide variety of media, Warhol seemed more interested in tracing than creating, in the automatic rather than the thoughtful or planned, in appetite rather than disinterest. At the limit, Warhol didn't just prioritize animals and plants in his art; he became an animal- or vegetal-machine to those around him. In the process, he attempted to reconcile two of his most important edicts—his drive "to be a machine" and his sense that Pop Art is "liking things"—with his concurrent awareness that these ambitions marked his work as "queer." When his public efforts to communicate this queerness were censored, he turned to the strange possibilities of ecological, vegetal, and mimetic production, defined by collaboration, reuse, and hoarding rather than the humanist and capitalist ideals of individuality, creativity, and exchange. In each of these areas, becoming an animal- or vegetal-machine allowed Warhol to celebrate his instincts without worrying about their social acceptability in a homophobic world.

The fourth and fifth chapters form a pair focusing on Warhol's only two major projects that can be described as explicitly environmentalist. Produced in collaboration with Rupert Jasen Smith, they were intended to draw attention to the plight of species facing extinction: *Endangered Species* (1983), a portfolio of silkscreen prints, mostly of charismatic megafauna; and *Vanishing Animals* (1986), a series of silkscreen prints of mostly lesser-known creatures, some of which were used to illustrate a book by the scientist Kurt Benirschke. Although they have rarely been discussed by scholars, these projects epitomize Warhol's shifting attitudes toward animal suffering and political advocacy, and his unusually expansive, if inconsistent, empathy toward animal life. While *Endangered Species* and *Vanishing Animals* have typically been treated as interchangeably forgettable, chapter 4, "'Philosophy of the Fragile,'" will show that they represent disparate approaches to an explicitly advocatory form of artistic production, and that the second series broaches a resonant collection of queer themes.

Chapter 5, "Queer Beauty and Extinction," concentrates on a specific set of prints produced for the *Vanishing Animals* project: those depicting an okapi (*Okapia johnstoni*) dam and calf. As Benirschke's text emphasized, these extraordinary animals faced grave challenges when held in captivity. Provided with food, water, and security, and therefore without any competing threats or distractions, a dam would incessantly clean her calf's anus and rectum with her tongue, often to the point of rectal prolapse and lethal infection. The okapi prints, completed the year before Warhol's death, seem to have allowed him and Smith to return to some of the strange and challenging questions regarding animality, the abject, mortality, maternity, productivity, shame, taste, and retribution that had long troubled his career. In this regard, they form a constellation with related works by Leonardo da Vinci, Sigmund Freud, Julia Kristeva, Alfred Hitchcock, Michel Foucault, Toni Morrison, Judith Butler, and Ocean Vuong, and constitute one of the most sustained and provocative investigations of queer sexuality in Warhol's oeuvre.

The book's conclusion, "The Python Priestess," proposes one additional animal Warhol: the snake. Across his work, his career, and his personal life, Warhol explored and embodied a variety of serpentine qualities, including those catalogued by Aby Warburg in his research on the Hopi serpent ritual—camouflage, resurrection, unexpected strength and venom, phallic presence—but also others linking snakes to neoliberal individualism and queer ecologies. These serpentine qualities, widely remarked in positive and negative ways by Warhol's friends and acquaintances, are perhaps his most enigmatic link to animal otherness.

In his 1985 book *America*, cowritten with Craig Nelson, Warhol lamented television's tendency to provoke frustratingly inaccessible dreams in its audience. Unlike movies, which Warhol described as fundamentally unrealistic and thus harmless, television offered images of life that *seemed* to be attainable for its viewers. The fact that these images remained unattainable made television a deeply mendacious and disappointing experience: "People with television dreams are really disappointed with everything in their lives."[36]

In my work on Warhol and social class, I thought of this verdict as something like a foundational thesis for Warhol's understanding of US culture. Television, he seemed to be arguing, was like Lacan's mirror stage writ large: a series of experiences that installed a fundamental frustration in the viewing subject, who would always be striving to approximate an ideal that seemed realistic but could never actually be attained.[37] These powerful and frustrated dreams would become formative for the phenomenology of US culture: its ever-renewing and ever-profitable appeal, and the forever-deferred satisfactions it promises. Unlike movies, television dreams were reinforced through regular repetition, the same time every week, "like learning something by having it drummed into their heads over and over."[38]

At the time, I hadn't started considering Warhol as a biocentric artist, and thus didn't think much about the lines that followed. Now they are difficult to ignore:

> [S]ome people have found a way to satisfy their TV dreams. They have pets, and having pets is just like having a television family. TV parents never have any real problems with their children, and owners don't have too much trouble with pets. Pets make a family that's always loyal, will do just about anything to make you happy, never criticize, love you till the end of the earth, and never expect much in return. You can get a cat that calls to you every morning when you go out the door, just like a TV mother; a dog that always has that sad, cute face when you scold it, just like TV children; a pet that comes running to the door all excited just because you're coming home, like a TV wife; and one that sulks in the corner when it doesn't get its way, just like a TV husband or father. Most of the time one pet can even do all these things. So even if you're sort of poor, but you have all these television hopes and dreams, pets are really the answer.[39]

Just as the previous section of *America* seemed to sum up Warhol's theory of US cultural malaise, this section responded with a comforting proposal regarding the possibility of the pet as an accessible solution. Pets, Warhol argued, could solve these problems by providing a family that replicates the pleasures and satisfactions of a television family, providing loyalty, cheerfulness, acceptance, love, generosity—all the feelings Warhol apparently missed in his own family. Pets could also fulfill each family member's role, becoming the mother who says good-bye, the children who are "sad [and] cute" when scolded, the wife who greets, and the "husband or father" who mopes. These roles are revealing: the female adult is split into two loving roles (mother and wife), while the male takes the form of one sullen and withdrawn figure. The pet child is reminiscent of the regressive behavior Warhol's friends noticed in him when he was near his mother, with the "sad, cute face when you scold it." What's more, by the section's conclusion, Warhol is claiming that one pet can take on all of these various roles for economy's sake, "if you're sort of poor."

With its "wife" and "husband," the passage is at least superficially heteronormative, as was television in the 1980s. But, by posing the adoption of a pet or multiple pets as a satisfying alternative to the frustrating realities of the heterosexual nuclear family, Warhol was sketching out the possibility of pets as "companions in queerness" who can satisfyingly replicate the pleasures of a television family while bypassing its heter-

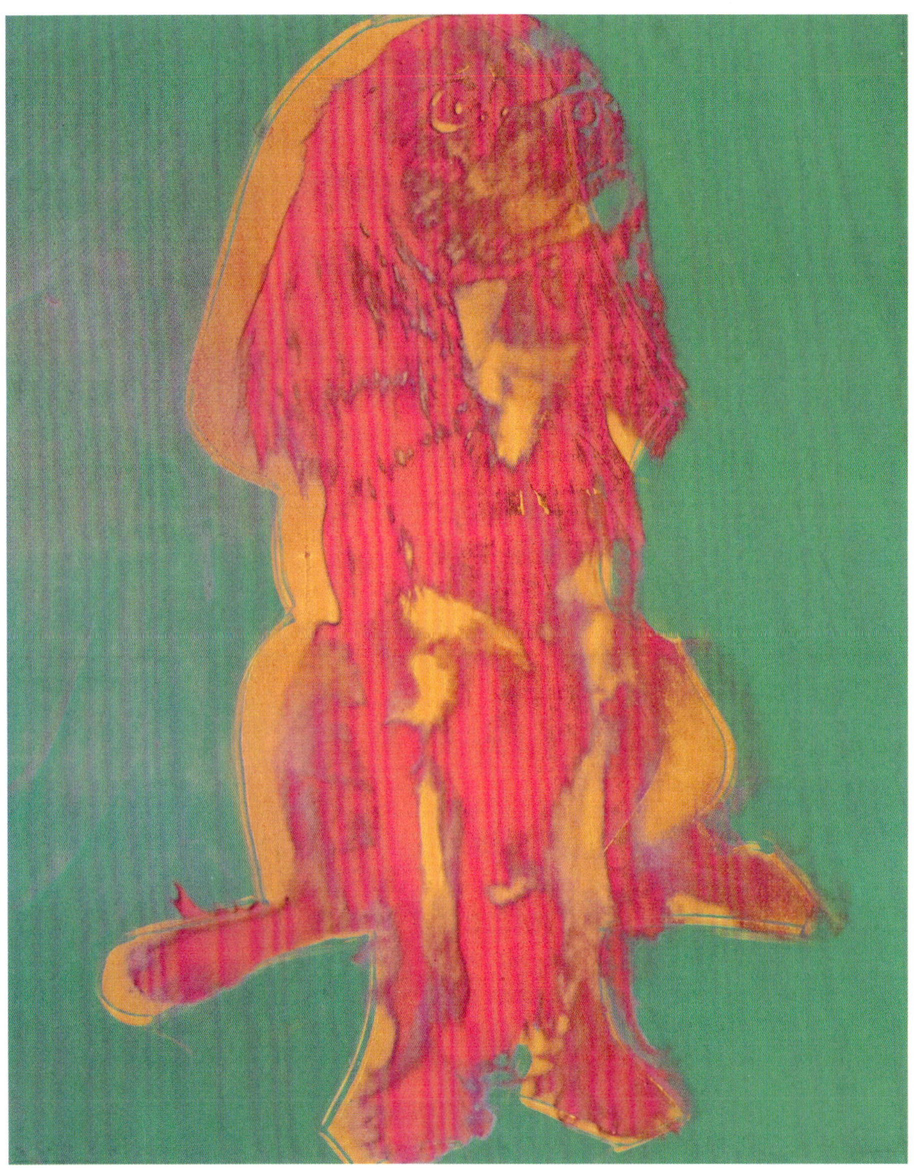

FIGURE 4
Andy Warhol, *Cats and Dogs (Pom)*, 1976. The Andy Warhol Museum, Pittsburgh; Founding Collection, Contribution The Andy Warhol Foundation for the Visual Arts, Inc. © 2022 The Andy Warhol Foundation for the Visual Arts, Inc./Licensed by Artists Rights Society (ARS), New York.

onormativity.[40] At the limit, one pet could fill the disparate roles of husband, wife, mother, father, and child, sidestepping all the messy requirements of human romance, exogamy, and reproduction. They would be "simple but reliable 'affection machine[s].'"[41] During the mid-1970s, Warhol had seemingly commemorated this perspective by expanding his profitable business in society portraiture to include paintings of his wealthy patrons' pets, granting these dogs and cats the same focus and attention that their owners expected. (See figure 4.) He practiced by painting portraits—or still lifes—of taxidermized animals.[42]

Warhol's book *America* contains a chapter called "Natural History." In it is the section on television dreams, illustrated exclusively with pictures of pets: a bichon frise alone in the back seat of a Mercedes; a pug on a desk posed with a Marlboro between its lips; Warhol's dachshunds, Archie and Amos, startled by the flash of his camera; a dapper man kneeling down to touch a parrot. *America*'s pets seem to be enjoying the pampering their humans bestow in their efforts at self-soothing—"getting into the spirit of a neoliberal order of things which grants them opportunities to flourish, in exchange for . . . their souls."[43] Tellingly, however, the passage on pets is juxtaposed with a very different photograph: an eerie Warhol snapshot of an anatomical model—male, with exposed musculature and, in the right leg, bone—arm upraised as if hailing the viewer or a cab. As is typically the case in Warhol, the possibility of animal/human intimacy is accompanied by an acknowledgment of the fundamental vulnerability of the biological human body—the precariousness it shares with nonhuman life-forms. These twin themes of biological precariousness and the possibilities of a queer animal or vegetal family—whose modes of relation "cannot be determined in advance"—persisted throughout Warhol's animal life.[44]

For his part, despite the fact that critics sometimes described him as being "obsessed" with "human presence" and "the human face and body," Warhol was painfully aware that he tended to see nonhuman life-forms everywhere, in himself and others; that they dominated his imagination; and that this tendency would be held against him as a limitation by many.[45] Asked by an interviewer what he saw when he looked at his own *Rorschach* paintings, he responded, "All I would see would be a dog's face or something like a tree or a bird or a flower. Somebody else could see a lot more."[46]

1

"LIKE A LITTLE DOG"

IN A VARIETY OF WAYS, Warhol's childhood, adolescence, and young adulthood demonstrate a persistent willingness to undermine the desirability and attainability of what Donna Haraway called "human exceptionalism," with its affiliated models of artistic production and reception, and to embrace his own animality—his implication in a transgressive and abject ecology.[1] Warhol was born into a lifeworld that disparaged him as the distinctively queer and sickly offspring of a poor, "ethnic," and therefore subhuman family in America's most economically stratified city. As the queer outsider in an already marginalized family, his status relative to white heteronormative humanism took the form of a double negative.[2] His childhood nicknames were the doglike "Spot" and the reindeer-themed "Andy the Red-Nosed Warhola."[3] Like his brothers and parents, Andy would pursue social acceptance through hard work and upward mobility, but unlike them, he would repeatedly reject normative standards of behavior, instead proposing what Kathryn Bond Stockton has called "an interval of animal"—a being-like or being-with nonhuman animals that could

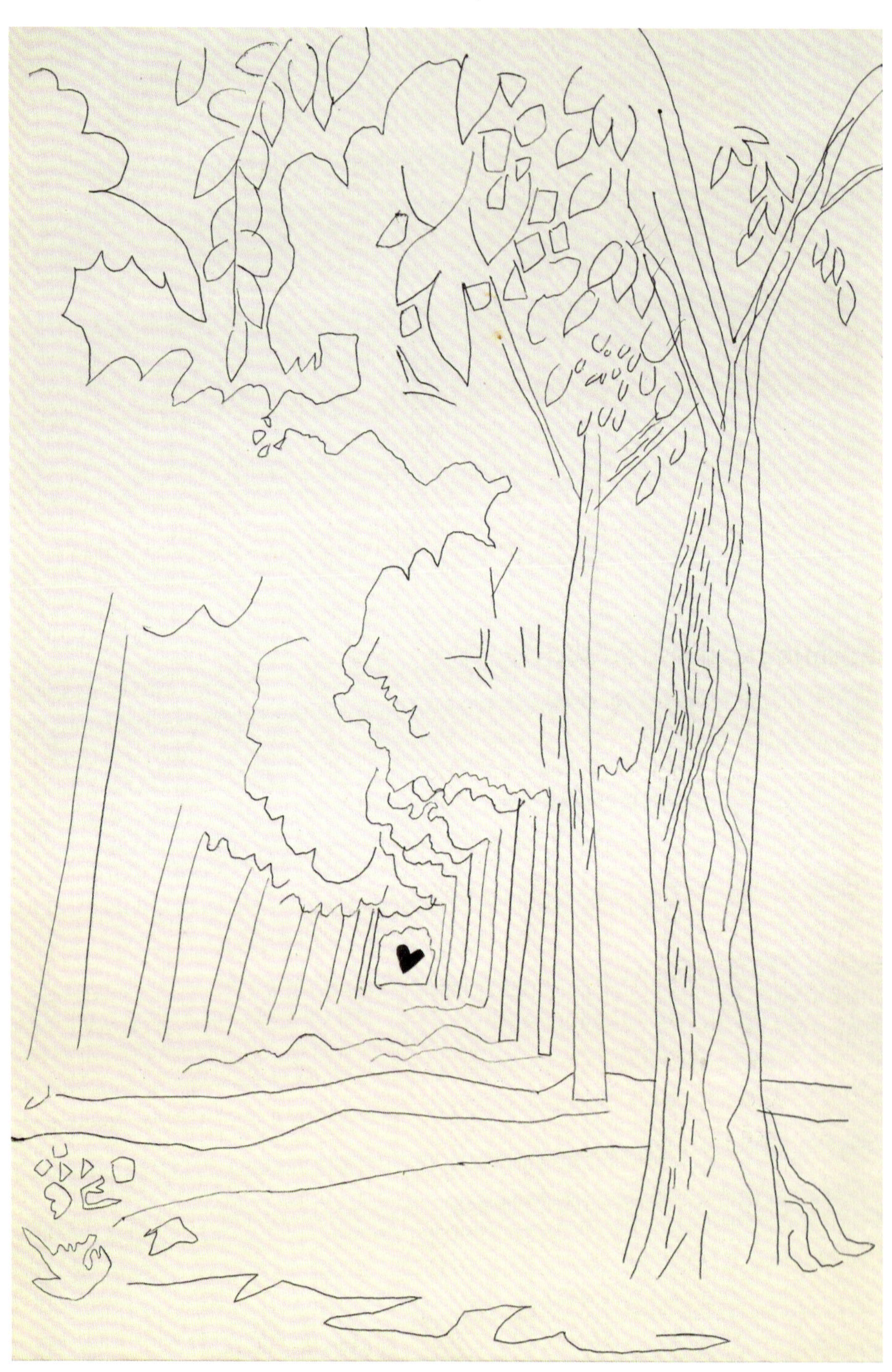

FIGURE 5

Andy Warhol, *Landscape with Heart,* c. 1956. The Andy Warhol Museum, Pittsburgh; Founding Collection, Contribution The Andy Warhol Foundation for the Visual Arts, Inc.

serve as a "vehicle for the child's strangeness," providing a "companion in queerness" in the face of social and familial approbation.[4] These intervals—which were often explicitly transgressive, and would sometimes take ecological forms as well—remained prominent throughout Warhol's life, as he continued to navigate a lifeworld that denigrated his socioeconomic background, bodily appearance, and erotic perspective. (See figure 5.)

The first section of this chapter traces the possible contributing factors to these animal and ecological intervals during Warhol's childhood—a period during which his life was rich with creaturely and vegetal interactions, but of which we have limited documentary evidence. The second and third sections focus on various documented and imagined ecological intervals from Warhol's years as a college student and advertising illustrator during the second half of the 1940s and the 1950s, respectively. In college, his direct exposure to nonhuman life seems to have waned, but animality became notably prominent in his paintings. And, during his years working as an illustrator, nonhuman life-forms again became prominent in his world, while taking on a centrality in his work that remains striking to this day.

CHILDHOOD AND ADOLESCENCE

Frailty, maternal-filial overinvestment, queerness, and animality seem to have been closely intertwined in Warhol's persona from an early age. Opportunities for animal and vegetal interaction were frequent, various, and intense: Warhol was surrounded by nonhuman life at home and at school in a way that would be uncommon for working-class children in the urban United States today. He tended an "award-winning flower garden" in his family's yard, along with a rabbit hutch, a pet chicken on the front porch, a cat until he was nine, and then a dog named Lucy, after Lucille Ball.[5] The science classroom at his elementary school housed an impressive variety of creatures, including lizards and young alligators, as well as an aquarium, and he practiced drawing by making observational sketches of these animals and of plants in nearby parks and conservatories.[6] As we will see, however, his ecological interactions and identifications were not exclusively positive. Warhol's childhood world was profoundly impoverished and precarious, and the animals that populated this world suffered as a result. They were kept in cages or the basement and not infrequently abused or killed. As Warhol's brother John remembered, "Me and Andy used to keep a chicken on the front porch as a pet till my mother killed it for soup"—an early resonance for the famous Campbell's chicken noodle soup cans that would bring Warhol fame years later.[7] Looking back on this period, he would confide to a friend that "as a child he always felt like a little dog"—a striking claim, since his childhood dog had been beaten until it became too vicious to live with humans.[8] In college he would commemorate this image in a remarkable painting.

Judged by its class and ethnicity, Warhol's family barely qualified as human at the time of his birth. The extreme disparities in wealth that characterized Pittsburgh during Warhol's childhood, which overlapped with the onset of the Great Depression, were often framed in terms of the human/animal dichotomy. As H.L. Mencken put it, "Here was wealth beyond computation . . . and here were human habitations so abominable that they would have disgraced a race of alley cats."[9] Warhol was born into these "abominable" conditions and would be branded by them for the rest of his life—by himself and by others. Misrecognized as "Polacks" or "Hunkies," his family fell into the category of "human draft animal[s] whose brawn could be enlisted to carry out the designs of the Anglo-Saxon intellect."[10] A contemporary foreman divided his list of accidents into two categories: "five men and twelve hunkies."[11] And yet, as Gopnik points out, in combination with his family's upward mobility, the obscurity of Warhol's Mikovan, or Carpatho-Rusyn, nationality allowed him to at least partially disidentify from these stereotypes—to embrace them as a style, rather than an inheritance.[12]

Within the context of this socioeconomic and ethnic dehumanization, Warhol was swiftly singled out as less masculine than his burly brothers and father—"a mother's boy" and "a sissy little crybaby."[13] The acting out that resulted may have been the first appearance of his lifelong transgressive avant-gardism—an early effort to turn rejection and discomfort into style. The Warholas' landlord's son remembered toddler Andy as "a holy terror" who intentionally urinated on him while they were standing on the family's front porch.[14] As his brother Paul later reported, he "picked up some bad language when he was about three. . . . We'd go to a relative's place and Andy'd say some of these things and it wasn't nice. It was really embarrassing."[15] These willful disruptions of proper human behavior carried animalistic connotations: compare a "wild and defiant" six-year-old "working-class" patient of Donald Winnicott's who "stamped and spat and cursed . . . just like a wild animal."[16] Warhol's intensely territorializing urination—effectively marking the building's owner as having crossed the boundaries of his family's space—only bolsters these associations. His precocious embrace of animality and the abject provided a glimpse of the power of the animal or ecological interval, the swerve out of human decorum that could captivate and enrage onlookers. To Warhol's family's chagrin, not even corporal punishment could curtail these transgressions of the bounds of propriety: "The more you smacked him the more he said it, the worse he got."[17] In the face of these challenges, and with his father mostly absent, Andy "turned to his mother for protection" from his relatives and peers.[18]

This disturbing disciplinary logic—in which bad behavior and corporeal punishment become both sexualized (through Andy's embrace of transgression) and mutually reinforcing—linked Andy to his childhood dog, all the more so since they both endured traumatic experiences in the family basement.[19] At the age of five, Andy had watched a "funny kid" being forced to give a boy head in this basement, surrounded by other boys. He would later tell William Burroughs that this sight of childhood abuse had been his first exposure to sex, and that he "never understood what it meant."[20] Four years later, Warhol's family brought home a puppy—half Chow, half

Dalmatian—to "replace" the family cat.[21] Andy's brothers and a friend of theirs would bring the "loveable mutt" down to the basement, where they would "take out their suppressed anger by kicking it around."[22] Ultimately, Warhol's brothers and their friend indirectly tortured the puppy to death: "When the dog got bigger, it became so vicious nobody in the family could go near it except [the boys' mother] Julia. . . . Eventually they had to get rid of it."[23] Like their younger brother, the dog turned to Julia for help; unlike him, Lucy was expendable. In both basement instances, Warhol occupied a position that was precariously close to that of the victimized body: strange and marked as a sissy, like the "funny kid"; smaller and weaker than his brothers, and beaten by them, like the puppy. Within the confines of this subterranean fraternal world, a space of pronounced decomposition and decay, the queer animal frailness of Warhol, Lucy, and the "funny kid" was shown to be simultaneously desired and detested. Lucy would not be the last queer and tortured dog that Warhol took under his wing.

Warhol's childhood was also marked by a series of challenging and unusual physical maladies that left him unusually desperate for allies. The list is daunting: at two, his eyes began to swell up. His mother would bathe them daily in boric acid.[24] At four, he broke his dominant arm; the injury went undiagnosed and untreated for two months, until someone finally noticed that "it had a pronounced curve in it" and took him to the doctor to have it rebroken and reset.[25] At eight, he had scarlet fever, which apparently progressed into rheumatic fever (a disease linked to poverty) two years later, and then Sydenham's chorea (Saint Vitus' Dance). This last condition manifested itself in physical shaking, which led to abuse at school, since, as his best friend remembered, "[t]hey always picked on the frail kids."[26] Soon, Warhol was "slurring his speech, touching things nervously with shaking hands, fumbling, and [having] difficulty sitting still."[27] A doctor was finally summoned, and Warhol was confined to bed for a month.

Julia moved Andy's bed into the dining room and dedicated herself to his recovery. Having already survived six of her fourteen siblings, lost her first child (who also suffered from convulsions) at thirty-three days, and endured severe trauma during World War I—when Russian and German troops fought in her village and she found skulls in the fields "like large white mushrooms"—Julia would come to rely upon Andy for comfort.[28] She doted on him all day and slept next to him in bed at night; the difficult relationships with men and boys that characterized his life outside of the home were replaced by her attention. One biographer describes this bed rest as "a golden time in Warhol's childhood."[29] Animals, movie stars, and candy—three of Warhol's ongoing obsessions—seem to have been central to Julia's recovery program. He acquired his first camera, a Baby Brownie Special that cost $1.25, and "his brothers . . . built him a darkroom in the basement fruit cellar"—perhaps as penance for the violence and abuse that had been doled out there.[30] Julia brought Andy comic books, coloring books, and magazines, moved the family radio into his room, and "[drew] colorful pictures of cats and other animals for him" while they listened to the radio, rewarding him with chocolate each time he finished coloring a page.[31] For Julia, appetite, creative production, and natural beauty went hand in hand: she would cut tin cans into flowers and sell them door-to-door in "the better sections of towns" to supplement her income.[32] His brothers felt he was exaggerating his illness in order to spend more time with her. The "mother's boy" stigma would soon become a prominent element of his "practices of self-fashioning," interwoven with his interest in animality and transgression.[33]

After four weeks of bed rest it was, his family decided, time for him to return to school; Andy resisted. John Elachko, a neighboring undertaker trainee who stood in as a paternal authority when necessary, tried to enforce the decision, pulling him kicking and screaming toward the street: "Andy tried to kick him . . . and then [Elachko] . . . just held his arms and legs and forced him and Andy's crying and trying to break away."[34] This altercation—in which a funereal father figure attempted to separate mother and son—triggered a relapse, and Warhol spent another month in bed. These various childhood ailments may have heightened Warhol's sense of his own animal embodiment, what Cary Wolfe calls "the physical exposure to vulnerability and mortality that we suffer because we, like animals, are embodied beings"—a quality he remained particularly attuned to throughout his life.[35] His family felt he was becoming vegetal as well, "like a clinging vine to Julia," and he was "accorded the position of an eccentric invalid who had to be treated with special care."[36] This seems also to have reinforced suspicions regarding Warhol's queerness. A family friend at the time said that Andy "was the daughter [Julia] never had. . . . We thought he was a little sissy."[37]

By the time Warhol was a teenager, his new sister-in-law had conclusively pigeonholed him as "a queer," and therefore inhuman or unearthly: "It came to me whenever he would wave his hand, that he was from another world—you know what I mean?"[38] Adolescence would bring a range of distressing skin problems, including severe acne, vitiligo, and rosacea, all of which must have served as painful reminders of Warhol's most secret and scandalous skin malfunction: a group of "very prominent hemangiomas . . . chiefly on the scrotum" that "looked like little collections of rubies, lots of them" and apparently had been "present since birth."[39] Warhol's long-term physician surmised that they caused him a great deal of bodily and sexual shame. He seems to have actively projected this shame onto others: a high school classmate assumed that Warhol's shyness marked the two of them as "about the shortest-hung studs in the shower," where Warhol "would point at him and say, 'Hee hee hee hee hee hee'" and "'euuuughh . . . euuuuughh . . . euggghhh.'"[40] In this instance, Warhol processed shame like a small child or Winnicott's "wild animal," using giggles and grunts instead of words.[41]

Warhol's father died of tubercular peritonitis in 1942, when he was fourteen. Andy's brothers suspected that the hospital staff had been more interested in running tests on their father than in treating him—a plausible suspicion given the subhuman stereotypes attached to their ethnicity and class.[42] In keeping with their religious traditions, the family kept his open casket in their living room, where Andy and Julia had slept, for three days. Andy refused to view the corpse, "hid[ing] under the bed upstairs" and then begging to stay at a relative's house because he was "frightened to sleep in the house with a body."[43] When his family returned from the funeral, a cousin of Andy's noted that Andy "was playing outside in the street. He didn't take it seriously."[44]

In refusing to face his father's death, Warhol was again adopting a hyperbolically animalistic position, and failing a specifically human responsibility, since animals and plants have long been held by anthropocentric thought "to be incapable of an authentic relation to death."[45] Something of this quality is visible in the photograph of the Warholas taken after the funeral, with Andy front and center, awkwardly obscuring the figure behind him, her two hands firmly gripping his upper arms as if to hold him back from running wild. Warhol's increasingly close relationship with his mother would have raised similar alarms with regard to the incest taboo, which, as Sharon Patricia Holland argues, "provides a neat separation between the human and the animal"—not to mention the human and the vegetal.[46] Already his mother's surrogate daughter after his sister's early death, Warhol became her surrogate husband as well; Julia would tell Warhol's brother that "she didn't think she would have made it without Andy."[47] Despite the threats posed by the neighboring undertaker's apprentice, the traditional oedipal family seemed to be at risk of collapse as Andy repeatedly refused to "grow out of" his regressive, animalistic behavior and his attachment to his mother.

Two years later, the Warholas were again hit with devastating news: Julia was diagnosed with colon cancer. A doctor informed the family that she had only a 50 percent chance of survival and recommended an experimental new treatment: a colostomy. Julia accepted the treatment without fully understanding it. She spent three weeks in the hospital and then refused to return to have the colostomy bag replaced with tubing, relying on a bag for the rest of her life.[48] Warhol seems to have developed a lifelong fear of hospitals in the wake of his parents' illnesses. And with good reason, one could argue: in both cases, hospital staff appear to have treated his parents as mere biological entities—"bare life," in Giorgio Agamben's terms—with little if any thought given to them as speaking or thinking subjects.[49] This seems to have been another dimension of Warhol's capacity for ecological empathy and identification: he recognized that, in the medical context, the line between human and nonhuman life was not as bright as it often appeared to be. His fears in this regard would prove well-founded.

Reviewing this childhood history, one might wonder whether Warhol's interest in and identification with nonhuman life corresponded—at least on a performative level—to a failed abjection from the overwhelming closeness of his mother. As Kelly Oliver has noted, these categories are closely linked in Julia Kristeva's theory of abjection, since abjection encompasses differentiation from both mother and animal: "those fragile states where man strays on the territories of *animal*" and "our earliest attempts to release the hold of *maternal* entity even before existing outside of her." [50] The "primal repression" of achieving separation from one's mother is culturally coded as vanquishing one's own animality, and thus advancing from the semiotic realm of drives to the symbolic realm of language and laws.[51] "The abject"—the biologically vital zone of excreta, decomposition, and decay—then becomes debased as "a space of contagion" subject to violence and repulsion but also captivation: "[f]ascination and rejection at the same time."[52] It underwrites every subject both historically and physically, and thus always threatens to return no matter how deeply it is repressed.[53] The political implications of this repression are profound, since, as Judith Butler and others have shown, the abject can be projected onto a range of "others"—subjects who have been marginalized on the basis of class, gender, ethnicity, sexuality, age, or ability—as well as the vast and disparate range of individual creatures categorized as subhuman "animals" or "lifeforms."[54] Of course, as Imogen Tyler and others have pointed out, the misogyny that permeates Kristeva's story needs to be recognized as historical and cultural rather than permanent and universal—as it appears to be for Kristeva.[55]

From this perspective, Warhol's hyperbolically close relationship with his mother strikingly correlates with his pronounced unwillingness to distance himself from the animal drives and ecological life he observed around him—his unwillingness to embrace the role of a civilized, speaking subject distinguished in part by a "disgust" with animality and "body excretions."[56] Julia's lifelong use of a colostomy bag would have exacerbated these associations, as might have the general absence of Andy's father (described by another son as a "shadowy figure"), who would be expected in Kristeva's schema to break up the bond between child and mother.[57] Warhol made a show of fighting neither battle: forgoing independence and boundaries; embracing bodily excretions and maternal and animal dependencies; prioritizing drives over language and rules, in himself and in others. Although they originated at what Rebecca Wanzo calls "[t]he nexus of abjection and precarity," in Warhol's work and life these refusals were distinctively performative—far more actively cultivated than they were passively absorbed.[58] Andy and Julia would both profit handsomely from these queer strategies, even as they consistently enraged—and quietly titillated—the figures of law and order who condemned them. In this respect, Andy and Julia participated in the political project described by Butler: "resignifying the abjection of homosexuality into defiance and legitimacy"; but they did so with great ambivalence, particularly since Julia seems to have consistently overlooked or denied her son's queerness.[59]

CARNEGIE TECH

We have little direct evidence of Warhol's childhood use of animals and plants as imaginary refuges from all of these social, familial, and bodily challenges. The funeral photograph offers some clues, as do the remembered scenes of animal and vegetal identification, transgression, sexual and physical abuse, and maternal interaction. But in the years that followed, Warhol would use his art to explore these childhood engagements retrospectively, testing animals and plants as avatars for navigating what would otherwise be a highly unwelcoming heteronormative lifeworld, and for imagining forms of nonprocreative sexuality in a society predicated on reproduction.[60] (See figure 6.) And

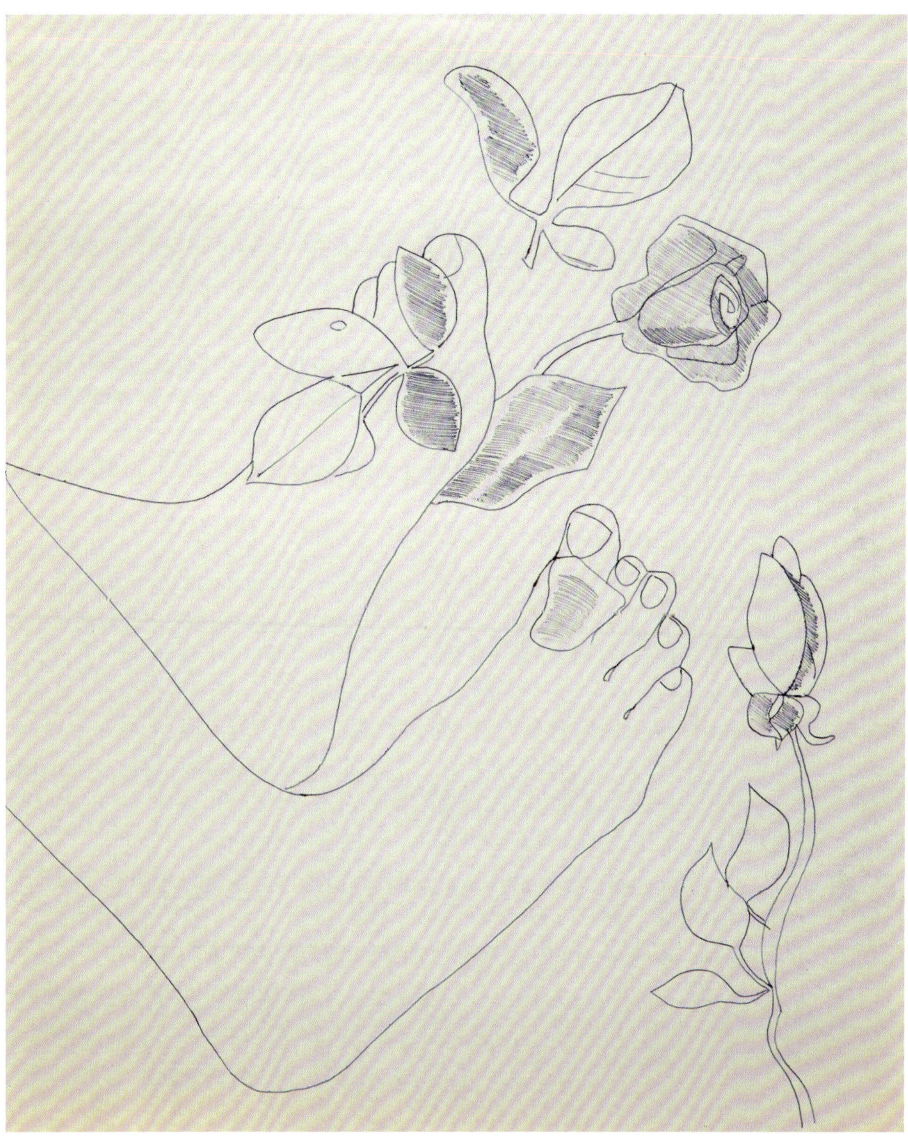

FIGURE 6
Andy Warhol, *Feet with Flowers,* c. 1956. Image and Artwork © The Andy Warhol Foundation for the Visual Arts, Inc./Licensed by ARS.

yet, as Stockton has shown, these identifications and imaginings can be dangerous as well, since homophobic voices have long argued that parahuman relationships can be used to identify the queer child: strikingly, "[z]oöphilia, or excessive love for animals," has been cited as one of the "stigmata for degeneracy" since Max Nordau's writings in the late nineteenth century.[61] Warhol would test the acceptability of these associations in the work he produced during the 1950s, highlighting what Nordau described as "strange birds," "blowsy flowers," and "vain butterflies," playfully hinting at a common thread linking maternal overinvestment, nonhuman life, and queer transgressions, and implying that animal and vegetal intervals could signal or even model queerness without directly illustrating it.[62] In the process, he would confirm Stockton's concerns, as these animal and vegetal threads in his work were frequently censored and condemned as degenerate.

As Gopnik has shown, college was statistically miraculous for someone from Warhol's background. No one else in his family had ever enrolled, and in Warhol's neighborhood "you graduated from high school and you went to the mill."[63] In addition to the possibility of upward mobility, college would have introduced Warhol to a powerful Freudian model for deciphering his childhood sexuality. At Carnegie Tech, his "favorite professor" was Balcomb Greene, a prominent painter and novelist who had met Freud, attended his lectures during the 1920s in Vienna, and adopted a Freudian model of interested, drive-driven, aesthetic production.[64] As Greene argued in a 1948 essay titled "Basic Concepts for Teaching Art," published in the same semester that Warhol attended Greene's mandatory Arts and Civilization course during his junior year, "It was Freud's considered opinion that the creative artist does not profit by suppression of his instincts"—a tactful way of saying that art must be fueled by "instincts" or drives in order to be successful.[65] In this essay, with young artists' drives in mind, Greene went so far as to broach the possibility that "a sexual revolution be stated [*sic*: started?] in college studios," and that art departments might "institute aggressive physical assaults upon the happier departments to compensate for frustration," although, pragmatically, he couldn't fully recommend either project.[66]

Warhol's extant paintings from college would follow Greene's Freudian lead, frequently returning to the anxieties and tensions that dominated his early years, and homing in on animalistic, vegetal, and abject subject matter. These paintings rejected the world of normative adult behavior and fixated instead on childhood, which was presented as a fundamentally grubby and disordered experience, distinctly subhuman, and characterized by almost hypnotic self-absorption. A number of them appear to be staged in a basement world, with its connotations of experimentation, decomposition, and menace. When Warhol explored alternatives to this world in these paintings, he leaned heavily on three possible sanctuaries: maternal affection, artistic expression, and nonhuman life forms. Taken together, the Carnegie paintings mobilized longstanding associations between pleasure, regression, and homosexuality, since, as Nordau argued in 1892, "[h]e who places pleasure above discipline, and impulse above self-restraint, wishes not for progress, but for retrogression to the most primitive animality."[67] Warhol's trademark style fits neatly into Nordau's racist and homophobic description of a degenerate: "Degenerates lisp and stammer. . . . They draw and paint like children, who dirty tables and walls with mischievous hands. They compose music like that of the yellow natives of East Asia. They confound all the arts, and lead them back to the primitive forms they had before evolution differentiated them."[68] Warhol

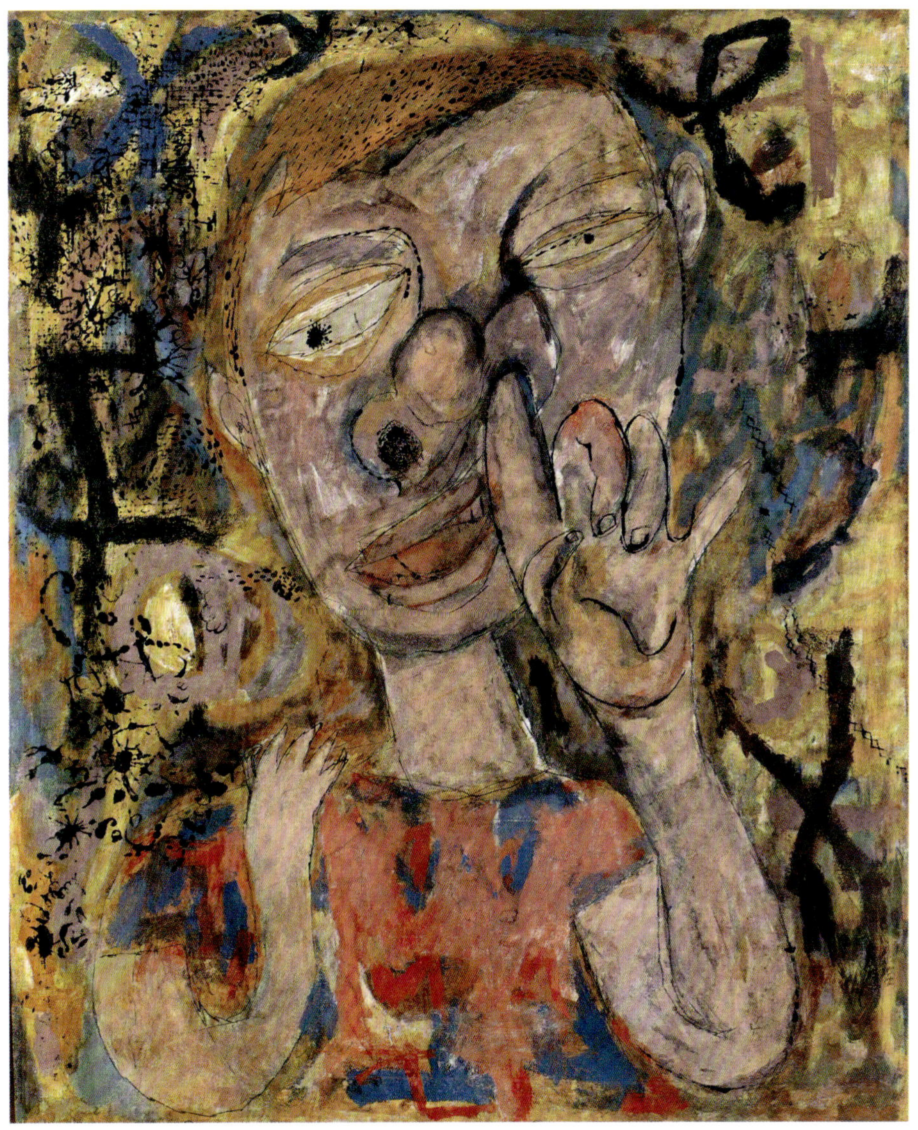

FIGURE 7
Andy Warhol, *Nosepicker 1: Why Pick on Me* (originally titled *The Lord Gave Me My Face but I Can Pick My Own Nose*), 1948. Paul Warhola Family Collection. © 2022 The Andy Warhol Foundation for the Visual Arts, Inc./ Licensed by Artists Rights Society (ARS), New York.

cultivated this image at least as much through his behavior as he did through his paintings; one classmate described him as "an innocent" who "appealed to the maternal and paternal instincts in people," while another remembered him as "very shy and cuddly, very much like a bunny rabbit."[69]

The Lord Gave Me My Face but I Can Pick My Own Nose (1948) and other similar works may be the first recorded paintings in Western art to focus exclusively on the autoerotic pleasures of nose picking: penetrating, digging, scraping, extracting. (See figure 7.) The enormous left hands of the figures depicted there, with their thick, phallic index fingers and raised pinkies, signal the intensity of these pleasures, as do the unevenly somnolent eyes. Like other bodily orifices, the nose allows access to the interior of the body in a potentially transgressive way. Psychoanalytic theory has long linked nose picking with sexual pleasure and masturbation; Sándor Ferenczi described it as expressing "insufficiently repressed tendencies to onanism," while D.W. Winnicott offered a more specific reading: "Nose-picking really stands for anal masturbation."[70] Melanie Klein contended that it "turned out to represent . . . an anal attack on the bodies of [the] parents."[71] Gopnik describes one work from this series in which Warhol made these homoerotic connotations even more explicit, depicting a naked boy with "an adult's chest hair" wearing "girlish Mary Janes . . . a brazen self-portrait by an unrepentant homosexual, the pinky finger up his nose being a stand-in for a middle finger raised in general defiance."[72]

Throughout their scratchy, gestural surfaces, these paintings propose mark making as an analogue or substitute for these transgressive pleasures—albeit one that is neither wholly satisfactory nor sublimated. They are aggressively shameless paintings, flaunting their contraventions of adult norms and values and proposing the child as an indecorous creature, animal rather than human in their willingness to live without shame, although touched by an echo of shame in the aggressiveness of their transgressions. Most of Warhol's professors found them unacceptable, and they were rejected from an annual exhibition (although the painter George Grosz argued for their inclusion). Warhol remained optimistic: a related drawing from this period, *Female with Ribbon Extending from Nose* (ca. 1948), proposes that abject extractions from the nasal orifice could serve as objects of aesthetic interest: a shimmering ribbon that turns the girl's eyes to stars, redeeming her otherwise jagged and misshapen body and crossed-out mouth. (See figure 8.)

Three Children explores similar themes and affects, but here they are staged as potentially intersubjective and incestuous. (See figure 9.) The painting is thought to be a group portrait of Warhol's nieces and nephews, who would later repay its maker by using some of his college paintings, stored in the family attic, as dartboards.[73] The figures are shown from the chest or shoulders up, although in each case their "mischievous hands" (Nordau) wriggle and claw toward and around their heads. All three figures seem focused either partially or entirely on their tongues, which thrust out from their mouths in various directions, reaching forward, or down toward the chin, or up toward the nose. In concert with the nose-picker paintings, *Three Children* emphasizes the irreducibility of corporeal experience and polymorphous perversity. The figures' rapt expressions suggest that they are at least partially absorbed in these adventures, but their seeking and grasping hands foretell an anxious yearning for objects around them that might be used for further pleasures, and the abstract, almost hieroglyphic patterning seems to track the vicissitudes of these desires beyond their

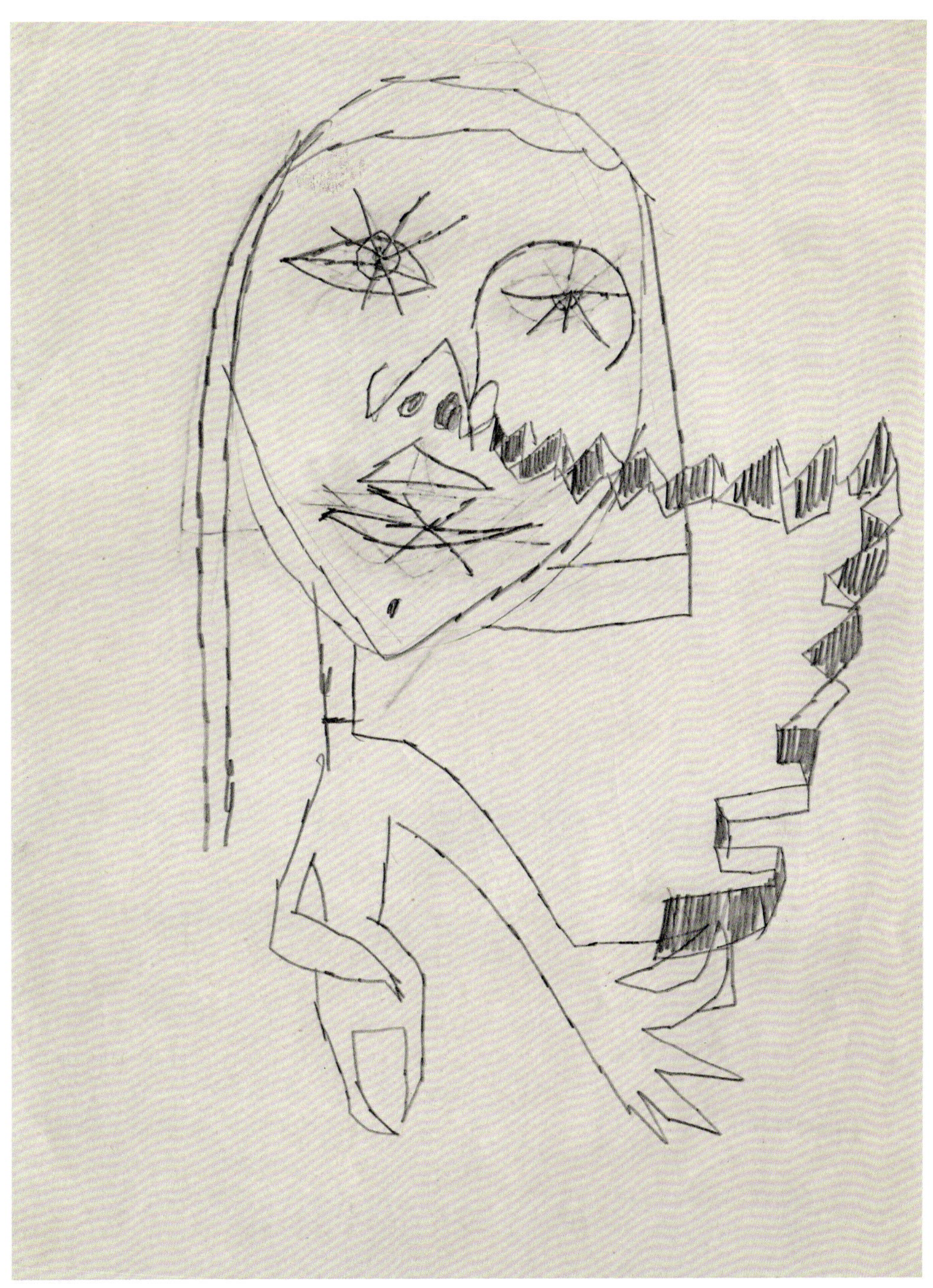

FIGURE 8

Andy Warhol, *Female with Ribbon Extending from Nose,* c. 1948. The Andy Warhol Museum, Pittsburgh; Founding Collection, Contribution The Andy Warhol Foundation for the Visual Arts, Inc. © 2022 The Andy Warhol Foundation for the Visual Arts, Inc./Licensed by Artists Rights Society (ARS), New York.

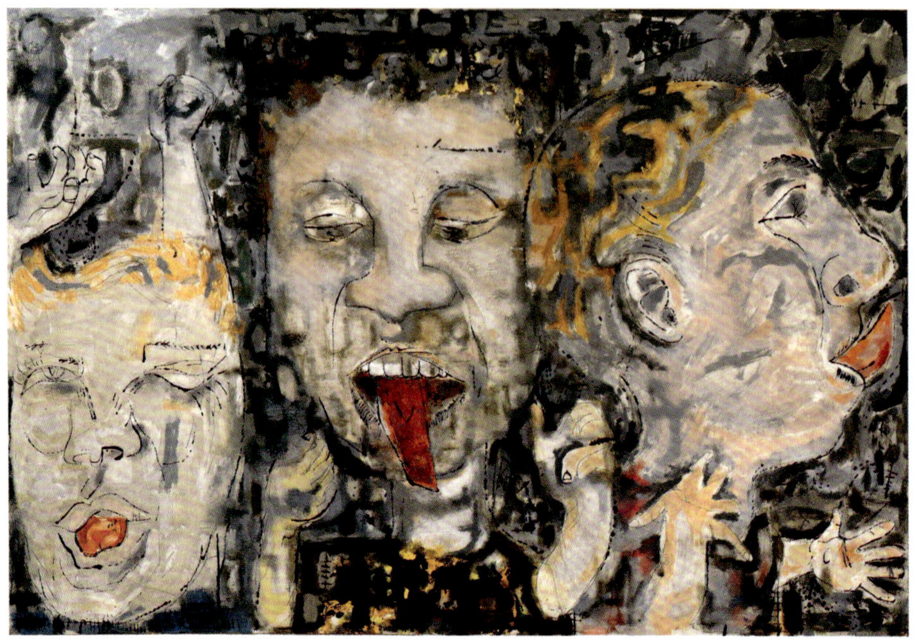

FIGURE 9
Andy Warhol, *Three Children,* c. 1948. Paul Warhola Family Collection. © 2022 The Andy Warhol Foundation for the Visual Arts, Inc./Licensed by Artists Rights Society (ARS), New York.

originating bodies.[74] Warhol would continue to embrace these expressions throughout his life; a 1978 photo of him in Studio 54 by Carrie Boretz captures him, camera in hand, tuxedo clad, eyes darting, tongue coltishly extended to the side.[75]

Other college paintings—such as *Boy and Tree, Girl in Park,* and *I Like Dance*—seem to offer escapes from this solipsistic world of picking and licking. At first glance, *Boy and Tree* (1947) and *Girl in Park* (1948) might chart a favorable future for these children, who, having escaped their basements, are now able to enjoy a larger world. (See figures 10 and 11.) But closer inspection shows that this optimistic tone applies only to the latter painting, in which the world of culture appears to its young protagonist as a pair of beautiful, multifaceted domes surrounded by a golden sky, as enticing and sustaining as a mother's bosom. Here, Warhol is exploring distinctly Kleinian territory, wherein the outside world appears as "the mother's body in an extended sense."[76] The boy's world is, by contrast, much more constrained. He lies prone on the ground, his head toward us, surrounded by a sickly green laid down in anxious scrawls, his hands and face completely absorbed in something that we will never see or understand—a worm, an insect, or a blade of grass? His foreshortened and thickly silhouetted legs protrude behind him awkwardly, forming a clumsy "V" near the painting's center that points directly to his skull. This open shape is on the verge of being invaded by an aberrant triangular tree that seems to be menacing the boy from behind, edging

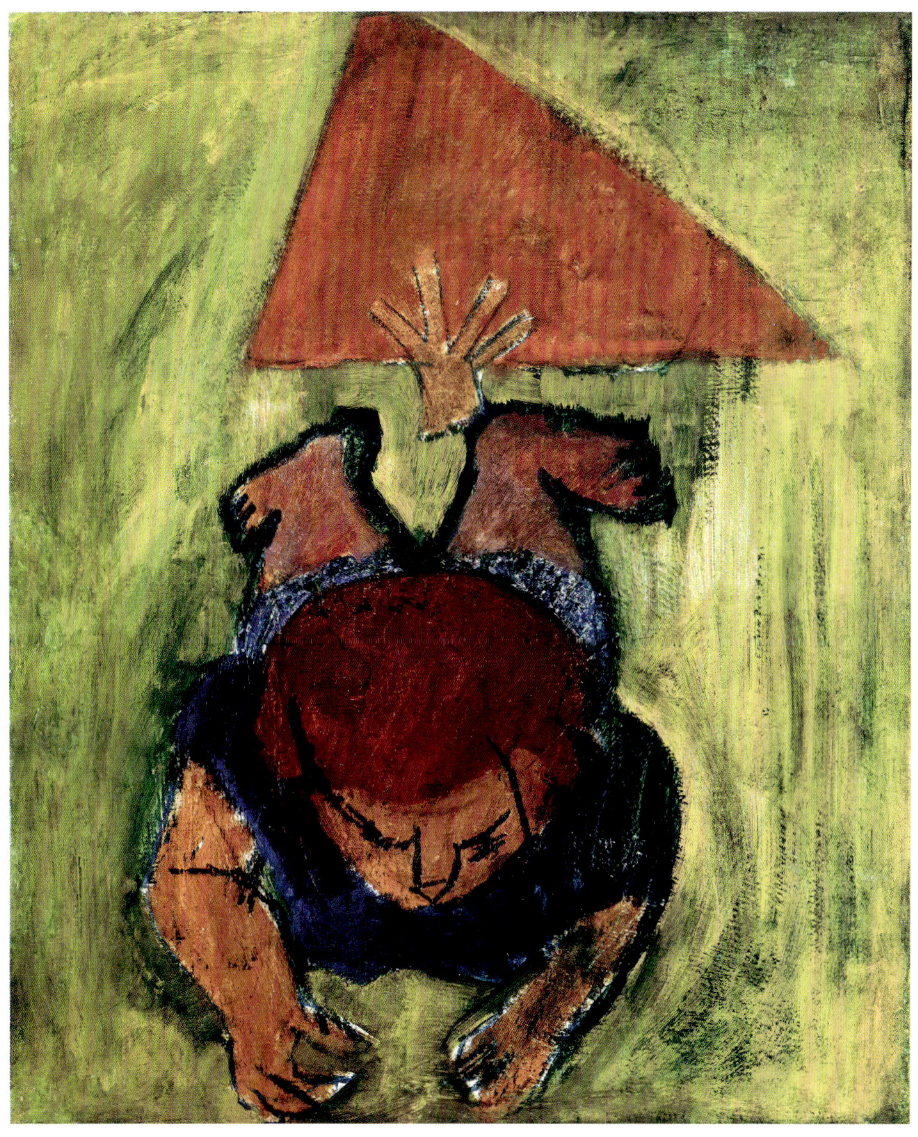

FIGURE 10
Andy Warhol, *Boy and Tree,* 1947. Paul Warhola Family Collection. © 2022 The Andy Warhol Foundation for the Visual Arts, Inc./Licensed by Artists Rights Society (ARS), New York.

between his heels, profiting from his preoccupation. Environmental absorption is figured here as an opportunity for erotic—and, more specifically, anal—transgression, like the various forms of abuse and violence targeted at frail creatures during Warhol's childhood.

I Like Dance is the lightest and most cheerful of these early paintings, eclipsing even *Girl in Park* in its positivity. (See figure 12.) Six lithe male figures of various sizes

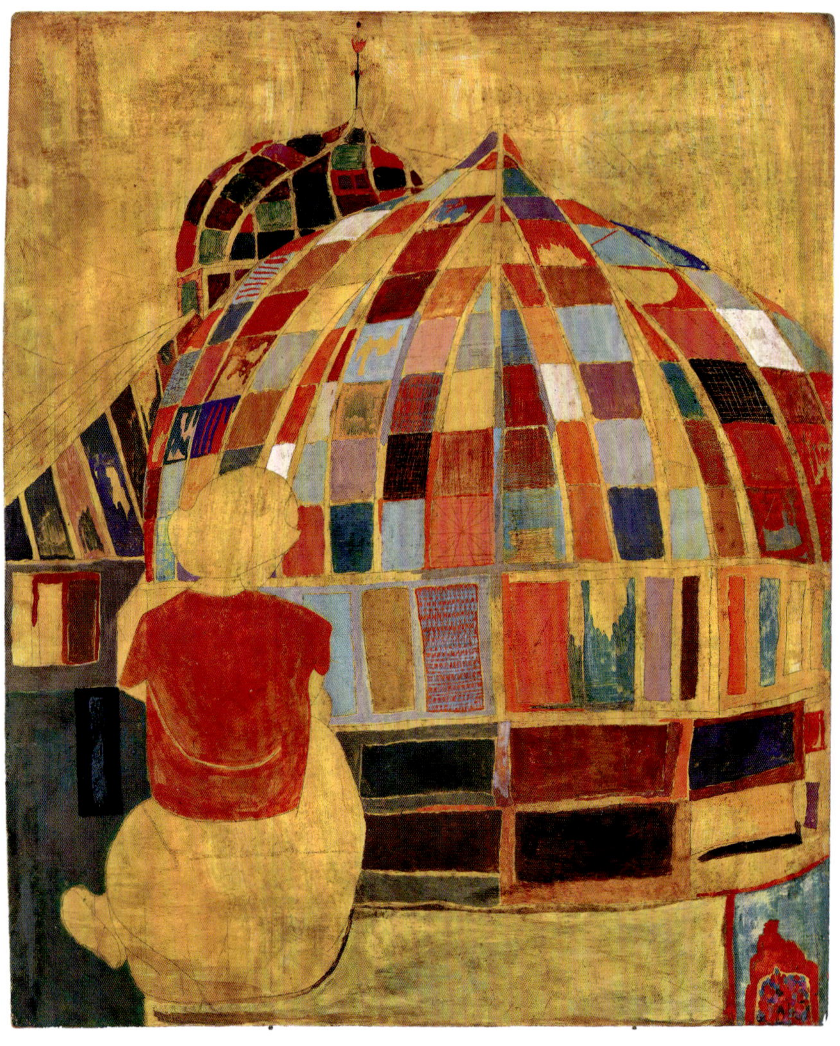

FIGURE 11
Andy Warhol, *Girl in Park,* 1948. Paul Warhola Family Collection. © 2022 The Andy Warhol Foundation for the Visual Arts, Inc./Licensed by Artists Rights Society (ARS), New York.

stretch, pirouette, and support each other, forming an elegant spiral from depth (upper-right red figure) to surface that culminates in a series of three dancers grounded in the lower register whose bodies elegantly counterweigh each other. Along the right-hand side, a lavender figure balances along the outstretched arm of a brown dancer beneath him. Reminiscent of Picasso's beachgoers of the late 1920s—particularly of the smallest figure in *Bathers with Beach Ball* (1928), from which Warhol seems to have cribbed his phallus head and the figures' triangular crotches—this almost perfectly symmetrical H-shaped figure stretches nearly the height of the painting. (Gopnik has shown that Warhol probably saw MoMA's *Picasso: Forty Years of His*

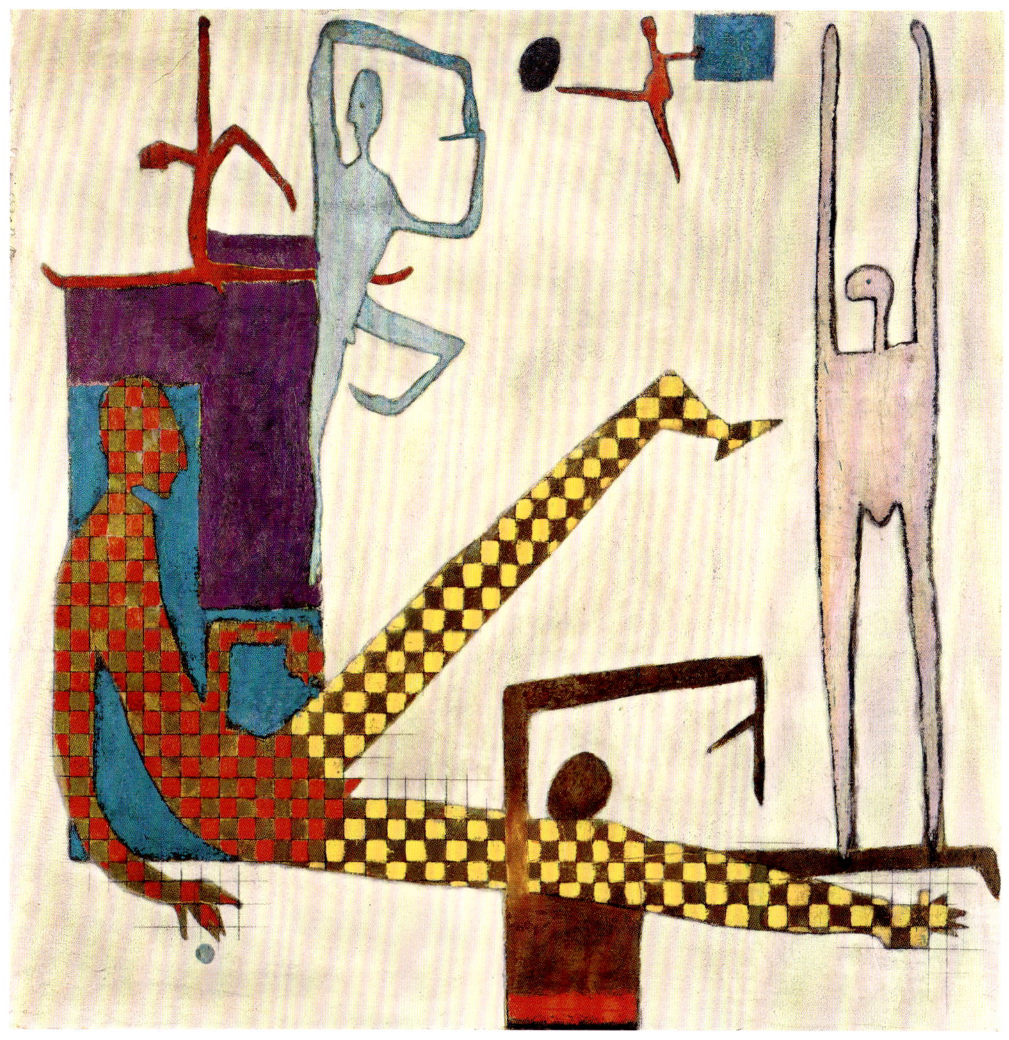

FIGURE 12
Andy Warhol, *I Like Dance*, 1947. Paul Warhola Family Collection. © 2022 The Andy Warhol Foundation for the Visual Arts, Inc./Licensed by Artists Rights Society (ARS), New York.

Art exhibition in 1941 when it traveled to the Carnegie Institute, which included the related work *On the Beach, Dinard* [1928].[77]) This figure imaginatively embodies an equalized world, in which arms and legs, having been unburdened of hands and feet, become equivalent. Its phallus seems to have been displaced to the head, where it can survey the other dancers without apprehension. The troublesome fingers of the *Nosepicker* paintings have here been tamed *and* sexualized, as in the pale blue dancer at upper left whose outstretched finger rhymes with the phallic foot of the red dancer behind him, or the brown dancer at lower right whose triangular hand echoes the triangular crotches of the dancers above him.

No wonder Warhol "likes" dance: it may have been the first human arena he found where homoeroticism could thrive unencumbered, if also partially sublimated. Warhol's cousin describes seeing a ballet with him in Greenwich Village in 1953: "Andy was completely in a trance, the whole time he was literally sitting on the edge of his seat. . . . [He] was in ecstasies. 'Wow, that's wonderful! Aren't the dancers beautiful?'"[78] Even homoerotic and racial aggressiveness could be aestheticized: the red figure near the painting's top edge kicks an oblong ball that almost perfectly duplicates the head of the brown figure at the lower margin—no one flinches. One thinks of Eve Kosofsky Sedgwick's crucial definition of Warhol's shame as "a kind of free radical that . . . attaches to . . . almost anything: a zone of the body, a sensory system a . . . behavior, another affect such as anger or arousal."[79] In this otherwise relatively shameless and harmonious painting, shame can be seen as adhering to the sole brown body, producing a barely disguised moment of violence.

The power of aestheticization to tame and normalize homoerotic energies is perhaps most directly figured in the painting's large, reclining, checkered figure, reminiscent of Picasso's harlequins (a number of which were also included in the Carnegie show). Here the great modernist trope of "the grid" is rendered handmade and decorative. Warhol took pains to show his work near the figure's edges—right hand, right foot, crotch—letting the grid eclipse the figure's silhouette, as if intimating that its graceful patterning could someday extend everywhere. There are unexpected limits, however, to this figure's exemplary elegance. The checkered dancer's graceful right leg culminates in a very awkward foot; Warhol seems either to have had difficulty deciding on its angle or to have clumsily attempted to paint it with its toes splayed. Whatever the intention, the result looks distinctly nonhuman, more like a paw than a foot. The figure's left arm is similarly bizarre: it emerges vertically from the torso, takes a sharp right turn, and culminates in a downturned fist. The resulting half rectangle echoes the checkerboard pattern but has no human anatomical equivalent. It much more closely resembles a horse's foreleg and hoof than any standard human arm. These abnormalities hint at an anxiety that not even aestheticization can render homoeroticism completely acceptable within a homophobic world.[80] Even its most beautiful adherents will still be rejected as monstrous or bestial, exceeding the boundaries of the human. That said, the painting seems to have inspired or been inspired by real-world experimentation among Warhol and his cadre. A contemporary photograph shows a group of them striking angular poses together in a park.[81]

I Like Dance's anxiety regarding the social acceptability of homoeroticism takes on a comic-utopian tone in *Two Dogs Kissing*, which imagines two bipedal male dachshunds grasping each other's arms and locking lips, eyes wide. (See figure 13.) As Alice Kuzniar has shown, "the relationship with the dog, or even being a dog, [often] serves as an allegory of homosexuality"—an association that becomes quite literal in this painting.[82] The symmetry evidenced by the lavender figure in *I Like Dance* has now been bisected into these two strange figures, who—alone among Warhol's early creations—

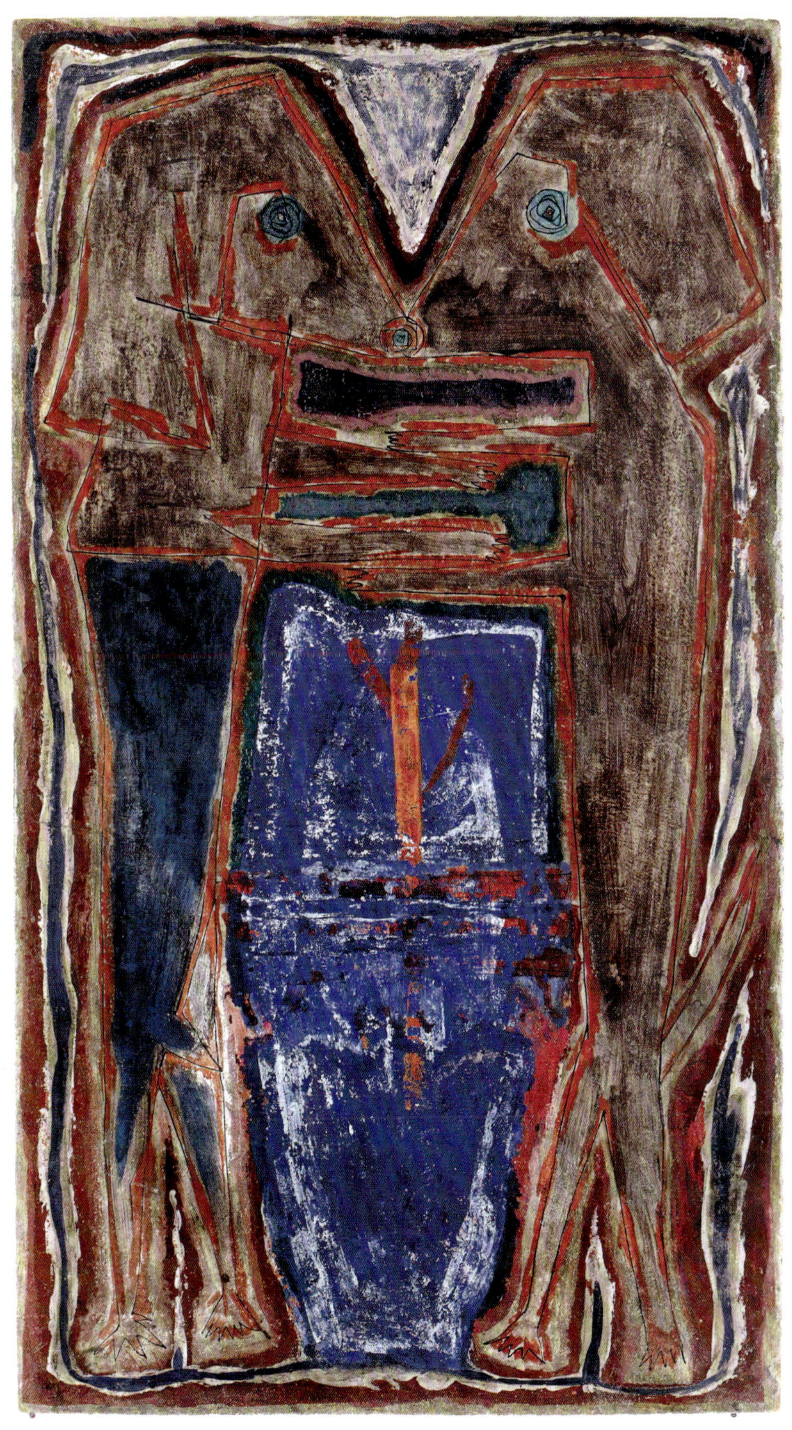

FIGURE 13

Andy Warhol, *Two Dogs Kissing*, 1948. Paul Warhola Family Collection. © 2022 The Andy Warhol Foundation for the Visual Arts, Inc./Licensed by Artists Rights Society (ARS), New York.

are able to express homoerotic affection openly. The kissing dogs seem almost to reconcile the two primary iconological meanings of dogs in Western art—lust and fidelity—but only outside the bounds of human reproduction. Their long torsos and stubby legs resemble the *Nosepicker* paintings, where, absent a partner, the titular figures are forced to explore their own bodies, brazenly and insolently.

Warhol's kissing dogs are nevertheless not without their own ambivalence. Their embrace is undermined by the chasm of mostly blue negative space that separates all but their arms and snouts, and by the ways in which this blue infiltrates their bodies—strikingly in the two visible eyes, and perhaps more distressingly in the left-hand figure's torso—such that the difference between interior and exterior becomes uncertain. We are close, here, to Warhol's memory that "as a child he always felt like a little dog," and therefore to Freud's claim that "[u]ninhibited as they are in the avowal of their bodily needs, [children] no doubt feel themselves more akin to animals than to their elders."[83] But Freud also noted the use of "dog" "as a term of abuse," and proposed that "the dog incurs [human] contempt through two of its characteristics: . . . it does not shun excrement, and it is not ashamed of its sexual functions."[84] Although Warhol may have known about animal homosexuality from personal observation, he probably would not yet have known about it from a scientific perspective, since no popular books on the subject would be published until Bruce Bagemihl's *Biological Exuberance: Animal Homosexuality and Natural Diversity* in 1999. But he clearly sensed an uninhibitedness in animals relative to the human world. Sometimes, as in this painting, nonhuman creatures could serve as an unfettered avatars for him; at other times, as when he later decided that "nobody liked" him and he might as well "eat worms," they could bear the brunt of his shame and self-loathing.

Strikingly, in these early paintings, truly intersubjective and erotic same-sex communion is limited to two spheres: the world of artistic performance, as figured in *I Like Dance* (where it is arguably plagued by racist aggressivity), and the world of animal or cross-species affection, as in *Two Dogs Kissing* (where it is troubled by interior/exterior instability). Many of these questions and tensions were reportedly collated in the painting Warhol chose for his first exhibited work in college—a work that is undocumented, and whose location is currently unknown. The painting is described as depicting a woman nursing a dog. Its subject matter, which borders uncomfortably on zoophilia, was so controversial that a Carnegie Tech professor successfully demanded its removal, providing Warhol with an early taste of succès de scandale. A related drawing from the period, *Female with Animal at Breast* (ca. 1948–49), survives. (See figure 14.) Through their focus on a maternal interaction between human and dog, these works strikingly reinforce Kristeva's claims regarding the closeness of animality and the maternal as abjected states. The dog's somnolent eye echoes Warhol's nose-picking figures and, in its closeness to the silhouette of the woman's breast, forms a strange second nipple, connoting what Kristeva called "the archaic dyad": mother and child intertwined.[85] The nexus of canine mouth and tongue and human

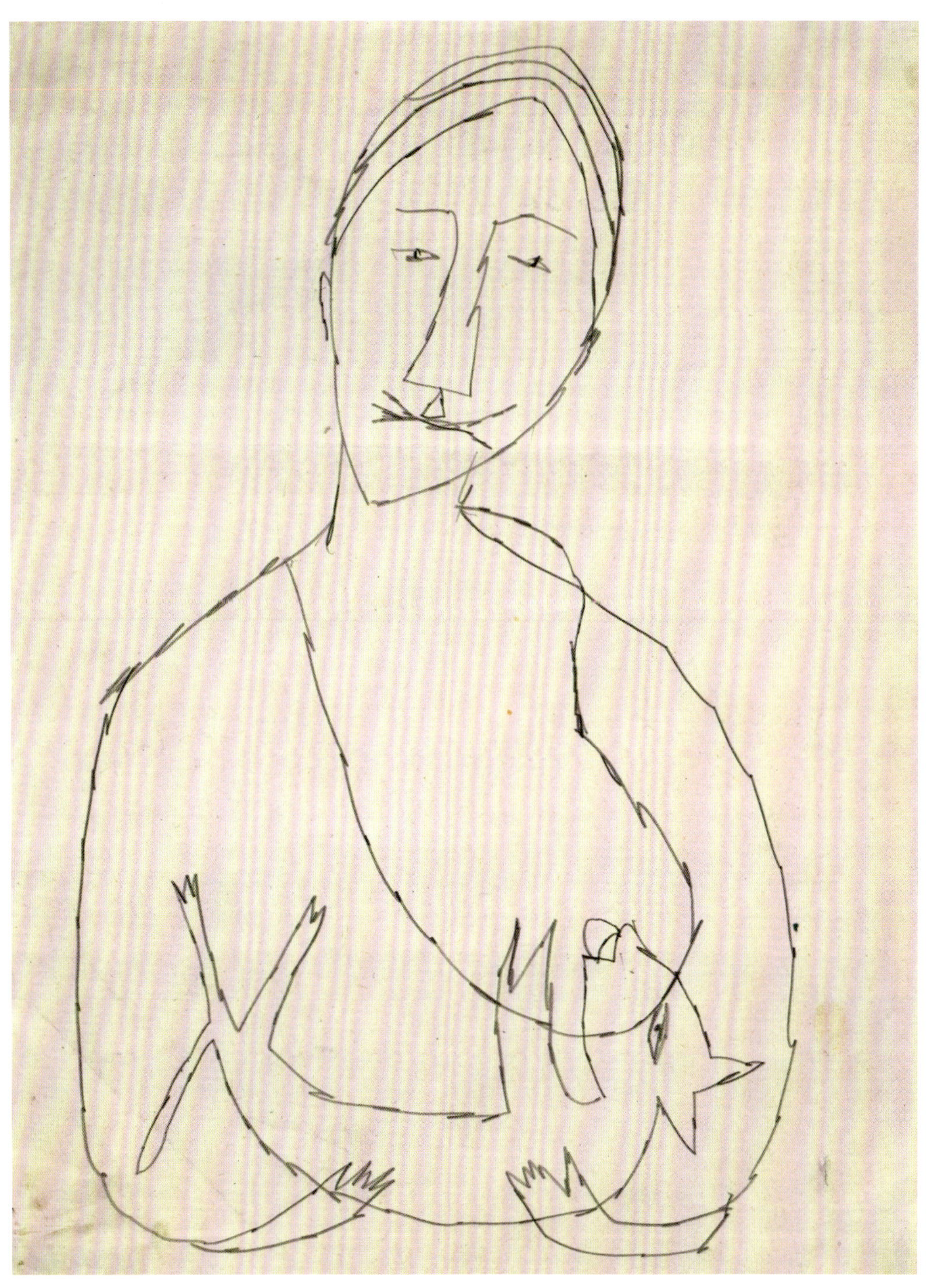

FIGURE 14

Andy Warhol, *Female with Animal at Breast,* 1948–49. The Andy Warhol Museum, Pittsburgh; Founding Collection, Contribution The Andy Warhol Foundation for the Visual Arts, Inc. © 2022 The Andy Warhol Foundation for the Visual Arts, Inc./Licensed by Artists Rights Society (ARS), New York.

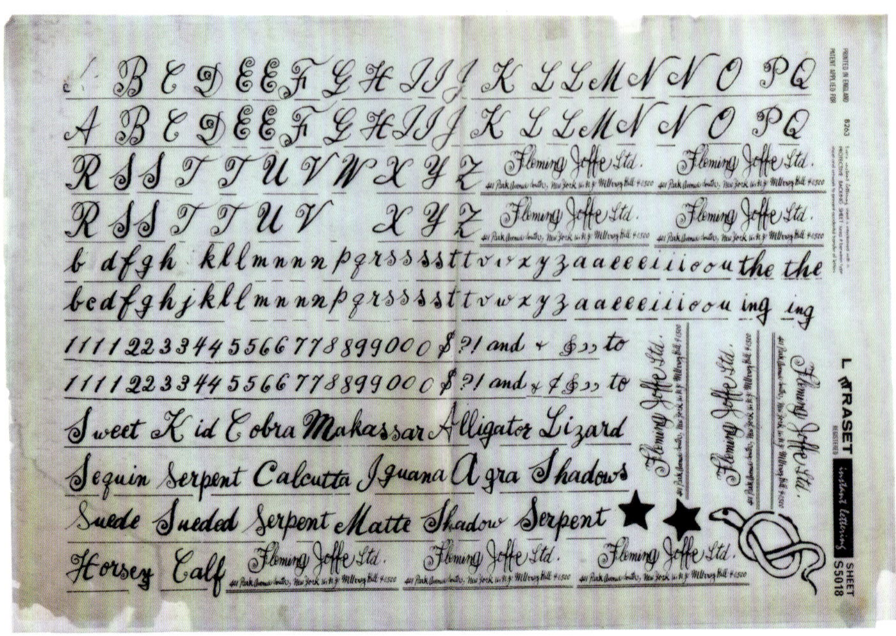

FIGURE 15
Julia Warhola, *Letraset (Julia Warhola's Handwriting)*, c. 1963. The Andy Warhol Museum, Pittsburgh; Founding Collection, Contribution The Andy Warhol Foundation for the Visual Arts, Inc. © 2022 The Andy Warhol Foundation for the Visual Arts, Inc./Licensed by Artists Rights Society (ARS), New York.

breast is equally intricate; it is hard to tell where one ends and the other begins. But the woman's mouth disavows this blissful merging. Figured here as the blocked site of language, it is puckered and ungenerous, communicating something like disapproval for the creature who is cradled by paltry, jagged, unwelcoming hands and flat, twisted arms. The wordless delight in the abject expressed in *Female with Ribbon Extending from Nose* has here become an unspeakable embarrassment for the mother.

The strange connections these works proposed between artist, animal, and mother would recur throughout Warhol's work, perhaps most strikingly in the late series of prints depicting an okapi dam and calf (chapter 5). What's more, through their imaginative identification of the mother as the source of the dog/artist and his sustenance, they seem to corroborate Elissa Marder's claims that "the maternal function operates at the very outer limits of the human" and that "the maternal body tends to become associated and confused with other forms of cultural labor that are defined . . . by their reproductive capabilities."[86] Marder singles out two of Warhol's favorite technologies—the camera and the telephone—but her insight can be extended to virtually every reproductive technology that Warhol utilized. He would be quick to embrace this association between the maternal, the nonhuman, and technological reproduction: he referred to his beloved portable cassette recorder as his "wife"—a designation he would later bestow upon a dachshund.[87] Throughout the 1950s, he would ask his mother to do the lettering on his illustrations, and often even to sign his name or produce drawings for him.[88] Christopher Schmidt memorably called Julia Warhola a "writing machine," and Warhol commissioned a custom-made Letraset of her handwriting. Many of the prewritten words were animal names, and the page was decorated with a serpent tied in a knot.[89] (See figure 15.) Andy and Julia lived together from 1952 to 1970. For much of this time, she resided in his basement.[90]

Carnegie Tech does not seem to have offered Warhol a viable homosocial atmosphere; as one fellow student put it, in Warhol's college world, "[a]nyone who talked openly about homosexuality would have been considered insane."[91] Gopnik has conclusively shown that Pittsburgh was a terrifying place to be gay during this period, with vice squads roaming the city, and sodomy punishable by up to ten years of hard labor; by 1951, the maximum penalty would be increased to life in prison.[92] Warhol's friend Betty Asche Douglas remembered pervasive homophobia: "One of the prejudices of the day was all artists are gay and to be gay is wrong or bad."[93] Art gave Warhol a safer outlet for his feelings and desires: the hyperbolic embrace of transgressive and animalistic modes he had developed during childhood could, at Carnegie Tech, be sublimated and at least partially accepted.

One of Warhol's college jobs—producing window displays for the upscale Joseph Horne department store—did, however, provide a glimpse of another social world. It was there, surrounded by what one of his gay professors described as "a number of flaming queens," that he met display director Larry Vollmer, whom he would later refer to with uncharacteristic enthusiasm as "a wonderful man" and "an idol to me."[94] Vollmer immediately sensed something avian in his young assistant, describing him as "really a wild bird, an odd duck."[95] A photograph of the two of them captures Vollmer on the left—nattily dressed, hands crossed at the wrists, almost preternaturally dapper—addressing the camera or its bearer. (See figure 16.) Warhol—smirking, left hand on hip—has turned his face away from him. His right arm is operating a large hand puppet, a dark-furred monkey, who raises one hand toward Vollmer in a gesture that looks like a benediction or an oath. The three figures have been caught by the photographer in the middle of something hilarious and now forever unreadable. In a life incessantly documented on film, this shot nevertheless feels unusually candid: Warhol was rarely captured smiling this way. And yet, as was so often the case during Warhol's early years, when confronted by a situation in which his desires and/or anxieties were activated, he seems to have chosen to fall back on an animal avatar. This voiceless monkey can speak for him, facing his desires directly. The photograph resonates with a number of other dual or multiportraits and self-portraits of Warhol: Michael Cooper's extraordinary multi-exposure portrait (with its strong resemblance to Titian's *Allegory of Prudence*); the many portraits of Warhol and his Factory coworkers with dogs, cats, and rabbits;

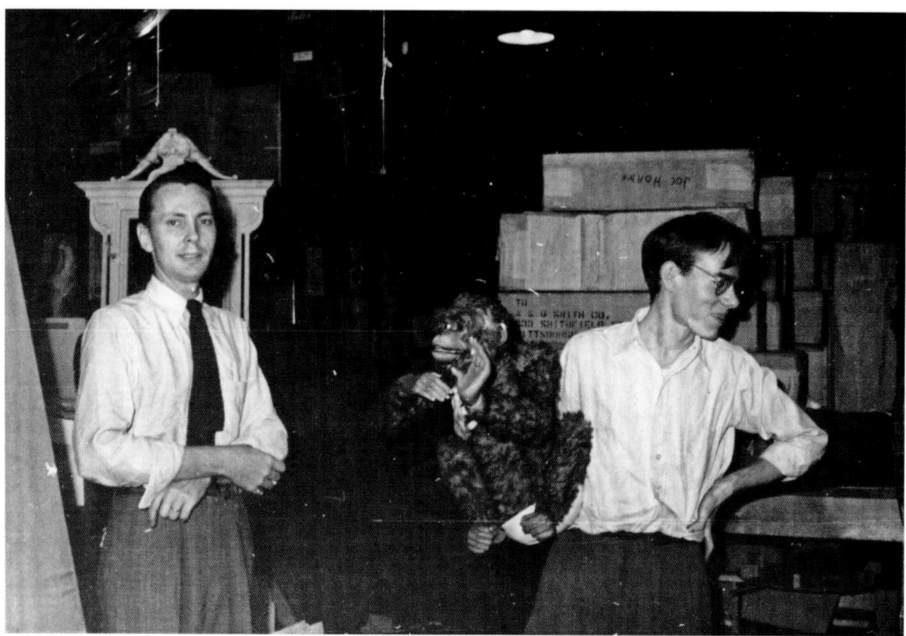

FIGURE 16
Photographer unknown, *Larry Vollmer and Andy Warhol,* 1947. The Andy Warhol Museum, Pittsburgh; Founding Collection, Contribution The Andy Warhol Foundation for the Visual Arts, Inc. © 2022 The Andy Warhol Foundation for the Visual Arts, Inc./Licensed by Artists Rights Society (ARS), New York.

Jack Mitchell's striking dual portrait, *Andy Warhol and His Dog Archie* (1973); Thomas Hoepker's *Double Exposure of Andy Warhol in His "Factory" at Union Square, New York City, 1981;* Dennis Hopper's 1964 *Warhol with Flower;* and Bill Redic's 1985 portrait of Warhol with Brigid Berlin's dog, Fortune.

But the Vollmer photograph is even more reminiscent of another portrait of Warhol taken during this period. (See figure 17.) Here, Warhol is shown posing on his family's Dawson Street porch. Someone must have asked him to stand in the sunlight and given him at least a moment or two to prepare. In response, Warhol has grasped Lucy, the family dog, in both arms, cradling her hind legs in his right forearm and drawing her upper body toward his chest. She faces the camera, alert, ears up, eyes wide, just below and to the right of his face. Again, Warhol has a proxy animal to face the world and the camera—a shield and an avatar. What Benjamin Fong has described as "the primary conflict of childhood," the tension between "urge to union" and "need for independence"—a particularly challenging puzzle for the queer adolescent—is here negotiated by way of a canine companion.[96] Off to the left, in the shadows, stands Julia, scowling, her body leaning away from her son's, as if recoiling from his decision to be portrayed this way. Over time, she would learn to embrace his animal and ecological identifications.

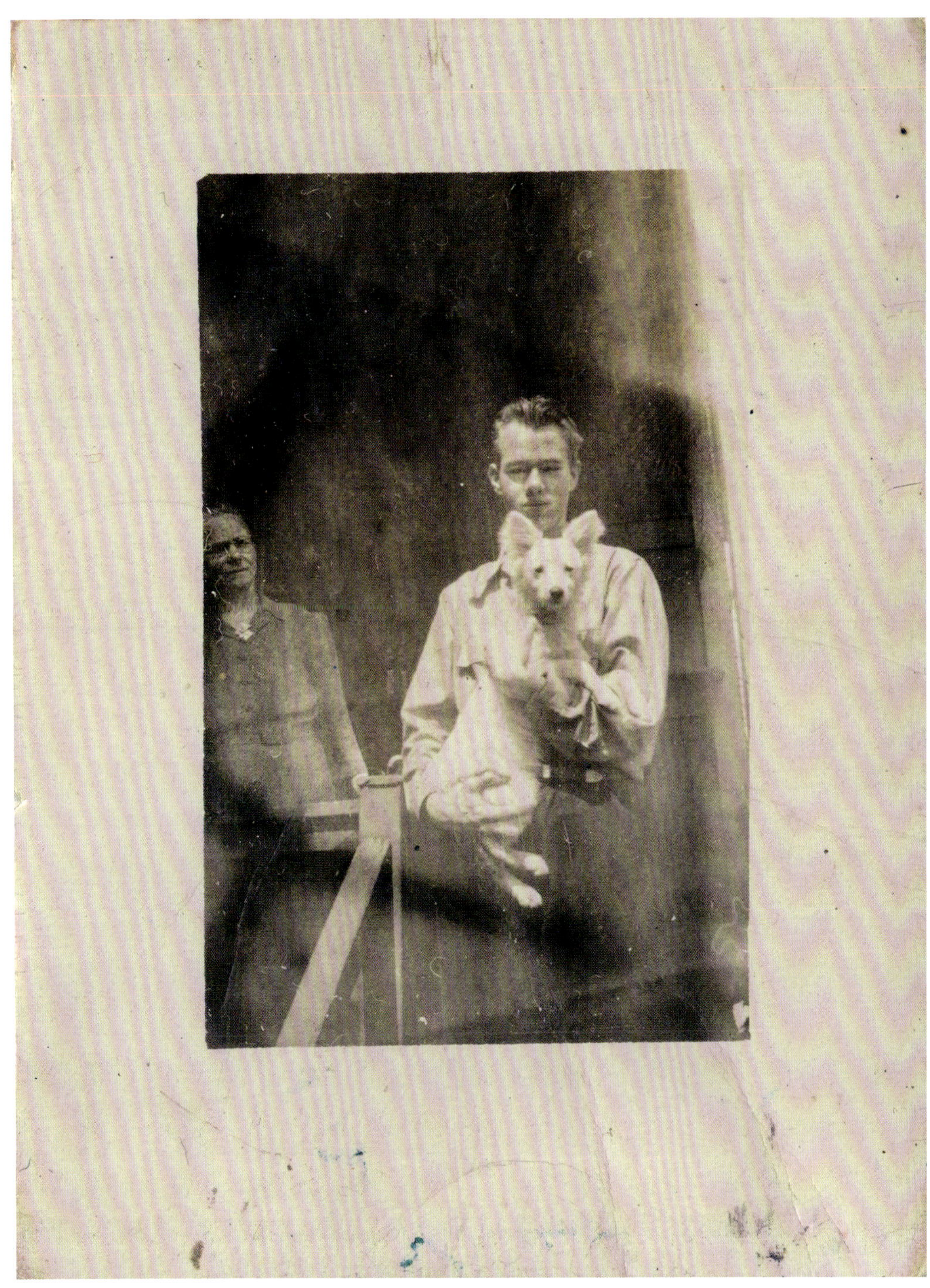

FIGURE 17

Photographer unknown, *Andy Warhol with the Family's Dog, Lucy, and Julia Warhola at Dawson Street,* c. 1946. The Andy Warhol Museum, Pittsburgh; Founding Collection, Contribution The Andy Warhol Foundation for the Visual Arts, Inc. © 2022 The Andy Warhol Foundation for the Visual Arts, Inc./Licensed by Artists Rights Society (ARS), New York.

NEW YORK

In the summer of 1949, after periodic trips by bus during college and a couple of brief sublets, Warhol and his Carnegie Tech classmate Philip Pearlstein began renting a room near the Chelsea Hotel from the dancer and dance therapist Franziska Boas, sharing space with her "stupid castrated Persian Cat" and a huge sheepdog and eight puppies—"a scene of true bohemian chaos."[97] Boas fell behind on the rent, however, and everyone was evicted, puppies included. Warhol was "heartbroken" to lose them.[98] One friend reported that it was only in 1950, when Warhol moved into a basement apartment with seventeen roommates—"artists, writers, dancers"—at 74 West 103rd Street, near Central Park, that he "began tentatively, exploring the homosexual underground."[99] The subterranean metaphor is striking. During Warhol's lifetime, basements, which had figured so powerfully in his traumatic animal and sexual experiences, would become known as sites for adult sexual experimentation where socially proscribed erotic encounters could be pursued.[100]

But Warhol's initial results in this arena seem to have been disappointing. One Halloween, Warhol and his new roommates dressed up as "a garland of flowers," slyly referencing the sexual slang term "daisy chain," and using vegetal figures to screen a queer meaning.[101] However, the dance scene he had idolized in college failed to provide the lifeworld he had envisioned in *I Like Dance*. Warhol would later complain that while he had hoped the roommates "could become good friends and share problems," it turned out "they were just interested in another person sharing the rent."[102] Perhaps in response to these disappointments, he immediately retreated into a hyperbolic incorporation of the basest sort of animal life. A friend remembered Warhol tacking a painting to the living room ceiling "that was all these white squiggly lines that resembled worms." Warhol told her it "was inspired by the lyrics of the children's song 'Nobody Likes Me, Everybody Hates Me, Guess I'll Go Eat Worms.'"[103] One can imagine it looming over every party, every common-room conversation, communicating alienation and disappointment, decomposition beneath the guise of abstraction. Would any of these audiences have been aware of Darwin's claim that even worms exhibit intelligence and "small agencies," which, as Jane Bennett and others have remarked, ultimately produce large ecological effects—effects that might be magnified if humans joined more fully in their causes?[104] Through its clever mixture of subterranean, carnal, fecal, decompositional, and depressive connotations, the work effectively summarized sexual frustrations in ecological terms. Warhol's friend got the sense that the work "somehow seemed important to him."[105]

Around a year later, Warhol moved into his own apartment for the first time, a "mouse- and louse-ridden" basement flat under the train tracks at 216 East 75th Street.[106] During the brief period of solitude that followed, he purchased a black-and-white television and, in the summer of 1951, a male Siamese cat he named Sam.[107] Sam was, according to one of Warhol's boyfriends, "an incredibly dumb, weird and distorted-looking cat," who Warhol claimed had been driven cross-eyed by the sirens of the nearby fire station—traumatized by modernity, like so many of Warhol's forthcoming heroes and antiheroes: Marilyn, Elvis, Jackie, the Velvets, the Superstars.[108] Julia and Warhol's brother John came to visit the following spring and found Andy nearly destitute, eating mostly just "cake and candy" and smelling "as if he had not taken a bath in days."[109] It was as though, after his failed experiment in communal dance living, Warhol had retreated not just to eating worms but to embracing decay and living "like an animal"—surrounded by other creatures (cat, mice, bugs) rather than humans, indulging his appetites for sugar and television without restraint, and refusing to adhere to social conventions of hygiene.

Julia was appalled and decided to relocate from Pittsburgh to live with Warhol and take care of him: "I come here to take care of my Andy, and when he's okay I go home."[110] They had been separated, as Gopnik points out, for only three years, and she would stay for the next twenty.[111] A "nonstop talker" and diligent homemaker, she would reintroduce housekeeping, home-cooked meals, and human sociability into his environment, along with (feline) sexual reproduction.[112] She woke early every day, donned "a simple cotton dress, a long apron, and a babushka," and began taking care of the household: preparing meals, doing laundry, sweeping the sidewalk, helping Warhol dress.[113] His friends noticed that he seemed to revert to childlike behavior in her presence: "I saw situations between them that were typical of a mother/son relationship. Andy would start wining [*sic*] like a little boy (imitating voice) 'Oh Ma.'"[114] Warhol would later identify this voice with animality, telling an interviewer that he talked to his dachshunds "in dog talk," by whining.[115] As far as his friends could tell, Julia was "oblivious to his homosexuality" and surprised that he hadn't yet married: female visitors were appraised "as potential wives. She'd say things like 'You'd be a good wife for my Andy, but he's too busy'"—using a surfeit of economic productivity to justify an absence of reproductive productivity.[116] Julia would worry, literally to her dying day, that Andy had never grown up. Her last words to his brother Paul were "'I want you to look after him because sometimes I wonder if he don't have a childish mind.'"[117] But she seems also to have recognized Warhol's need for animal companionship. Around this time, a second Siamese cat, Hester, moved into their apartment. She and Sam began breeding.

During what he described as his "cockroach period," Warhol used animal imagery and associations to cultivate a specific image to potential clients, who would refer to him as "Raggedy Andy" or "Andy Paperbag."[118] He purchased Brooks Brothers suits and Italian brogues but "encouraged his cats to pee on his shoes" to give them "the right patina," implying that he existed on their territory.[119] Perhaps thinking back to Anliker's portrait of him with a mechanical bird, Warhol would call potential clients and coyly pitch them vegetal animals instead of illustrations: "'I planted some birdseed in the park yesterday,' he would say in a whispery voice. 'And would you like to order a bird? And do you have any work for me?'"[120]

As Lucy Mulroney has demonstrated, Warhol used book production during this period "as a pretext to create collaborative projects with other men," projects "expressing, recognizing, and creatively envisioning themselves and their desires amid the homophobic culture of the 1950s."[121] Wayne Koestenbaum notes that Warhol would invite his "comely male friends" to "coloring parties," where they would "hand-tint the pages."[122] Some of these books, like the first of Warhol's two collaborations with Ralph T. Ward, *Love Is a Pink Cake* (1952), directly addressed homosexual desires through recondite references to George Sand, Oscar Wilde, and André Gide. As Mulroney shows, Warhol's efforts to render these desires more specific—like his illustrations based on Truman Capote's *Other Voices, Other Rooms*—tended to be met with critical disapprobation. But animals remained an effective device—as they had been in the college work—for referencing these desires without resorting to venerable figures or risking overt specificity. In one drawing of a toddler and a butterfly from this period, Warhol wrote: "Here is Andy at the age of two—Looking wistfully at you—He has wings like a butterfly—And if you ask the reason why—He will say: I'm a butterfly you see—Won't you come and fly with me."[123] The second book Warhol and Ward produced, *A Is an Alphabet* (1953), paired Warhol's spare and yearning blotted line drawings with a series of twenty-six short stanzas written by Ward and inscribed in pen by Julia Warhola, each of which described an encounter—typically playful, aggressive, and/or erotic—between an animal and a "young woman" or "young man." The animals are arranged alphabetically and seem to have been selected for maximum weirdness and whimsy (albatross, bat, cricket, Dalmatian, eel).

The first half of the book is mostly chaste and playful, but the second half becomes increasingly erotic and suggestive. Three of these sheets are particularly relevant to the themes of animal homoeroticism discussed so far. "O was an otter /," one begins, "Who slept in the same bed with this young man / And there never was an odder otter." (See figure 18.) The clever wordplay that closes the stanza might almost overshadow the sexual innuendo that precedes it, were it not for Warhol's accompanying drawing. Here one long and graceful blotted line fashions and joins two heads seen in profile—one apparently male, the other androgynous and vaguely serpentine—their noses and mouths brought into almost jigsaw-like proximity, their eyes left blank and empty. The negative space beneath their chins forms a strange shape of its own, biomorphic and duck-like. Animal homoeroticism is broached by this image and its accompanying rhyme but, through the use of androgyny, left vague and deniable.

Four pages later, these provocative connections are made even more explicit. Here, Warhol's drawing of two male human figures takes up nearly the entire page. They stand close together, almost touching heal to toe; the right-hand figure's visible foot encroaches upon the other figure's pair of feet. This left-hand figure has twisted his head around to face his companion and seems to be smiling at something he has just said. The blotted line, which everywhere else in this drawing is free of folds and crossings, curls around itself at this figure's crotch, opening a suggestive negative space

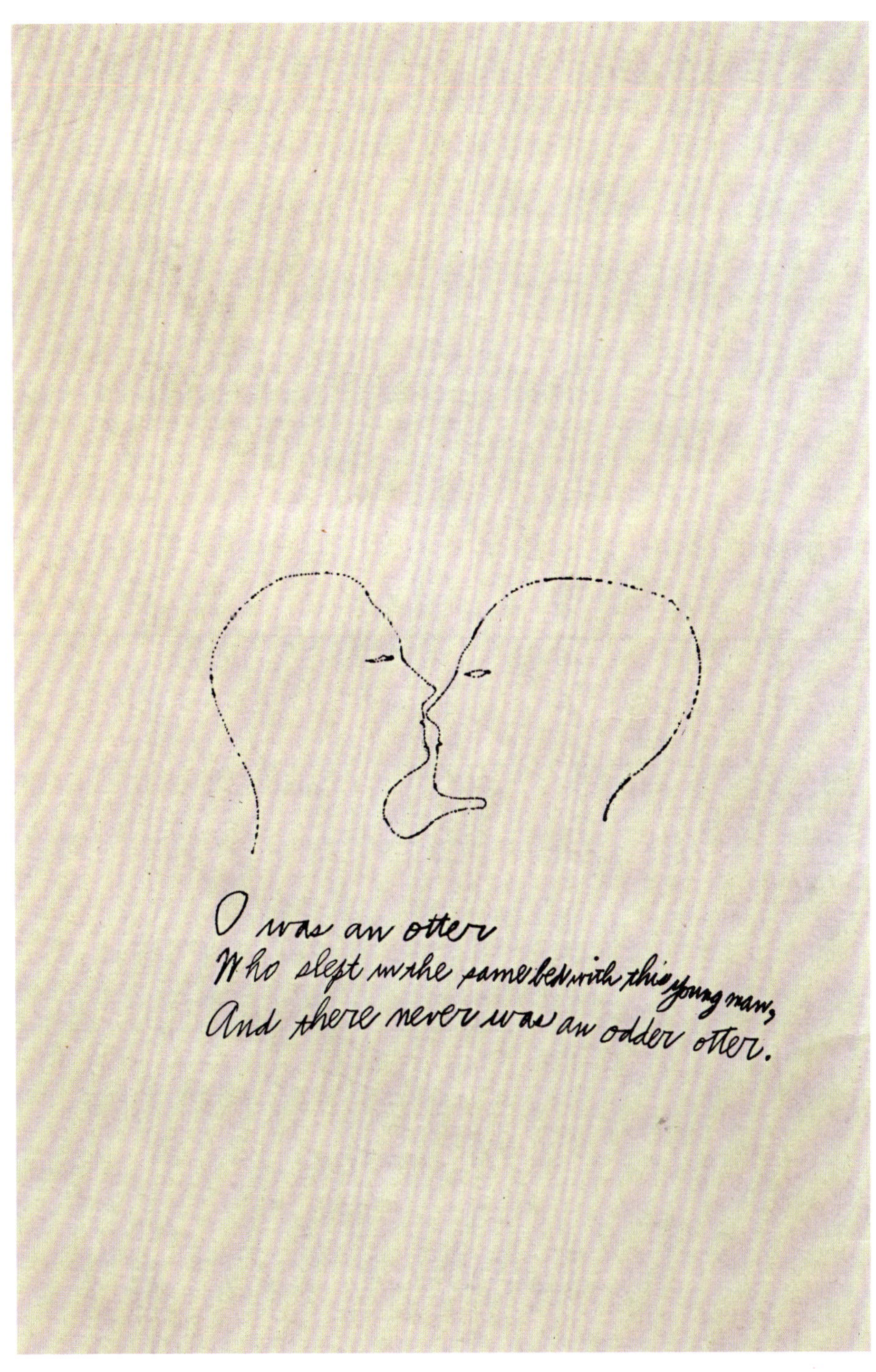

FIGURE 18

Andy Warhol, *A Is an Alphabet*, 1953. Image and Artwork © The Andy Warhol Foundation for the Visual Arts, Inc./ Licensed by ARS.

between his thighs. Beneath the figures, the stanza reads: "S was a snake / who played with this young man until his mother chased it with / a rake." Here, in addition to the standard association between snakes and homosexuality, the rhyming wordplay accentuates the innuendo, since the secondary meaning of "rake" (a playboy) reintroduces the threat that the primary meaning (a garden tool) ostensibly wards off.[124] Warhol's kissing dachshunds have almost become men in these two images, nearly lip to lip in one, nearly crotch to crotch in the other.

If "O" and "S" introduced the emotional and physical themes of animal homoeroticism, "R" proposed their possible origin. Its accompanying drawing depicts the partial silhouette of a young woman's head and torso seen in profile, with the breast centrally placed, and the nipple emphasized with a thicker blot of ink. (See figure 19.) The caption reads: "R was a rabbit / Who was fed everday [*sic*] by this yg. lady / they both thought it an agreeable habit." On first read, the verse might be taken to describe the regular dispensation of vegetables, but its emphasis on pleasure and addiction ("everday . . . an agreeable habit") and the prominence of the figure's breast and nipple in the drawing quickly complicate this reading. Placed in dialogue with Warhol's lost *Female with Animal at Breast,* and with future works that would return to this theme, the page and its proximity to "O" and "S" again evoke long-standing associations between overly affectionate mothers and homosexual sons who supposedly never get over what Freud called "this first and most significant of all sexual relations."[125] According to this etiology, which Elizabeth Lunbeck has shown to be tremendously influential, these boys "narcissistically identified with their mothers and put themselves in her place, fated forever to love boys as their mothers had loved them."[126]

In an uncanny irony, none of these pages' risqué allusions—not even those regarding the erotics of maternity—would have been fully legible to the woman who literally wrote them and had physically nursed the artist who produced their accompanying drawings. Julia Warhola could transcribe English words, but she had difficulty reading them.[127] This immunity may have been at least partially contagious: Julia's antiquated and occasionally indecipherable script could screen Warhol and Ward's innuendos from casual readers while adding another layer of intrigue to the works' etiological associations. But whatever their success aesthetically, Warhol's collaborations with Ward were not successful romantically. His crush on Ward was never reciprocated, and a mutual friend reported that Ward later described Warhol as "a boorish peasant"—from an impoverished background, obviously, but perhaps also too attached to agrarian worlds and bodies.[128]

At the height of his career as an illustrator, Warhol filled his work with images of animals, particularly of cats. Had he never successfully transitioned from commercial to fine art, he would probably have been known in large part for these images and his fashion illustrations. (These latter illustrations had become massively successful,

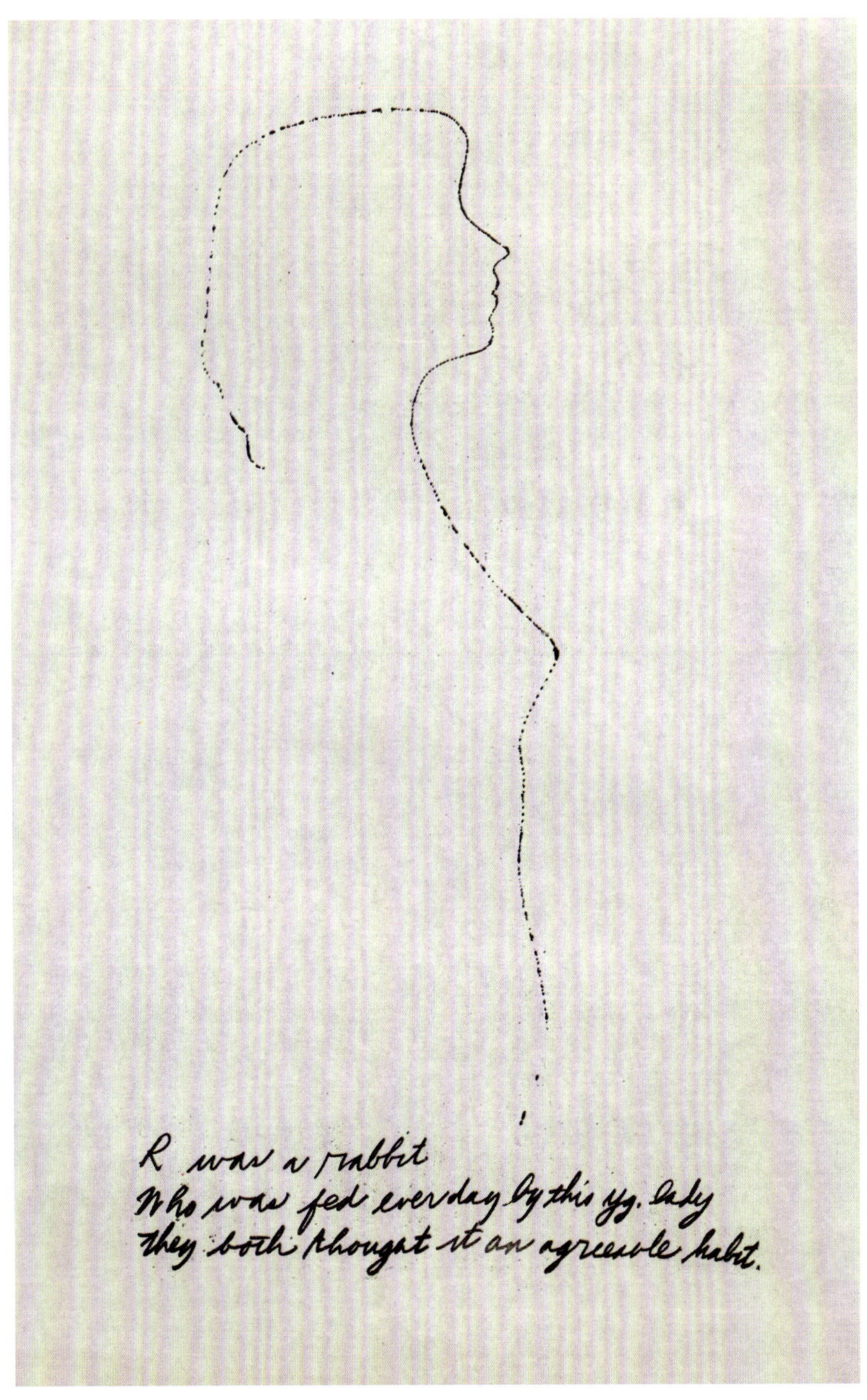

FIGURE 19

Andy Warhol, *A Is an Alphabet,* 1953. Image and Artwork © The Andy Warhol Foundation for the Visual Arts, Inc./Licensed by ARS.

even earning him inclusion in MoMA's 1965 exhibition "Recent Drawings USA.") His homoerotic works—full of flowers and butterflies and beautiful boys—remained mostly uncelebrated during this period, despite his efforts to frame them as naturalistic by dubbing them *Landscapes*.[129] But the brood of Siamese cats he cultivated during the 1950s served as more than merely models for the work. As Gopnik's research suggests, Warhol's working method incorporated feline production: his studio was typically strewn with works in progress, which would become ink-stained and paw-printed over time.[130] Warhol marketed himself and his work as being dominated by cats: made in their image, produced in part by their activity, redolent of their world (as with his urine-soaked shoes).[131]

Many of Warhol's trademark creative strategies were tested out with his cats during this period. As Matt Wrbican has argued, while the almost identical rows of soup cans were still a decade away, Warhol foreshadowed them by naming all but two of his cats "Sam," playfully undermining common notions of identity and singularity, and raising the question of a "branded" cat.[132] In typical Warholian fashion, this mischievous branding was tied to an actual effort to monetize the cats' fecundity. Siamese cats were in vogue, his were reproducing rapidly, and Warhol thought he might be able to supplement his income by selling them to friends for ten dollars each (roughly equivalent to one hundred dollars today). Proceeds from selling kittens were directly used to fund care packages for impoverished relatives in Europe.[133] Absent buyers, Warhol would attempt to give the kittens away.[134] The alternative was brutal: one friend recalled that Julia killed some of their unwanted kittens during the 1950s.[135] As was so often the case in Warhol's work, the origins of stylish nonchalance can paradoxically be traced to desperation and impoverishment.

Also typical of Warhol's emerging style, however, was the prominence of imperfection in these commodified reproductions. As Gopnik has discovered, "Warhol's idea of feline birth control was to wrap an old sweater around Hester's loins."[136] Warhol's commercial-art assistant, Nathan Gluck, noted that the kittens tended to be "highly neurotic and inbred"—like young Warhol according to his family, prone to incestuous impulses and misbehavior.[137] As he would in his advertisements, prints, and paintings, Warhol cultivated a loose and undisciplined reproductive style in his cat breeding that resulted in noticeable flaws for which he refused to apologize. One client recalled that Warhol "hated" to do the exacting work required for color printing: "A lot of that stuff was accidental, and then, he used it, and then that became his style."[138] Originality and uniqueness (ideals closely linked to heterosexual reproduction) were refused in favor of messy, irregular, haphazard replication. Even Warhol's famous book of cat prints, *25 Cats Name Sam and One Blue Pussy*, was found to have been copied in large part from two previous photo books.[139]

These queer themes of incest and inbreeding raise a third trademark Warholian concern in his approach to the Siamese cats: sexualization. At every turn, Warhol and his collaborators found ways to link the cats to sexual innuendo, deploying them as flirts and avatars whose innocence could not be questioned. Here the slang term "pussy" was indispensable, as in 1954's *Holy Cats,* for instance: "Some pussys [*sic*] . . . play with angels / Some play with boys / Some play with themselves."[140] Upon learning that Warhol had a cat, his friend Tommy Jackson remarked, "i knew things was good / but I didn't know you had a pussy."[141] As Koestenbaum has shown, Warhol would make the most of this double entendre, drawing out its implications of sexual and artistic reproductivity: in a love poem to a friend, he promised that "my kittys [*sic*] going to have a baby" and that "my kitty lies between my legs."[142] A boyfriend remembered, "[Warhol would] call me up sometimes . . . and say please talk to my cat, she's very lonely."[143]

But the sexualization of Warhol's cats extends beyond the opportunities that "pussies" provided for wordplay. The twenty-five cats—all allegedly male, all with the same name—also cunningly foreshadow the gay clone culture that Warhol would explore in works like *Elvis I* (1964) and *Thirteen Most Wanted Men* (1964) during the 1960s.[144] This human-feline sexualization literally permeated Julia and Andy's shared living space. Carl Alfred Willers remembered that the cats "left messes on the drafting table, in the bathtub, everywhere. Andy's poor mother was always mopping up after the cats."[145] If, as Koestenbaum and Christopher Schmidt intriguingly argue, Warhol's sexual interest in the abject can be traced to the results of his mother's battle with colon cancer, then the squalor of their overpopulated and under-cleaned apartment may have served to screen this queer interest, deflecting the abject events and sensations from human bodies to feline ones.[146]

But the most powerful and intriguing link between Warhol's feline sociability and the rest of his career wouldn't become public until decades later. In a remarkable diary entry from September 1980, Warhol made the case that his transition from advertising to Pop Art was fueled by his attachment to his cats and his reaction to their traumas. He described these feelings as having provoked the affective shift that made the Pop style possible:

> I once gave [Bettie Barnes] a kitten and the kitten was crying and I thought it wanted its mother so I gave him the mother. We had two cats left, my mother and I had given away twenty-five already. This was the early sixties. And after I gave [Barnes] the mother he took her to be spayed and she died under the knife. My darling Hester. She went to pussy heaven. And I've felt guilty ever since. That's how we should have started *Popism.* That's when I gave up caring. I don't want to think about it. If I had had her spayed myself I just know she would have lived, but *he* let her die.[147]

"That's how we should have started *Popism*": the book, which Warhol cowrote with Pat Hackett, had been published a few months earlier. Its narrative begins in the early 1960s and singles out Emile de Antonio as having initially discerned the superiority of Warhol's cold, mechanical style over his rough, expressionistic style while examining two paintings of the same motif: "One of these is a piece of shit. . . . The other is remarkable—it's our society, it's who we are, it's absolutely beautiful and naked, and you ought to destroy the first one and show the other."[148] This snap judgment became a key episode in the Warhol myth; it is frequently mentioned in discussions of the artist's adoption of his mature pop style.[149] It casts Warhol as a fundamentally passive artist, vacillating between styles but canny enough to trust an expert. "That afternoon was an important one for me," he concludes.[150]

And yet Warhol's reconsideration of this chapter in his diaries suggests that he had second thoughts about assigning so much responsibility to de Antonio, and that it was the trauma and guilt attached to the experience of losing Hester that convinced him to forge an aesthetic of emotional indifference. The guilt seems to have resulted from at least two sources. First, Warhol's own failure to take responsibility for having Hester spayed ("If I had had her spayed myself I just know she would have lived"), which was likely attached to Warhol's lifelong fear of hospitals and medical treatment more generally but also to his long-standing commitment to maximizing production and profitability: why spay a cat who could still profitably produce offspring, particularly when his mother and their relatives were relying on this support? (Warhol mendaciously mentions having "given away" the kittens, not selling them.) And second, the unresolved pain of his mother's death in 1972, long after Hester's death but before his reconsideration of it in the 1980 diary entry—another situation in which Warhol had entrusted a beloved matriarch's care to others only to have her die without him (see chapter 4).

No wonder Hester's death proved too painful to process, and painful enough to provoke a style predicated centrally on apathy. "That's when I gave up caring"—the expression resonates with Warhol's infamous pronouncements of indifference: "I still care about people but it would be so much easier not to care . . . it's too hard to care . . . that's why my work is so distant from myself."[151] Or again, in *a: a novel:* "Well I've been hurt so often I don't even care any more."[152]

Finally, the saga of Hester and her Sams also anticipated a fascinating cluster of observations posed by Jacques Derrida in his late book *The Animal That Therefore I Am.* This section ponders the biblical story of Genesis and the powerful mythic and ideological connections between naming, sexual difference, anthropocentrism, sacrifice, and shame that are proposed and canonized therein. Derrida shows that Adam's capacity to name other beings—"Eve," "woman" more generally, and the nonhuman animals—is inextricable from his "human" powers to differentiate, dominate, and experience shame.[153] Julia and Andy's playful and eccentric decisions to name all the cats "Sam," regardless of gender, to allow them to proliferate so wildly and incestuously, and to refer to them repeatedly and suggestively as "pussies" all amount to a hyperbolic refusal of the human exceptionalism promised in Genesis, including the distinction of feeling ashamed.[154] Freed of the father figure, with "nothing left but [their] own complicity," mother and son turned naming animals into something strange.[155] The traditional dichotomies between male and female, human and beast, and reproduction and incest were each at least partially disrupted. This sense of radical sexual egalitarianism would prove extremely seductive and marketable. Dotson Rader described Warhol as "a parental figure, a father to the young," but one who "represents limitless tolerance, deliverance from loneliness and alienation."[156] Asked in the 1980s whether he thought of himself as "a father figure to anyone," Warhol was quick with a witty response: "Just to my dogs."[157]

If *Female with Animal at Breast* is Warhol's great lost college work, then his great lost collaborative project with Julia, the effort that I think ties the others together most compellingly and preposterously, is the homemade performance art they concocted by clothing their unfixed cats in handsewn pants. Warhol would describe their interactions as "more interesting to watch than television"—high praise indeed, coming from one of the medium's great admirers.[158] The hijinks that resulted mark the intersection of so many of Warhol's signature themes: seduction, reproduction, the "primitive," the abject, the possibilities of a drive-based aesthetic practice. In the early 1960s, Warhol was still struggling with how to make these intersecting themes public as art. He proposed enlarging a "Ben Shahn–ian illustration of his, of cute birds roosting on rooftop antennas" to the size of a mural—the animal and the machine, not quite eroticized, not quite conflated, but nowhere near as fascinating as his and Julia's horny, dopey, incestuous cats.[159]

In the years leading up to Warhol's emergence as a Pop artist, we see nonhuman lifeforms occupying a variety of pivotal and compelling positions in his life, his work, and his imagination. On the one hand, and perhaps most obviously, plants, dirt, cats, dogs, mice, insects, rabbits, and chickens are physically, emotionally, and imaginatively prominent in Warhol's life throughout much of this period. They are repeatedly described as being some of his closest companions, and Warhol is charged (by himself and others) with resembling them. We have seen that, in the face of numerous traumas and anxieties—sexual, physical, linguistic, financial, existential—Warhol turned for comfort to his mother and to these nonhuman others, who tended to be closely connected to her. His mother would literally produce animals and plants for him, either by procuring them, breeding them, buying him images of them, or drawing them herself. She administered the overwhelming broods of animals that lived with them: cleaning, feeding, organizing.[160] Nonhuman life forms allowed Warhol to imagine a world without bodily or sexual or oedipal or ethnic or class-based shame, without linguistic awkwardness, without abjection, without the foreknowledge of death—a world of "blowsy flowers," kissing dachshunds, snakes who are rakes, odder otters. Their overwhelming prominence in his work during this pre-Pop period speaks to the effectiveness of this strategy for him. At important moments, these two sources of comfort—maternal and nonhuman—were explicitly linked in his imagination and his work: the uncanny images of dogs suckling from human bosoms; the earthworm ceiling; the drawings of flowers sprouting from beautiful feet; the rabbit in *A Is an Alphabet* and its "agreeable habit" of nursing a young woman's breast; the portrait with Lucy and Julia; Warhol's insistence that, as a child, he had felt like a little dog. Mother and nonhuman others seemed to offer intertwined refuges from the adult rules that Warhol found so unappealing: speak and read properly; face death solemnly; be "manly" without desiring men; be comfortable in your body by controlling your shame; keep your private parts and fluids hidden; let go of your mother so that you can move on to exogamous heterosexual relationships; obey your father and his surrogates.

And yet we have also seen that the interrelations between these refuges—maternal and ecological—were by no means consistently reliable, harmonious, or altruistic. There were times when Julia seemed to have the magical capacity to soothe savage beasts like Lucy, whose temperament had been ruined by Andy's brothers' beatings. But Julia was also the main administrator of death in Warhol's natural kingdom. She eventually got rid of Lucy (who trusted only her), fed Warhol's beloved pet chicken to him in a soup, and would apparently kill their surplus kittens when Warhol couldn't sell them fast enough. Julia and Andy: the undertaker's apprentice who lived next door to them in Pittsburgh said that neither of them would hurt a fly: "If you were going to kill something, a bug or a fly, she'd say, 'Loving one, don't do that.'"[161] But when the chips were down, they both did, sometimes just for the sake of aesthetic pleasure. Warhol would later insist that a "red lobster's beauty only comes out when it's dropped into the boiling water."[162]

What's more, there are troubling hints in Warhol's biography that Julia's capacity for coldhearted pragmatism could extend to her son as well. Joseph Giordano, a close friend from this period, was sure that "the crux of Andy Warhol is that he felt so unloved, so unloved." He sensed that "it came from his mother," that "she was doing something wrong. . . . She made him feel that he was the ugliest creature that God put on this earth."[163] At some point in the late 1950s, Julia unexpectedly left their shared apartment and went back to Pittsburgh. Giordano believed the departure was a form of punishment, since "his mother thought of Andy as a source for money to give to her other children" and "he wasn't shelling out enough."[164] This queer boy, this "ugliest creature," with his "childish mind," was framed by Julia as a productive and servile earner, a bit like Hester, having or being "a pussy," producing kittens for the profit of his human companions.[165] Eventually Andy convinced his mother to return. As Giordano remembers, "[H]e finally called her back. She insisted that I be there that night. She came in and slammed her suitcase on the ground and turned around. She looked at him and said, 'I am Andy Warhol.' And there was a big discussion about why she was Andy Warhol. But I guess she convinced him that she was."[166]

Shame, Martha Nussbaum writes, "dogs our footsteps": it certainly dogged Warhol's.[167] The canine metaphor is not accidental: as Nussbaum shows, "disgust has been used throughout history to exclude and marginalize groups or people who come to embody the dominant group's fear and loathing of its own animality and mortality," including women, the poor, ethnic minorities, and homosexuals.[168] Julia encouraged and administered the abject and animal in Warhol's life—his various pets and pests and companions—and she also encouraged and administered an abject animal life *in him* as and through shame and transgression. By holding him close to her and treating him as ugly and "unloved"—disgusting and shameful—she helped to form a child who simultaneously relied on her for comfort *and* would constantly seek attention from others through his embrace of the abject and transgressive. Transgression produced shame, which in turn could be mollified by the earnings produced by new transgressions, which brought with them renewed shame; the process could be self-perpetuating, mechanical. In this way, Warhol's shame became, in Sedgwick's words, "a nexus of production"—"of meaning, of personal presence, of politics, of performative and critical efficacy," certainly, but also of profitability, all fueled by animal/maternal transgression: an animal-machine, an ecology.[169] From peeing on the landlord's son's shoes to soaking his own shoes in cat urine, beginning at an early age Warhol cultivated a profitable style of animal/ecological appetite and volatility that seemed to flaunt all human propriety.

At the limit, Julia seems to have thought that her son *belonged* to his mother the way pets, livestock, or crops belong to a farmer, so that she could plausibly claim his productivity as her property: "I am Andy Warhol." (Maybe they both remembered that she had sketched a Campbell's Soup can in 1952, almost a decade before Warhol introduced the motif in his work, and that she had transformed empty soup cans into salable flowers to support her family.)[170] Warhol's ability to communicate intense and unusual animality and shame *was* his profitability, for Julia. She saw Andy not just as her surrogate daughter and husband but also as her abject *animal,* the "ugliest creature" with the "childish mind" who would lucratively captivate various segments of American society during his career of almost four decades, and for at least a quarter century after that.[171] Warhol would broadcast and reiterate this relationship throughout his career, perhaps most pointedly in his images of dogs nursing at women's breasts—a perfect Kristevian conflation: breast and beast, mother and other—but also in his prolific *Flowers, Silver Clouds,* and *Cows* of the 1960s. Their codependence seems to have mostly been "an agreeable habit" for Andy and Julia. In any case, there were mouths to feed in Pittsburgh, and abroad.

This collaborative project would have strange and powerful consequences. As a wide variety of artists—including Chryssa, Marisol, Yayoi Kusama, Allan Kaprow, Pauline Boty, the Fluxus group, and Robert Rauschenberg—championed conflations of art and a "life" that was often all too human, Warhol's emphasis on an art grounded in animal and vegetal life promised to offer something deeper and less sublimated: rooting art in a larger and more profound queer ecology.[172] At the Silver Factory, he would replicate and radicalize the mother/animal relationship with his Superstars, encouraging them to pursue their own inner animality through intoxication and disinhibition.

These relationships would prove tremendously fertile and hazardous. And, in the decades that followed, Warhol would continue to pursue the model he and Julia had inaugurated, branching it out to challenge many of the fundamental hierarchies that underwrote traditional aesthetic production. At the limit, this ecological orientation would dispute everything that "art" was meant to protect: life (in opposition to death), creativity (in opposition to replication), disinterest (in opposition to appetite), propriety (in opposition to every form of transgression), preservation (in opposition to entropy and decomposition). And, in his final years, a pair of explicitly advocatory projects would unexpectedly return Warhol to the mother/animal relationship that had formed him as an artist.

2

FACTORY BADLANDS

WARHOL'S SILVER FACTORY REMAINS one of the truly problematic sites in twentieth-century art history. On the one hand, it is widely recognized as a wellspring of prodigious cultural production. Some of the century's most iconic avant-garde films, paintings, photographs, and sculptural objects were produced there: the *Screen Tests* (1964–66), *Blow Job* (1964), and *Chelsea Girls* (1966), for starters, but also the *Flowers, Most Wanted Men,* and *Brillo Boxes* (all 1964), the last of which Arthur Danto called "a philosophical masterpiece," and a "profound" one at that.[1] What's more, Warhol somehow found time between these projects to cultivate one of the century's preeminent rock bands, the Velvet Underground, described by Lester Bangs as "the most advanced experimental group in the world," and their remarkable early multimedia experiences, the *Exploding Plastic Inevitable* (1966–67).[2] It is difficult to overstate the cultural impact of the Silver Factory during this period, and particularly its commitment to a truly unprecedented egalitarianism of production, content, and reception.[3] The Silver Factory proposed that any creature (no

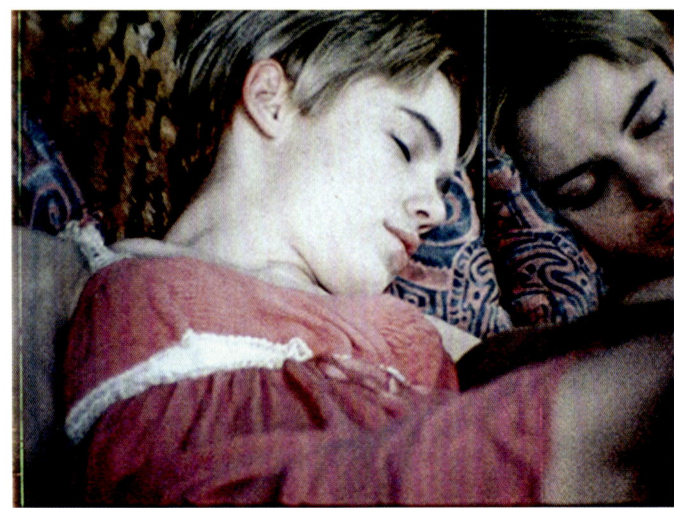

FIGURE 20
Edie Sedgwick in the film *Lupe* (Andy Warhol, 1966).

matter how degenerate) could make art, anything (no matter how "vulgar") could be the subject of art, and anyone (no matter how marginalized) could enjoy art. Situated across the street from the Grand Central YMCA, a queer landmark of the period, it was also, as Blake Gopnik has shown, a nexus for sexual experimentation and libertinism.[4] And yet, to a much greater extent than most art studios, or than many of Warhol's admirers would care to acknowledge, the Silver Factory was also the site of extensive and intense suffering: emotional, sexual, and physical abuse; overdoses; and suicides. As Fran Lebowitz recently observed, "Andy encouraged bad behavior by people who were already unstable. I noticed a very high mortality rate of people near him."[5] Ondine, one of Warhol's central Superstars, apparently said of his director (using his primary Factory nickname): "Drella, she's not good to her friends."[6] (See figure 20.)

Recent Warhol scholarship has attempted to reconcile this troubling coincidence of brilliance and cruelty by acknowledging the prominence of drug use—particularly amphetamine use—in the Silver Factory, and by charting its aesthetic, psychological, and ethical consequences.[7] Chelsea Weathers, Juan Suárez, and others have added immeasurably to our sense of this dimension of Warhol's collaborative production. Warhol was certainly willing to acknowledge amphetamine's link with productivity, although he claimed to be unsure whether it was a cause or an effect: "I could never finally figure out if more things happened in the sixties because there was more awake time for them to happen in (since so many people were on amphetamine), or if people started taking amphetamine because there were so many things to do that they needed to have more awake time to do them in."[8] He was widely reported to have taken Obetrol daily from at least the early 1960s until his death (with a brief break while he recovered from his assassination attempt).[9] Peter Plagens memorably described him as "de Tocqueville on thorazine."[10] And yet, the Silver Factory's emphasis on amphetamine use, and drug use more generally, raises as many questions as it answers, since, to paraphrase Jean-Paul Sartre (himself a voracious consumer of drugs), not every speed binge resulted in *Chelsea Girls* or the *Brillo Boxes*.

This chapter will propose that, for a variety of reasons, animality, queer ecology, and the animal-machine are apposite concepts for thinking through this difficult and prolific period in Warhol's work.[11] On a practical level, the emphasis on animal transgression that Warhol had cultivated since early childhood—hyperbolically becoming an animal-machine, allowing himself to be driven by appetites without the constraint of human morality or reason, working with and among nonhuman life-forms—logically culminates in an embrace of drugs, beyond any concern for legality or safety. Inebriation, we now know, is practically ubiquitous among animals. Ronald Siegel, a pioneer in this field, has described it as "the fourth drive," alongside hunger, thirst, and sex—a "behavior that is consistent across time and species."[12] Thoroughly exploring animality and its unrestrained drives *meant* exploring intoxication, because, although traditional science chooses mostly to ignore it, "the action of an animal in seeking out intoxicants [is] a natural behavior in the animal kingdom."[13]

What's more, Warhol and his collaborators believed that intoxication promised regressions into animality they found fascinating and desirable. At the limit, they would use drugs to explore what they thought of as animal forms of sexuality and violence that were completely unmoored from traditional understandings of biology and evolution. This emphasis on regression also had stylistic consequences in Warhol's paintings, as when "the face is effaced" through sloppy and irregular silkscreen printing, and "subterranean becomings-animal occur . . . over-spilling the limits of the signifying system."[14] Warhol's collaborators graded each *Screen Test* participant on a ten-point scale for soullessness; the ideal sitters would be "like moths pinned to a board."[15] Contemporary observers agreed that, in these works, Warhol was exploring the collapse of human signification: "These objects express a deep doubt about man's ability to communicate anything, except his own failure as a creator."[16] Beneath this failure was the merely animal or ecological.

Connections between animality and the amphetamine use that abounded in Factory life were remarked by some of its less inhibited observers. Reviewing a Kraftwerk album in 1975, Lester Bangs observed that "methamphetamine . . . of all accessible tools has brought human beings within the closest twitch of machinehood," and that without it, "we would never have had such high plasma marks of the counterculture as Lenny Bruce, Bob Dylan, Lou Reed and the Velvet Underground, Neal Cassady, Jack Kerouac, Allen Ginsberg's 'Howl,' . . . as well as all of the fine performances in Andy Warhol movies not inspired by heroin."[17] This machinelike production was, for Bangs, explicitly bestial: "American archetypes ground out by holloweyed jerkyfingered mannikins locked into their typewriters and guitars like rhinoceroses copulating."[18]

As we will see in chapter 3, Bangs's animal-machine analogy (in this case, a cyborg that performs like a rhinoceros fucks) is by no means aberrant: it joins a venerable lineage, stretching back before Descartes, that equates the nonhuman animal and the machine, proposing both as distinctively subhuman in their supposed automaticity and soullessness, and linking them to "primal" sexuality.[19] But Bangs's perspective also introduces an important new component. Amphetamine, which he rightly identifies as a prominent technology within countercultural production and particularly within Warhol's Factory, is the terrifying substance that turns humans into animal-machines, sex-crazed and empty-eyed beasts who mindlessly and soullessly pour their libido into their production. Within the human/animal hierarchy, drugs seem to offer the charged possibility of regression, moving backward along the evolutionary ladder. Drug use in the Factory resulted in a highly violent and sexualized environment, but one that contested what Michael Lundblad has called "the discourse of the jungle"—an imperialist ideology that imagines all life forms as being driven by narrowly evolutionary imperatives: "'naturally' violent in the name of survival, and heterosexual in the name of reproduction."[20] At the limit, Factory drug use offered the annihilation of rationality, growth, and individualism: intoxication could instead promise what Theodor Adorno described as "a form of oceanic regression."[21]

Bangs was not alone in remarking a connection between the Factory's drug-fueled film production and animal life. Describing Warhol's 1965 film *My Hustler,* Stephen Koch claimed that its "camera movements are . . . informed with something that is almost primordial . . . like the movements of cats or birds."[22] In Koch's account, Warhol's camera becomes an animal: probing, attacking, caressing, but ultimately nonchalant, like the human mind in its preconscious state, as in Warhol's *More Milk, Yvette* (1966), where the camera becomes "a very inattentive dog, constantly distracted by the fly on the ceiling."[23] A similarly prerational perspective seemed possible for Koch while watching *Blow Job:* "In this vague state, the personality becomes diffuse, lax, attentive, merely open, waiting for that sharp singular instant . . . when authentic desire will leap at the screen like a dog snarling for its gratification."[24] For his part, Parker Tyler could at least vaguely and dismissively link what he called "drugtime" with both animality and sadomasochism: in Warhol's 1965 film *Vinyl,* he argued, "We are witnessing a snailpaced fantasy in which familiar homosexual sadism, enhanced by drugtime, is putting on some kind of an act."[25] But in an early draft of this famous essay, he was able to intuit that Warhol's cinema depended on "an intuitive appeal to that common, ever-ready domain of human susceptibility: the beautiful badlands of sadomasochism."[26] Sadomasochism as a harsh terrain that shadows human experience: this remarkable vision was excised from Tyler's published text.

Some of these insights regarding the centrality of amphetamines to the Silver Factory's production have been extended in recent articles by Weathers and Suárez. For Suárez, amphetamine use intensified the machinic aesthetic that Warhol is perhaps best known for: "Noise . . . floods the mind on speed" like the "automatic read-write protocols . . . [that] register and emit sense and non-sense, information and the murmur of the world."[27] Along the same lines, amphetamine could stimulate a new world of nonnormative sexuality, "sex without genital fixation."[28] As a result, the machine/amphetamine Factory produced a complete overturning of the traditional filmic hierarchies, "inverting the usual hierarchy between signal and noise, center and periphery, and message and sensory massage"; this, for Suárez, was its exceptional achievement.[29]

Weathers proposes an equally provocative reading of amphetamine's effects on temporality and emotion. The drug offered Warhol and his collaborators access to a "*ludic temporality*," which "allows a person to live a life beyond the confines of conventional temporal structures." The result was a refusal of "a long-term temporal trajectory of childhood, adolescence, maturation, procreation, and then death," a rejection of what Elizabeth Freeman has called "chrononormativity."[30] Ultimately, Weathers proposes that Factory amphetamine use resulted in an "amphetamine community," in which "love and affection . . . was borne . . . out of cruelty, paranoia, and a sense of singularity" in the absence of "a narrative of redemption."[31] This insight into Factory life offers an important counterweight to the persistent temptation to heroize Warhol, and to disregard the suffering over which he presided.

Together, Weathers's and Suárez's provocative analyses greatly illuminate the aesthetic, erotic, epistemological, and ethical consequences of amphetamine use at the Silver Factory. And yet, as Bangs, Koch, and Tyler all noticed, this use also had distinctively animalistic connotations: these critics saw something dog- or cat- or birdlike in Warhol's camera, something canine in his spectators' attention, something snaillike in his pacing. Warhol apparently recognized this ecological connection quite clearly. As he put it in *Popism:* "People on amphetamine didn't really have 'apartments,' they had 'nests.'"[32] Factory–animal intersections were not as obvious and direct as they were in Warhol's pre-Pop life: we don't have dozens of animal and vegetal companions to reckon with, as we did there, or hundreds of drawings of cats and flowers. Instead, the Silver Factory provided Warhol with an opportunity to encourage his collaborators to embrace their own animality in various ways: erotically, cinematically, interpersonally. Intoxication was among these forms of becoming-animal, and so were sadism and masochism—ways of "test[ing]—and potentially escap[ing]—one's psychic and existential boundaries via a sympathetic circuit with another creature."[33]

Only two companion animals—both cats—seem to have lived at the Silver Factory long-term; their names, Black Lace and White Pussy, telegraph the strange and smutty ways in which Warhol and his colleagues cultivated these new forms of human animality. So does the ephemeral Factory bathroom graffiti apparently drawn by Richard Stringer (a friend of Name's who went by "Binghamton Birdie," and who would costar in Warhol's homoerotic film *Couch* [1964]). A photograph by Stephen Shore captures a Boschian tableau of gross indecencies—bestiality; a gymnastic male threesome; a rocket cock, ascending; Superman, erect, heading the opposite way; a proud aristocrat in an armchair, penis peeking out from his lap; a Picassoesque bull raining golden showers onto a supine human (ineffectually protected by an umbrella added by some

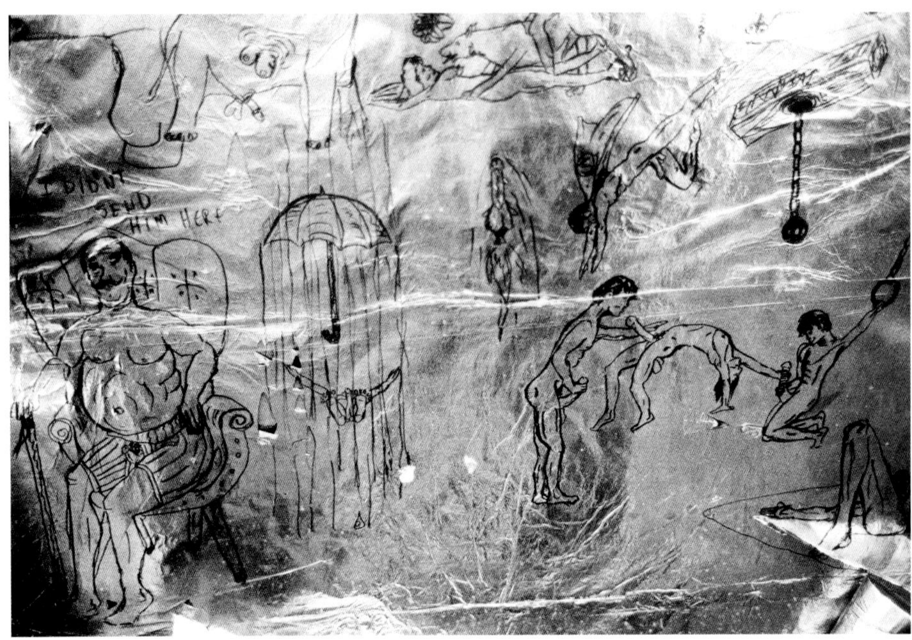

FIGURE 21
Stephen Shore, *Factory Toilet, The Factory, New York, New York,* 1965–1967. © Stephen Shore. Courtesy 303 Gallery, New York.

subsequent graffitist)—all in black Sharpie on aluminum foil, one of the only close-up views we have of the "silver" that covered the Factory walls, with its unglamorous wrinkles and perforations finally visible. (See figure 21.) The umbrellaed golden shower may have been a direct reference to the Factory's main amphetamine source; Ondine would later claim that their dealer "sold them Mason jars of speed for $25, but first he had them get under a plastic sheet so he could piss on them."[34]

Warhol's inspirations for linking narcotics with animal-machinic production seem to have been widespread and various. In his 1963 film *Flaming Creatures,* Jack Smith (who Warhol later claimed "makes the best movies") paired a delirious opening orgy scene with a soundtrack of animal noises.[35] The film's risqué title set the tone for many of Warhol's animal investigations during this period, and Warhol and Smith would go on to collaborate on a variety of projects. Reva Wolf has shown that, during this period, Warhol was also influenced by the communities around mimeographed journals like *Floating Bear, Sinking Bear,* and *Fuck You / A Magazine for the Arts,* with whom he shared "a fascination with the bestial dimension of human behavior and, by extension, relations between human beings and animals."[36] She points to Marlowe's stroking of a tiger skin in Warhol's film *Alan Marlowe and Diane di Prima* (1964); the "allusions to the bestial side of humans" in Warhol's first sound film, *Harlot* (1964); and, most suggestively, Warhol's filmic adaptation of Michael McClure's notorious play *The Beard* (1965).[37] Critics described *The Beard* as "a reduction of all male-female spats, courtships, fetishes, etc., to simple animal circling, snarling, sniffing, teasing."[38] Factory Superstar Ultra Violet recalled that Warhol found *The Beard* intensely inspirational: "Andy said, 'God, it is beautiful.' . . . 'That's how all my movies should be. My movies should be as beautiful as that play.'"[39] By 1966, and without McClure's blessing, Warhol had produced his own filmic version. When McClure complained after the first screening, Warhol gave the poet a print of the film and promised never to show it again.[40]

The Warhol film that would most directly engage the human-animal relationships that preoccupied McClure would be *Horse* (1965), the second-longest of Warhol's cinematic collaborations with screenwriter Ronald Tavel. Searching for someone to write dialogue for his films, Warhol had heard Tavel read at an East Village coffeehouse in November 1964. Tavel described his trademark vocal style as being "like the Serpent . . . in the Garden of Eden," and Warhol immediately invited him to join the Factory.[41] Tavel was not shy in describing its ambitions regarding human-animal themes: he hoped that *Horse* would "demythologize the Western novel and film and introduce the hidden in the anthropometric [*sic?*] image and stale ethnography of cowboys: their phallic worship, Levi competition, homosexuality, bestiality, onanism, racism, and institutionalized ignorance."[42]

A horse named Mighty Bird was rented and transported to the Factory. Four actors—Gregory Battcock, Tosh Carillo, Dan Cassidy, and Larry Latreille—in stereotypically "Western" garb (later removed to reveal jockstraps) were employed, uttering a mixture of clichéd dialogue and Tavelian provocations like "Beat it, beat it, beat it all day long."[43] The script was fed to the actors via "idiot sheets," large cue cards deployed off-screen: "[O]ne of us would hold up a card. It would say, 'Kid', 'Sheriff', 'Mex', or 'Tex' . . . and the other would hold up the line."[44] The result was stiff and mannered; as Douglas Crimp observed, in *Horse*, "[d]ialogue and interaction never constitute anything like recognizable intersubjectivity."[45]

According to Tavel, the film's origins and production were closely tied to drug use, sadism, and bestiality. Tavel had set out to produce a "*genuine* Western," revealing "cowboys" as "celibate, asexuals, and homosexuals" who were "in love with their horses" and "[p]robably screwing them. Not 'probably', they were."[46] All four actors would caress the horse erotically during filming, professing their desire and competing for his attention; Mex would repeatedly mount Mighty Bird as though sexually. Beneath this theme, Tavel's deeper interest, inspired by Konrad Lorenz's recently translated *On Aggression*, was in "how easily . . . a group of people under pressure [would] be moved to sadistic . . . [and] genuinely inhuman acts toward each other and perhaps the horse."[47]

Tavel saw *On Aggression* as having proposed that humans had "evolved as aggressive, flesh-eating beasts," that this remained as a "racial memory still in the genes," and that this accounted for sadists' and masochists' interest in "fur and leather and rubber and whatnot."[48] *Horse's* four human actors were "using [drugs] like mad": poppers and marijuana and "who knows what else."[49] Inebriation allowed them to be "oblivious to the danger of the horse throughout," despite its having kicked one of them—Carillo—on set. But Tavel thought that this repressed animal danger produced human aggression: "[T]hey went at each other to release that tension when I told them to start beating each other up on that concrete floor of the Factory!" The other actors "started pounding [Carillo's] head on the concrete so that I had to stop them, and it took a *very* long time of screaming."[50] The film was, for Tavel, a laboratory for investigating the intersections of regression, drug use, and cross-species eroticism and aggression. His grim suspicions about the causative relations between these forces were proven out; it took "about four minutes" for people to be "reduce[d] to a bestial state!"[51]

Two of *Horse*'s three reels record these semiscripted, highly sexualized human/animal interactions. The third reel, however, would be shown sandwiched between these two. This middle reel comprises a thirty-three-minute shot of the horse accompanied by his trainer, who offers him hay and sugar. The man holds a microphone to the horse's mouth and tries to prod him to communicate; he tells passersby that the horse has been sharing "dirty jokes": regression, humor, sexuality, and animality are again closely linked. Mighty Bird is positioned in a busy spot between the elevator and stairwell doors; Warhol, Ondine, Edie Sedgwick, and other Factory denizens make cameos. We are left with the silent ghost of a horse, as Factory life proceeds around him. Crimp has astutely remarked the resemblance between this reel and Warhol's classic "silent, minimal" films, like *Empire* and *Henry Geldzahler*. For Crimp, the "imposition of a recognizably 'Warhol' film reel between the two 'Tavel' reels serves straightforwardly to mark the 'failure' of the Warhol–Tavel collaboration."[52] The middle reel "is pure Warhol," whereas the other two are adulterated by Tavel's perverse obsessions.[53]

When Warhol's considerable animal interests are taken into account, however, the three reels of *Horse* become less discordant than Crimp suggested.[54] If Tavel was preoccupied primarily by animalistic perversions of human behavior, Warhol added an interest in the possibilities of animal expression and their compatibility with various reproductive technologies, including film and photography. What's more, as we have seen, Tavel's transgressive interests were by no means foreign to Warhol. He, too, was fascinated by experiences of violence, suffering, and cross-species eroticism, and had pursued them extensively in his work. Already in 1963, in the transcript of his well-known interview with Gene Swenson, he was asking friends about the relationship between marijuana, poppers, and sadism, and wondering whether "being a sadist and being beaten and stuff, if you can really do it well, it really doesn't hurt, does it?"[55] (The exchange would be censored from the published version.) What's more, Tavel certainly didn't think that Warhol's reel had ruined the film; he called *Horse* "the most interesting and the deepest" of their collaborations and "perhaps, the best of all

[Warhol's] films."[56] In many ways, it would set the tone for Factory life during this bizarre and fecund period.

Horse is almost a primer on the intersections between animality, drug use, and non-normative sexuality that made the Silver Factory such a fertile and dangerous creative site. None of Warhol's other films from this period rival it in this regard, and yet almost all of them would touch on these intersections in some way. In *Tarzan and Jane Regained, Sort Of*... (1963), dogs and cats play the roles of jungle creatures, and Jane is transformed into a dog who nevertheless retains Tarzan's erotic attention.[57] The unfinished *Batman Dracula*, codirected with Jack Smith, features Taylor Mead "pretending to be attacked by a dog."[58] In *Beauty #2* (1965), Edie Sedgwick wonders why her dog won't talk to her, and then is reminded by Chuck Wein that, as a child, she "beat [her] horse all the time ... the one [she] loved so much." Wein also accuses her of beating her dog, and implies that, in so doing, she is punishing her father for their allegedly incestuous relationship.[59] Warhol would later claim that the sole time he received substantial interest from a Hollywood studio, including a phone call from Rita Hayworth and a meeting with executives, the studio backed out when they learned that one of the characters was "going to have an affair" with a Great Dane, even though "the sex with the dog would be off-camera." Warhol could tell "that the roof had fallen in," and the invitation was withdrawn.[60]

Even when these intersections between animality, intoxication, and deviant sexuality were not explicitly thematized, canny observers would remark their presence. Documenting the filming of the rarely shown *More Milk, Yvette* in 1966, the novelist Donald Newlove homed in on a moment of incestuous and homoerotic animal appetite as Mario Montez, playing Lana Turner, eats a burger from one side as Richard Schmidt, playing Turner's daughter, Cheryl Crane, eats it from the other. Midway through, the two gender-bending characters are mouth to mouth, hand in hand, locked together in incestuous appetite. (See figure 22.) Something about the scene breaks Newlove's previously cavalier and homophobic tone. He writes, "They chewed, into each other's eyes and out into the camera, chewing, existence a cud, their cheeks sweet aphorisms of family. They were, mother and daughter/son, together."[61]

As Sharon Patricia Holland has argued, part of the function of the incest taboo is to separate human sexuality from its animal counterparts.[62] Julia Kristeva posited that the decision to embrace rather than abject the maternal or filial also entails an embrace of one's own animality.[63] This remarkable filmed moment, spurning all norms of incest and gender, prompted Newlove to see the two actors as bovine, their "existence a cud" to be chewed. Their worldly concerns had been reduced to a purely appetitive act—chewing—which is readable through their cheeks as "aphorisms of family." These aphorisms seem to signify the incestuous and postgendered *togetherness* of "[cross-dressing] mother and daughter/son," recalling the "the primal autoerotic or narcissistic wish" described by Whitney Davis: "I want all these, and more!"[64]

Fittingly, in this instance of Newlove's imaginative projection, the "cud" the incestuous cows are chewing is hamburger—cow flesh—crossing the incest taboo with the

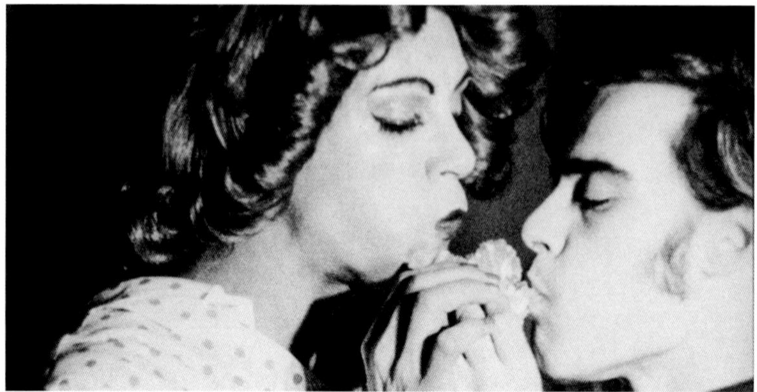

FIGURE 22
Mario Montez and Richard Schmidt in *More Milk, Yvette* (Andy Warhol, 1966).

taboo against cannibalism, and grimly foreshadowing the horrors of bovine spongiform encephalopathy (BSE, or mad cow disease), which has been "traced to the tautological practice of feeding protein meals rendered from animal remains back to livestock."[65] All told, the filmed romance was transformative for Newlove. By the end of the essay he had decided that *Yvette* was "one of the most profound, beautiful and original films ever made," and was openly pining for Montez's Turner: "I wanted to make love more than win the world."[66] Similar themes would recur in *Lonesome Cowboys,* produced in 1967, shortly after the closing of the Silver Factory. One character, expressing remorse for raping another, says, "We were like beasts. . . . I lost control. . . . I was slobbering like a horse . . . with a mouth disease."[67]

Mary Woronov's remarkable memoirs (which Lou Reed has called "the best book on Warhol") offer further confirmation that, even when it was not thematically emphasized, animality was in fact a powerful force in Factory life, closely associated with deviant sexuality and drug use.[68] Woronov visited the Factory on a school trip from Cornell, sat for a *Screen Test,* was cast as the dom to Gerard Malanga's sub in the *Exploding Plastic Inevitable,* and became a prominent sadistic presence in Factory life more generally. (See figure 23.) Tavel would describe her as "a top contender"—along with Nico, Ondine, and a few others—for "'mirror of the sixties.'"[69] As Woronov saw it, the energies that fueled her sadism were vividly and distinctively animal: she chronicles a "black dog" of sadism named "Violet, for violence," "that lived in my stomach growling away until . . . I attacked whatever was in front of me."[70] It would come to dominate the Silver Factory during Woronov's tenure.

Violet's childhood origins echo and extend the traumas that Warhol suffered as a child. Violet, Woronov explains, "was a house pet":

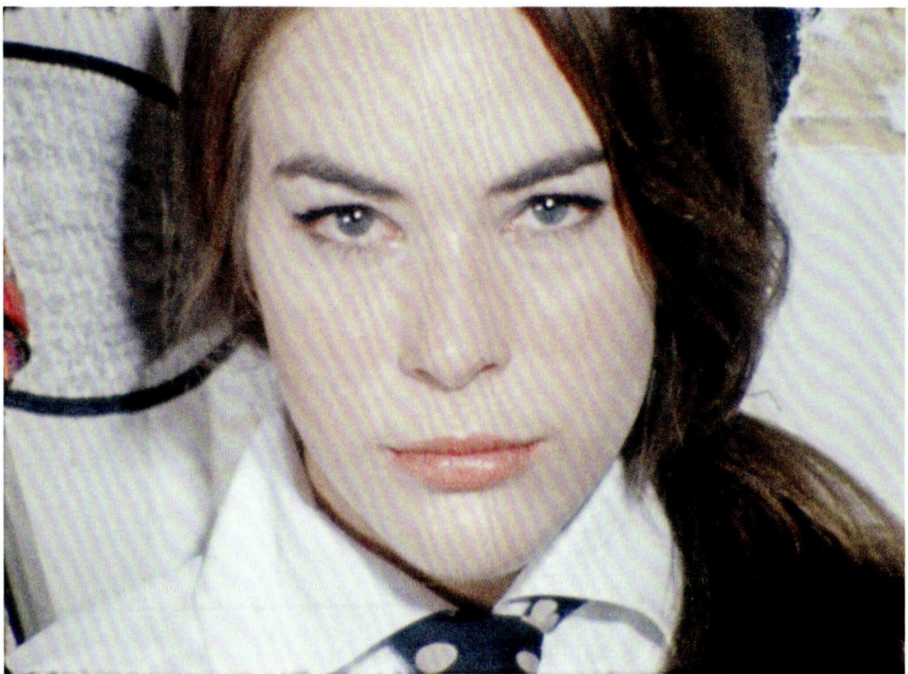

FIGURE 23
Mary Woronov in the film *Chelsea Girls* (Andy Warhol, 1966).

> I got [Violet] at home when I couldn't stomach breakfast anymore. Every morning Mum ended up hitting my kid brother, Victor, in the head because he wouldn't eat his eggs. His eyes blamed me from across the table (normally I ate his food for him . . .), but I couldn't eat those eggs. He would put syrup on them hoping they would turn into pancakes . . ., then he'd gag, then she'd scream, then he'd cry, then she'd hit him, then we'd go to school. . . . I could feel my stomach grinding up inside me on the way to school, while Victor trotted along beside me completely happy. . . . If I turned on him and yelled, "Don't you remember how you were sobbing twenty minutes ago?" he'd just look at me in that baffled, hurt way. So I didn't yell at him, I just ground my teeth and dreamed about how I was going to beat up Valerie during my lunch break, smash her head until she looked at me in that same baffled, hurt way and started crying. Valerie was also my best friend, which made this daydream particularly satisfying (35).

Woronov learned from an early age that Violet's targets could react to aggression in unpredictable ways, including by embracing sadistic and masochistic positions. Her best friend and first victim, Valerie, "decided to remain my friend after all, not because she was a forgiving person but because she fell in love with Violet" (35–36). The two girls became partners in sadism, luring classmates to the bathroom to beat them up. But Woronov reached her limit after Valerie "walked into our tiled web dragging . . . a shy epileptic child." (36). Terrifyingly, it wasn't this decision that convinced Woronov to "put Violet down"—it was Valerie's masochistic pleasure when Woronov attempted to punish her for her transgression. Woronov knew she had to make Violet stop: "her new cage looked like a coffin buried deep between my liver and stomach" (36). She would reappear briefly during fights with boys in high school, but a painful defeat left her "shell shocked . . . just daydream[ing] about killing people." (36–37).

It would take the Silver Factory to bring Violet back out of her cage: Woronov "forgot about Violet until I started making movies with Andy" (37). Warhol and his collaborators recognized Woronov as "a budding dominatrix"; the Factory drag queens "loved her" since "she could be so dramatic," and they talked Woronov into believing that it would be all right to unleash Violet on camera (37). In addition to her inner dog, she had an unnamed "rage rat," "a voice in my head that never shuts up" and that was constantly scrounging for drugs. The only way to turn the voice off was to find "something even more enraged," which Woronov assumed was "impossible" until she "met my first drag queen" (47). Factory queens, she discovered, were "so wired if you just touched them they would go off into a torrid movie affair" (53).

Amphetamine and animal violence became even more closely intertwined during the filming of what MoMA describes as Woronov's "showcase piece," *Queen of China (Hanoi Hanna)* (1966), which would become one section of Warhol's seminal *Chelsea Girls*.[71] In preparation for shooting, Woronov "did speed till I thought my head would explode and my heart shriveled to a pinprick."[72] When Ingrid Superstar started "trying to hog the camera," Violet "wanted to crack a few of her ribs," but Woronov restrained her. Repeatedly referring to International Velvet (Susan Bottomly) as "pig face" and disparaging her body, Woronov/Violet snapped when Velvet attempted to escape. Violet went "completely nuts," becoming "Godzilla . . . attack[ing] Velvet's makeup as if it were a miniature replica of Tokyo" (41). Velvet returned, but Woronov and Warhol's camera had shifted their attention to Angelina "Pepper" Davis, and again the victim immediately became animal: "With every question Violet was making a meal of Pepper's ego, ripping it apart like raw meat. . . . Pepper tried to rebel . . . but it was too late, her willpower hung like a dead chicken between my teeth" (41). It was as though Woronov's ampheta-sadistic imagination translated everything it saw into animal relations, just as Tavel had predicted. Critics could see it too: Koch described "the icy but beautiful Hanoi Hannah snarling in voiceless sadism at various girls draped around her room."[73]

As with her childhood collaborations with Valerie, the unexpected appearance of a victim's masochistic pleasure could disrupt Violet's attacks: "It was too easy, she was enjoying this. . . . I recoiled from her where she lay on the bed like a piece of rotting meat."[74] A victim's masochistic satisfaction nullified Violet's pure sadism: Violet wanted to give pain, not pleasure. As Deleuze observed, "[A] genuine sadist could never tolerate a masochistic victim."[75]

Woronov's narratives demonstrate a profound link between animality, amphetamines, and the tone of life in the Silver Factory that exceeds the phenomenologies of camera, viewer, and community described by Koch, Tyler, Weathers, and Suárez. Drug use allowed at least some of Warhol's central performers to see themselves and others as animals, engaged in sadistic battle for the camera's attention. One anonymous Factory newcomer noticed this environment immediately: "You were either a predator or a victim. . . . You were like a snake. You looked around and if something cropped up you lanced at it."[76]

Woronov's childhood narratives also offer interesting resonances with Warhol's. In both cases, we see troubled children turning to animals for support in a world that seems overwhelmingly threatening to them, and then performatively embracing animals and animality as a transgressive stance. But where Warhol's animals mostly provided queer avatars, administered by the artist's mother, that could at least partially escape homophobic censorship, Woronov's animals were born as a form of retribution for her mother's abusiveness. In this respect, Woronov and her childhood friend Valerie integrated two of the strategies Kathryn Bond Stockton attributes to the queer child: the use of animals as queer avatars, and the "prob[ing] of ideas of suffering in ways that are emotionally generative and bold."[77] And, in so doing, they were unknowingly replicating a long history of such linkages, which are already present, for instance, in the Marquis de Sade's claim that "cruelty is stamped in animals," and in the "becoming animal" that Deleuze and Félix Guattari would identify as "essential to masochism."[78]

However, read in tandem with what we have learned about Warhol's mother's manipulation of his animal shame and transgression for profit, Woronov's narratives further suggest that Warhol had found a way to replicate this relationship in the Factory: taking his mother's supervisory role for himself (the "clucking mother hen," with her simultaneously loving and critical tone), fostering "sibling rivalry," and encouraging his superstars to ramp up the stakes of the animal transgressions that he had tested throughout his pre-Pop years.[79] Asked in 1969 "[w]hat part of the human anatomy" he would be, Warhol responded, "A teat."[80] In Woronov, Warhol found an artist who could "become animal" in the most terrifying and vivid ways, chewing up the scenery and her costars, and dominating the camera in the process. The psychic costs of these attacks, both for their perpetrator and for her victims, do not seem to have been considered relevant so long as the resulting products were marketable. Warhol had become what his friend Henry Geldzahler called a "sadist-voyeur . . . he doesn't go around hurting people, but they do get hurt."[81]

Geldzahler's verdict is all the more appropriate since, as Georges Bataille insisted, abjection is central to sadism: the sadist takes pleasure in hyperbolically occupying the position of the purifying father, so that "the general tendency to exclude impurity then manifests itself in the form of the cruelty exercised on a person."[82] Sadism thus allowed Warhol to occupy two positions at once with regard to the abject. On the one hand, he could wallow in its shameful pleasures, monetizing them for shocked audiences eager for a dirty thrill. On the other, through his own sadistic actions and those of intermediaries like Woronov and Tavel, he could supervise the abject in others, and thus "feel (temporarily) secure in [his] own sense of self."[83] The primal (fascist) father could keep everyone in line.

Gopnik has revealed that the Silver Factory's sadistic culture pervaded Warhol's private life as well, sometimes taking on racist, homophobic, and fascist undertones. In 1967, Warhol dated a young man named Rod La Rod, who "would slap and punch [him] even in front of others," and who told a journalist that his two heroes were the white-supremacist politician George Wallace and "the Great White Father," Andy Warhol.[84] As Taro Nettleton has shown, this racist sadism infected Warhol's filmmaking, notably when Warhol cruelly "zoomed in" to emphasize "the thick, dark masculine hairs and veins" on the arms of his cross-dressing Latinx star, Mario Montez.[85] When George Harris, who had gained notoriety as the "sensitive young hippie" sticking a flower into a gun in the famous 1967 photo from the March on the Pentagon, came to the Factory for a "date" with Warhol, he was apparently subjected to sadistic humiliation and brutality—beaten, and burned with cigarettes by Warhol's friends "while Warhol looked on with pleasure."[86] The attackers allegedly told Harris not to report them to the police because they "won't listen to a faggot"—weaponizing the heteronormative state to protect themselves from culpability.[87] In this respect, the Factory's sadistic tendencies troublingly foreshadow a Trumpian approach to the abject, in which the figure of "the ultimate sovereign white male subject" can sustain its power only by ceaselessly projecting its own abject qualities and dependencies (its venality, incontinence, and fragility) upon others under the signs of disgust, titillation, and hatred, as when the "toilet obsess[ed]" Trump insisted that America's flushing problems applied only to others: "Not me, of course not me. But you."[88]

Emile de Antonio, one of Warhol's early confidants, worried that sadism had come to define the Silver Factory: "Andy was like the Marquis de Sade in the sense that his very presence acted as a kind of release for people so they could live out their fantasies, get undressed, or in some cases do very violent things to get Andy to watch them. . . . He loved to see other people dying. This is what the Factory was about: Andy was the Angel of Death's Apprentice."[89] By perpetrating this manipulative sadistic voyeurism, Warhol became for de Antonio "the devil"—the Beast, devoid of empathy or morality, "beyond love and hate," the worst possible animal—a judgment Warhol would inscrutably commemorate in a late series, *The Mark of the Beast* (1985–86).[90] (See figure 24.)

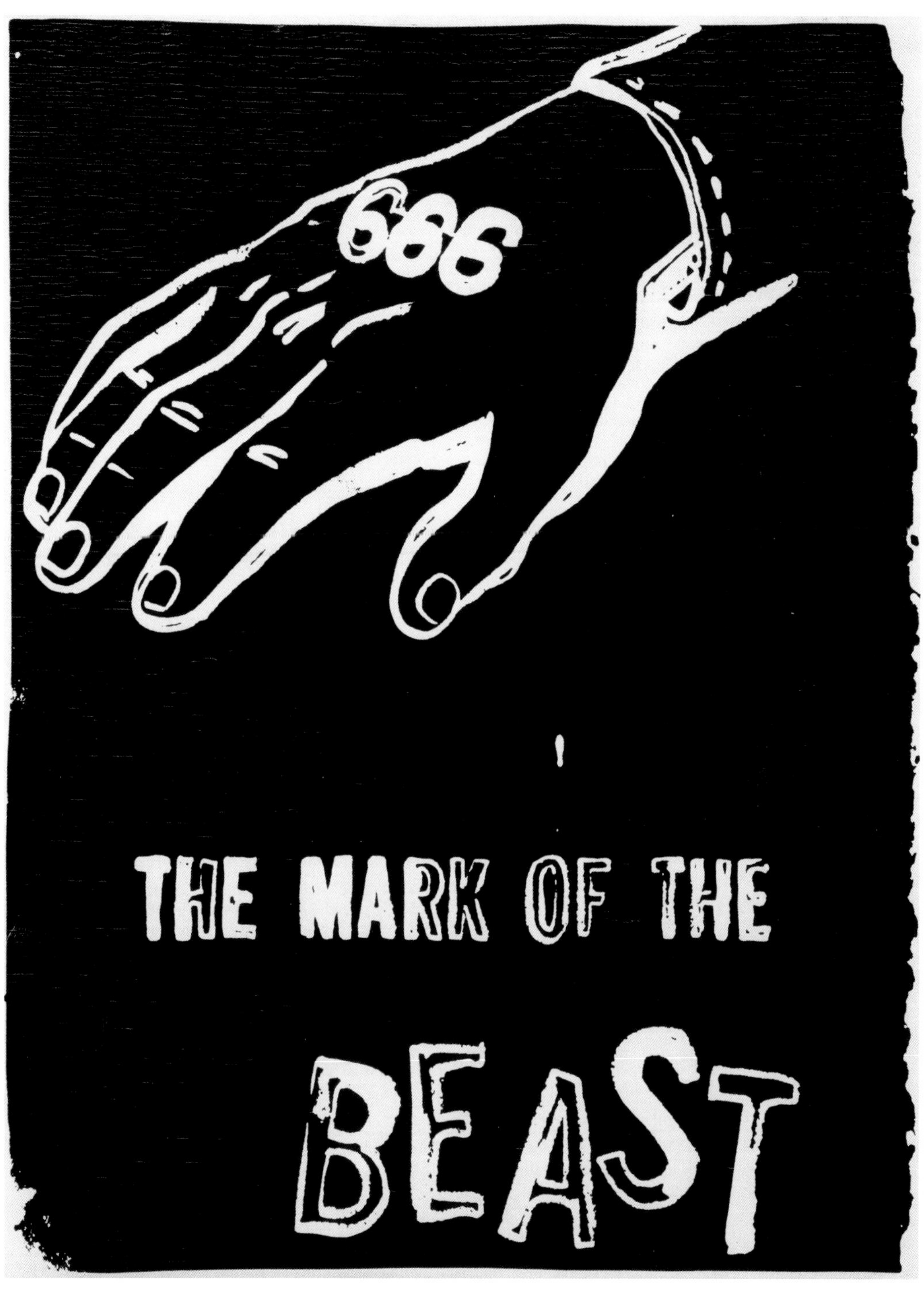

FIGURE 24
Andy Warhol, *The Mark of the Beast,* 1985–86. Image and Artwork © The Andy Warhol Foundation for the Visual Arts, Inc./Licensed by ARS.

Alongside Woronov and Tavel, the third and most prominent animal/ecological/amphetamine force in the Silver Factory was Billy Name. Ondine said that Name's name "should be synonymous" with Warhol's.[91] The Factory, Geldzahler would memorably claim, "was a Billy [Name] environment."[92] Name had been instrumental in designing the Factory "magpie" look.[93] Woronov recognized Name as "the protector of the Factory," the one denizen whom "everyone trusted."[94] He was the ringleader—"sort of like Andy's boyfriend," something more than an employee, "his principal architect and decorator, his secretary, his archivist, his studio manager, security man, night watchman and bouncer, his casting director, his handyman, his photographer, his electrician, his magician."[95] Name organized the other animals, "provid[ing] Andy with an entire stable of performers."[96] Warhol credited him with naming the Factory, but Name always claimed it had been a collaborative effort.[97] His photographs made up the bulk of the catalogue for Warhol's first retrospective. He managed the flow of drugs and kept Warhol shielded from its excesses; unlike other Factory stars, Name seemed able to live with speed. He claimed that "it was like a magic powder" for him and that "[f]or a lot of people, speed kills, but for me speed lives."[98] In 1964, Warhol listed Name as his son in *Who's Who in the East,* extending his queer family tree.[99]

Name was "like a dog, a poodle . . . he is loved for the reasons a poodle is loved."[100] He embodied the best and most treasured qualities of the domesticated canine: loyalty, intelligence, good humor—a perfect counterweight to the aggressivity and resentment embodied by Woronov's Violet and the paranoid lasciviousness of Tavel's screenplays. Valerie Solanas would intuit this canine pattern in Warhol's life when she referred to his Factory collaborators as "your trained dogs."[101] Warhol said that "Billy was different from all the other people on speed because he had a manner that inspired confidence: he was quiet, things were always very proper with him, and you felt like you could trust him to keep everything in line, including his strange friends. He had this way of getting rid of people immediately if they didn't belong." The final phrase ("getting rid of people") twists unexpectedly back toward the violence perpetuated by Woronov and Tavel. At the limit, Name could be ruthless too.

Through these custodial qualities, Name provided Warhol with what seemed to be an exemplary and shameless creative ecology, an ecosystem of production and reuse. Warhol saw Name as the consummate recycler, an example of what Gustavus Stadler calls "managerial animals," efficiently able to manage the waste that Warhol found so fascinating and repulsive.[102] Warhol called him "a perfect custodian" and "a good trasher; he furnished the whole Factory from things he found out on the street."[103]

Name created what Ondine described as "a certain nebula, like a chaos," that Warhol could "make . . . into a thing that could be seen."[104] With Name's help, Warhol thought he had monetized the recycling process: as he told Brigid Berlin, referring to her father, the newspaper tycoon Richard Berlin: "Your father is just, uh, exactly like me: he's making money out of trash!"[105] He claimed to have based his filmmaking business on this model, "recycling work and . . . recycling people," and "running [the] business as a byproduct of other businesses."[106] "I'm becoming a factory" working with other "non-people," Warhol told an interviewer in 1964.[107] But he also seemed to worry that he could never match Name's zeal for trash—it was too dirty: "That's another conflict. I want to throw things right out the window as they're handed to me. . . . But my other outlook is that I really do want to save things so they can be used again someday."[108] Here again is Warhol's abjection dilemma: torn between wallowing in waste and the abject, banishing them, and administering their use by others. In 1976 he said that he once devised footprint paintings, but was too disgusted to profit from them: "Then there were the canvases that I used to leave on the street and people used to walk on them. . . . Then I thought they were all diseased so I rolled them up and put them somewhere."[109] Hallucinogens may have occasionally loosened his inhibitions, allowing him to catch a glimpse of the "ecological imbrication" that Richard Doyle has argued is sometimes "cultivate[d]" and "enhance[d]" by psychedelics.[110] Gerard Malanga remembered that Warhol and his entourage had once been dosed with LSD on Fire Island: "I found [Andy] at six in the morning rummaging through the garbage cans. I asked, 'What are you doing?' He said, 'I'm looking for something.'"[111]

In 1967, when Warhol decided to move the Factory after an attempted robbery at gunpoint there, Name disagreed with Paul Morrissey about the new location, arguing that it ought to be "on the ground floor and . . . accessible to the public."[112] Warhol sided with Morrissey, and they found a clean and elegant sixth-floor studio near Union Square. This was where Valerie Solanas almost assassinated Warhol in 1968, firing a bullet that damaged his spleen, liver, stomach, esophagus, and both lungs. Her manifesto had made trenchant use of the animal-machine metaphor, reducing it to one of its logical extremes: "To call a man an animal is to flatter him; he's a machine, a walking dildo."[113] Her letters to Warhol addressed him as "Toad."[114] Name had cried out when he saw Warhol lying on the floor, bleeding. Warhol mistook the cry for laughter and worried it would be contagious: "'Billy,' he said softly, 'don't laugh. Don't make me laugh.'"[115] Shortly afterward, apparently in response to Solanas's attempt on Warhol's life, Name became nocturnal; he "retreated from the daytime activities of the Factory and began emerging from his darkroom only at night and only after everyone had gone."[116] Ondine claimed that he lived there for three years, growing feral. Reading in black light, suffering from retinal colic, his eyes turning yellow, scabs growing on his face, fingernails lengthening: "There was some kind of fire going on in Billy's brain."[117]

Name left the Union Square Factory in 1970. As Warhol's subsequent creative collaborator, Paul Morrissey, put it, with profound condescension, "The drug types had their time, they did some things, but it's all gone now. Now it's stupid."[118] Warhol apparently had the locks changed.[119] But a decade later, Warhol was still dreaming about the collaborative, clownish, swarming, subterranean, amphetamine-fueled, machinic possibilities that Name had broached, where "everything was loose, flexible. The people in the studio were there night and day. Friends of friends."[120] Truly collaborative, barely attached to a proper name: "Since I was paying the rent for the studio, I guessed that this somehow was actually *my* scene, but don't ask me what it was all about, because I never could figure it out."[121] Egalitarian and level, through the aid of pharmaceuticals: "Drugs helped a little there. Everybody was equal suddenly—debutantes and chauffeurs, waitresses and governors."[122]

In the late 1970s and '80s, Warhol's employees gave him a new nickname: instead of "Drella"—linked, at least in Tavel's mind, to his image as "a clucking mother hen"—they began to call him "Pop," a perfect double entendre of the paternal and proprietary.[123] As Deleuze and Guattari warned, swarms can be "undermined by extremely varied forces that establish in them interior centers of the conjugal, familial, or State type, and that make them pass into an entirely different form of sociability, replacing pack affects with family feelings or State intelligibilities."[124] By the 1980s, Name's swarm had become an embarrassing memory for Warhol—poor, ratty, letting itself go, hanging on to the past: "I can just see it if Billy Name comes to New York. Oh he won't, he's too shy, he won't want us to see him fat. Oh but if he does—I can just see it—he'll come on the bus with a YMCA satchel."[125] The final image is telling: where the YMCA across the street from the Silver Factory had once promised wild queer libertinism, its brand now connoted only grime and privation.

And yet, for all its menace and destructiveness, and despite the luster it had lost over the years, the animal spirit of the Silver Factory remained a powerful force in Warhol's imagination for the rest of his life, always available to be reactivated when something reminded him of it. In 1986, he told an interviewer that he had neither dreams nor fantasies.[126] The *Diaries'* eight hundred pages seem mostly to confirm this claim, recounting only a handful of dreams. But then, one night in Vienna,

> I'd dreamt about Billy Name, that he was living under the stairs at my house and doing somersaults, and everything was very colorful. It was so weird, because his friends sort of invaded my house and were acting crazy in colorful costumes and jumping up and down and having so much fun and . . . they took over my life. . . . Everybody was a clown in a funny way, and they were just living there without letting me know, they'd come out in the morning when I wasn't there and they'd have a lot of fun and then they'd go back and live in the closet. And so I got up and Christopher had left all the lights on, and the windows were open and it was very beautiful.[127]

Warhol dreamed a tribe of insect-men, "Mole People," a swarm, a bug factory that hid under the stairs (like Warhol's first exposures to both sexual activity and animal abuse) when he was at home, and came out to party when he left for work. Clown-animal-artists—an apt amalgam since, as Adorno observed, "the constellation animal/fool/clown is a fundamental layer of art."[128]

In 1987, a month before Warhol's death, Name called to say he wanted to see him:

> Have I forgotten to say that he's been calling? He's up there in Poughkeepsie and he's organizing a sixties reunion and he has like three jobs up there, deputy sheriff and everything, and he was just chattering away—"You know how deeply I love you, honey"—about how Gerard is coming up and Ingrid Superstar and how I'd be picked up and taken to Stephen Shore's house . . . and all this stuff. But I'm going to just have to tell Billy that I can't face the past. And I'd walked into the house and didn't look where I stepped and so I was talking to him with dog poop all over my shoes.[129]

"I can't face the past": Name's swarms remained an appealing but uncomfortable memory for Warhol after the first Factory shut down—something exciting, dangerous, unsustainable, to be explored occasionally but always at the risk of stepping in shit: much like his family, his friends who had "gay cancer," or having to hear about the lives of his aging Superstars ("kids/no kids"), all of which he also told his diaries he "can't face."[130] Name's drug-fueled ecological egalitarianism—in which the entire world awaits swarms of creative recycling—was a lost dream from Warhol's Silver Factory.

Another dream, much grimmer, might be described as biotechnological. Warhol wouldn't live to see it, but the centrality of amphetamines in the Silver Factory, and their links to animality and sadism, foretold a biotechnology of living bodies. Since the late twentieth century, as Dawne McCance has shown, "genetics . . . has come to apprehend animal bodies as factories . . . [and] animals themselves have become biotechnologies"[131] Weren't Warhol's Superstars at least primitively biotechnologically productive? Trading golden showers for amphetamines that would trigger the chemical reactions that could provoke and sustain the dramas that would be filmed and sold? Understanding themselves as animal-machines to be dosed, so that their reactions and interactions could be measured and recorded by what Woronov called "the black hole lens of the camera"—"Next to the muzzle of a gun . . . one of the coldest things in the world"?[132] Forever at risk of melting down, burning too brightly, becoming unsustainable? Truly biopolitical, since, under this regime, everyone "work[s] all day long," and "one's whole life (one's identity, sexuality, diet, health) is saturated by power's effects."[133] In its unleashing of animal-machinic energies, the Silver Factory was heaven and hell all at once.

Silver Clouds versus *Cow Wallpaper,* then: two of the Silver Factory's late masterpieces (both 1966). (See figure 25.) On the one hand, mylar pillows set adrift. The beginnings of an open world of movement, interaction, reflection, polymorphous perversity. A portable Silver Factory, where everyone and everything could be reflected in motion. An intoxicating new ecosystem in which any life-form could transgress every human rule and become a star in the process. Warhol wondered whether the *Clouds* might free him of the burden of being an "artist": "while I was making them . . . I felt my art career floating away out the window, as if the paintings were just leaving the wall and floating away."[134]

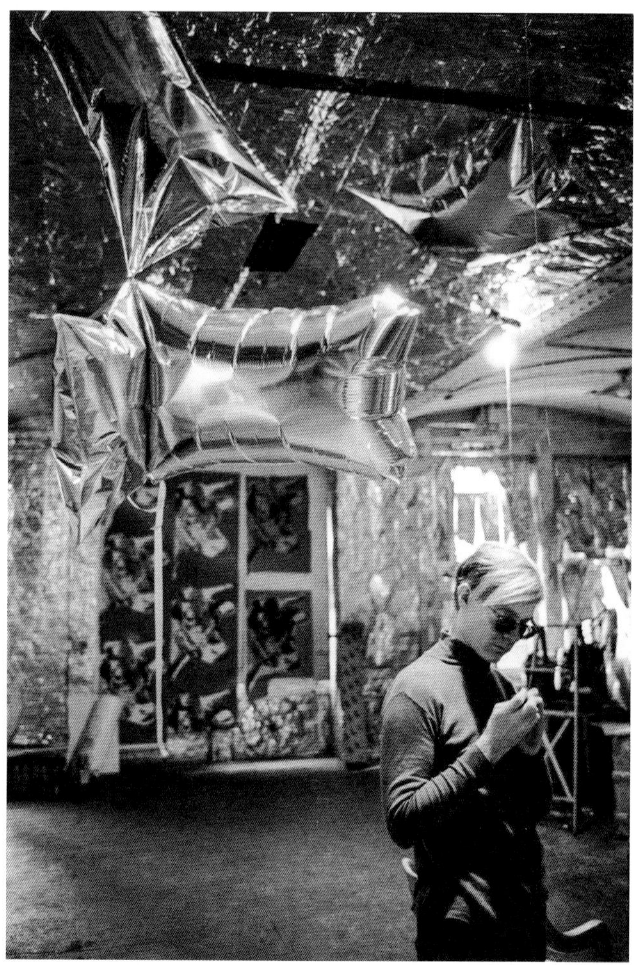

FIGURE 25
Stephen Shore, *Andy Warhol with Silver Clouds, the Factory, New York, New York*, 1965–67. © Stephen Shore. Courtesy 303 Gallery, New York.

And, on the other hand, the endless neon cows plastered onto walls: "[B]lazingly bright and vulgar!" as Ivan Karp immediately recognized, "They're *super*-pastoral! They're ridiculous!"[135] (See figure 26.) From a narrowly art-historical perspective that's all they were: a droll avant-garde provocation. But, seen as one of the last gasps of the animal life of the great Silver Factory, they are also a prescient image of the biotechnological animal, subject to human greed and sadism: a beast in harness, restrained in a fluorescent world, chewing its cud—perhaps the flesh of another cow—waiting to be beaten, molested, milked for content, cut, eaten, and finally boiled down into gelatin for industrial use.[136]

It is through their dependence on gelatin, as Shukin has brilliantly shown, that every photograph and film has been deeply if unknowingly entangled in animal suffering. "[T]he animation effects of modern cinema," its ability to produce the illusion of life on a screen, are directly dependent on film's "carnal origins": the animal "byproducts,"

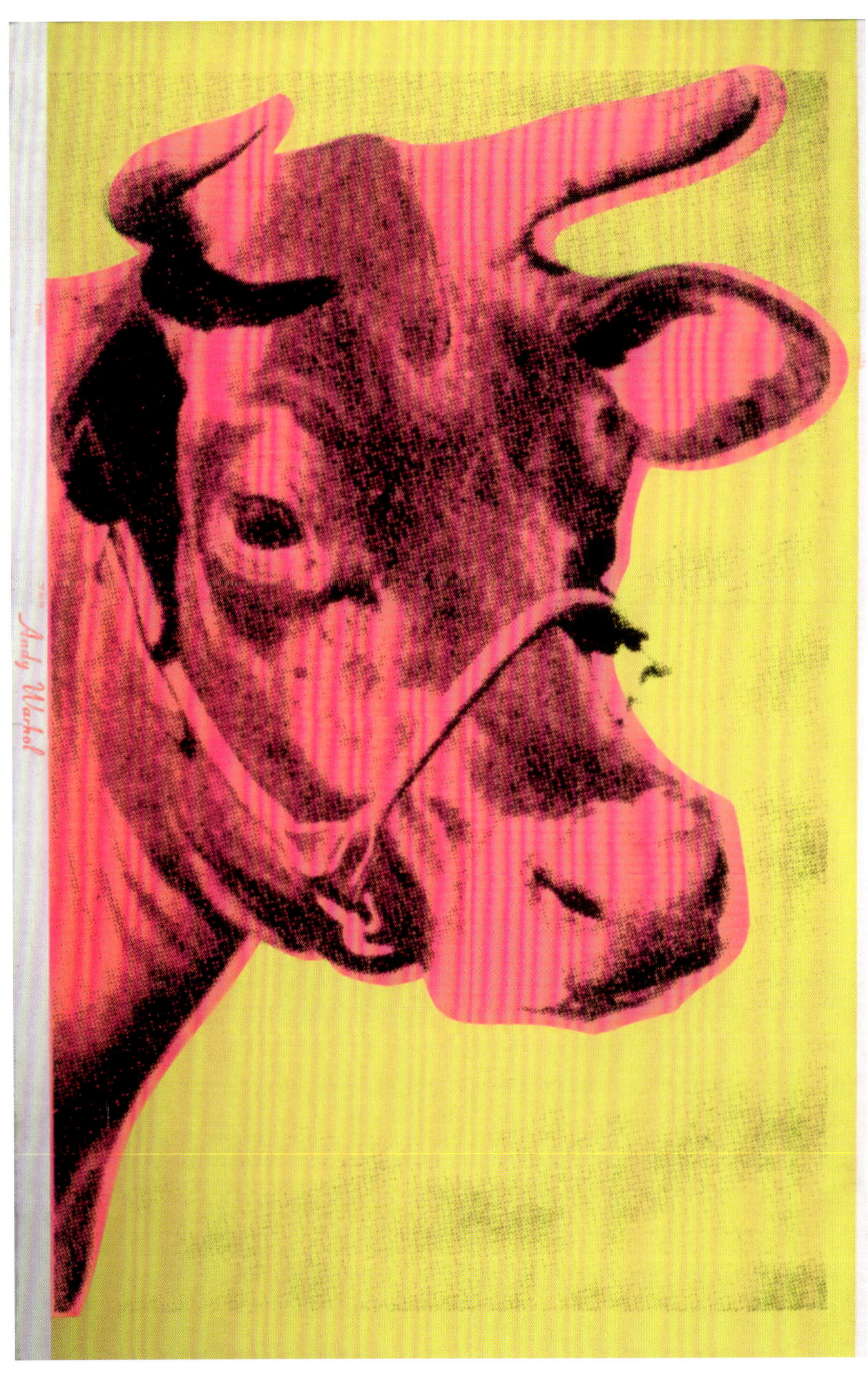

FIGURE 26

Andy Warhol, *Cow*, 1966. The Andy Warhol Museum, Pittsburgh; Founding Collection, Contribution The Andy Warhol Foundation for the Visual Arts, Inc. © 2022 The Andy Warhol Foundation for the Visual Arts, Inc./ Licensed by Artists Rights Society (ARS), New York.

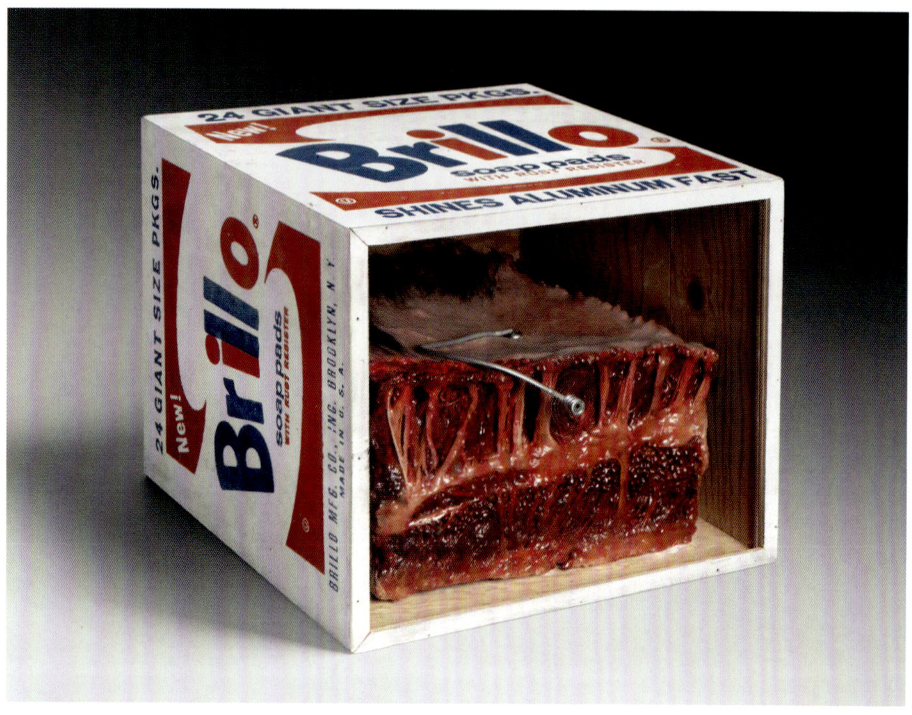

FIGURE 27
Paul Thek, *Meat Piece with Warhol Brillo Box*, 1965. Philadelphia Museum of Art: Purchased with funds contributed by the Daniel W. Dietrich Foundation, 1990, 1990–111–1 © The George Paul Thek Estate, New York

"the leavings of tanneries and slaughter-houses," that are used to produce gelatin, "[t]he coating of choice for photographic and film stocks today as it was at the turn of the century."[137] "Film," Shukin points out, was originally a euphemism for "gelatin." Gelatin was so critical to the film industry that Kodak would purchase a US rendering plant in 1930; by 1969, they were sourcing gelatin from all over the world.[138] In this respect, every filmic image, even one that explicitly promotes environmental causes, "actively render[s] unconscious [its] material contingency on slaughter."[139] Warhol's "super-pastoral" cow wallpaper, filmed by and glued to the wall with animal by-products, emblematizes this tension between "'sympathetic' technologies of representation and 'pathological' technologies of material control."[140] Paul Thek seems to have recognized these animal dependencies in Warhol's work.[141] His *Meat Piece with Warhol Brillo Box* (1965) installs animal slaughter at the heart of Warhol's signature box. (See figure 27.)

For his part, Warhol would continue to affiliate his own body and its production with these ambivalent properties; when Henry Geldzahler invited Warhol to the Capote Masked Ball in 1966, Warhol chose for his mask an "electrified cow's head"—proposing himself as an animal-machine to New York's high society.[142] The mask proved uncomfortably heavy and was removed early on. Four years later, on the occasion of his first international retrospective, Warhol lobbied for the entire show "to be one image—the wallpaper with the cows' heads."[143] He was overruled.

———

"[E]veryone was constantly in a crisis," Billy Name said of the Silver Factory, "constantly being destroyed."[144] Ondine remembered that "[a] Warhol creation released from its master is hopeless. . . . You went to Warhol to be exploited."[145] Tavel called this process "the exploitation of human flesh."[146] He would sometimes refer to Warhol with an impersonal pronoun ("It was an artist"), and thus as something that eclipsed the boundaries of the human completely, having truly become some type of machine: "I do not remember him as somebody loved. . . . He began to become a humanoid, which is what he was thought of as at the time. . . . [H]e thinks of himself as being inhuman."[147] For his part, Warhol seems to have sometimes seen others as "its," and to have had difficulty empathizing with those who suffered under his management. "When you hurt another person," he told Leticia Kent in 1968, "you never know how much it pains."[148]

3

MACHINES, ANIMAL AND VEGETAL

ALONGSIDE THE CONTEMPORANEOUS VOICES who described him and his work as subhuman and animalistic, observers have long emphasized Warhol's interest in the machinic, and its persistence throughout his work. Across a wide variety of media, Warhol seemed more interested in tracing than in creativity, in the automatic rather than the thoughtful or planned, the mechanism rather than the soul. At the limit, Warhol became a machine to those around him: Danny Fields said, "He was like *I Am a Camera*. You, sort of, played to him."[1] John Wilcock "[thought] of him as a seismograph, thin, like something that bobs on the waves and tries to be neutral and records."[2] For Ultra Violet, interviewed in the early 1970s, Warhol "is a computer."[3] Considered together with his persistent interest in animal and vegetal life, this emphasis on the machine in Warhol's work anticipated both Derrida's critique of the traditional Western concept of the nonhuman animal as "a machine that doesn't speak, that doesn't have access to sense" and Michael Marder's analysis of similar conceptions of plants as "photosynthesizing biological machines."[4] These traditions define animal- and vegetal-machines as subhuman, driven by instinct and appetite, unreflective and mechanical.[5] Where the human (supposedly) writes, speaks, and draws, the animal and plant (allegedly) leave only traces.[6]

Warhol challenged this hierarchy from both sides. He often wondered about the possibility of animal and vegetal creativity: when he claimed that the cats he and his mother kept were more interesting than television; in *Horse* (1965), with its full reel featuring a horse accompanied by a microphone; when he declared that "[l]and really is the best art" and that "the plants are screaming";[7] and, near the end of his life, when he repeatedly proposed that a talking dog would render him obsolete as an artist. In all of these ways, he anticipated contemporary interest in animal and plant languages.[8] But he also questioned his own supposed ability to make meaning, to leave anything more than traces and grunts. Even his "mother tongue" was a problem: "I only know one language, and sometimes in the middle of a sentence I feel like a foreigner trying to talk it because I have word spasms where the parts of some words begin to sound peculiar to me."[9] Similar doubts plagued his attempts at traditional artmaking: "My instinct about painting says, 'If you don't think about it, it's right.' . . . Usually all I need is tracing paper and a good light."[10] This was the lesson he drew from Hester's untimely death: in the face of a "human" world defined by greed and false nobility, he would hyperbolically embrace the position Frantz Fanon called the "the machine-animal-m[a]n" that likes but does not care; "an automaton," in Derrida's words, "deprived of a 'me' or 'self,' and even more of any capacity for reflection, indeed of any mark or autobiographical impression of its own life."[11]

Wayne Koestenbaum called this Warhol's "charm": "his connection to the mute, the animal, the 'retarded.'"[12] Many of his contemporaries felt that it rendered him despicable or subhuman. Bob Colacello described him as being "like a child, the way a child keeps repeating the same stupid thing."[13] Eleanor Ward would "never forget the sight of [Warhol]" arriving at her haut bourgeois Stable Gallery for his first big New York gallery show "in his dirty, filthy clothes and his worn-out sneakers with the laces untied, and a big bunch of canvases rolled up under his arm. 'Look what the cat dragged in,' he said."[14] The canvases he delivered would establish a new benchmark for unfettered appetite in art: soup cans, soda bottles, sultry celebrities, tabloid disasters—images that were fuckable or edible or morbid or transfixing, and so tainted by mechanical reproduction that, for many viewers, they failed to qualify as paintings. And yet, from a contemporary biotechnological perspective, Warhol's emphasis on reiteration and replication might also be described as profoundly astute and demystified, since "*life, before it is anything else,*" as Richard Iveson reminds us, drawing on contemporary work in thermodynamics, "*is a copying machine.*"[15] At the limit, Warhol's refusal of humanistic notions of creativity verged on the vegetal—"the mute affirmation and reaffirmation of existence in all its finite materiality."[16]

The animal-machine model involves three fundamental reductions. The first is that it amalgamates the vast diversity of nonhuman earthly creatures into a single category: "animals." In so doing it accomplishes a breathtaking simplification of an immeasurable range of beings, each with its own irreducible perspectives, powers, and eccentricities, cramming them into one, completely human and arbitrary, concept: millions of species that meet certain basic requirements regarding movement, growth, and sustenance, but are not human. The second reduction is that, by understanding these "animals" to be essentially machinic—incapable of creativity and critical thought—the animal-machine paradigm thereby establishes a rigid hierarchy, with all these creatures forever installed *beneath* their human counterparts, inferior to them in a variety of essential ways. According to the animal-machine paradigm, all nonhuman creatures are "animals," and all animals are subhuman, as are any humans who are relegated to this category through various forms of discrimination and oppression (by class, gender, sexuality, race, age, ability . . .). Finally, in a wide range of areas, the animal-machine is also described as being driven merely by appetite, whereas the human being is distinguished by its access to abstract thought, its ability to consider things and experiences in themselves, "as such," without interest or appetite. These things and experiences include many of Warhol's most consistent themes: creativity, death, sexuality, food, the abject, profit, communication. In each of these areas, Warhol's interventions anticipated problems investigated by the field of animal studies at the turn of the century. These interventions continually asked the two questions posed by Norris in her definition of biocentric artists: Do humans actually have access to the rational and disinterested position they espouse? And are other living beings as limited to the "poor" world of appetite as many humans imagine them to be?

As Jeffrey T. Nealon has pointed out, "ethically similar" questions apply to vegetal life as well, and in both cases we are faced with the task of grappling with "the power effects" and "forms of violence" that result from "differentiat[ing] ourselves from other forms of life."[17] Issues of classificatory reductionism and hierarchy apply here as well, exacerbated by the fact that "plants" are typically treated as "deformed, deficient, or inverted animals" by humans.[18] For Warhol, these were pressing and eternal questions, since "having land and not ruining it is the most beautiful art" and "*everything's* alive—the plants are screaming."[19] This vegetal empathy pervaded his everyday life. He knew that the smoke at parties made his skin feel "awful," and wondered whether the same was true for the flowers in bouquets, having to "fend off all that cigarette smoke."[20] Worse yet was the "tree in a treepot in Times Square" having to "hustle" like human New Yorkers "to make oxygen for a million people."[21]

This chapter explores a range of Warhol's disparate but related investigations of the animal- and vegetal-machine as models for artistic production. In each case, these models offered a powerful challenge to the priorities of traditional Western aesthetics. They disrupted principles of disinterest, creativity, and heteronormativity, suggesting alternate principles of interest, ecology, and queerness. Warhol explored each of these principles intrepidly in his work and thought, but he was often unable or unwilling to embrace their challenging consequences completely.

The reasons for this unwillingness are various, but here I would like to highlight one that might be seen as dominant: Warhol's dependence on the tense and ambivalent constellation that Nicole Shukin has defined as "animal capital"—and in this case, vegetal capital as well. Warhol, as we have already seen, was profoundly aware of the ways in which other life-forms could be commodified. His mother seems to have commodified him as an animal, as she had the animals he loved, and he in turn commodified the animals around him and within his cadre. The eco-political implications of Warhol's attention to animal and vegetal life are thus profoundly contradictory: even as he did as much as any major artist of his time to explore these areas in his work, he also consistently pursued their monetization and fetishization, anticipating what Shukin describes as "a new spirit of capitalism," which, instead of merely harvesting nonhuman life, "appreciates other species as vital subjects . . . who are . . . more value-adding when they are flourishing."[22] Throughout his life, Warhol was intensely attuned to the commodification of nonhuman spirit that Shukin describes, but the "flourishing" he commodified took on a variety of strange and troubling forms.

———

Warhol's most profound and persistent challenge to humanist aesthetics was his lifelong commitment to interest rather than disinterest, appetite rather than contemplation. In his 1975 essay "Economimesis," Derrida showed that Kantian aesthetics is secretly theological: it promotes a system of disinterested pleasure that is reliant upon a postulated God and available only to humans. God endows an artist with genius, and that endowment flows through the artist into their work, which becomes a shared sacred resource for humanity: beautiful, irreplaceable, untouchable. In order to be properly perceived, this precious beauty must also be received with disinterest—independence from all appetite and desire. As Kant put it, "beautiful art must be free art in a double sense: it must not be a matter of remuneration [for the artist] . . .; but also, while the mind is certainly occupied, it must feel itself to be satisfied and stimulated (independently of remuneration) without looking beyond to another end."[23] In this respect, the artist and the audience serve as guarantors for each other in the purity of their disinterest. Just as the artistic genius makes art without anticipating profit, the viewer enjoys art without seeking purpose. In each case, Kant's ideology of art requires an impossible subject who can work and play purely, without thought of needs; as Derrida points out, "The free man, the artist in this sense, is not *homo oeconomicus*."[24] If the Kantian artist is untouched by need and the Kantian audience is uncorrupted by desire, then artworks can transcend the narrow boundaries of self-interest, enabling free and true communication between otherwise constrained individuals and communities. In this way, the artist's work is their gift back to God, a tradition Warhol homoerotically satirized in 1965 when he sent a twenty-five-foot-long Mylar phallus filled with helium "up to God, all the way up."[25]

This subtly theological model of artmaking, still so pervasive in everyday definitions and institutions of art, is mutually reinforced by the allegedly impermeable barrier between human and nonhuman life-forms. Plants and animals, we are told, are fundamentally appetitive and reactive, driven by their needs. Humans, even though many of their mundane behaviors are characterized by appetite, have the (God-given) capacity to surpass and transcend these needs, and produce and appreciate beautiful things merely for the sake of beauty. Human exceptionalism guarantees the possibility of artistic beauty, and artistic beauty demonstrates the validity of human exceptionalism. Despite being a plant's reproductive organ, the flower's beauty epitomizes this sublimatory system, since, according to Kant, "[h]ardly anyone other than the botanist knows what sort of thing a flower is supposed to be; and even the botanist, who recognizes in it the reproductive organ of the plant, pays no attention to this natural end if he judges the flower by means of taste."[26] We can appreciate beauty only when we set all desires and appetites aside.

Throughout his career, Warhol questioned the possibility of any disinterested aesthetic position, and thus the plausibility of human exceptionalism in this area. In direct contradiction to Kant, he considered flowers to be pornographic—"a real sex movie"—and always rooted in, and destined for, the abject matter of excrement and decay: "Risen from the stench of the manure pile," as Bataille argued, and doomed to "rot . . . indecently in the sun."[27] Warhol's work returns almost compulsively to imagery that is fundamentally and unapologetically *interesting* (commodities, celebrities, mass media, transgression, erotica, disasters), presenting it in what were taken to be unartistic and mechanical ways (silkscreen, tracing, photography, film). It could be argued that this sustained rejection of disinterest is the defining feature of Warhol's work. He embraced an artistic worldview that was forever alert to appetite—sexual, pharmaceutical, culinary, financial, ecological—incessantly repudiating the idea that anything artistic could be disinterested. As he told an interviewer in 1972, "I've got a lot of mouths to feed. I've got to bring home the bacon."[28]

What's more, Warhol sensed early on that disinterestedness had implicit economic connotations, and that it was widely assumed to be an exclusively human privilege. In a remarkable 1963 interview, Warhol and Gerard Malanga brought these questions into close proximity:

GM. If you are happy doing what you do, should you be paid for it?
AW. Yes.
GM. If so, why?
AW. Because it will make me more happy.
GM. And how much?
AW. As much as I want.

GM. Are you human?
AW. No.[29]

Although pithy and informal, Malanga's questions were nevertheless remarkably canny. They immediately identified a central tension in the Kantian tradition: if artists are driven to create out of sheer generosity, and without thought of recompense, why should they ever be paid? Warhol quickly and effectively resolved this dilemma: money makes him happy, so the more the better. But Malanga's next question was truly ingenious. Without a Kantian framework, the shift in topic from profit seeking to the question of humanity would appear abrupt and unmotivated. But within this framework, it could not be more pressing: the artist's ability to separate artmaking from profit seeking is precisely what makes them distinctively human. Warhol's failure to do so renders him sub- or antihuman, something more akin to an animal or a plant.

Similar themes emerged in another 1963 interview, with John Giorno:

JG. Tell me more about your painting.
AW. I am going to stop painting. I want my paintings to sell for $25,000.
JG. What a good idea. What are you working on now?
AW. Death.[30]

There are two important connections to note in Warhol's responses here. First, by emphasizing that the law of supply and demand applies in the artistic realm, he explicitly rejected the Kantian disaffiliation of art from profit.[31] (This rejection would grow more extreme as the 1960s progressed. By the end of the decade he would tell *Playboy*, "The new art is really a business. We want to sell shares of our company on the Wall Street stock market."[32]) And second, he again tied this rejection to a sub- or antihuman position: that of the lifeless or the deathly. Warhol seemed to sense that death is the impossible boundary that separates existence from the ideal of disinterestedness. As Derrida would later argue, a completely objective standpoint would ultimately require a disembodied spectator—a body beyond all interests, dead to all interests.[33] (Despite his oft-mentioned Catholic upbringing, Warhol had no time for the afterlife: "I believe in death after death" was his answer to that mystery.[34])

These, then, are the impossible poles of Western aesthetic theory: on the one hand, a nonhuman—perhaps vegetal or animal—body completely dominated by its instincts and appetites; on the other, a corpse that has left such impulses behind completely. Warhol's epochal paintings from the early 1960s were crammed with subject matter that conjured these two poles. Celebrities, grocery-store commodities, currency, brand names—all of which were thought to appeal to America's basest appetites, but also morbid scenes of "death and disaster": suicides, assassinations, car crashes, electric chairs. Many of the paintings that fit neatly into neither of these categories found ways to bridge them: the cans in *Tunafish Disaster* that fatally poisoned their consum-

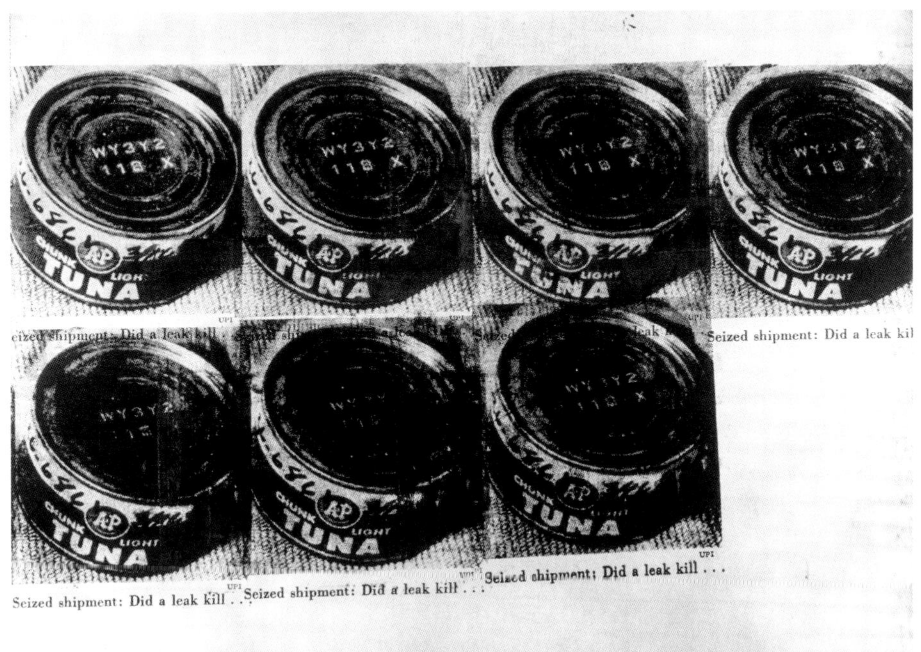

FIGURE 28
Andy Warhol, *Tunafish Disaster,* 1963. The Andy Warhol Museum, Pittsburgh; Founding Collection, Contribution The Andy Warhol Foundation for the Visual Arts, Inc. © 2022 The Andy Warhol Foundation for the Visual Arts, Inc./Licensed by Artists Rights Society (ARS), New York.

ers; the *Most Wanted Men* who infamously blurred the line between erotic and juridical enthusiasm; the *Flowers,* which brought eroticized celebrity style to the reproductive organs of plants; and, perhaps most pointedly, the *Race Riots,* where the underpinnings of racist police control were revealed as animal violence.[35] (See figures 28 and 29.)

Through their attention to the edibility of the human body, these last paintings highlight an even more radical dimension of Warhol's antihumanist aesthetics. As Bénédicte Boisseron has shown, the "habit of launching dogs on the racialized Other" has persisted from the mid-sixteenth century well into the early twenty-first, when police unleashed attack dogs on Native Americans at Standing Rock, and on Black protesters in Ferguson, Missouri (where a subsequent investigation showed "a blatant correlation between race and the use of attack dogs" by Ferguson police).[36] The underlying "carnophallogocentrism" of these works, in which "the master enacts the symbolic act of eating the slave," touches on various memories and fantasies upon which Warhol fixated, including his brothers' beatings of their childhood dog in the basement, the forced oral sex he also witnessed there, and his sadistic and masochistic relationships and activities. Crucially, in these various areas, Warhol's role alternated between eater and eaten, beater and beaten, voyeur and participant.[37] Something similar might be said to happen in the *Race Riot* paintings, which leave openings for

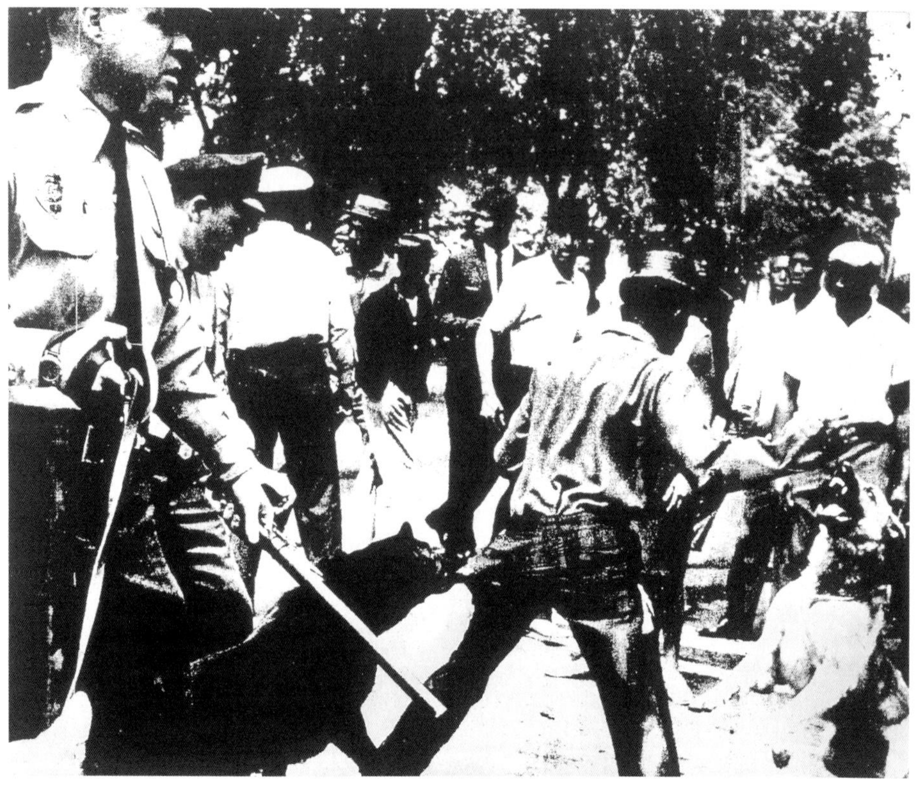

FIGURE 29
Andy Warhol, *Birmingham Race Riot,* 1964. The Andy Warhol Museum, Pittsburgh; Founding Collection, Contribution The Andy Warhol Foundation for the Visual Arts, Inc. © 2022 The Andy Warhol Foundation for the Visual Arts, Inc./Licensed by Artists Rights Society (ARS), New York.

viewers to identify with the dog or the protester or both. For a 1964 photograph by William John Kennedy, Warhol even converted one of the *Race Riot* paintings into the front half of a "sandwich board" advertisement, strapped over his shoulders as a perverse spur to appetite.

These fantasies of human and maternal edibility persisted throughout Warhol's work, forming a blood-red thread from the early, lost *Female with Animal at Breast* through the *Race Riots* and *More Milk, Yvette* all the way to the memorable okapi images explored in chapter 5. As Boisseron points out, since the dog "is the only animal that dares bite humans on a regular basis," dogs' capacity to attack "brings to mind the fetishistic nature of human nonedibility; it shows that human consciousness is based on the disavowal of being an (edible) animal."[38] The *Race Riot* paintings thus resurrect the Kristevian theme of a subject who transgressively flaunts his oral attachments and appetites—both maternal and animal—in the face of powerful social approbation. Put another way, not only does Warhol's work emphasize appetite and desire against the Kantian aesthetic rule of disinterest; it doubles down by emphasizing appetites and desires that are particularly prohibited: violent, bacchanalian, coprophilial, incestuous, bestial, anthropophagous.

Just as Derrida suspected, rejecting the Kantian system of aesthetic disinterestedness meant abdicating the privileges of the human and becoming a "craftsman," an animal or plant, a naïf or a monster.[39] Robert Indiana saw the connection early on: "Warhol's auto-death transfixes us; DIE is equal to EAT."[40] David Bowie and William Burroughs recognized it too: "[Bowie]: [Warhol] was the living dead. . . . He's . . . the wrong colour to be a human being. [Burroughs]: "I don't think that there is any person there."[41] Stephen Koch, who studied Warhol closely, thought that this effect was intentional, that "he wasn't really a person in the ordinary sense of the word."[42]

And yet Warhol's relationship to humanist aesthetics was not entirely negative. On the one hand, his entire worldview could be said to have been predicated on a rejection of disinterest, a turn toward appetite, which he and his audience frequently associated with "beastly" voices: female, queer, immature, and/or working-class subjects, people of color. Throughout his career, he would seek out, and be sought out by, artistic collaborators from marginalized groups. His responses to their appeals would vary: Valerie Solanas found his lack of interest violently intolerable; Jean-Michel Basquiat asked that Warhol's portrait of him be silkscreened over a urine oxidation painting, implicitly acknowledging their shared investment in the abject and the refusal of disinterest.[43] In 1984, they collaborated on an untitled painting featuring two happy dogs, one pissing, the other shitting.

But Warhol was also canny enough to recognize that, in a post-Duchampian art world, this rejection of the theological model could and would be reappropriated as an act of genius in its own right. Even his most transgressive actions—like embracing the profit motive and "quitting" painting for film, fashion, and publishing—could ultimately be recuperated as the brave actions of a genius, willing to sacrifice anything (even, paradoxically, the position of genius) for their art. What's more, he knew that "sophisticated" audiences could take great pleasure in "slumming," enjoying their interests even as they pretended not to, or choosing to abandon this pretense temporarily. A great deal of Warhol's success was predicated on his ability to play both sides of the interest/disinterest binary, perpetually finding new ways to pursue animal- or vegetal-machinic production without ever fully forfeiting the rights and privileges of the artist.

During his early career, Warhol experimented with various sly and playful animal transgressions, constructing a collaborative system with his mother in which abject themes and the shame that accompanied them could be converted into titillation and profit. At the Silver Factory, he developed a method of encouraging and overseeing these transgressions in others, managing their desire and shame and aggression, profiting by marketing these experiences to various audiences. And, throughout the rest of his career, he would seek out new ways to use animal- and vegetal-machinic production to expand the capacities of the artist. Warhol was always quick to explore the

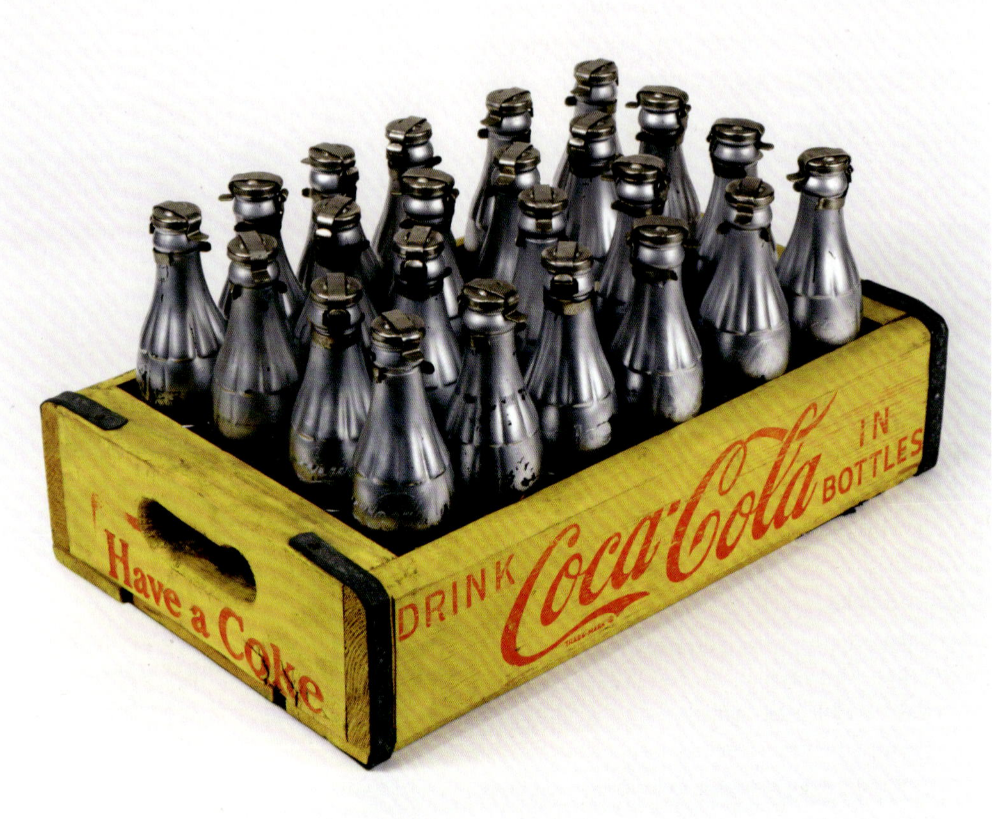

FIGURE 30
Andy Warhol, *You're In*, 1967. The Andy Warhol Museum, Pittsburgh; Founding Collection, Contribution The Andy Warhol Foundation for the Visual Arts, Inc. © 2022 The Andy Warhol Foundation for the Visual Arts, Inc./ Licensed by Artists Rights Society (ARS), New York.

possibilities of integrating previously taboo appetites into his artistic production: the *Death and Disaster* series, with its unusually explicit renderings of the loss of life; the *Cock Book*; the proposed celebrity-underwear store (which would have charged a premium for dirty garments); the repeated attempts to record Ondine's use of the toilet in *a: a novel;* the *Invisible* paintings with breasts visible under blue light; pornographic films like *Three* and *Couch* and *Blow Job* (all 1964), *Eating Too Fast* (1966), and *Blue Movie* (1968), the first theatrically released film to include explicit sex acts; the bright yellow perfume called *You're In* (1967), packaged in silver spray-painted Coca-Cola bottles; the *Cum Paintings* and *Piss Paintings* and *Oxidation Paintings* and *Landscapes* and *Torsos* and *Sex Parts*—in each of these disparate projects, Warhol was eager to breach the borders between taste and transgression.[44] (See figures 30 and 31.) What's more, he would continue to wonder over the possibility of actual animal and vegetal

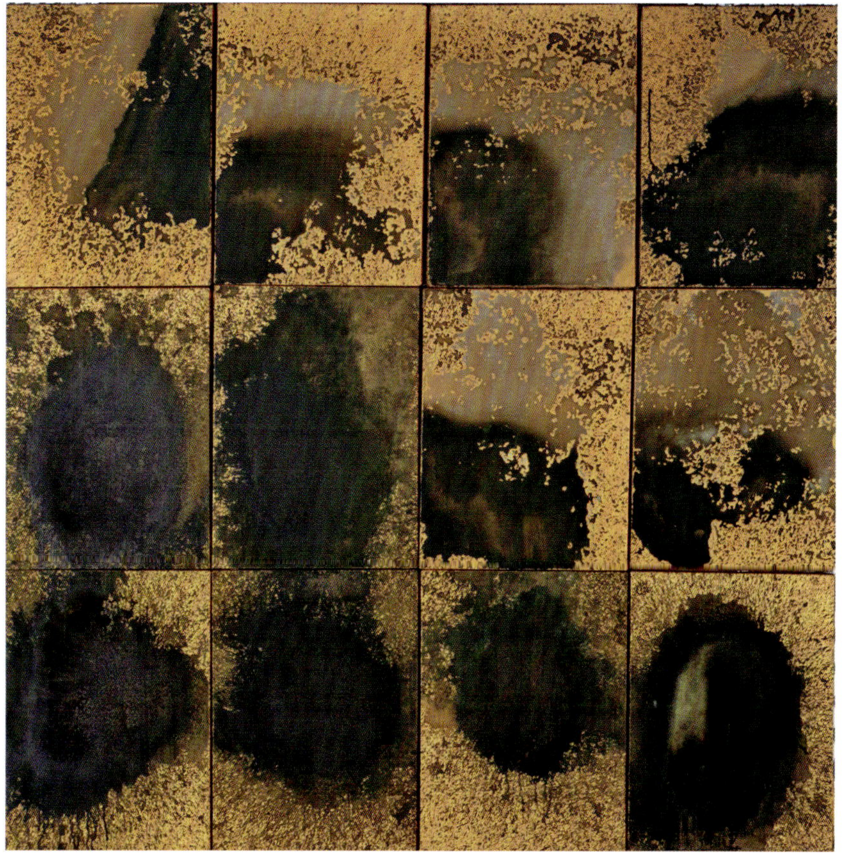

FIGURE 31
Andy Warhol, *Oxidation*, 1978. The Andy Warhol Museum, Pittsburgh; Founding Collection, Contribution The Andy Warhol Foundation for the Visual Arts, Inc. © 2022 The Andy Warhol Foundation for the Visual Arts, Inc./Licensed by Artists Rights Society (ARS), New York.

creativity—not humans learning from or becoming like nonhuman life-forms, but finding ways to highlight the creativity of these life-forms directly. He maintained that the ultimate pornographic film would be "a flower giving birth to another flower," and "the best love story" would be "two love-birds in a cage," and was apparently inspired to create the *Piss Paintings* when Brigid Berlin's pet pug urinated on one of his blank canvases.[45]

Strikingly, however, one central opportunity for animal- or vegetal-machinic production remained problematic throughout most of Warhol's career: an explicitly queer mode of production that could be palatable for a "mainstream" audience. As a result, Warhol's classic pop paintings—the Marilyns and soup cans—have often been understood as a way of screening the artist's homoerotic interests and strategically embracing a universally "American" and impersonal iconography. This reading has been buttressed by Warhol's 1963 interview with Gene Swenson, where he famously declared that "everybody should be a machine"—a recommendation that seemed to sidestep the problem of sexuality altogether.

Through her groundbreaking archival research, however, Jennifer Sichel has established that the published version of this interview was drastically and homophobically censored. Sichel's transcript of the recorded conversation shows that Warhol posed "be[ing] a machine" as a solution to a specifically eroto-political problem: how to acknowledge the importance of homosexuality in pop art—to have a "whole interview on me [that] should be just on homosexuality"—without relying on the tired tropes of symbolism ("Does your can represent a penis?") or fetishism ("Why did you like to draw women's shoes?").[46] For Warhol, "be[ing] a machine" brilliantly resolved this dilemma. Machines make their connections automatically and (at least potentially) without the influence of social approbation. If one were to "like things" like a machine, one could like everyone, regardless of gender, without fearing homophobic repercussions, and "without any discrimination."[47] Pop Art would have bypassed heteronormativity, and perhaps suggested a cure for it. Instead of using animal avatars to hint at queerness, or commissioning others to act out queer-bestial fantasies, the pop artist could directly embrace a machinic transformation that would render homophobia obsolete.

Unfortunately, Warhol's proposed pop solution to the pressures of homophobia would remain buried in an archive for fifty-five years, unremarked until Sichel discovered it.[48] The censored version of the interview would contribute to multiple generations of scholarship that overwhelmingly minimized—and often didn't even mention—Warhol's sexuality or the queer dimensions of his work. He remained "almost but never quite out," and complained about gay friends who were more open.[49] Queerness was mostly expressed among friends and confidants; the institutional heteronormativity of museums and books and magazines could be lightly mocked, and contravened in sexually explicit work that was typically shared with smaller audiences, but rarely contradicted in major works. This discretion was reiterated in the headquarters he established in 1974, which had two studios—one public (for commissions), one private (which was reserved for "[f]oreplay and sex acts, including masturbation, fellatio and anal intercourse.").[50] As late as 1987, a gossipy remembrance of the artist in *Vanity Fair* entitled "The Secret Warhol" was still referring to his longtime boyfriend, Jed Johnson, as his "roommate."[51]

Although his proposal for an explicitly queer-machinic version of pop art remained mostly censored or covert, Warhol would continue to explore alternatives to traditional humanist thought in the decades that followed, and to draw heavily on animal and vegetal life for inspiration. While "be[ing] a machine" remained primarily an individual model, in which a pop artist could train pop fans to direct their desire toward a wider range of things and gender identities, over the course of his career Warhol would also propose collaborative modes of queer ecological production that might ultimately transcend the individual entirely. In contrast to the idea of an artist endowed with

God-given genius, these models explored the possibility of a collaborative creative ecosystem, in which everything is recycled into something else, and nothing is created sui generis or "divinely."

As we saw in chapter 2, the Silver Factory, with its legendary commitment to openness and social mixing, was in many ways Warhol's most sustained experiment in an ecological model of creativity. By the time it closed down, as Ondine recalled, "Warhol had been told that commercialism means you can't bother with the freaks any more. You have tintypes. Whatever sound somebody did originally, well—you can duplicate it."[52] In subsequent decades, this managerial component would become more prominent: "At the office, [Warhol] was grumpy, penny-pinching and suspicious, a small-business owner convinced that the people on his payroll were slacking off."[53] But he would continue to wonder about the possibilities of the type of artmaking he facilitated during the mid-1960s: animalistic, swarm based, unfazed by death, grime, decay, and the abject.

Perhaps humans could become more like insects: more cooperative, less individualized.[54] Warhol greatly admired the ecological model, but often claimed it was too grimy for his tastes, too unhygienic. When he allowed himself to think abstractly, however, he could delve more freely into the possibilities posed by creative ecologies. Midway through *The Philosophy of Andy Warhol* (1975), he reflected on the subjects of nourishment, defecation, and bees:

> I think about people eating and going to the bathroom all the time, and I wonder why they don't have a tube up their behind that takes all the stuff they eat and recycles it back to their mouth, regenerating it, and then they'd never have to think about buying food or eating it. And they wouldn't even have to see it—it wouldn't even be dirty. If they wanted to, they could artificially color it on the way back in. Pink. (I got the idea from thinking that bees shit honey, but then I found out that honey isn't bee-shit, it's bee regurgitation.)[55]

Warhol's interest in bees echoed a long-standing trope in aesthetic theory: the bee as a figure for the noncreative creator, a creature who produces beauty without actually attaining to the status of an artist.[56] Despite its capacity to produce beauty and sweetness, the bee was long seen as a machine rather than an artist: automatic and unreflective, devoid of true creativity. As Derrida observed, this line of thought helps to ground the classed distinction between art and craft: "The craftsman, the worker, like the bee, does not play."[57]

Andrew Carnegie, Warhol's earliest artistic benefactor, was more willing to grant a resemblance between the artist and the bee in order to emphasize the social and economic merits of patronage. Addressing the Carnegie Institute's commitment to art education, he proclaimed in 1932, "[W]e shall search out and find the potential artist. We shall nurture him, like the queen bee, on special artistic food . . . [s]o that a leader in this field shall not be lost."[58] The metaphor is striking: it is as if Carnegie imagines himself (or his institute) as a beekeeper, identifying and "nurturing" a queen from among the drones—one who, through their artistic genius, could become a "leader" for the others. A relatively small investment would thus produce enormous dividends with regard to social stability. The limitations of this generosity were strict, however, and egalitarianism was not its goal. As the Carnegie Institute clarified in 1940, "Not all these children will become artists, such a state of affairs would be distinctly undesirable."[59] In Carnegie's vision, workers could occasionally become artistic leaders, but statistically this would be a rare anomaly. The vast majority of drones had nothing creative to contribute.

Warhol's bee-people universalized and radicalized Carnegie's vision, and dramatically disputed the anthropocentric priorities of traditional aesthetics. These coprophilial drones imaginatively collapsed the distinction between the human and the animal: they would now be governed completely by utility, in a closed system requiring only the occasional replenishing of pink dye. They also modeled a regression to life in the womb, a reunification with mother, during which the fetus's waste is recycled as sustenance. And they overcame the limitations Freud bemoaned in humanity's attitude toward excrement: they were no longer "embarrassed by anything that reminds them too much of their animal origins," having learned to treat their bodily by-products "with the attention and care which [they] might claim as an integrating component of their essential being."[60]

In this deeply abject and demystified vision, Warhol was also anticipating one of Derrida's most memorable insights regarding animal life, which would be published two decades later. Having raised mulberry silkworms as an adolescent, Derrida later learned that their "*serigenous* [silk-producing] *glands . . . can . . . be labial or salivary, but also rectal.*"[61] Each caterpillar "*secreted absolutely, it secreted a thing which would never be an object to it, an object for it, an object it would stand over against. It did not separate itself from its work.*"[62] Like Derrida's silkworms, Warhol's bee-people are therefore "[a]bsolute nature and culture": excretion is sustenance, nature *is* culture, the body is a closed loop.[63] Billy Name saw something similar in Warhol, describing him as being "like one of those mulberry caterpillars, the silk caterpillar who spins a cocoon to enclose himself in, and lives his life inside that cocoon, and spins silk webs."[64] Perhaps he was thinking of Marx's description of Milton—that he "produced *Paradise Lost* as a silkworm produces silk, as the activation of *his own* nature."[65]

Warhol's work—frequently produced with synthetic silkscreen—certainly was understood to have a similar animalistic automaticity. But the Warhol/silkworm image also raises interesting sexual and reproductive connotations, since, as Derrida also pointed out, silkworms have often been seen to exist "beyond any sexual difference or rather any duality of the sexes, and even beyond any coupling."[66] A similar asexual and nonbinary quality was often ascribed to Warhol—first disparagingly as "sissy" or "momma's boy," then later, more generously, as "all woman [AW]," "all witch," "Pop," or "Drella."[67] Once closed-loop, nature/culture unification is achieved, gender binaries and reproductive expectations immediately become less meaningful. Each body becomes reproductive on its own.[68]

Warhol presented his own dietary proclivities as automatic, like those of the bees he described. Nourishment—and more specifically the synthetic sweetness of sugar—replaced even wealth as an ultimate motivation for labor:

> When I was a child . . . what I had a fantasy about having was candy. As I matured that fantasy translated itself into "make money to have candy," because as you get older, of course, you get more realistic. Then . . . my career started to pick up . . . and now I have a roomful of candy all in shopping bags.[69]

Kathryn Bond Stockton argues that the fantasy of limitless candy is "the dream of manufacturing what you will profusely and on the spot consume," indulging childhood curiosity regarding economics, destruction, and the abject.[70] In Warhol's case, candy carried animal resonances as well, since his candy fantasies seem to have been perfectly embodied in the bee-people, who could process their waste *as* sweetness, skipping the awkward and time-consuming steps of design, manufacture, exchange, and profitability. Warhol's candy fantasy is also an animal fantasy.

Abject substances were accepted in Warhol's model as integral features of life. The bee-people—Boschian or Bataillean in their shameless transgression—would close the loop between consumption and waste. No one would go hungry, and no embarrassing by-products would be created; everything would happen "behind their backs," where waste—first shit, then vomit—would be converted into nourishment. For Kristeva, any human found "wallowing in their vomit" is "caught flush with their animality."[71] Warhol's imagination effortlessly took him beyond the traditional (and in this case scientifically accurate) version of the disgusting—vomit—to excrement, the absolutely unassimilable object/action. In this respect, as in so many others, he radically undermined the priorities of traditional Western aesthetics, anticipating Derrida's claim that "vomit" is both a limit of, and a protective seal for, the aesthetic system, since it "substitutes . . . oral for anal," that which is "more disgusting than the disgusting."[72] Any animal that violated this prohibition would be deemed sub-animal, like the rats Freud had singled out as "dirty animals" for their propensity to eat excrement.[73]

Warhol's artificial coloring was crucial here, since it staged the aesthetic as a disguise for an otherwise unthinkable system. But, from a broader perspective, the refuse/nourishment system Warhol imagined is just a miniaturized version of the earth's ecosystem, in which there would be no nourishment without the fertilization provided by waste and decay, no flowers or food without shit and rot, since "rotting both makes possible and invariably succeeds growth."[74] As unthinkable as it appears on first glance, Warhol's closed-loop ecological system was also timely. In an effort to cut back on food weight during space travel, the US government had been funding research in the late 1960s on the possibility of deriving sustenance from bacteria grown on human waste.[75] The possibilities of recycling waste as food were by no means outside the bounds of biotechnology.

Translating these ecological ideals to the everyday world proved difficult, however, particularly for an artist who was notoriously anxious and germophobic. The New York subway offered one plausible model. As Warhol explained in 1975, "The kids who spray graffiti all over the subway cars at night have learned how to recycle city space very well. They go back into the subway yards in the middle of the night when the cars are empty and that's when they do their singing and their dancing on the subway. The subways are like palaces at night with all that space just for you."[76] These typically overlooked subterranean "palaces" appeared to promise a new model of creativity, in which every form of artmaking could be pursued openly and collaboratively, without gatekeepers or fees. But the ethnic diversity that characterized the subway also intimidated Warhol. In 1983, he told his diary, "The day had been mostly black. Originally, the city was having Puerto Rican Day, so that was one of the main reasons to get away. But P.R. Day was 98.9 percent black. The subway was 85 percent black. The zoo was 80 percent black, the park was 99.5 percent black. Whites are really a minority."[77] In this instance, Warhol's rarely remarked racial biases—here delivered with the casual scientificity of a meteorologist—counterweighed his commitment to creative egalitarianism, rendering the subway ecology simultaneously fascinating and frightening.

The closed-loop apiarian system Warhol imagined deeply unsettled the distinctions not just between "human" and "animal," but between life and waste, "living" and "dead." For the rest of his career, Warhol would investigate this area as another opportunity to challenge the boundaries of humanist aesthetics, and to propose animal or vegetal alternatives. Here, again, Warhol anticipated contemporary currents in ecological theory, which have singled out this seemingly foundational distinction as ideological; as Timothy Morton has recently argued, "The life-non-life distinction is impossible to maintain; all beings are better thought as undead, not as animate or as inanimate."[78] "Life" and "death" are constitutively intermixed—interdependent, indistinguishable. Warhol apparently sensed these connections in an unusually visceral and universal way, insisting that "*everything's* alive" and that "the plants are screaming."[79] Lamenting the impact of "drugs" on the nation's topsoil, in 1985, and recognizing that "when the topsoil is gone, you starve," Warhol advocated adding trenches to movie theaters and washing down their "sticky floors" after each screening—"[j]ust like a barn," all the candy and pop and excreta reintegrating into the landscape.[80] It was in these moments that Warhol came closest to recognizing what Marder calls "the unacknowledged vegetal background of human knowledge," with its roots in earth and decay.[81]

Dying with living, living with dying, each feeding the other; artistry, in Warhol's model, might ultimately just be a way of prettying up this messy process—putting some pink in it. The recording technologies that he embraced—photography, film,

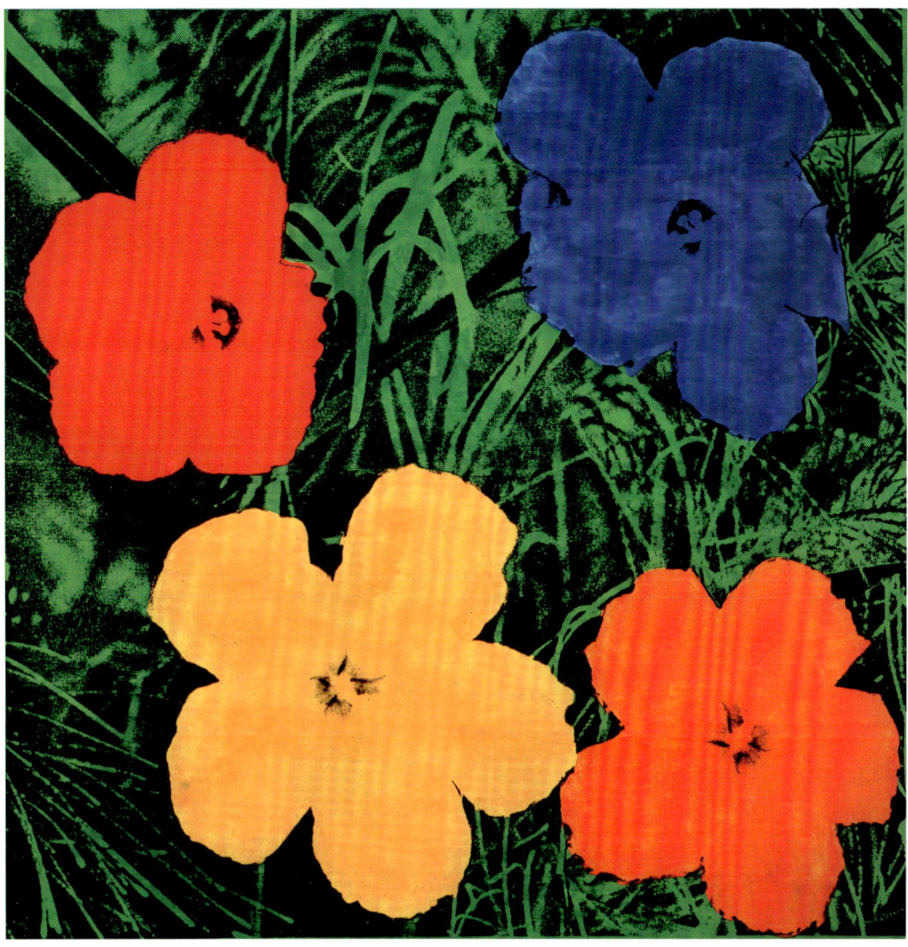

FIGURE 32
Andy Warhol, *Flowers*, 1964. The Andy Warhol Museum, Pittsburgh; Founding Collection, Contribution The Andy Warhol Foundation for the Visual Arts, Inc. © 2022 The Andy Warhol Foundation for the Visual Arts, Inc./ Licensed by Artists Rights Society (ARS), New York.

video, television, audio recording—were constantly testifying to the intermixture of the living and the dead.[82] John Coplans saw this quality immediately in Warhol's massively prolific *Flower* paintings, which "perish under one's gaze, as if haunted by death" and would be shown alongside the *Jackie* series when it debuted.[83] (See figure 32.) These paintings highlight what Marder calls "a peculiar mediation between the living and the dead," in which the plant, "caressing the dead with its roots and obtaining nourishment from them . . . makes them live again . . . . through the roots to the stem and on to the flower."[84] Introduced to a camera cable release by a journalist in 1965, Warhol immediately imagined a terminal self-portrait, whereby "if a person were dying he could photograph his own death." He bragged that in a previous film, his "first color movie," entitled *Suicide,* he had "found" a "star . . . who has 13 scars on one wrist and 15 scars on the other wrist from suicide attempts . . . all different shades of purple." The life/death interface was this important to Warhol: its colors were the first thing he chose to capture when he finally got access to color film: "We just focused the camera on his wrists and he pointed to each scar and told its history."[85] Someone asked him if he would ever film an actual suicide: "Ohh, wouldn't that be something. One of my friends committed suicide recently, but he didn't call me. . . . He was a dancer and had been in a couple of my films. He got high and just danced right out the window."[86] The dancer was Fred Herko; he had jumped from a window the previous October.[87]

Warhol's artistic interest in the interface between life and death applied to his own mortality. After Valerie Solanas shot and almost killed him, his emergency-room scars qualified as another source of beauty: "The scars are really very beautiful; they look pretty in a funny way."[88] In a little-known interview printed in 1976, he attributed his retreat from the subjects of death and disaster to his own "death":

> AW. And then I stopped because I died.
>
> OX. —because?—
>
> AW. Then I stopped because I died.[89]

Reflecting on the aftermath of this near-death experience, Warhol described a perpetual state of confusion: "Since I was shot, everything is such a dream to me. I don't know what anything is about. Like I don't even know whether or not I'm really alive or—whether I died."[90] Those who knew him best agreed that he had changed dramatically: "When Andy came back . . . he was like a stand-up cardboard Andy. He had been so injured. . . . He would just shrink away from anybody who tried to touch him."[91] At the limit, he would present himself as just another object among objects, standing still within a glass vitrine, "ANDY WARHOL, USA, INVISIBLE SCULPTURE, mixed media, 1985."[92]

The ability to identify and process death, to sequester it away from life and move past it, has long been deemed a specifically human capacity. This is the anthropocentric distinction between human dying and animal perishing that Derrida would later criticize in Martin Heidegger's philosophy, where "only *Dasein* has a relation to death *as such,* and this relation is not dissociable from its ability to speak, the animal being deprived of both possibilities or abilities."[93] As in Kant's aesthetic theory, access to the "as such"—abstraction from the messy world of drives and decay—is used to distinguish human from nonhuman life. Just as artists can create "as such" (without thought of recompense), artworks can be purposive "as such" (without an actual purpose), and audiences can enjoy "as such" (without the interference of interest), *Dasein,* according to Heidegger, can reflect on death "as such"—abstractly, disinterestedly. And yet, as Derrida would point out (and here it seems clear that he and Warhol would have agreed): "[A]nimals have a very significant relation to death . . . even if they have neither a relation to death nor to the 'name' of death *as such*. . . . But neither does man [have such an abstract relation], that is precisely the point!"[94] Death "as such" is unthinkable, for human and nonhuman lifeforms alike, but this doesn't mean that any being lives without a relation to it.

In the aftermath of his father's death, Warhol had learned that the abdication of this "human" capacity for establishing a disinterested attitude toward death would provoke outrage and titillation in others. He seems to have grasped the close relationship between the abject and the deathly, since "nothing is more abject . . . than the raw literalness and materiality of the corpse," and the "return of the dead animal body" it entails.[95] He would continue to explore this provocative constellation throughout his career. In his discussion of Warhol's refusal to acknowledge his mother's death, Koestenbaum homed in on a videotaped letter to Man Ray that Warhol recorded after the surrealist's passing in 1976: "Nobody told me what to talk about. You mean write a letter to May Ray? Oh. Man Ray was this wonderful person. . . . And he was really cute: he took a picture of me, and I took a picture of him, and then he took another picture of me . . . [repeats]."[96] Koestenbaum persuasively argued that the passage demonstrates that photography—and technological reproduction more generally—was Warhol's substitute for conversations he found too difficult to have. When Warhol did attempt to address Man Ray directly in this "letter," the results were mostly negative and hazy: "I don't know what else to say to you. I never really had much to say to you before. All I did was take pictures." There are, however, two companions that Warhol felt had no difficulty addressing the dead artist directly: "My dogs say hello to you. Archie and Amos."[97] Once again, when we think of Warhol (as Koestenbaum does) embracing a machinic or technological reaction to avoid facing the things and people he had difficulty facing, we have to acknowledge the frequency and intensity of his reminders that his personal, creative, emotional machine is an animal- and sometimes vegetal-machine—"subhuman," defined by instinct and appetite, unreflective, unable to access the abstract "as such"—and that, although technological reproduction could provide a shortcut to this mode of living, plants and animals (and humans becoming plants and animals) continually provided him with its ultimate exemplars. By the mid-1970s, he was describing Victor Hugo Rojas—the Factory collaborator who would scout models for, and coordinate the logistics of, the *Torsos* and *Sex Parts* series—as "the greatest artist in the world," having "covered the feet of live chickens in red paint and then released them to 'sign' the floors, and stairs, and walls of a borrowed country place."[98]

Warhol long dreamed that his beloved dachshunds—whom he seems to have pre-envisioned in his college work *Two Dogs Kissing*—might do the difficult work of socializing and even artmaking for him, just as he had called on various creatures to do so throughout his past: "Andy gave himself a dog for Christmas, a black dachshund puppy he named Archie, after Archie Bunker, the lower-middle-class loudmouth on the new sitcom *All in the Family*. He carried it around in his arms at the office party, whispering in its ear, 'Talk, Archie, talk. Oh, Archie, if you would only talk, I wouldn't have to work another day in my life. Talk, Archie, talk.'"[99] Waiting to meet Imelda Marcos in 1974 to solicit her patronage, Warhol repeated this supplication: "Archie . . . you're going to meet Mrs. Marcos. Oh, if you'd only talk, Archie, we wouldn't have to do things like this."[100] There is no more powerful image for Warhol's self-understanding as an artistic animal-machine during the 1970s. He had worked his entire life to demonstrate the bestial and vegetal core of aesthetic experience, and to market it to the rich and powerful; how much less unpleasant it would be if he could finally find a nonhuman life-form that could communicate this truth for him directly. Posing with Archie for a photograph, he eerily echoed the youthful portrait that was painted of him with a mechanical bird, except now instead of whispering in his ear, the animal snout supersedes the human mouth, as if it should speak first. Archie would even take center stage with Warhol at his most corporate: photographed with the "leadership team" of Andy Warhol Enterprises, for instance, in 1973. Friends thought Warhol had actually named the dog after "a black man named Archie who cruised Union Square and was known for his oversize penis," again covertly intertwining creativity with animality, the abject, and queer desire.[101]

If the ecological and the deathly constituted two appealing but difficult directions for Warhol's ecological aesthetics, his practices of collecting provided a much more palatable alternative. Warhol was a passionate and comprehensive collector across a wide range of media. His time capsules and audiotapes and snapshots and antiques, clothing, cock drawings, taxidermied animals, and perfumes constitute some of the century's most impressive and eccentric private collections. Collecting offered a highly administered method of simultaneously jettisoning *and* protecting the ephemeral while avoiding the grime and decay that comes with it, and potentially profiting from the result. Once the daily detritus was boxed up properly in *Time Capsules,* it could be forgotten and preserved without anyone having to deal with the mess until much later. What's more, as Blake Gopnik illustrates, shopping trips could be deducted as business expenses, since almost anything Warhol purchased could be justified as a "prop" for his creative work.[102]

Jonathan Flatley has shown that "the logic of the collection seems to permeate Warhol's aesthetic practices fairly thoroughly," encouraging "identity games" that emphasized likeness and singularity. Each addition to the collection loses its "identity" and gains its "singularity," its specific similarities and differences from other members of the group. Instead of the "system of universal equivalence" advanced by capitalism, Warhol helps us to see "likenesses"—similarities without equivalences. For Flatley, these practices were "a way for [Warhol] to imagine being-similar, to imagine himself belonging to a community of *semblables*"—modeling and developing what Walter Benjamin described as the mimetic faculty, "the once powerful compulsion to become similar and also to behave mimetically."[103] This unlikely resurrection of the mimetic faculty is, for Flatley, part of what makes Warhol's work so consequential.

As it turns out, there are strong links between the mimetic drive Flatley noticed in practices of collection and Warhol's animal and vegetal imagination. Although he believed that humans have "[t]he highest capacity for producing similarities," Benjamin recognized that the mimetic drive was decidedly animal in origin: mimicry arises when "the obscure impulse of the animal . . . detects, as danger approaches, a way of escape that still seems invisible," blending into its surroundings by mimicking them.[104] Benjamin bemoaned modernity's repression of the mimetic faculty, and argued that antipathy toward animals signaled a fear of the creaturely origins of mimesis.[105] And, as Joyce Cheng has remarked, Benjamin's observations can be traced back to surrealist sources that explored "a world of ambiguous, indistinct beings," "[p]art-man, part-beast, part-plant."[106]

Kristeva proposed an ontogenetic explanation for these animal/mimetic connections, tracking the origins of human mimesis to infancy, a period during which the bond between mother and child approaches complete mimetic union.[107] Only when—and if—the mother sublimates her passion for the child can the child abject the animal/maternal other and begin to engage creatively with the world and its laws: "*It is because the maternal passion is a continual sublimation that creativity is made possible for the child.*"[108] This transition from passion and unity to "paternal laws" draws the child away from their fundamentally mimetic relationship with their mother—the nuzzling, burrowing closeness in which "[t]he infant becomes the breast through its incorporation."[109]

As we saw in chapter 1, Warhol and his mother seem to have relished their unwillingness to perform this socially prescribed transition from "the archaic dyad" to "language and law."[110] Warhol's nuzzling, infantile, appetitive, animal closeness remained a prominent dimension of his personality and work. Instead of enthusiastically abjecting the animal/maternal other as a normative white American male is expected to do, Warhol hyperbolically embraced all of its components—animality, the vegetal, maternal affection, transgression, the abject in its various forms—and the mimetic drive itself. In opposition to language and law, which are structured around difference, evaluation, and exchange, mimesis prioritizes similarities and likenesses, a drawing together and holding close that is supposed to be left behind with childhood, and that Warhol pursued with great enthusiasm in his practices of collecting.

"Liking things" Warhol once claimed, was appealing because everything in life is "hard."[111] The "florid . . . hording" that Gopnik traces from the late 1950s to the end of Warhol's life was an attempt to circumvent this immutable difficulty.[112] Collecting—people, receipts, trash, precious gems, artworks, antiques—offered the possibility of holding everything close, not having to choose between one pleasure and another, not ever having to let go of something precious. Never abjecting, keeping one's mother and one's animal and vegetal others close by—in the basement, in the spare bedroom, in the back studio. Orchids, houseplants, horses carved out of wood, taxidermied dogs and peacocks and moose heads, the marzipan cow Warhol kept among newspaper clippings and crumpled paper towels in a small box of mementos after his mother died in

1972.[113] Liking indiscriminately, without thought of consequence or judgment, death or growth, so that "every image [could] be clear and simple and the same as the first one."[114] Something like the pansexual liking-machine that he had attempted to explain to Swenson in 1963, where even style—that most personal of artistic qualities—could be abandoned and made multiple, "[w]ithout feeling that you've given up something."[115] Finally, perhaps, embracing what his mother called his "childish mind," and finding the position advocated by Kristin Dombek: just "being the animal you are, born of other animals, made of mirroring them."[116]

4

"PHILOSOPHY OF THE FRAGILE"

DURING THE LAST FIVE YEARS of his life, Warhol worked on two projects that specifically advocated for nonhuman animals facing extinction: a series of ten silkscreen prints entitled *Endangered Species* (1983), and a group of prints illustrating a book by the scientist Kurt Benirschke called *Vanishing Animals* (New York: Springer-Verlag, 1986). Both were produced in close collaboration with Rupert Jasen Smith, who had been working as Warhol's master printmaker since 1977, and who would die from AIDS-related complications in 1989. It is common among Warhol's biographers and critics to group the two series together, and to dismiss them as faddish and embarrassing attempts to profit from a passing zeitgeist.[1] Arthur Danto's view is representative: these series were "dreamt up as commercial propositions," characteristic of the spirit of "Andy Warhol Enterprises."[2] This dismissive gesture has been at least partially justified by the paradigm of the animal-machine discussed in chapter 3: if every nonhuman creature is "just an animal," then everything Warhol produced that focuses on these "animals" can fairly be merged and subordinated beneath other work that takes on more serious or worthy subjects. This chapter and the next will make the case that these projects actually propose two very different approaches to the problem of animal advocacy in art, and that, in disparate ways, they made substantial and provocative contributions to this cause.

As Keri Cronin has conclusively shown, visual representations have long been central to animal advocacy, "playing an important role in shaping dominant ideas about and attitudes toward nonhuman animals."[3] Recent scholarship by Julia Bryan-Wilson, Elizabeth Sutton, and Aloi Giovanni has demonstrated that nonhuman animals were becoming increasingly prominent in the work of Warhol's contemporaries, including Simone Forti, Hiroshi Sugimoto, VALLIE EXPORT, Jannis Kounellis, Tim Rollins and KOS, Mimmo Germana, Robert Rauschenberg, Helen Chadwick, Bill Viola, Vettor Pisani, Ana Mendieta, and Joseph Beuys.[4] Bryan-Wilson compellingly establishes that this new prominence "had the potential to register as politically inflected," since the idea of "animal rights" was gaining momentum in Europe and the United States—most prominently in legislation such as the US Animal Welfare Act (1966) and the European Convention for the Protection of Animals during International Transport (1968).[5]

Endangered Species and *Vanishing Animals* both ostensibly contribute to this emergent tradition of animal advocacy. And yet their relationship to this tradition is problematic in a number of ways. As Peggy Kamuf has argued, the word "advocacy" is typically understood to be specifically verbal, and to imply a power differential between the defendant and the advocate, who "is called to speak in place of the other, to lend his/her voice to the other's cause, thereby to act as an aid or supplement to the one who stands accused."[6] Warhol's work with animals undermined every element of this definition. Where advocacy is generally expected to be verbal, Warhol was borderline nonverbal: one contemporary commentator described "[t]he absolute flatness [of his voice], the affectlessness [which] meant you couldn't see behind it at all."[7] Where advocacy requires force and resilience, Warhol was notoriously weak and vulnerable, besmirched as a feeble animal or insect himself, with a "hypnotized voyeuristic stare of smarmy whitened worminess [that] inspired much fascinated talk about what you find under rocks."[8] And, while advocacy implies inequity (one who must advocate for another who is unable to), Warhol had deeply egalitarian ambitions: "The Pop idea, after all, was that anybody could do anything."[9] Warhol apparently sensed the weight of these challenges. Rather than speaking for animals, he wished they could speak for him. The question remains: do these tensions undermine Warhol's projects or redeem them?

The *Endangered Species* series seems to fall prey to many of the weaknesses we associate with Warhol's late commercial production. (See figure 33.) The series looks opportunistic, faddish, and mercenary. Warhol's recorded comments on its production do little to assuage these concerns. Writing in his diary on the day he finished printing, Warhol focused on compensation: "Worked on the Endangered Species portfolios and talked on the phone to Ron Feldman . . ., and Ron was excited, really excited,

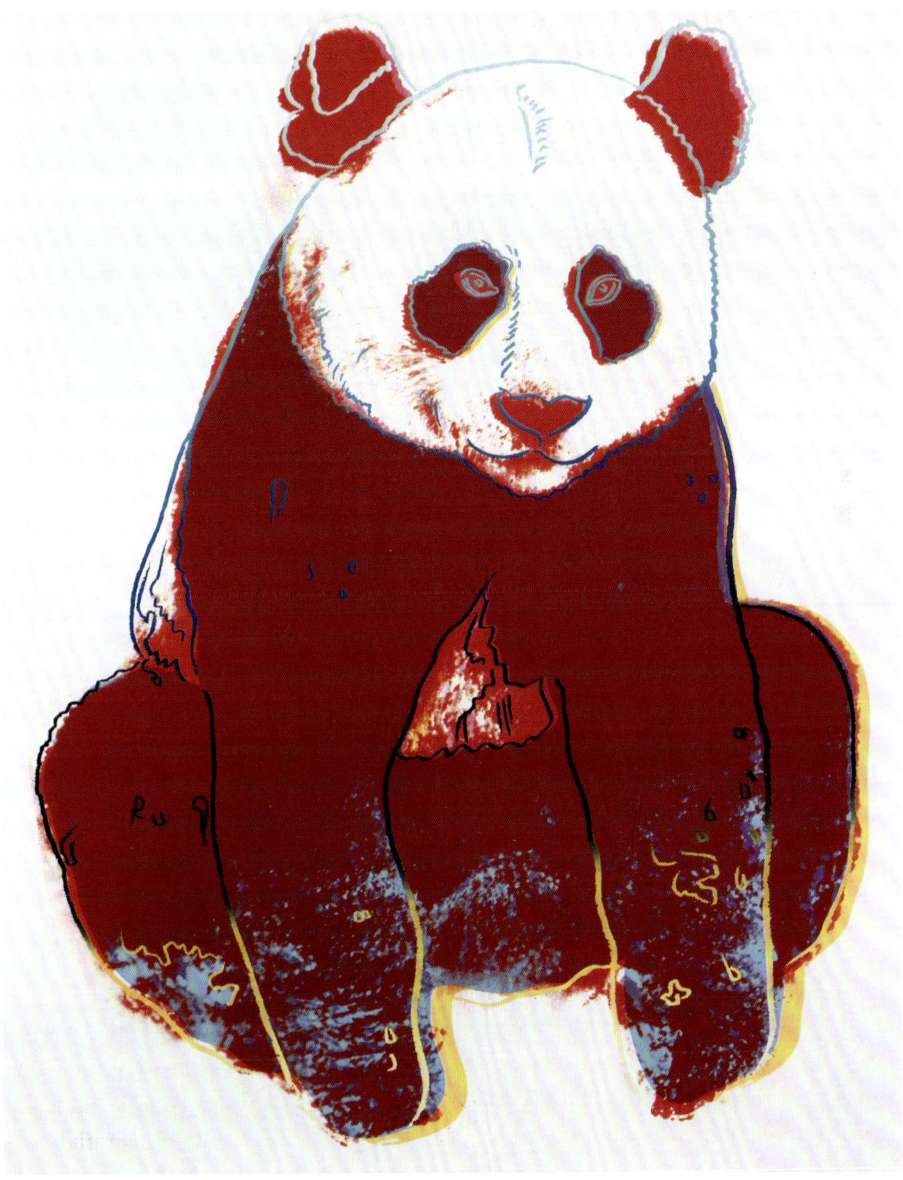

FIGURE 33
Andy Warhol, *Endangered Species (Panda)*, 1983. Image and Artwork © The Andy Warhol Foundation for the Visual Arts, Inc./Licensed by ARS.

and now we have to figure out how to market them."[10] It was Feldman, an art dealer, who had dreamed up the idea, and provided Warhol with a list of possible animals.[11] The prints would be shown at the Museum of Natural History in 1983, and would end up earning Warhol over a million dollars.[12] Later, he apparently described the series as "Animals in make up."[13]

There's a troubling obviousness about Warhol's approach to these images: eight of the ten chosen animals are charismatic megafauna, while the other two, smaller creatures—the San Francisco silverspot and the Pine Barrens frog—are deeply beguiling in their own right. It is hard to imagine Warhol selecting animals that would have been more blatantly appealing than these. It is as though he has converted these glamorous creatures into celebrities, wilder versions of Marilyn Monroe or Troy Donahue. Even the silverspot butterfly, which echoes a long-standing homoerotic trope in Warhol's work, appears here generic and uninflected by feeling.[14] And the style of these images seems similarly obvious or sure-fire. In each case, the image is based upon a photograph, which is then traced in a subsequent layer. Their lines are so glitchy and digitized, however, that they can barely be taken to register a human hand. This series could be used to illustrate Linda Weintraub's claim that "Warhol's process is a tribute to the machine and its takeover of natural occurrences."[15]

And yet, ironically, Warhol traced this "tribute to the machine" to a moment of deep animal trauma in his past. As we have seen in chapter 1, Warhol located the origins of his mature Pop style in the death of his beloved cat Hester, a death he blamed himself for: "I've felt guilty ever since. That's how we should have started *Popism.* That's when I gave up caring."[16] Many of the recriminations he leveled against himself for the cat's death could equally be applied to his mother's, in 1972. Didn't he seem to avoid taking care of Julia as her health deteriorated, sending her to live with his brothers? Wasn't he in Los Angeles when she died, promoting a film, *Heat,* whose star, Andrea Feldman, had killed herself after being frustrated in her efforts to marry Warhol and become "Andrea Warhola," as his mother had always hoped someone would?[17] Couldn't he be described as having been greedy with his mother's love and care, profiting from it as much as possible and then abandoning her when she became a nuisance? From this perspective, the kitten crying for its mother is Warhol, but so is the figure who selfishly separates, reunites, and then permanently sunders mother from kitten. What's more, these intertwined problems had recursive effects: if Hester's death in the late 1950s permanently taught Warhol not to care, as he claimed it did, couldn't this change in affect have played a role in his shockingly apathetic response to his mother's death—his refusal to attend her funeral, his apparent inability to say anything to his brother John regarding the death other than "Uh" and "Aaahhh," his decision not to tell anyone at the Factory about it for years?[18] Asked by a reporter how he was feeling shortly after his mother died, he could speak only of their mynah bird: "I think about my bird that died. If it went to bird heaven. But I really can't think about that. It just took a walk."[19] By 1980, with his mother's death far more proximate than Hester's, it is remarkable to see Warhol again singling out the animal death as the one that was truly pivotal.

Mechanical indifference and animal empathy were therefore not dichotomous in Warhol's work, and both were closely tied to the realm of the maternal. Since he could no longer risk caring for others after losing Hester, Warhol pursued a mechanical style that distanced him from his subject matter. A surplus of empathy produced a defense mechanism that was itself hyperbolically animalistic, since it involves an introjection of the stereotypical "animal-machine" that would be critiqued by Derrida: "a machine that doesn't speak, that doesn't have access to sense, that can at best imitate 'signifiers without a signified.'"[20] In the *Endangered Species* series, Warhol performed this animal/mechanical lack of compassion all too convincingly.[21]

Warhol's diaries, however, show us that this denial of compassion was exaggerated and defensive. He cared deeply about nonhuman animals; in fact, it often seems that he felt more compassion toward them than he did toward other humans. In 1979, in Manhattan, he had seen a taxi hit a dog: "a woman was screaming, and we offered her the limo to take the dog to the hospital, but she said her husband was getting the car, and it ruined the whole night. It made me feel funny."[22] The passage resonates with Warhol's well-known response to witnessing injuries from a cherry bomb exploding in a crowd of people near 42nd Street, during which he "felt like [he] was bleeding all over."[23]

This compassion also extended to, and perhaps even gravitated toward, animals and elements of animal existence that were traditionally shunned or ignored. In interviews and in his diaries, Warhol repeatedly worried over killing the cockroaches and water bugs that inhabited his living space. He thought one water bug that he cornered in the kitchen every night had been eating his food for at least three years.[24] He had difficulty discerning the difference in value between human lives and water-bug lives, and worried that if he killed a bug it would be just like "mugging someone."[25] When he did kill a roach, "it was a trauma. A very big trauma. I felt really terrible."[26] Ultimately, he identified with these creatures' vulnerability: feeling "like an old timer" on his birthday, Warhol remarked that he "can't even squish a roach anymore because it's just like a life, like living."[27] In these more marginal areas of Warhol's practice, we thus start to glimpse a "compassion in impotence and not from power" from which, Derrida would argue, "we must start when we want to think the animal and its relation to man."[28] As Warhol told a reporter in 1969, "I've been thinking about the philosophy of the fragile."[29]

Warhol doesn't seem to have been able to summon this "compassion in impotence" for the *Endangered Species* series, but there is evidence to suggest that it did inform the *Vanishing Animals* project. Benirschke, a world-renowned expert in animal and human medicine, gave a speech on endangered species in 1984 in New York, which Warhol attended. Warhol was reportedly "deeply impressed" by Benirschke's presentation, and accepted an invitation to collaborate on a book.[30] It seems to have been the first such collaboration—book length, between a prominent artist and a scientist, focused on endangered species—published in the United States. Benirschke moved quickly, sending Warhol a list of animals in January 1985 that closely resembled the final set. Their intervention was timely: the National Forum on BioDiversity would take place the following year—an event that, as David Sepkoski notes, "is widely credited with launching biodiversity preservation as an organized movement."[31]

It is immediately apparent that the species depicted in *Vanishing Animals* are far less familiar and marketable than those in the *Endangered Species* group. Among these fifteen are a condor (*Gymnogyps californianus*), an armadillo (*Chlamyphorus retusus*), a giant Chacoan peccary (*Catagonus wagneri*), an okapi (*Okapia johnstoni*), and a douc langur (*Pygathrix nemaeus*). Of course, this is Benirschke's list, reflecting his research interests, but it prompted Warhol to reflect on animals he might not otherwise have considered, and to adjust his working methods as well. Correspondence between the two men preserved in the Warhol archives shows that they were thinking collaboratively about each of the images, with Benirschke making suggestions and even supplying Warhol with his own drawings in an effort to facilitate his process. Their differing approaches to the project might be epitomized by Benirschke's desire to have an "outrageously exclamatory" cover image of "the 'ugly' head of a condor shedding a brightly sparkling tear." ("Of course [condors] don't cry or shed tears," Benirschke admitted, "but the message would be strong and clear.")[32] He followed up a few days later with a mournful and melodramatic postcard painted by Karel Havlíček of a crying lemur surrounded by litter, proffering a skeletal hatchling in a cracked egg, as a possible reference point for the cover.[33]

Instead of following Benirschke's maudlin suggestions for this series, Warhol returned to a technique he first explored in 1975, for his groundbreaking *Ladies and Gentlemen* series of prints: silkscreen over collage.[34] (See figure 34.) In many cases, the images were printed directly onto collaged paper, which was uniquely composed for each individual print. What's more, in *Vanishing Animals* he relinquished the photographic layer that structured the *Ladies and Gentlemen* and *Endangered Species* images, instead building the images from his tracings of other images—tracings that communicate a supposedly animalistic tendency to follow another's tracks without dissimulating one's own.[35] The roughly collaged paper gives these prints a precariousness that seems appropriate to their subjects' status. Like each animal, each print is a unique instance of a species—"inherently singular and . . . irreducible to each other"—attempting to make a place for itself in a world that may or may not be able to support it.[36]

The text of Benirschke's 1984 speech does not survive, but we can get a sense of his interests, and of what Warhol might have known of them, from his essays in *Vanishing Animals.* The book offers accessible but detailed descriptions of the challenges facing each of its fifteen species. It quickly becomes apparent that many of these challenges would have resonated with Warhol for a variety of reasons relating to his personal history and the threats that he faced as a gay man in the 1980s. What's more, Blake Gopnik's conclusive repudiation of long-standing assumptions regarding Warhol's "illiteracy" means that it is no longer plausible to assume that Warhol would have illustrated a book without having read it.[37]

Given Benirschke's expertise in reproductive medicine, it is no surprise that eleven of the book's fifteen essays touched on sexual challenges related to mating and reproduction.[38] Perhaps less predictable was the provocative range of issues Benirschke

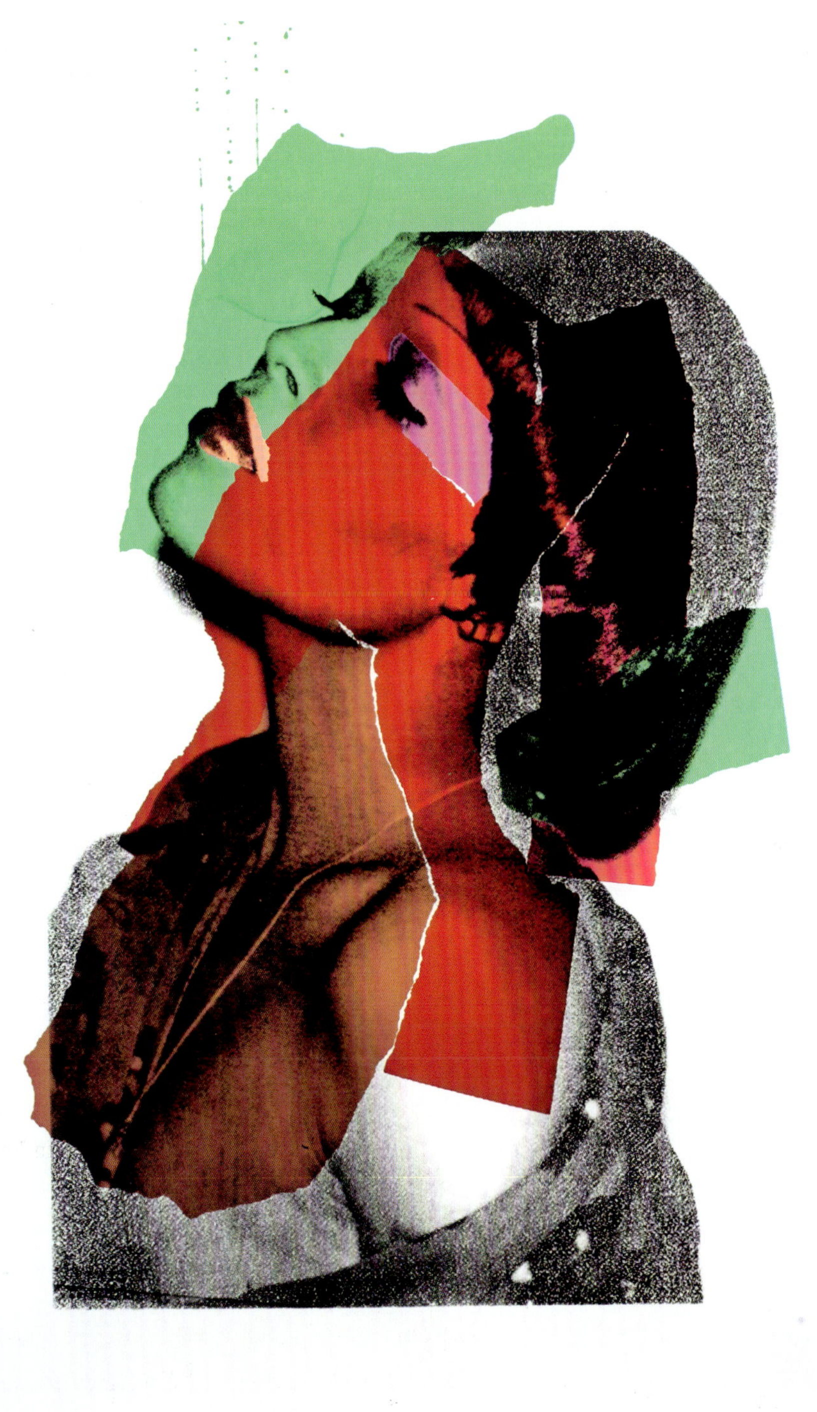

FIGURE 34
Andy Warhol, *Ladies and Gentlemen,* 1975. Image and Artwork © The Andy Warhol Foundation for the Visual Arts, Inc./Licensed by ARS.

covered, including same-sex bonding and biotechnological reproduction, maternal/newborn trauma, synthetic pheromone production, cross-species sexuality, infanticide, and sex fluidity and illegibility. Each of these concerns would have rung bells for Warhol, who had already expressed interest in them, or their rough equivalents in human behavior, in his previous work and writing—perhaps most directly in the *Ladies and Gentlemen* series. As Joan Roughgarden has pointed out, the more we learn about nonhuman species, the more traditional assumptions about the "naturalness" of sexuality, sex, and gender roles come into question. Even the most basic inference—that "[a]n organism is solely male or female for life"—becomes completely untenable, since "the most common body form among plants and in perhaps half of the animal kingdom is for an individual to be both male and female at the same, or at different times during its life."[39] What's more, as their social and erotic worlds were being ravaged by the AIDS epidemic, the precariousness that Warhol and Smith emphasized in their prints for the volume would not have been abstract for them. In many cases, Warhol and Smith seem to have coordinated this visual precariousness with the threats described in Benirschke's essays.

Perhaps the most familiar of the species described in *Vanishing Animals* are the birds: the condor, the parrot, and the crane. Warhol would learn from Benirschke that they were also the most explicitly queer. Warhol seems to have been aware that birds formed strong bonds; as he had put it in 1975, "[T]he best love story is just two lovebirds in a cage"[40] Benirschke's text emphasized that all three of the species it described "almost always form permanent pair bonds," and that "it is not in the best interest of a bird lover to keep single parrots as they are social animals and can become extremely lonely."[41] It must have been painful for Warhol to discover that, when opposite-sex mates are unavailable, parrots form permanent same-sex bonds.[42] He and his mother had kept a lone mynah bird named Echo in their apartment for decades—another species that pairs for life and was thought to be lonely without a partner.[43] Through his work with Benirschke, Andy would have learned that he and Julia had inadvertently kept a potentially queer bird unloved.[44]

To make matters more complicated, parrots and mynahs are both "monomorphic"—their sex cannot be distinguished visually, even by scientists. Benirschke reported that "[a] 'pair' [of parrots] donated to the breeding program . . . eventually was discovered to be a pair of bonded females. Such mistakes could have tragic results when so few birds were left."[45] In an effort to avoid this situation, Benirschke's colleagues discovered a new method for sexing parrots: "the fecal pellet method," which involved testing bird feces for estrogen and testosterone, but only when the bird in question was "healthy" and "turned on." Ultimately, scientists were able to determine sex in condors from "the remnants of incubation that stay in the shell after hatching," since "the sex organs are shaped by sex hormones in embryonic life and excrements accumulate in the egg."[46] These problems and solutions would have been vivid for Warhol, since he had so often been described by observers as ambiguous in gender, and since cross-dressing and the abject had long been keen interests for him.[47] What's more, monomorphism as a threat to these endangered species directly linked extinction to nonreproductive sexuality—a linkage that would have been pressing for Warhol and Smith as their erotic and social worlds were being decimated by AIDS.[48]

The print that Warhol and Smith constructed for the parrot essay is murky, particularly given the vividness of its subject matter, and uneven. Unusually for this series, it was constructed on two sheets of identical amber-colored paper, calling to mind a matched pair or its absence (since both sheets are almost completely obscured by the printed image). This sense of doubling and absence is reiterated in the print itself, where the various layers of color obscure at least as much as they reveal. The resulting image feels tragically palimpsestic, built on a succession of rough and uneven layers that can never be retrieved to consciousness without destroying the artwork. This effect is perhaps most apparent in three places: in the bird's gripping claws, which communicate action and desire and are partially rendered in a lavender that appears nowhere else in the print; in the roughly torn paper scraps that vaguely echo the silhouette of the parrot's body but are completely obscured by paint and remain visible beneath it only as texture and edge; and by the strangely highlighted section of the bird's chest, approximately where its heart would be. Here, through some trick of overlap and exposure, the amber paper peeks through almost unobstructed, forming something like a sector of the bird's breast. Intertwined themes of mortality, pairing, and queer desire are vividly recorded in this image.

Another likely point of connection for Warhol and Smith would have been Benirschke's account of the whooping crane. These birds were among the most flamboyantly precarious creatures discussed in *Vanishing Animals*. Among the qualities that make them vulnerable in the face of human threats are their territorial loyalty, their lifelong pair-bonding, and the "loud trumpeting calls [they make] when courting and during flight."[49] The essay notes that, as with parrots, the sex of cranes is difficult to identify. It does not mention, as later research would emphasize, that they "often form . . . stable homosexual pairs" in captivity.[50] But it does offer a variety of details that resonate with the trope of the "queer child" or "queer animal"—ideas that had long captivated Warhol. Benirschke noted that whooping cranes tend to produce two eggs each year, separated by a two- or three-day interval. Typically, however, only the elder chicks survived: "Being slightly older and stronger, the first chick has a decided advantage over its sibling, and since young cranes are known to squabble and fight fiercely, the second chick often dies, being trampled to death or thrown out of the nest."[51] Concerned about species survival, scientists in the late sixties decided to snatch twenty-six of these "second" eggs over a three-year period, and hatch them in incubators at the Patuxent Wildlife Research Center. Hatching was successful, but rearing was not: the scientists "simulated . . . the natural conditions of light and environment" and the birds initiated their "well known and ritualistic" premating dances, but nevertheless did not mate.[52]

In 1975, scientists began artificially inseminating cranes, and by 1978 the birds began producing fertile eggs. Eventually, eggs produced through artificial insemination were transferred to a sandhill-crane population to be raised by cranes of another species. These biotechnological interventions were successful in boosting population—the eggs hatched, and were raised by the foster parents—but Benirschke worried that these fostered whooping cranes might lose their species-specific behaviors and adopt the behaviors of their new flock, perhaps even mating with them.[53] He was right to be concerned: mis-imprinting could even occur between cranes and humans. In 1982, as Thom Van Dooren has shown, a prominent crane biologist named George Archibald visited *The Tonight Show* "to tell the story of his relationship with a Whooping Crane named Tex" who had been unable to produce offspring, and who "showed little interest in other cranes."[54] Scientists surmised that Tex "had been imprinted on a human" and could not process a fertile egg unless her hormones were reactivated by attraction. Archibald built an office in Tex's pen and spent seven years with her. Their relationship eventually produced a fertile egg that hatched and sired "many offspring."[55]

Unlike most of the other images in the book, Warhol and Smith's print for the whooping-crane essay is not based on a photograph. It was derived instead from one of John James Audubon's paintings reproduced in his *Guide to American Birds*.[56] The painting depicts a whooping crane hunting lizards on a rock; Warhol and Smith omit all but the bird, mouth agape, planted on one foot with the other aloft. Absent its prey, the crane appears to be whooping rather than feeding. It is printed in slightly irregular layers of red and black ink on teal paper, with two overlapping scraps of paper attached, light blue and pale green. The irregularly cut pale blue scrap establishes a ground plane around the bird's foot, but this plane quickly becomes unreliable as, above the foot, it seems to flatten visually against the paper behind it. This flattening effect is exacerbated where the two scraps overlap, since they clearly provide a backdrop rather than a ground for the lifted foot printed upon them. The larger pale green scrap forms something like an interior frame within the crane's body, intersecting its boundaries at a variety of vulnerable points: ankle, foot, vent, and repeatedly at the neck. (A similar sense of peril might be noted in Warhol and Smith's dolphin print for *Vanishing Animals,* where overlapping scraps of paper may refer to Benirschke's account of dolphins inadvertently being caught in gill nets.[57] This morbid association is reinforced by Warhol and Benirschke's decision to base that print on a photograph of a preserved dolphin carcass.)

The various ambiguities introduced into this image during its conversion from painting to print emphasize a creature whose world has become unwelcoming to it. Its sole place of grounding is perpetually revealed to be a false promise. The background that should encompass it and ideally provide a refuge is instead incomplete and full of bodily threats. Warhol, who had suffered as the last and smallest child, the sickly boy, queer and presumed to be incapable of reproduction, might have empathized with the plight of the second chick: statistically dead on arrival; prone to be bullied and killed by its siblings; subject to overseers who attempted to impose heterosexual reproductivity and failed.

The resonances of these various predicaments and discoveries for Warhol must have been profound, particularly during the late 1980s: here were many of his sexual preoccupations and imaginings, surprisingly confirmed by scientists as problems and possibilities in the animal kingdom. What if sex were in fact not essential, but determined by environmental factors, with "the *vast* majority of cells in human bodies [being] intersex"?[58] What if sexual excitation were a requisite for a being's ability to be sexually identified, and sex hormones could be detected in feces, even at the embryonic stage? What if "like-sex" bonding was natural rather than perverse? Warhol had broached many of these possibilities in his 1983 print *Cells*, and in his own, nonscientific, writing: "I think I'm missing some chemicals and that's why I have this tendency to be more of a—mama's boy. A—sissy. No, a mama's boy. A 'butterboy.' I think I'm missing some responsibility chemicals and some reproductive chemicals."[59]

Warhol would have discovered similarly evocative problems in Benirschke's chapter on the Galapagos turtle, another species in which sex identification is difficult for scientists to determine, to the point where "it is not unusual to find a tortoise that has been thought to be a 'male' laying eggs!" What's more, as Benirschke noted, the sex of each individual turtle is determined not by chromosomes, but by ambient temperature during certain phases of incubation. While the layering in Warhol and Smith's Galapagos-turtle print is far less complex and obscure than it is in the parrot print, it nevertheless introduces a similar range of tensions. A magenta sheet was overlaid with two roughly rectangular green scraps of slightly different tones, and a single black screen was then printed onto these three overlapping sheets. In the resulting image, the turtle is presented as a divided being, its head existing in a different world than its body, both mostly isolated from their surroundings. The scraps' two tones of green read as similar on their own, but the almost sickening contrast with the magenta background makes their difference pop strikingly. Like many used in the *Vanishing Animals* prints, these are institutional rather than ecological colors, reminiscent of the walls of a hospital café. The turtle that they bisect might be seen to suffer from a mind/body problem, split at the neck between mental and physical life—a creature in flux, at the mercy of its environment.

Although Benirschke does not dwell on this point, the plights of the turtle and the parrot speak not just to the illegibility of animals for scientists, but also to these creatures' abilities to sense things in ways that could not be detected by humans—specifically, the sex of their potential mates. There are other moments in *Vanishing Animals* that directly emphasize these parahuman abilities. In his essay on the Mongolian wild horse, Benirschke relates a story that began with a surprise pregnancy and ended with attempted infanticide undertaken by what appears to be a jealous father. Benirschke's zoo traded wild horses with an institution in Russia. One of the three horses they received was unexpectedly found to be pregnant. Benirschke and his colleagues "congratulated [themselves] on what [they] considered to be a fine bit of horse trading, getting four for three."[60] The mare was "well received" by Basil, the zoo's "reigning stallion." When she gave birth, however, "Basil, in a display of uncharacteristic behavior, fiercely attacked the youngster, nearly killing it instantly." A human attendant's arm was crushed when he tried to rescue the foal. The mare, "still in 'foal heat,'" "was promptly served by Basil"; she gave birth to another foal eleven months later, "under the now caring eyes of Basil."[61]

Benirschke goes on to pose the obvious questions: How could Basil have known that the first foal was not his? "Could he smell it? Did he know when [the mare] arrived that she was pregnant by someone else? Surely he cannot count."[62] Again, the accompanying print homes in on these strange and pressing questions. (See figure 35.) It is composed of a sheet of teal paper with three partially overlapping paper scraps—orange, then red, then pink—that culminate near the center of the page. The wild horse's head is depicted in profile in overlapping prints of black over red. The resulting palimpsest presents the horse's head as divided into three distinct zones: visual, nasal/oral, and mental. The image eerily reiterates Benirschke's strange questions: How might sense inform knowledge in the mare? How could he know something he couldn't see? Did the foal have a foreign smell that gave his patrimony away? Through its attention to filicide, the print also resonates with one of Warhol's enduring preoccupations: "the concealed impulse" that Freud, in attempting to analyze his own filicidal dream, called "the envy which is felt for the young by those who have grown old, but which they believe they have completely stifled."[63] This envy certainly seems to have characterized Julia's relationship with her son, but it also tainted Warhol's interactions with his younger peers and collaborators, "kids right off the street getting these prices!"[64]

Themes of intraspecies violence and filicide returned even more eerily in Benirschke's essay on the Komodo dragon (*Varanus komodoensis*). Here was an animal with which the "Drella" in Warhol could certainly identify: a monstrous cannibal—"thought to eat each other, or at least adults may devour young animals"—with vampiric qualities to boot: "[I]f by chance the prey escapes after being bitten, so many vicious bacteria have been injected with the monitor's saliva that the poor animal will soon die from blood poisoning anyway."[65] The scarred and ragged old creature reproduced alongside Benirschke's essay—hissing tongue extended as a younger dragon ambles by—emblematizes the menace described therein.[66] (See figure 36.) These vampiric and filicidal qualities may have reminded Warhol of his own history: his mother's efforts to appropriate his production; his own reputation as an appropriator of his "stable's" work; and the terrifying threats of "blood poisoning" posed by the AIDS epidemic. There is no photograph documenting the essay's other, strangest detail—"that eversion of the hemipenises (male reproductive organs) induced intense tongue flicking by females," suggesting that "pheromonal attraction occurs before mating"—but it cer-

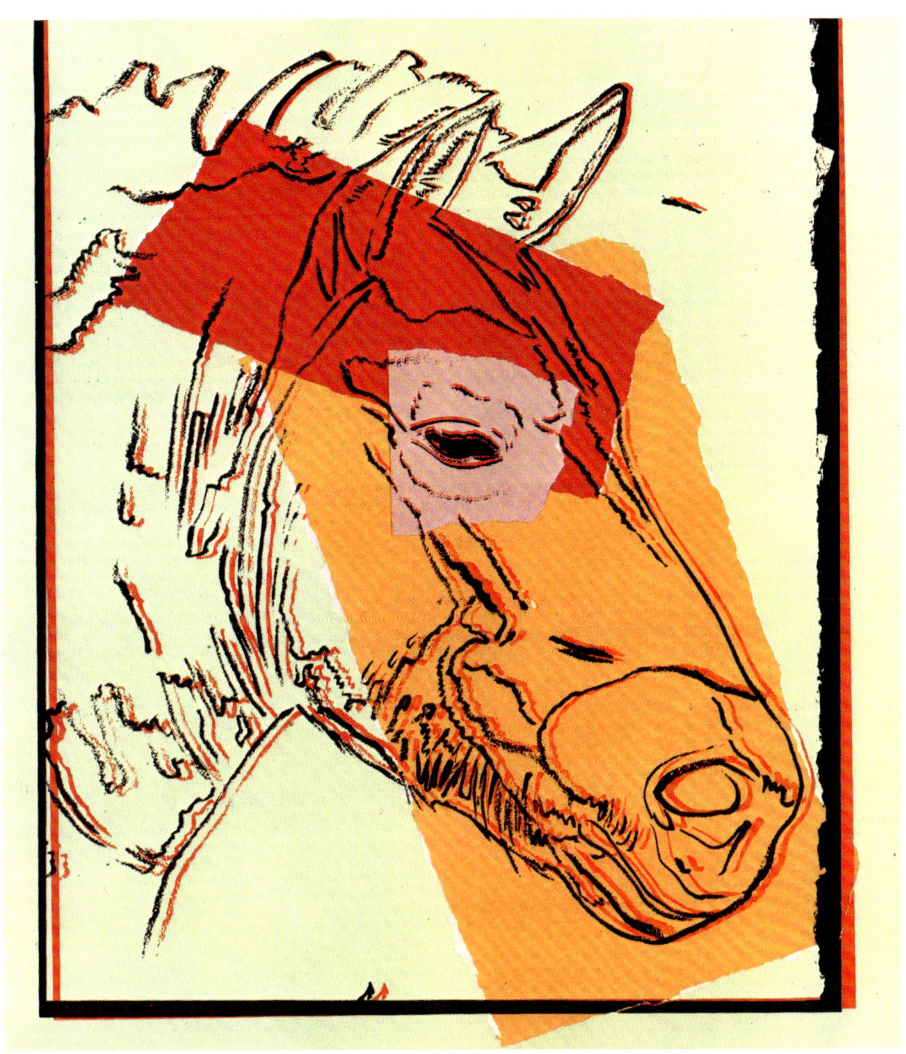

FIGURE 35
Andy Warhol, *Vanishing Animals (Mongolian Wild Horse)*, 1986. © 2022 The Andy Warhol Foundation for the Visual Arts, Inc./Licensed by Artists Rights Society (ARS), New York.

tainly resonates with Warhol's long-standing interest in the chemical dimension of sexuality.[67] The accompanying print produced by Warhol and Smith homes in on the tension between vampirism and pheromonal attraction, framing the dragon's eye, nose, and mouth in a blood-red paper scrap that is dramatically juxtaposed to the pink background tone, suggesting a fatal viciousness lurking within a general zone of lurid sexuality.[68] Scientists would not learn until decades later that female Komodos are capable of parthenogenesis—asexual reproduction, a truly queer power that raises the monstrous threat of incest.[69]

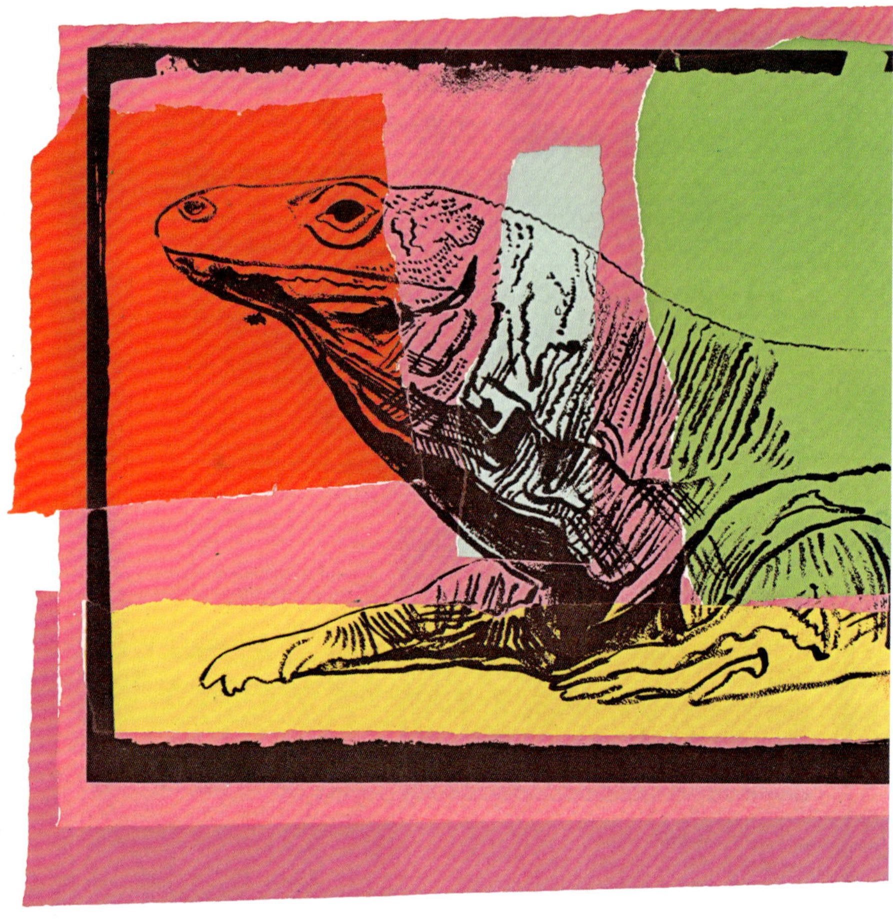

FIGURE 36
Andy Warhol, *Vanishing Animals* (*Komodo Monitor*), 1986. © 2022 The Andy Warhol Foundation for the Visual Arts, Inc./Licensed by Artists Rights Society (ARS), New York.

Benirschke's essays occasionally touched on questions of biotechnology. If sexual attraction had chemical components, might they possibly be synthesized, manipulated, and sold? The essay on butterflies broaches these possibilities directly, highlighting both their costs and their potential, while sidestepping their political implications. The word "pheromone" had been coined in 1959, after the German chemist Adolf Butenandt—one of the "eminent biochemists" Donna Haraway described "prowling around nonhuman animal slaughter floors"—killed a half million moths to extract six milligrams of "bombykol."[70] Scientists went on to implant micro-electrodes onto moth antennae, and to measure the signals produced by pheromones distributed via wind tunnel. Having identified the compounds, scientists were hopeful they could "be manufactured synthetically" to "attract male moths of a given species," who could "be lured into sticky traps and destroyed," or "confuse[d] . . . so drastically that they will never be able to find a 'real' female to fertilize!"[71] Researchers would eventually come to believe that female butterflies produce male pheromones as "antiaphrodisiacs" in order "to keep males away."[72]

Although his essay doesn't mention it, Benirschke probably would have been aware that the "German chemist" in question had been linked to the Nazi party and that, during the early 1930s, he had gathered fifty milligrams of human pheromones by collecting twenty-five thousand liters of urine in men's restrooms in Berlin's police barracks—a deliriously sado-fascist fantasy if there ever was one.[73] Intended to shore up the concept of sex-specific hormones, similar research would eventually lead to the discovery of "cross-sex hormone[s]": "female" hormones present in men, and vice versa.[74] We don't know whether Benirschke shared these further nuances and their sexual implications with Warhol while they discussed the butterfly's plight; neither could have known about recent research that conclusively demonstrates the prevalence of "same-sex courtship and copulation in butterflies and moths."[75] We do have ample evidence, however, that Warhol had linked butterflies with homoeroticism throughout his work, and that he was fascinated by the chemical dimension of sexuality and its possible economic and political consequences.[76]

In 1981, on a visit to Colorado State University, Warhol had encountered the strange powers of same-sex and cross-species excitation firsthand as a research lab attempted to harness and ultimately commodify bull semen:

> [T]hey brought the biggest bulls with flies on them that you could ever imagine. They had this poor little animal—he had his head stuck in a thing—and the guy said, "This is a steer, and when he was young, other male steers would jump on him, he's just one of these strange animals that give off the wrong hormones." And so . . . now he's being used in this experiment to get fucked by a big bull. And there was a big bull sitting there, waiting.
>
> Christopher [Makos] ran out of film and he was going nuts, he wanted to get the big cock out. So they get the bull over and let him mount the steer and he gives out some juice but they don't want *that* juice. His cock is like a two-foot pencil. It's pointed. So the guy said, "Wait, I have to get the artificial vagina." So he ran in and got the glove and everything, and then the bull mounted again and he ejaculated really fast and the whole thing was over. Then we went into the office and watched while the guy took the sperm out of the artificial vagina.
>
> All of us slept on the way to the airport for some reason except Chris, he said he was going to spend the night in Denver and go to the baths. Watching the bull must have got him really hot.[77]

The episode was clearly transfixing for Warhol; it is one of the more focused narratives in the otherwise spasmodic diaries, vacillating dramatically between fascination and repulsion, and implicitly linking desire and artistry through its phallic/pencil imagery. Throughout, Warhol highlighted the ways in which animal homoeroticism stirred passions in its human observers.[78] It is also one of the many places in the diaries where he adopted a condescending attitude toward friends and acquaintances whom he deemed "too gay."[79] But the restrained steer posed a possibility that apparently impressed Warhol: a homoeroticism that was chemical, innate, passive, and animal, and could be exploited biotechnologically, in the interest of expedience and profit. This innate and chemical homoeroticism also raises the specter of segregation—a threat that Warhol would return to in 1985 as he watched his friends and acquaintances fall ill with HIV/AIDS: "You know, I wouldn't be surprised if they started putting gays in concentration camps. All the fags will have to get married so they won't have to go away to camps. It'll be like for a green card."[80]

Alongside all these ambivalent themes, however, the passage demonstrates a quiet and persistent sympathy with the bound steer, resembling what Vanessa Lemm has described as a "[p]ositive biopolitics [that] sees in the continuity between human and animal life a source of resistance to the project of dominating and controlling life-processes."[81] The sight may also have reminded Warhol of his basement exposure to animal and sexual abuse (discussed in chapter 1): watching boys abuse his beloved dog, and "ma[k]e this funny kid suck this boy off."[82] The three scenes resonate strongly with each other. All trapped creatures; two of them, "this funny kid" and "this poor little animal," forced into same-sex intercourse in front of a crowd. "I never understood what it meant." It is as though these traumatic childhood scenes were reactivated in the university laboratory: "[H]e gives out some juice but they don't want *that* juice."

Warhol and Smith's butterfly print for *Vanishing Animals* seems to draw on similar themes. Like most in this book, it is printed on torn scraps of paper glued to a rectangular sheet. In this instance, however, these scraps are unusually small and haphazardly arranged. They don't correspond to particular figures or sections of figures as they tend to in other prints. This lack of correspondence is most radically apparent in one yellow scrap that remains outside the boundaries of the printed image, and in a nearby scrap of the same hue, the edge of which peeks out from beneath it. Strikingly, in this minor "butterfly brigade," the underlying scraps of paper are bright enough to alter the perceived color of the printed ink, so that the color of the images shifts as it crosses from scrap to background paper.[83] The resulting image is a remarkably effective visualization of creaturely contingency: the "essence" of every creature being in large part determined by forces that exceed its control and its perception, and that may even be technologically manipulated in the pursuit of profit or control.

As we have seen, the specter of the AIDS epidemic haunted *Vanishing Animals* without ever being named directly. This grim theme recurred in Benirschke's bat chapter, and its accompanying print. The scale of bat colonies and their feeding habits directly raised the question of mass extinction, as when Benirschke cited "the disappearance of a colony of over 250,000 [bats] in Alabama."[84] But, given his documented attention to—and empathy for—insects, Warhol would also have been interested to learn that a colony of this magnitude required "a million pounds of insects per night" for its survival. Assuming an average insect weight of three milligrams, this would entail the daily deaths of over 150 *billion* insects. (Benirschke's essay emphasized the positive effects of this consumption, referring to bats as a "natural insecticide.")[85] All of these menacing implications would have been inflected, for Warhol, by the bats' remarkable machinic/technological "auditory system," which can "accurately analyze" the movements of even "the smallest insects . . . as if it possessed a computer."[86] A truly superhuman animal-machine, powerfully alert and discriminating, computational, as others had accused him of being.[87] We don't know whether he or Benirschke would have been aware of emerging research that would ultimately link bats to a wide range of devastating human viruses, including Ebola, Middle East respiratory coronavirus (MERS-CoV), severe acute respiratory syndrome coronavirus (SARS-CoV), and SARS-CoV-2, the virus that causes COVID-19. The spread of these viruses has now been closely tied to capitalist practices of deforestation, through which "formerly isolated microbiological reservoirs of the rain forests and mountains have been inadvertently integrated into the food economy of the cities"—a process that also directly contributed to the onset of HIV/AIDS.[88]

The accompanying print is probably the most menacing image that Warhol and Smith produced for this book. (See figure 37.) A single bat is captured in profile, flying from left to right, wings spread, eye gleaming, teeth bared. A rectangular scrap of green paper frames the bat's upper body, including its head, chest, and arms. This framed section depicts the bat as almost canine or lupine: a carnivorous beast of prey. Scale becomes distorted; it is difficult to tell whether the creature we are looking at is small or massive. Instead of the sympathetic images that Benirschke hoped the book would produce, Warhol and Smith have rendered the endangered bat aggressive and dangerous. The various menacing themes in Benirschke's essay—extinction, destruction, contagion, and superhuman surveillance—seem to have infected the image with an ominousness that is otherwise mostly absent from *Vanishing Animals*, with the exception of the Komodo-dragon chapter.

As we will see in the subsequent chapter on the okapi essay and its associated images, it is difficult to overestimate the importance of the AIDS epidemic in Warhol and Smith's production of these works. This massively devastating disease remained subtextual in many responses to Warhol's work; Warhol generally chose not to speak about it publicly as it ravaged his community and took the lives of his boyfriend, Jon Gould, and Smith himself. As Gopnik notes, when *Vanity Fair* published a grid of fifty photos of artists who had died of AIDS, in 1987, ten were in Warhol's circle; his boyfriend, Gould, had been mentioned anonymously in the article because he remained closeted until he died.[89] Warhol had long worried he could catch AIDS from beard stubble or a sandwich.[90] He participated in fundraising but was anything but an outspoken advocate (at least in the traditional sense) as his friends and colleagues succumbed to the disease.[91]

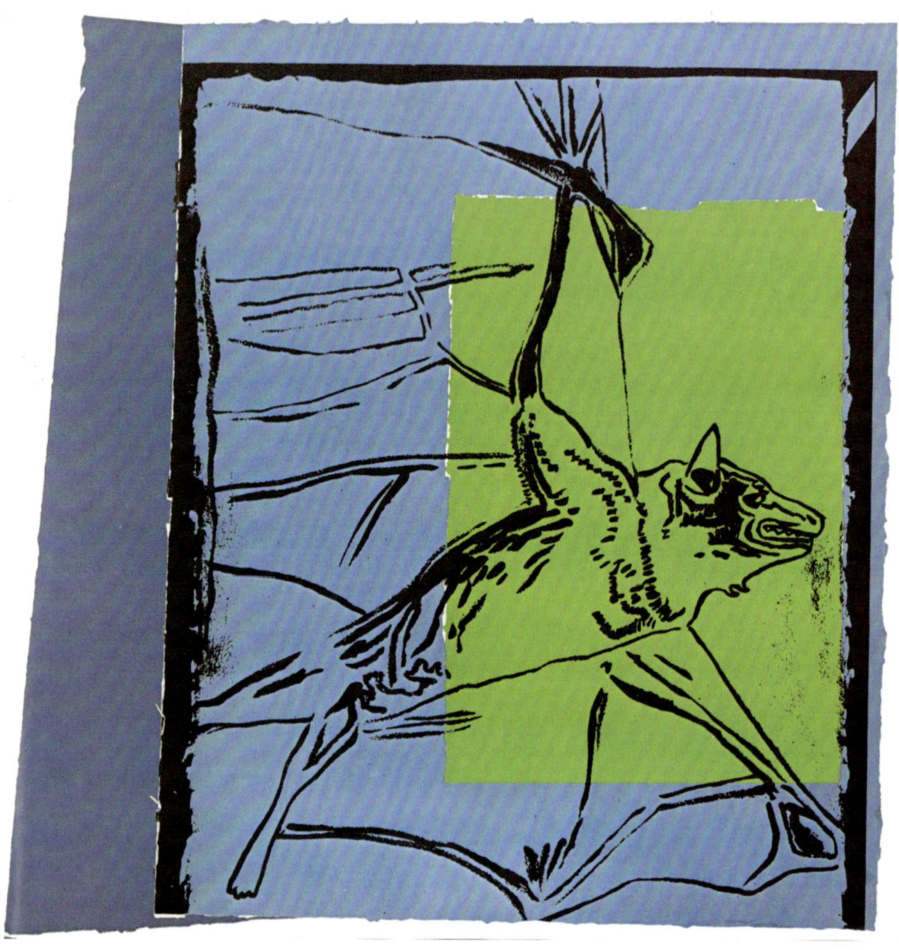

FIGURE 37
Andy Warhol, *Vanishing Animals (Bats)*, 1986. © 2022 The Andy Warhol Foundation for the Visual Arts, Inc./ Licensed by Artists Rights Society (ARS), New York.

The AIDS epidemic cast a tragic light on *Vanishing Animals*, and particularly on the dragon, bat, and okapi prints, imbuing these images with a deathliness that Benirschke did not anticipate when he invited Warhol to collaborate with him. Although he does not mention them in this book, Benirschke certainly would have been aware of long-standing suspicions among scientists that captivity somehow encouraged homosexuality among animals—a possibility already pondered by French entomologist Henri Gadeau de Kerville in his studies of scarab beetles in 1896, and in studies of "baboons, garter snakes and gentoo penguins, among other species," by other observers during the first half of the twentieth century.[92] Scientists regularly used lobotomies and castration to "cure" these animals of their homosexuality.[93] As Vinciane Despret has shown, many believed that "[h]omosexuality remained a rare phenomenon in the animal world . . . just a few pathological cases observed here and there on farms and in zoos and thus assumed to be due to conditions of captivity—which fell into perfect agreement with human psychopathological theories that equated homosexuality with mental sickness"—a misconception that began to be challenged in the 1980s.[94] If Warhol and Smith learned of this history from Benirschke, it would have contributed to the tragic resonances of extinction, homoeroticism, and human/animal relations that characterize many of their prints, particularly since all three men would have been aware of the fact that HIV crossed from primates to humans.

But there was another, more mundane, physiological risk that directly pervaded the production of these images: Warhol's collaborative print production involved the covert outsourcing of hazardous working conditions. As Gopnik has documented, prior to selling a print, "Smith and Warhol had an elaborate charade worked out whereby Smith would deliver the still-damp canvases to the back rooms of Warhol's studio, without being seen by the client, and Warhol would then fetch them out, 'as though he had worked for ages on them himself.'"[95] Of course, this type of subterfuge was not unusual: Warhol outsourced many of the tasks associated with "his" artistic production for the sake of expediency. But in the case of Smith's printmaking, he was apparently motivated by safety concerns as well: "Ventilation was pretty much nonexistent in [Smith's] loft, despite noxious fumes from the inks and solvents, and even on the hottest summer day Smith would turn on the heat in the room to make works dry more quickly," in order to expedite production.[96]

Warhol was allegedly well aware of these risks. As one worker told Gopnik, the boss they called "Mrs. Warhol" "never walked through the door in that place. He was getting to be a health freak, and would never have exposed himself to those chemicals"—which had caused him distress since he started using them in the early 1960s.[97] Frequently inebriated, Smith reportedly treated his subordinates "like a dictator."[98] One of them, Horst Weber von Beeren, described the studio as "an abortion on a kitchen table" and apparently "smoked cigars as he pulled prints—with a can of gasoline sitting nearby, as solvent"—a slap in the face to Warhol, who had grown up in a "veritable fire trap" and was terrified of fire.[99] We cannot know all the complex ways in which these working conditions might have influenced these workers as they visualized these vanishing animals, and did so in a world in which their own precarity was so pressing—vanishing animals inhaling toxic fumes to produce images of *Vanishing Animals* who were themselves ravaged by industrialization, and who sometimes passed their animal diseases to human hosts, as HIV had been passed. None of them seemed willing to become an outspoken advocate for themselves or other workers or gay men publicly. But it does seem plausible that, the more they learned about these vanishing animals, and the ways in which these creatures "dramatize emergent worlds of desire, action, agency, and interactivity," the more these artists empathized with their predicaments, and registered this shared precarity in the images they produced.[100] Perhaps, in turning to the *Ladies and Gentlemen* series as a formal precedent, these various collaborators were attempting to include at least some of these vanishing animals in their pantheon of "queer heroes," or even in their "queer families."[101] The subsequent chapter will explore the most remarkable instance of this unusual and underrecognized form of animal advocacy.

5

QUEER BEAUTY AND EXTINCTION

THIS CHAPTER WILL FOCUS on one group of prints from the *Vanishing Animals* series, depicting an okapi (*Okapia johnstoni*) dam and calf, giraffid artiodactyl mammals native to the rain forests of the central and northeastern Democratic Republic of the Congo, in Central Africa. Reaching back to Caterina di Meo Lippi, Leonardo da Vinci, and Sigmund Freud; out to Toni Morrison, Alfred Hitchcock, Michel Foucault, and the AIDS epidemic; and forward to the work of Ocean Vuong and some central questions of queer theory and animal studies—including what Neel Ahuja has called "an ecological dimension of queer critique"—Warhol's work on these images constitutes one of the most sustained and provocative investigations of queer and animal sexuality in his oeuvre, and arguably in the artistic production of this period.[1] They strikingly demonstrate his unusual interest in animal queerness, desire, precariousness, and suffering, and mark the culmination of his attention to animal life more generally.

In his accompanying essay for *Vanishing Animals,* Benirschke took pains to emphasize the okapi's obscurity and peculiarity from the outset. This "wondrous beast" unknown to "even the more erudite of my friends," weighing up to four hundred pounds, "the last large mammal discovered [*sic*]" by Western scientists in 1901, "deep purple in color" with "zebra stripes to boot!"—the okapi seems almost impossibly flamboyant. The uniqueness of each stripe pattern, which allows a researcher to identify an individual animal via photography without the use of tagging, only adds to this effect.[2] In the wild, however, this flamboyance paradoxically served as camouflage. One early British researcher, on the hunt for specimens to send home to London, reported that the okapi were "so ghost-like, wary, and elusive" that he "only succeeded in shooting two."[3] In 1911, the *New York Times* called them "the rarest of all known living animals."[4] The poet Eugenio Montale described them as "too delicate to exist among beasts like us . . . a mistake, a misprint that escaped from the Great Printer, but . . . an ineffable hope for the heart."[5] Attilio Gatti, who hunted the okapi extensively, offered an evocative description of their eyes: "blue, large, gentle" when calm, "but glassy and sinister in moments of danger or fury, and possessing the extraordinary convenience of rotating independently, like those of a chameleon, so that he can look in two directions at the same time."[6] He described the okapi's cooked flesh as "the most delicate and exquisite one can find in Africa," and its skull as "almost indistinguishable from that of the Samotherium . . . a prehistoric creature vanished from the earth some fifteen million years ago" (11). Each okapi, he argued, is "a 'living fossil'" and a "freak of nature" (11).

After spending two and a half years tracking them, Gatti became convinced that the okapi possessed unusually sharp vision, smell, and hearing, observing that "the remarkable thickness of [their] skin" allowed them to navigate "a network of vegetation which for man is impenetrable," grazing on tender leaves and flowers, which "Great Mother Forest" ("as the pygmies call it") provides in abundance (17). Each okapi, Gatti concluded, is "a confirmed solitary, living isolated except during the short mating season and the few months in which a mother nurses her young" (17). Nevertheless, owing to its powerful kick, bony head plate, and "determination ten times stronger" than a horse, the okapi "has nothing to fear from the denizens of the jungle" (17).

And yet, as Gatti and others noted, okapi specimens also constituted a significant source of income for the native Mbuti people, since European colonialists paid them to capture or kill the animals for zoos and display. The economic incentivization of violence that characterized this relationship was simultaneously acknowledged and renounced in many accounts, with authors like Gatti instead disparaging the "ravenous appetites" of the "Mambuti [*sic*]," and the alleged savagery of the strategies they proposed for capturing the elusive prey (11). Ultimately, Gatti and the Mbuti agreed to try to trap the okapi in *zemu*, pits "ten feet deep, three feet wide and eight feet long," disguised with elaborate coverings of forest debris and surrounded by walled perimeters (11). During one hunt, Gatti was attacked by a trapped male okapi, which leaped out of a pit, charged, and sent him ten feet through the air, before "resum[ing] his queer rolling gallop" (17).

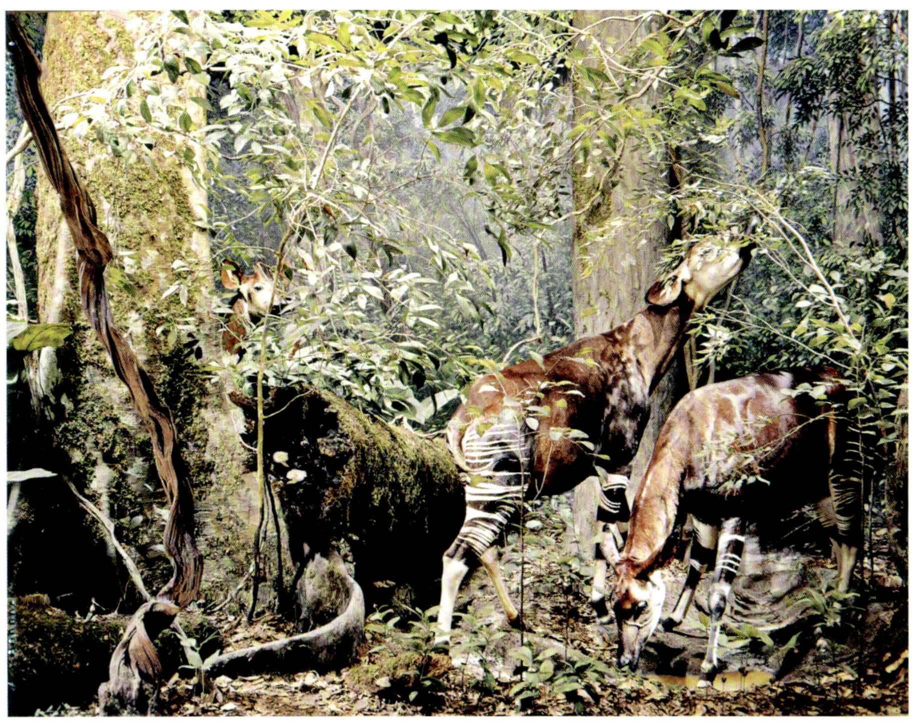

FIGURE 38
Okapi diorama in New York's Museum of Natural History, 1938. American Museum of Natural History Library.

"[A] strange creature," Gatti concluded, "to be set down in this city of the New World," New York (17).[7] This was where Warhol—an enthusiast for taxidermy—would have encountered a diorama featuring stuffed okapi at the Museum of Natural History. (See figure 38.) The exhibition "Warhol's Animals: Species at Risk," featuring the *Endangered Species* prints, had premiered there in 1983.[8]

In addition to facing significant threats from poaching and deforestation, the okapi posed an unusual challenge for conservationists in their attempts to preserve captured specimens. Later research would show that even wild okapi calves have "an extremely low newborn body weight" relative to their mothers, and exhibit unusually prolonged nesting behavior, spending 80 percent of their first two months hiding with their mothers, and nursing without defecating (which scientists surmise helps keep them concealed from predators).[9] During this period, the mother communicates infrasonically with her calf, as elephants do.[10] Gatti had already noted that the okapi's "fastidious cleanliness" was "one of [its] most striking peculiarities."[11] Benirschke outlined the implications of this tendency for animals in captivity as delicately as he could:

> [Okapi] deposit their young in hiding while they forage and nurse at intervals. But there are no infant-hiding places in zoos and since food is supplied (with the best of intentions),

> there is no need to browse. So what does the mother do with her spare time? Cuddle the infant of course, and lick its rectal area. The result is rectal prolapse, which is an eventration of the terminal bowel with ensuing infection. It frequently resulted in death. . . . Because of boredom—so our behaviorist concluded—the mother (in captivity) much extends the duration of an otherwise brief and less frequent behavior. With her long harsh tongue her prolonged licking would in due time cause the prolapse.[12]

Benirschke's final sentence was perhaps slightly understated: the mature okapi's "long harsh" and potentially fatal tongue is lengthy enough to clean its own ears, up to eighteen inches.[13] Gatti had described it, a bit fantastically, as "some twisting, headless, two-and-a-half foot blue snake."[14] The okapi section of *Vanishing Animals* included a tactful photograph labeled "Young okapi sucking while mother cleans rear," in which neither tongue nor rear was visible.

Noting that infant animals are often born without developed immune systems—an issue that can become exacerbated with animals in captivity—Benirschke surmised that "[b]y sampling the infant's anus with her tongue, perhaps once a day in nature, [the mother] perceives with her own immune system the harmful intestinal flora that upsets the baby's digestion, quickly produces antibodies . . . and delivers these with the next day's milk to her young."[15] The Mbuti also seem to have surmised these healing powers; according to Gatti, they believed that belts made from the okapi's skin could "cur[e] dysentery . . . and the other disturbances of the digestive system which seem to afflict them for the rest of the time."[16] In his essay, Benirschke noted that conservationists became so concerned about the okapi calf's prolonged constipation that they would resort to "laxative treatment."[17]

Given his personal history, it is easy to imagine that Warhol found the calf's plight captivating. As we have seen, rectal and maternal trauma, and their potentially fatal interconnectedness, were by no means unfamiliar to Warhol. His family's first taste of celebrity seems to have arrived when his mother was recruited to visit prospective patients as a "star example" of the efficacy of colostomy. In the 1940s, Warhol produced a remarkably indelicate drawing labeled "Constipated Woman," which seems almost grandiose in its pretensions to gritty realism. (See figure 39.) Surely the infant okapi's strange maternal/rectal peril would have reminded Warhol of his mother's troubles, but also of the enemas she regularly gave him as a child to treat constipation associated with his Saint Vitus' Dance disease. Mrs. Warhola had already lost an infant daughter who suffered from constipation, and "always believed in giving her children enemas" when they were ill.[18] Blake Gopnik reports that in the 1980s, Warhol's strange eating habits and addiction to Valium combined to "caus[e] constipation so bad that he needed a daily enema," and that he was still being treated for anal warts and tearing he had suffered from since the late 1950s.[19] Warhol's long-standing digestive and rectal problems echoed his mother's, and were eerily mirrored in the plight of the okapi calf.

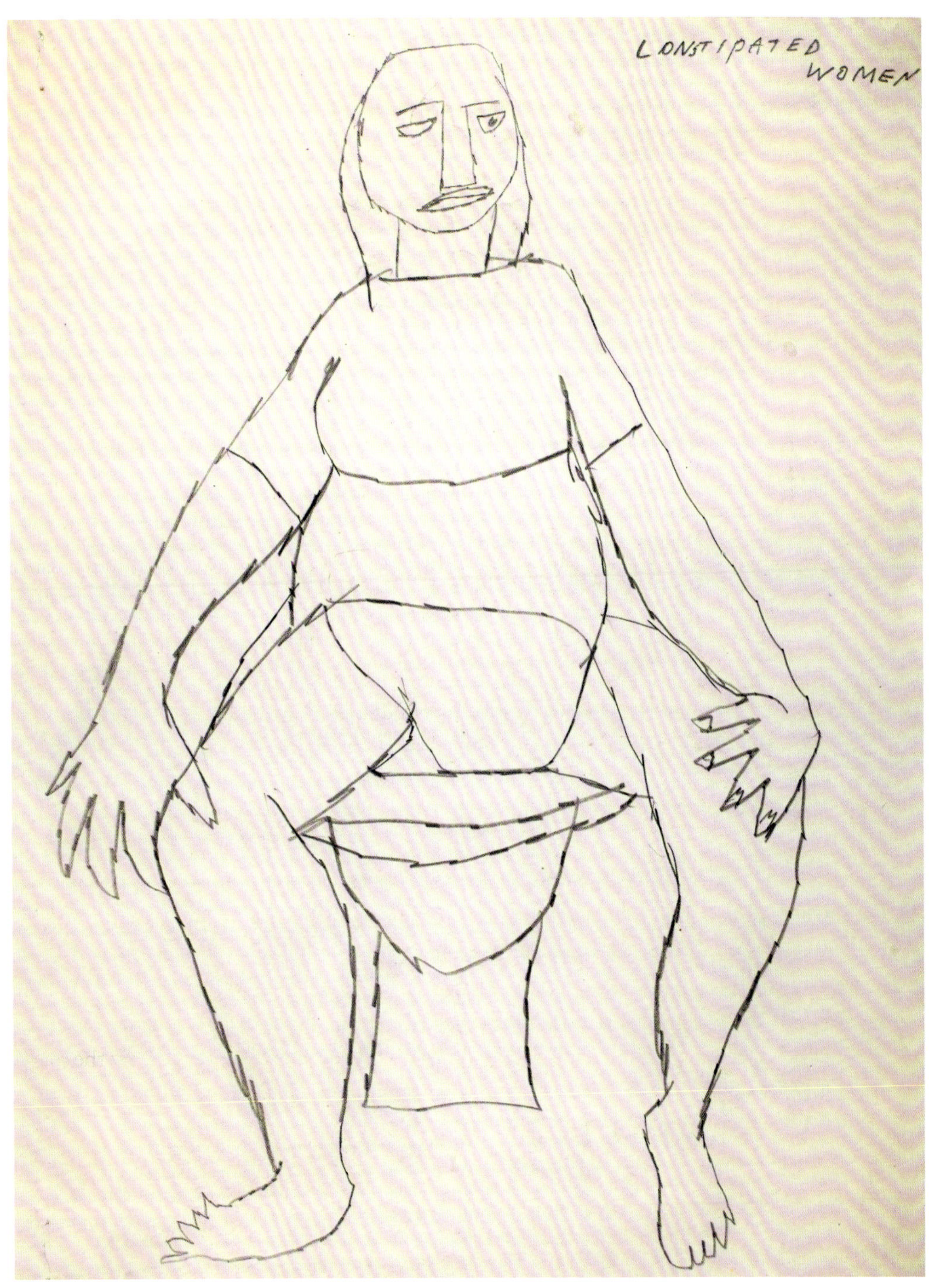

FIGURE 39

Andy Warhol, *Constipated Woman,* 1940s. The Andy Warhol Museum, Pittsburgh; Founding Collection, Contribution The Andy Warhol Foundation for the Visual Arts, Inc. © 2022 The Andy Warhol Foundation for the Visual Arts, Inc./Licensed by Artists Rights Society (ARS), New York.

Enemas, excrement, and anality also interested Warhol erotically and artistically throughout his life; some of his observers sensed this interest, including one critic who claimed that he "makes all of life seem like a soiled diaper."[20] Gustavus Stadler has shown that, in 1965, Warhol was captivated by the idea of having Steve Schapiro "[p]hotograph Ondine shitting on the toilet with [Warhol] holding the microphone," so that his interest in these matters could be publicized. Ondine demurred.[21] In 1967, in an attempt to woo Warhol, a model named Ivy Nicholson decided that the best way to ensure that "a part of her would remain with Andy" was to shit behind the Factory's main couch, and then, after being ejected by Billy Name, to try again in the Factory elevator. Warhol was duly impressed: "No one ever did that before! Please come back."[22] Frank Cavestani, who played a construction worker attacked by "feminists" who forcibly attempted to give him an enema in downtown Manhattan in Warhol and Paul Morrissey's 1971 film *Women in Revolt,* remembered the artist Wynn Chamberlain telling him that "Andy has a whole collection of asses being given enemas [on film]" that he kept for private enjoyment.[23] When an artist visiting the Factory in 1971 painted a portrait of Warhol using a brush clenched in his rectum, Warhol asked him whether he "ever [had] to go to the bathroom when you are doing this?"[24] Warhol's *Torsos* and *Sex Parts* series (1977) included some of the most explicitly anal-erotic images produced by a major artist during this period. The "[h]arness made for infant okapi to prevent rectal injury by mother's tongue," also illustrated in *Vanishing Animals,* would have tied all these themes together with Warhol's long-standing interest in leather and bondage.[25]

In addition to these biographical, erotic, and artistic resonances, however, for Warhol and Benirschke the maternal affection and peril that characterized the captive okapi might also have called to mind long-standing etiological associations between overaffectionate mothers, absent fathers, and homosexual sons—a homophobic trope that circulates to this day. As Whitney Davis has shown, these associations have been prominent not just in Freudian theory—where it is the mother "who has set the bar of his interest in [the boy's] own sex far higher than it would otherwise have been"—but in the homosexualist culture that preceded and coexisted with it as well.[26] Walter Pater had referenced this association in 1873 when he described *Mona Lisa*'s model as "like the vampire," embodying "[t]he fancy of a perpetual life, sweeping together ten thousand experiences."[27] Pater's "oceanic doctrine," Davis argues, with its emphasis on a "perpetual life," "often served in the later nineteenth century to represent . . . nonstandard eroticisms in a publicly acceptable pseudo-spiritualism of pansexual cosmic synthesis."[28] Rectal prolapse was also frequently cited as an identifying trauma of the gay male body.[29] By Warhol and Benirschke's time, these associations were deeply embedded in Western culture.

To the extent that the adult female okapi was understood by Warhol as overbearing, oversexualized and oversexualizing, vampiric, and even literally death dealing, and her calf as rectally activated and chemically altered as a result, the tragic pair thus would have reminded him of almost a century of homosexualist and psychoanalytic etiologies of queer desire. Warhol might have imagined the dam as indulging in a potentially fatal interest in returning to a state when "[m]other and child, indeed . . . were really one—mother *with* child," provoking in her calf a yearning for narcissistic unity and oneness with another who is just like oneself—the type of "agreeable habit" that Warhol had already acknowledged in his work of the early 1950s (see chapter 1).[30] Here the pleasure principle seems to join forces with the death drive, and we are forced to reckon with the situation, described by Judith Butler, wherein the "psyche seeks to return . . . to a time before the individuated life of the . . . organism."[31]

Warhol's double entendre also prefigured contemporary neurochemical understandings of motherhood, which propose that "[o]piates," produced by mammalian bodies in the form of endorphins, "are the chemical linchpins of the emotional apparatus in the brain that is responsible for protecting and nurturing infant life," since they flood both mother and child during their attachment process.[32] This blissful and transgressive symbiosis also recalls Julia Warhola's possessive attitude toward Andy's work: her remarkable claim that "I am Andy Warhol," her efforts to monetize her son's transgressive creativity, and the production of shame in her son—the "ugliest creature" with a "childish mind"—that apparently underwrote it. What's more, Benirschke's hypothesis regarding the dam's "sampling" could also have resonated with Warhol's frequently expressed opinion that "missing chemicals" had rendered him "a sissy" or a "mama's boy."[33]

We do not know whether Warhol discussed any of these queer associations with Benirschke, but if he did, he might have learned that homosexual behavior is by no means foreign to the okapi. Like the males of the only other living species of Giraffidae ungulates, the giraffe, male okapi are known to partake in what scientists call "necking," described by Bruce Bagemihl as "a multifaceted activity that incorporates elements of play-fighting, courtship, and sexuality, in which they rub their necks along each other's body while also licking, sniffing, and becoming sexually aroused by one another." Bagemihl further noted that "[i]n Giraffes and other species, these types of activities sometimes involve multiple animals interacting simultaneously in near 'orgies' of bodily contact."[34] At least in some observed giraffes, these behaviors were the norm rather than the exception. One "exhaustive study" of giraffes in Tanzania, lasting over a year, concluded that "94 percent of all observed mounting activity was same-sex."[35] These behaviors support Elizabeth Grosz's striking claim that "[r]eproduction is the side effect or by-product of sexuality, not its purpose, aim, or goal."[36] And yet many researchers still refused to report findings of this type in their publications, since "they were afraid of homophobic reactions and of being seen as homosexuals themselves"—a powerful example of the ways in which queerness has been perceived as contagious, even among scientists.[37] Like animal intoxication, animal homosexuality radically challenged traditional evolutionist ideologies that see survival and reproduction as life's absolute goals, and touched on subjects so taboo that they put their observers' careers at risk by association.[38]

The numerous and wide-ranging queer resonances of the captive okapi also call to mind perhaps the most famous image of mother/son/animal eroticism in Western art history: the memory recorded by Leonardo da Vinci of being molested by a bird in his cradle:

> I recall as one of my very earliest memories that while I was in my cradle a vulture came down to me, and opened my mouth with its tail, and struck me many times with its tail against my lips.[39]

This dream would form the kernel of Freud's 1910 essay on the artist, which he later called "the only truly beautiful thing I have ever written."[40] According to Freud's reading (which was marred by his adoption, from a previous translation, of the English "vulture" instead of the more accurate "kite" [*Milvus milvus*]), this memory "conceals . . . a reminiscence of sucking—or being suckled—at his mother's breast . . . . which . . . has been transformed by the man Leonardo into a passive homosexual phantasy. . . . 'That was a time when my fond curiosity was directed to my mother, and when I still believed she had a genital organ like my own.'"[41] As Davis has shown, Freud would adapt and intensify Pater's formulation when he described Leonardo's mother as having taken "her little son in place of her husband, and by the too early maturing of his erotism robbed him of part of his masculinity."[42] But Freud argued that the violence of the mother/bird's striking action also registered anxiety and frustration on the part of *both* mother and child, who feared losing each other after having developed an unusually intense and erotic bond. This erotic bond, "which not only fulfills every mental wish but also every physical need," would, Freud thought, be sublimated and recorded in the signature "mysterious smile[s]" of the androgynous figures that graced Leonardo's paintings, "as if they knew of a great achievement of happiness, about which silence must be kept."[43] As Elizabeth Lunbeck has compellingly argued, despite its missteps and exaggerations, not to mention its probable function as a screen for Freud's anxiety regarding "his own homosexual currents," the essay established Leonardo's mother, Caterina di Meo Lippi, as "[t]he germ of the overbearing Mom of mid-century American analysis and popular criticism, who in her ministrations spawned a generation of homosexual sissies."[44]

It is not hard to imagine that a memory of Freud's analysis or its popular derivatives would have occurred to Warhol when he learned of the strange plight of the okapi. (He might even have been reminded of this connection by the fact that the California condor, a vulture, was the first animal profiled in Benirschke's book.[45])There are many resonances here between these two small families (okapi and da Vinci): the sense of confinement and social isolation, with the father absent (for both single peasant mother and animals in captivity); the centrality of both oral (mother's tongue and baby's mouth) and anal eroticism (calf's rectum, the kite's "tail," and Leonardo's "repressed libido" as "anal eroticism"[46]); the association between maternal love and animal desire seemingly embodied by the okapi and imagined in Leonardo's fantasy; and the violent or even fatal consequences of this desire (the okapi's death, the mother's striking tail). Even without the added stimulus of the "[h]arness made for infant okapi to prevent rectal injury by mother's tongue," it would not have been a great leap for Warhol to envision the young okapi as a queer creature in the making, seemingly activated by an overaffectionate mother. And he might also have known that, within the Freudian version of this narrative, the "brooding and doubting" provoked by this type of mother "becomes the prototype of all later intellectual work" that the son pursues.[47] Brooding and doubting were, of course, central to Warhol's self-projection as an artist and celebrity.

"SUCH A SOOTHING PASTIME"

Warhol's popular image as a quasi illiterate may dissuade readers from accepting his knowledge of these Freudian narratives. But, as Gopnik has conclusively demonstrated, this was a cultivated affectation, playing on stereotypes of working-class bestial inarticulateness. Warhol was in fact a canny and enthusiastic reader, and his calculated self-fashioning could not be more at odds with the image of unrefined obliviousness that he successfully projected.[48] What's more, in addition to his exposure to Freudian narratives at Carnegie Tech through the influence of Balcomb Greene (see chapter 1), Warhol would have known them well from their reappearances in popular culture, including the topos of "a queer male and his monstrous mother" that David Greven and others have identified in the films of one of Warhol's heroes, Alfred Hitchcock.[49] In many of these films, as Greven, Lee Edelman, and others have noted, Hitchcock codes queer desire as animalistic or bestial in nature. In *Strangers on a Train* (1951), for example, the aestheticist and animalistic propensities of the overmothered and villainous Bruno Anthony are continuously emphasized.[50] In one striking scene he affectionately nuzzles his mouth against the crook of his neurotic mother's hand, like a dog or a cat. As Jonathan Goldberg has noted, in this same scene, Bruno's hands come to "look like the claw of the lobster," and that "[v]isually, he's becoming a cold-blooded crustacean, a sinthomosexual"—a being focused on *jouissance* rather than futurity.[51] The film's climax, with its carousel horses spinning faster and faster into an erotic and ultimately disastrous frenzy, makes this association between animals and unrestrained desire even more explicit.[52]

Warhol's attitude toward Hitchcock was practically idolatrous. When he interviewed the filmmaker in 1974, Warhol agreed to be photographed by Jill Krementz kneeling at his feet, both men smiling.[53] His questions immediately eschewed obvious topics like art and filmmaking to home in on the psychology of murder: "Since you know all these cases, did you ever figure out why people really murder? It's always bothered me." Hitchcock began by offering a droll explanation (the high cost of divorce in England), but Warhol was searching for something deeper: "But what about a mass murderer." "Well, they are psychotics, you see," replied Hitchcock. "They're very often impotent. As I showed in *Frenzy*. The man was completely impotent until he murdered and that's how he got his kicks."[54] Like *Strangers, Frenzy* proposes the figure of the overbearing mother as the source for both sexual "dysfunction"—homosexuality, lightly disguised—and the psychosis that supposedly arises from its repression.

As was so often the case, Warhol's mind immediately turned to the human-animal relationship in order to process these difficult questions: "[S]o if you [dispose of the body] well, then you're on your way," he informed Hitchcock. "I always thought that butchers could be the best murderers."[55] With this hypothesis, Warhol's musings attempted to close another section of the etiological circuit. Unrestrained animal/maternal love produces either homosexual boys and men (with desires that are unabjected and therefore animalistic) or—if these desires are repressed—murderous men who get their "kicks" through slaughter, and who (as butchers) learn to slaughter effectively by killing animals—which directly embody the instincts they supposedly share—before they move on to killing humans. For Warhol, at least, nonhuman animals and animalistic desire reemerge at every stage of the circuit. He explored a similar connection in his diaries a few years later: "The Saturday newspapers were great. There was the bathtub murders, the guy says he kills things and doesn't remember—things like his wife and daughter—and that it used to happen to him with animals, too, that he'd wake up and look around and they'd be dead."[56] Animals are the practice targets, and Warhol chillingly objectifies the "wife and daughter" as "things."

There is another contemporaneous narrative that echoes the okapi's strange plight and its Freudian resonances even more directly. Although I have not been able to ascertain whether Warhol was aware of this work, its author clearly had a profound understanding of the Freudian problematics it engaged; at the very least, this text and Warhol's okapi prints are kissing cousins. This is Toni Morrison's 1973 novel *Sula*, which includes a storyline that eerily anticipates many of the concerns that predominate the okapi images, including maternal animality and filial anal care, queer children, and filicide. Despite its prominence in the text, Kathryn Bond Stockton has been the first and only scholar to highlight the importance of anality in *Sula*, brilliantly arguing that it contributes to a post-Freudian investigation of the advantages and disadvantages of anal eroticism for Black Americans. But, as we will see, what Stockton calls "*Sula*'s anal focus" also closely echoes themes from Freud and Kristeva regarding the animal and avian associations of intense maternal affection, and its potentially fatal consequences.[57]

In the indelible chapter titled "1921," Eva Peace, a destitute single mother of three in the aptly named Ohio neighborhood of Bottom, takes her baby son, Ralph, "whom she called Plum,"—the nickname neatly conflates sweetness with excrement and "plumbing"—to an outhouse on a bitter winter's night in a desperate attempt to relieve his constipation:

> She wrapped him in blankets, ran her finger around the crevices and sides of the lard can and stumbled to the outhouse with him. Deep in its darkness and freezing stench she squatted down, turned the baby over on her knees, exposed his buttocks and shoved the

last bit of food she had in the world (besides three beets) up his ass. Softening the insertion with the dab of lard, she probed with her middle finger to loosen his bowels. Her fingernail snagged what felt like a pebble; she pulled it out and others followed. Plum stopped crying as the black hard stools ricocheted onto the frozen ground.[58]

The contemplation of this strange and intimate moment of filial anal maintenance, probably unprecedented in American fiction, prompts in Eva a moment of reckoning: "She shook her head as though to juggle her brains around, then said aloud, 'Uh uh. Nooo'" (34). She leaves her three children with a friend, promising to be back in a day, and then returns a year and a half later, hobbled, having devised a way to support her family and outwit capitalism by sacrificing her leg to a train and collecting the insurance settlement, just as she has sacrificed her finger to "the grave" of her son's rectum (a "radical disintegration and humiliation of the self") in order to relieve his discomfort.[59]

Plum, who had seemed "like he didn't even want to be born," remained a beloved child "to whom [Eva] had hoped to bequeath everything": he "floated in a constant swaddle of love and affection, until 1917 when he went to war" (71, 45). He returns traumatized, addicted to heroin, stealing from his family, but still with "a sweet, sweet smile," like Leonardo's androgynous beauties (45). Like Warhol, who had "wallowed in" undecorated rooms full of pop music and magazines during his early New York years, Plum has become smitten with popular culture, surrounded by magazines, "sleep[ing] for days in his room with the record player going" (45).[60] In his addiction, he remains infantile, unable to control his excretions, and closely attached to his mother: "Being helpless and thinking baby thoughts and dreaming baby dreams and messing up his pants again and smiling all the time" (71). Eva dreams that Plum's regression is a sign of his incestuous inability to detach from her: "[W]hen I closed my eyes I'd see him . . . six feet tall smilin' and crawlin' up the stairs quietlike so I wouldn't hear . . . and he'd be creepin' to the bed trying to spread my legs trying to get back up in my womb" (71–72). She decides one night that these dreams are premonitions, and that their implications are unacceptable: "I done everything I could to make him leave me and go on and live and be a man but he wouldn't and I had to keep him out so I just thought of a way he could die like a man not all scrunched up inside my womb" (72). She descends from her room, painfully, birdlike, on one leg—"swinging and swooping like a giant heron, so graceful sailing about in its own habitat but awkward and comical when it folded its wings and tried to walk"—to visit her son (46).

Like Warhol, and true to his nickname, Plum has been living on sugar, surrounded by "balled up candy wrappers and empty pop bottles" and "a half-eaten store-bought cherry pie" (46).[61] He, too, seems to sense the narcotic pleasures of maternal affection, initially mistaking his mother for his dealer, and jumbling up the maternal and narcotic meanings of "holding"—"Hey, man. Hey. You holdin' me, Mamma?"—a conflation he finds "amus[ing] . . . . [like] some private joke" (46).[62] When Eva laughs along, Plum reiterates his attraction to her: "Mamma, you so purty. You so purty, Mamma" (47). Eva's response is to raise her tongue to her lip, "to stop the tears from running into her mouth"—drinking and tasting herself like Warhol's bee-people, briefly a self-sufficient system, nature and culture. This taste turns quickly, however, first to thirst and then to disgust: "Suddenly she was thirsty and reached for the glass of strawberry crush. She put it to her lips and discovered it was blood-tainted water and threw it to the floor" (47). Self-taste has become cannibalism, a bitter sacrament. This is for Eva the final straw.[63] Inadvertently "both incestuous and cannibalistic," corrupted by the failure of abjection, Eva has become a "monster."[64] She leaves Plum's room to go to the kitchen.

The chapter's final scene, a filicide that ties together the various Freudian and Warholian strings discussed in this chapter, is unforgettably harrowing. As Plum lies in bed, "still chuckling" about his "private joke," "on the rim" of sleep, he feels "some kind of wet light . . . with a deeply attractive smell" on his midsection—"his legs and stomach," and therefore his genitals and anus as well. Opening his eyes, he sees "what he imagined was the great wing of an eagle pouring a wet lightness over him. Some kind of baptism, some kind of blessing, he thought. Everything is going to be all right, it said. Knowing that it was so he closed his eyes and sank back into the bright hole of sleep" (47).

The "wet light" is kerosene. The "eagle" who administers it is Plum's mother. The "bright hole" that the "rim" surrounds, and in which "Plum lay in snug delight"—such a resounding set of anal figures—will soon be set aflame.[65] For Plum, intense maternal love is figured in this scene as the bliss of regression: sugar and narcosis and anal eroticism. For Eva, a surfeit of filial affection has resulted in the deadly threat of a queer son who remains a sweet baby, who seeks bliss and sameness, who never becomes "like a man," who attempts to return to the womb, who can be made truly masculine only by being cooked, set ablaze. Like Julia, Eva worries that a mother's closeness to her son can pervert him. Like Leonardo's mother, a kite in his dream, Eva appears to the reader and her son as if she were a bird—first "a great heron," then "an eagle." Like the dreaming Leonardo, Plum first feels his mother's presence as a caress (an "opening" in Leonardo's case, a "baptism" or "blessing" in Plum's), and only later as an attack (a "striking," an unspeakable burning). Like the okapi dam, Eva has tasted her son's insides. What first appears as a sweetness ("strawberry crush") becomes deadly: the blood that presages his murder.

Morrison has underscored the economic deprivation that delineated her life during the writing of *Sula*: "In 1969, in Queens, snatching liberty seemed compelling. Some of us thrived; some of us died. All of us had a taste." She described the novel as an attempt to explore the "desperate and desperately creative strategies of survival" devised by "outlaw women" who have "escape[d] from male rule."[66] In different ways, all of the mother–son relationships discussed in this chapter (dam/calf, Julia/Andy, Caterina/Leonardo, Mrs. Anthony/Bruno, Eva/Plum) exist in a state of deprivation and lawlessness; these mothers might each, in their own strange ways, qualify as what Morrison called "outlaw women."[67] Outside the bounds of a "functional" heteropatriarchy, with its systems of exploitation and domination, and across the boundaries of ethnicity and

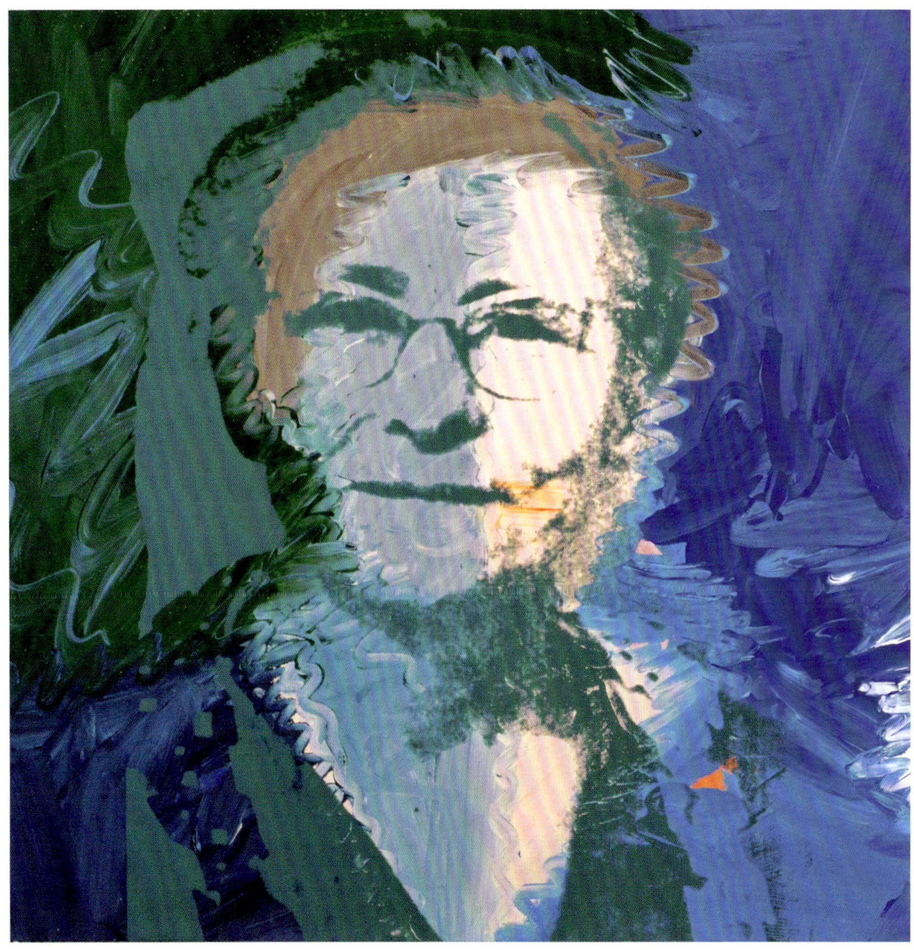

FIGURE 40
Andy Warhol, *Julia Warhola*, 1974. The Andy Warhol Museum, Pittsburgh; Founding Collection, Contribution The Andy Warhol Foundation for the Visual Arts, Inc. © 2022 The Andy Warhol Foundation for the Visual Arts, Inc./Licensed by Artists Rights Society (ARS), New York.

species, these figures are thought to overinvest emotionally or erotically in their mostly male offspring—and perhaps in this relationship to "taste" liberty in a young male who belongs to them—in a way that curtails their children's heteronormative "development." These effects can be physically fatal (as for the okapi), or result in queer tendencies that are repressed into psychosis (Bruno), partially or fully sublimated into art (Leonardo, Andy), or diverted into addiction (Plum)—forms of failure to "be a man" that may be judged radically unacceptable by their mothers, resulting in punishment or humiliation (Andy, Plum, Bruno). Warhol's extremely ambivalent portraits of his mother, in which (as Gopnik notes) her image is alternately "caresse[d]" and "cross[ed]-out," speak to the intensity of these relationships.[68] (See figure 40.)

Freud, Hitchcock, and Morrison thus lead us to the intersection of three of the core political trajectories in Warhol's work: his sustained interests in queerness (and, more specifically, anality and the abject), class (and its interplay with race), and nonhuman animality. They intersect here because in each of these areas, Warhol had a similar difficulty: seen as a "weird cooley little faggot," "a hunky," and a "boorish peasant"—"a white rabbit," "a silk caterpillar," and "a reptile"—he had trouble occupying the disinterested position that was widely expected of him as an artist and a white male human.[69] As Stockton has shown, anality, race, and economic precarity are unconsciously linked in the Western imagination, since "[t]he presumed physical and moral dirtiness of anal sexuality offends sensibilities in a way not entirely distinct from that dirtiness (physical and moral) that is presumed to attend (black) life on the economic bottom."[70] But, in addition to these intersections, *Sula* also insists that these debased terms are directly linked to animality and sub-animality in the white American unconscious: "When, [a white bargeman] wondered," contemplating the Bottom and its citizens, "will those people ever be anything but animals, fit for nothing but substitutes for mules, only mules didn't kill each other the way niggers did."[71]

It is as though, in their desperate investigations of infant anal maintenance and affection, Caterina di Meo Lippi, Eva Peace, and Julia Warhola discovered one of capitalism's impossible secrets: that (as Freud first argued and Stockton reemphasizes) money is shit and shit is money and the model for the hoarding of wealth is anal retention.[72] By literally or phantasmagorically digging deep into their sons' anuses, these mothers could either spur financial fortune through sublimation (through oceanic feeling, shame, and hyperproductivity in Andy and Leonardo, since "the aim to make money takes over for anal erotism") or gain a moment's peace through their sons' forbidden pleasure ("the shock was so great [Plum] was suddenly silent"), and perhaps catch a glimpse of capitalism's impossible solutions (the insurance payout secured through the sacrifice of a limb, lost like a finger in a forbidden anus, that Eva devises in the cold outhouse).[73] We return here to Kristevian territory, since, as Kelly Oliver points out, "[t]he boundaries between body and not-body are controlled by the mother."[74] For Kristeva, "a collapse of the Oedipal triangulation," such that the erotic bond between mother and son persists beyond its typical time frame, results in "a subject that is lacking its 'own and clean self,'" and for whom bodily fluids, including "excrement," can "suddenly become the sole 'object' of sexual desire."[75] When the abjection of the maternal and animal dimensions of selfhood fails, the subject can become fixated on an abject "object" itself: anality—"which," Kristeva argues, "precedes the establishment of the symbolic and is both its precondition and its repressed element."[76] As with both Plum (shifting between meanings of "holding"; babbling like a baby) and Warhol (stumbling over his words; muttering "um"), this results in the noticeable disruption of language, since "nonsublimated, nonsymbolized anality breaks up the linearity of the signifying chain."[77] This disruption in turn "provokes . . . and unveils repressed sadism—the anality underlying social apparatuses": Eva's attack on Plum; Julia's descriptions of Andy as the "ugliest creature" with a "childish mind"; the Factory traditions of violence and spite; Hitchcock's preening psychopaths.[78]

In different ways, and from different perspectives, Warhol and Morrison seem to have succeeded in processing or sublimating these strange dynamics into their work. In Morrison's case, this sublimation was highly conscious and intentional: having "tasted" the "liberties" of outlaw life, she chose to render them in fiction rather than to replicate them in her own biography. In Warhol's case, by contrast, as we saw in chapter 2, much of this processing seems to have been highly marketable *and* tragically repetitive: taking on his mother's maternal/managerial role as "Mrs. Warhol," attracting "a stable" of new Factory daughters and sons, and profiting from the imbalanced and violent relationships that resulted. But it is my sense that working on the okapi image granted him and Smith a clearer view of these strange dynamics and their possible consequences. The okapi, and the prints he and Smith made to ennoble and protect the species, offered a condensed emblem for this connection between deprivation, maternal/filial anality, queer precariousness, and (through their African origins) Blackness. This work may have marked a moment of recognition for Warhol, a spur that helped him to glimpse the power of these narratives, but also their potential alternatives. To this extent, these prints contributed to what Imogen Tyler calls "the social theory of abjection" by "examin[ing] the mechanisms through which norms of abjection are fabricated, operationalized and internalized," and then "begin[ning] to disarticulate the effects of abjection as lived."[79]

All of these trajectories would have been particularly troubling to Warhol during these years—from 1984, when he heard Benirschke's speech, to 1986, when *Vanishing Animals* was published, a few months before the artist's death. It was exactly during this period, as Jessica Beck has shown in her work on Warhol's contemporaneous *Last Supper* paintings, that Warhol was forced to face his boyfriend Jon Gould's contraction of, and death from, AIDS—one among over sixteen thousand such deaths between 1980 and 1986 in the United States.[80] The two men had started dating in 1981; Fred Hughes described it as "the most serious love affair in Andy's life"; it lasted for four years.[81] Warhol had starved himself to try to gain Gould's affection, dropping from his previously "proper weight" of 136 pounds to a dangerous 110 and describing himself as "so desperate [for Gould] I don't know what to do. I want to kill myself."[82] Gould was closeted, but agreed to move in with Warhol. In February 1984 Gould spent a month in the hospital for pneumonia, and Warhol "visited him nightly."[83] Both men seem to have known that Gould's illness stemmed from an HIV infection; when Gould left the hospital, Warhol asked his maids to wash their sheets and dishes separately.[84] Soon thereafter, Gould moved to Los Angeles and broke off the relationship. One friend remembered that he "kinda crawled off like a wounded animal."[85] He died in September 1986, the same year that *Vanishing Animals* was published; Warhol would die five months later following gallbladder surgery. Neither lived to see the introduction of AZT and the founding of ACT UP in 1987. Rupert Jasen Smith would die from AIDS two years later.

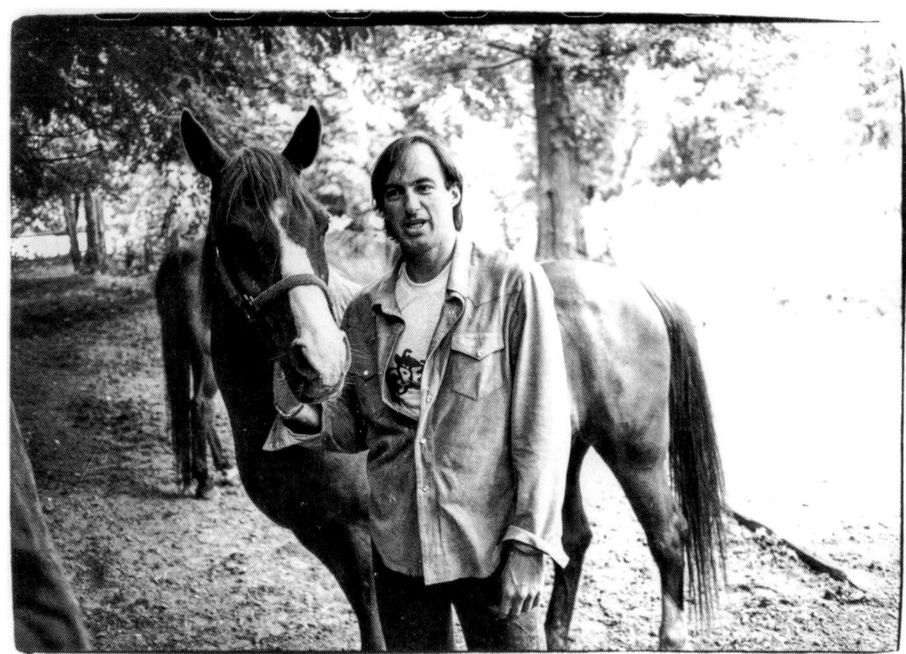

FIGURE 41
Andy Warhol, *Jon Gould,* c. 1983. Image and Artwork © The Andy Warhol Foundation for the Visual Arts, Inc./ Licensed by ARS.

Gould seems to have represented something like an ego ideal for Warhol—everything he craved and was not. He was tall, strong, handsome, a vice president at Paramount Pictures—"Old money, Harvard, Hollywood"—and able to pass as straight.[86] (See figure 41.) As Beck points out, Gould was "the most photographed subject of Warhol's late career," appearing in over 10 percent of the contact sheets he produced during his final decade.[87] Warhol hoped that his feelings for Gould could displace the persistent nihilism he claimed to have felt since the early 1960s, but he seems to have been perpetually disappointed in the results: "I've got these desperate feelings that nothing means anything. And then I decide that I should try to fall in love, and that's what I'm doing now with Jon Gould, but then it's just too hard."[88]

The strange paradoxes of the captive okapis' queer plight must have resonated with Warhol during this period. Here was an anally fixated pair of creatures seemingly addicted to beauty, pleasure, and a nonreproductive eroticism. By the time Warhol encountered the okapi image, it was commonly known that HIV originated in Africa and was animal in origin, having spread to humans through the hunting of primates.[89] Like the okapi, the first documented case of HIV infection was traced to the Democratic Republic of the Congo.[90] The same Belgian trading routes that would transmit AIDS in the second half of the twentieth century began transporting living and dead okapi specimens to Europe and the United States in 1901. King Leopold II knew that J.P. Morgan was on the board of the American Museum of Natural History, and hoped that his gift of over three thousand artifacts from the Congo would counterweigh the deaths of approximately 10 million native people he had overseen there between 1880 and 1920, "a death toll of Holocaust dimensions."[91] Leopold's regime had focused on rubber, but by 1937 the Belgian colonialists had found a new source of profit, again at the expense of millions of human lives and unfathomable environmental devastation: cobalt, the key ingredient in one of Warhol's frequently used paints. The okapi display would be installed at the American Museum of Natural History the following year.

The oral/anal locus of the okapi calf's traumatic care would have resonated with some of the most common visible symptoms of AIDS: sores on the anus, mouth, and tongue. Like Gould and Plum (and, Warhol feared, he himself), the okapi seemed to have been fatally punished for their transgressive, queer/anal/maternal, affections. Warhol had an eager eye for divine retribution. In 1978, in his diaries, he recalled that "[a] guy came over and said that he had the biggest cock in L.A., so I offered to sign it and Marisa [Berenson] got so excited she leaned over to look at the cock and her hair caught fire in the flames of a candle—it was like instant punishment."[92] By 1983, he would extend this retributive worldview to AIDS: "*The New York Times* had a big story on AIDS. The tourist business in Haiti is down to nothing. Probably the tourists were only there secretly for the big cocks. Because Jean-Michel [Basquiat] is half Haitian and he really does have the biggest one. Went to the Trump Tower and laid out a stack of *Interviews* and watched people take them for free. A lady was shaking when she asked me for an autograph, and she said, 'God bless you' and I hope she's right."[93] Here, creative productivity and generosity (Warhol's habit of passing out free copies of his magazine) are figured as a possible sublimation of queer desire (something to change the subject from cocks), and also as a penance for past sins and a safeguard against future "punishment." In his final year of life, Warhol focused his charitable giving on his nonhuman neighbors, "feeding the neighborhood pigeons every Sunday morning—early, so no one would notice him at it." "It's my charity," he explained to a friend.[94]

QUEER FAMILIES AND ZEBRA STRIPES

This link between Warhol and Freud's Leonardo by way of Hitchcock and Morrison also illuminates Warhol's profound interest in Leonardo's work, particularly in the last decade of his career. Warhol produced seven *Mona Lisa* paintings in 1963, when the original toured the United States, and then another series of *Mona Lisa*s in the 1970s. Then, between 1985 and 1986 he produced almost one hundred *Last Supper*s, including some that utilized the silkscreen-over-torn-paper collage format, like the *Vanishing Animals* prints. (See figure 42.) Beck's work conclusively demonstrates that these often-overlooked paintings, which outnumber any other theme he produced during this decade, ought to be recognized as one of Warhol's most sustained and sophisticated investigations of mortality and redemption.[95]

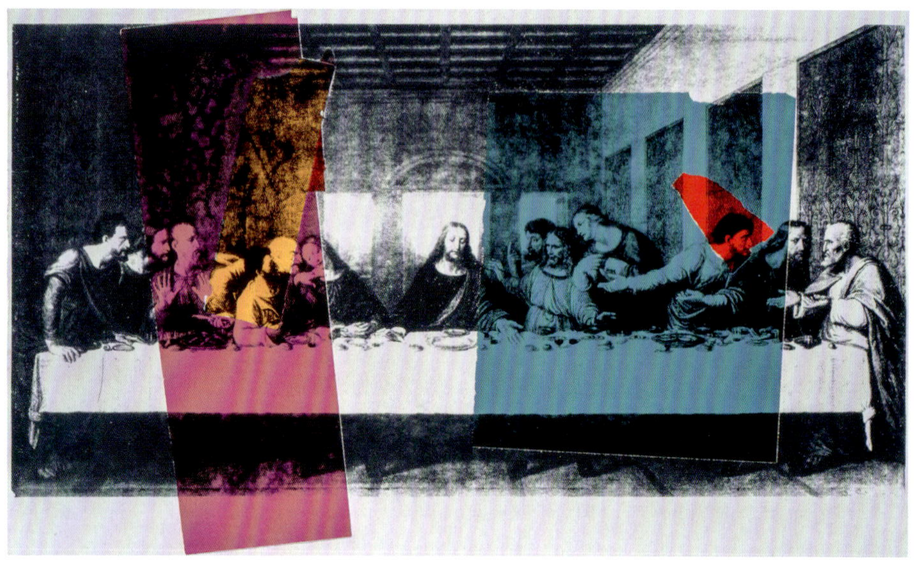

FIGURE 42
Andy Warhol, *The Last Supper,* 1986. The Andy Warhol Museum, Pittsburgh; Founding Collection, Contribution The Andy Warhol Foundation for the Visual Arts, Inc.

The themes discussed in this chapter buttress this claim. Jesus, as *Sula* reminds us, might be thought of as an imaginary or spiritual solution to the problem of maternal eroticism—a theme that Freud argued was also central to the *Mona Lisa.* In church, the women of Bottom, their hands moving "like pairs of raven's wings," "acknowledged the innocent child hiding in the corner of their hearts, holding a sugar-and-butter sandwich" and "remembered how dirty the room looked when their father left home and wondered if that is the way the slim, young Jew felt, he who for them was both son and lover and in whose downy face they could see the sugar-and-butter sandwiches and feel the oldest and most devastating pain there is: not the pain of childhood, but the remembrance of it."[96] Jesus is, for Bottom's women, both "son" and "lover." His "downy face" records the lawless sweetness of intense maternal love in the absence of the patriarch, without suffering its potential earthly consequences. Perhaps these resonances struck Warhol and Smith as well.

What's more, for Warhol and others who knew of Freud's "Leonardo," the *Mona Lisa* and *Last Supper* paintings may also have constituted a paean to his queer "grandfather" and the lineage he helped to initiate. In producing them, Warhol "professed a taste for images made by Leonardo," and thereby proposed himself and his lovers as members of what Davis would call Leonardo's "same-sex family . . . that existed only in cultural replications or only as a history of images."[97] One shared feature or generative principle of this family was "homosexual narcissism," the "interpersonal principle according to which the artist constituted his own generation, his own disturbed or deviant patriarchum."[98] The performance of homosexual narcissism was prominent in Warhol's Silver Factory, and in his production more generally.[99] As he and Pat Hackett put it in *Popism* in 1980, "[M]aybe more than anything, silver was narcissism—mirrors were backed with silver."[100] The okapi calf might then be thought of as a late addition to this family, expanding its reach beyond the human realm, particularly since another shared family feature was sensitivity to animal life. Leonardo, Freud remarked, "declined . . . to eat meat, since he did not think it justifiable to deprive animals of their lives," "took particular pleasure in buying birds in the market and setting them free," and "described man as not so much the king of the animal world but rather the worst of the wild beasts."[101]

But there were also elements of Warhol's work that seem to have provoked some of its viewers to imagine a future *beyond* the Freudian etiologies that codified "homosexual narcissism" as an inescapable feature of homosexual desire, and perversion and punishment as necessary results of maternal overaffection. As Lunbeck has shown, these etiological associations were relatively precarious: many of Freud's early followers had recognized narcissism as foundational for all love, and homosexuality as a force of sociability, but by midcentury these positive associations "had been definitively occluded by the figure of the narcissistic homosexual who is altogether incapable of sustaining relationships with others"—Eva's Plum, Mrs. Anthony's Bruno, Julia's Andy.[102]

By the time Warhol and Smith began working on *Vanishing Animals,* positive models of homosexual sociability were again gaining prominence; in one well-publicized case they were inspired by Warhol's animality itself. In his late work, Michel Foucault was proposing San Francisco and New York as "laboratories of sexual experimentation" in which "new pleasure" could be invented, potentially contributing, as Davis has shown, to an overthrowing of sameness and narcissism: "a spontaneity in consciousness and sensuous awareness . . . [a] shattering newness."[103] The ontological grounds for this ethical proposal had been developing in Foucault's thought since at least 1970, when he published "Theatrum Philosophicum," a review of Gilles Deleuze's *The Logic of Sense* and *Difference and Repetition.* It was in this essay that he first formulated the ideal of a "monstrous and lawless becoming," linking it to "genital thought" and the death of the "devouring Father-mother," but not explicitly to homosexuality or San Francisco's Castro district (which Foucault first visited in the late 1970s).[104]

For Foucault, the key to this new understanding would be a deep meditation on stupidity, a "magma" that escapes all categories, "await[ing], in the always-unpredictable conclusion to this elaborate preparation, the shock of difference."[105] Here Foucault proposed Warhol's work as a model for philosophy: "This is the greatness of Warhol with his canned foods, senseless accidents, and his series of advertising smiles. . . . In concentrating on this boundless monotony, we find the sudden illumination of multiplicity itself."[106] And, in his concluding words on Warhol's work in the Deleuze review, Foucault chose to sum up the artist's singular effect in the following way: "[S]uddenly, arising from the background of the old inertia of equivalences, the zebra stripe of the event tears through the darkness, and the eternal phantasm informs that soup can, that singular and depthless face."[107]

Warhol's "zebra stripe . . . tear[ing] through the darkness" is meant to foreshadow Foucault's bold claim at the essay's conclusion that "a lightning storm was produced which will bear the name of Deleuze: new thought is possible; thought is again possible."[108] But Foucault's Warhol/zebra stripe might now also be seen to prefigure the extraordinary stripes along the okapi's flanks, which, presumably for reasons of what Darwin called sexual selection, strikingly adorn the creature's coveted behind. And, as we saw in chapter 3, the "spontaneity in consciousness and sensuous awareness" that Foucault heralded seems already to have been championed by Warhol and his circle in the early 1960s, when—as Jonathan Flatley and Jennifer Sichel have shown—they proposed that Pop artists should be "queer," pansexual "machines," or animal-machines, liking people and things "[w]ithout any discrimination."[109]

STRIPING, BINDING, SCRAWLING, CROSSING

How did Warhol's okapi images deal with the disparate and competing possibilities for queer life proposed by Freud, Kristeva, and Foucault, and investigated by Hitchcock and Morrison? The original photograph upon which he based his drawing—and he and Smith their prints—caught the mother and calf in a moment of shared but not reciprocal attention: their gazes aimed away from each other, but not toward the photographer, directed instead toward a future object or threat, we might imagine, that has captured their attention. (See figure 43.) But the photograph's orientation, with the okapi facing left, makes them seem to be facing "backward" to human eyes accustomed to left-to-right script directionality, toward something "behind" them, in their past.[110] Warhol's preparatory drawing, upon which the prints would be based, preserves this orientation, but, despite its perfunctory quality, it also distorts and supplements the photograph in a number of intriguing ways, each demonstrating what Cronin calls "the power of sympathetic imagination."[111] (See figure 44.)

In Warhol's drawing, the interface between the calf's neck and the dam's right foreleg shows that, despite the dam's superior size, Warhol traced the calf first: its silhouette establishes the boundary that the mother's contours (mostly) cannot cross. Warhol seems to have begun with the calf's almost phallically upraised ear, central to the composition, neatly piercing and inverting the mother's upper leg. But the ear itself is broken, built out of two separate strokes—one upward, one downward—that are not joined at the tip where they ought to be. Similar broken contours demarcate both of the mother's ears, and both figures' muzzles, connoting the receptivity of those organs, but also the artist's apparent inability or unwillingness to trace a sharp corner neatly.

Warhol seems next to have proceeded down the calf's front edge, tracing the back of its head with a dark, sharp line, and then letting the pencil turn slightly onto its side as the line transitioned to the breast and forelegs, where it becomes lighter and rougher.

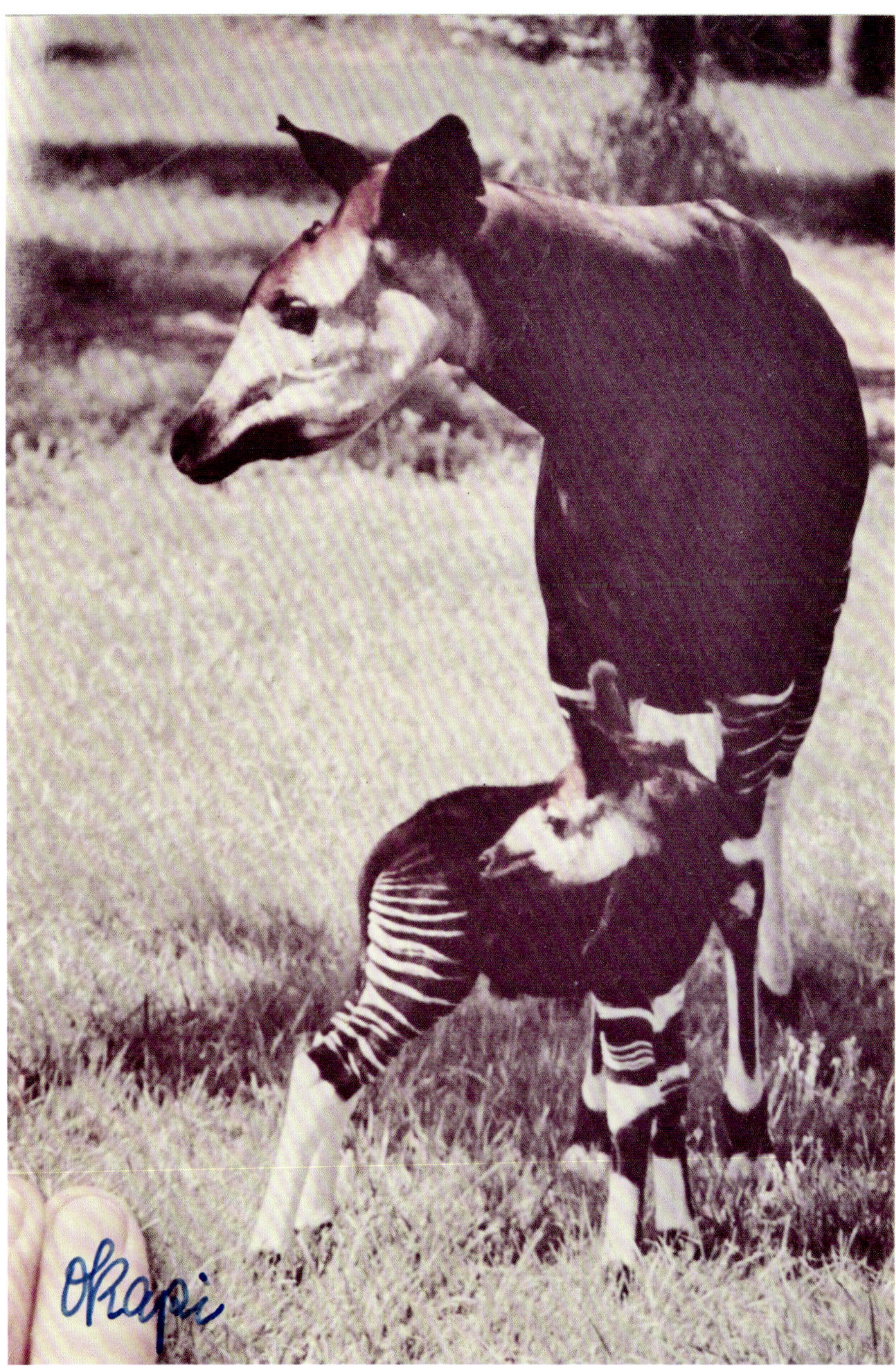

FIGURE 43

Photographer unknown, *Color Photograph of an Okapi and Her Young,* 1985. The Andy Warhol Museum, Pittsburgh; Founding Collection, Contribution The Andy Warhol Foundation for the Visual Arts, Inc. © 2022 The Andy Warhol Foundation for the Visual Arts, Inc./Licensed by Artists Rights Society (ARS), New York.

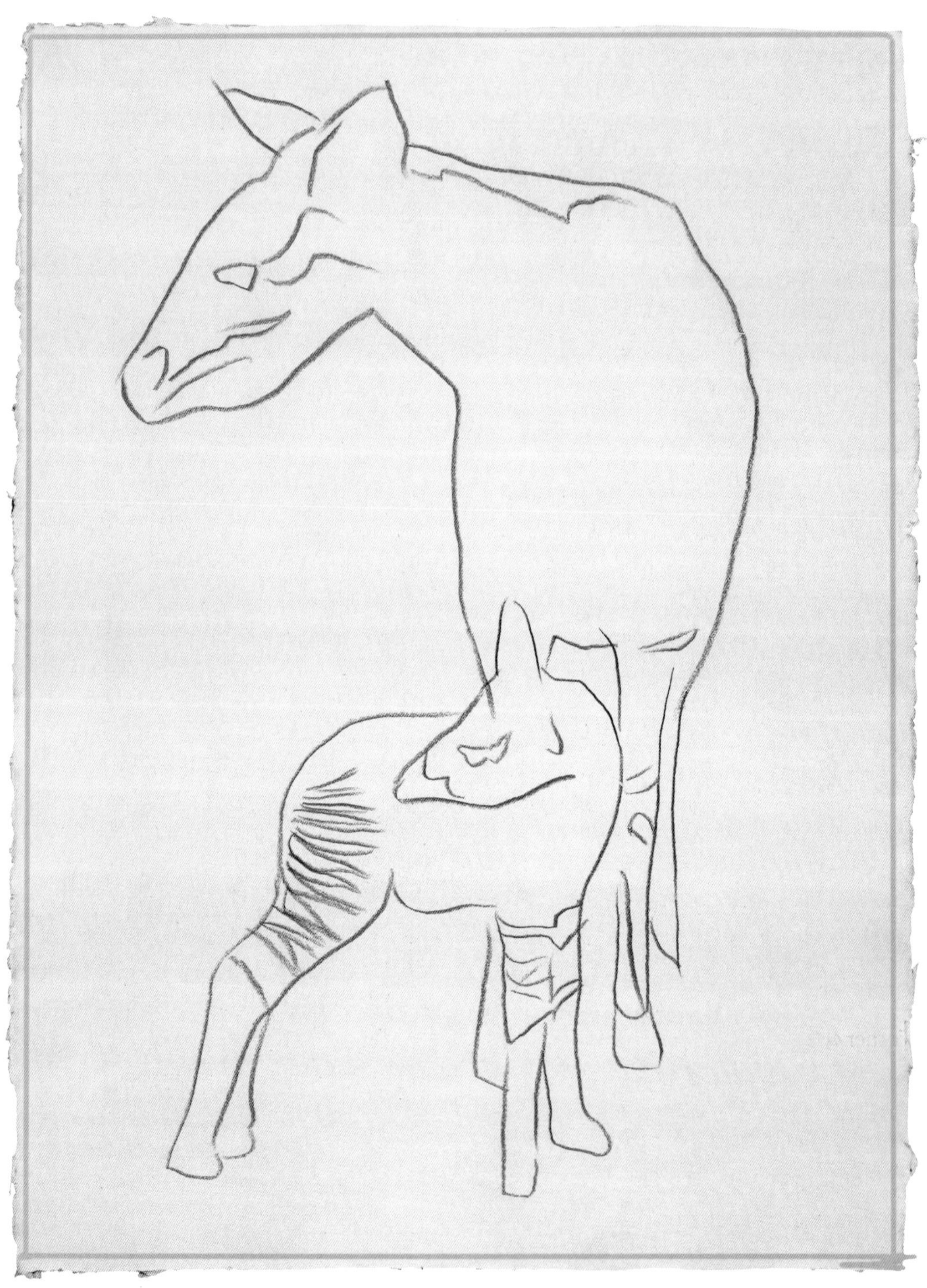

FIGURE 44

Andy Warhol, *Okapi Drawing*, 1986. Image and Artwork © The Andy Warhol Foundation for the Visual Arts, Inc./ Licensed by ARS.

The top of the calf's left foreleg hoof is strangely adjusted, made to curve down toward where its toes would be, becoming almost anthropomorphic. (A similar but less extreme revision is made to both rear hooves.) Warhol then made the remarkable decision to integrate the striping across the calf's upper forelegs, particularly the two uppermost striping lines, which are unbroken, and the lowermost, which seems to be formed from two connecting marks. These three lines effectively give the impression that the calf's striping has become a tether, and then immediately call to mind the "harness made for infant okapi to prevent rectal injury by mother's tongue" that Benirschke had described and illustrated in *Vanishing Animals*.[112] To the extent that the calf is read as fettered or bound, an ambiguity is introduced as to the source of this restriction: does it stem from the mother, who so dominates the scene, or from the calf itself, as a phantasmic result of its unique striping, or is it imposed by someone or something else, since okapi are not capable of binding each other? The zoo, for instance (as the resonance with the harness would suggest), or some other pernicious force?

This sense of striping as binding is restated more subtly along the calf's rear legs, where the lowermost striping line neatly connects the two legs just where they ought to separate visually. Above this line, the striping becomes more hectic and haphazard; Warhol draws here on the signature scrawling effects that had characterized his very earliest Pop paintings. (Although there are other prints in the series where similar scrawling is deployed, this is by far its most prominent use.) As I have argued elsewhere, Warhol used this scrawling line in his classic Pop work to connote the frustrations of working-class amateur cultural participation in its attempts to reproduce desirable objects that were socially proscribed or otherwise inaccessible to reproduction. In some cases, these desirable objects were beautiful women or men; in others, they were soda bottles or soup cans, which could be cheaply attained but never authentically reproduced by hand. In each instance, Warhol's scrawls conveyed the sense that his "hand" was too vulgar—too "impulse-following," too "non-rational"—to pursue the task of reproduction in a calm and controlled manner.[113] These were class stereotypes, of course, but they were closely tied to homophobic and anthropocentric prejudices as well. As one contemporary study put it, "From the point of view of other classes, [working-class Americans] 'live like animals.'"[114] Like the homosexual and the nonhuman animal, the working-class "consumer" was widely thought to be incapable of achieving and sustaining an acceptable level of disinterest; this perceived defect marked a vulgarity shared by worker, beast, and queer. All fell into Frantz Fanon's category of "machine-animal-men."[115]

Warhol appears to have drawn the calf's face next, again using the edge of the pencil to produce a lighter, grainier line that breaks briefly at the nose before tracing the jaw. The eye, which the photograph reproduced as essentially equine, is transformed in Warhol's drawing into the silhouette of a butterfly—a creature that had figured regularly in Warhol's work (and again in this series) as a symbol of queer playfulness and innocence. Reconfigured here as a grainy black silhouette, the okapi's butterfly eye suggests the negation of these qualities. The calf's and mother's "empty" eyes contrast interestingly with the eyes of most of the other animals in the series, where oculi or pupils are depicted.

Instead of completing the mother first, clasping her offspring like a creator and caregiver, Warhol depicts her second, like a superseding structure or constraint. Her body dominates the calf from every direction except from beneath: forming a reiterated barrier along the drawing's right-hand side, looming bulkily and blankly from above, nosing just past the back edge of the calf's rear hooves, as if to mark a plane of protection. Their relative positions also provide the mother access to her calf's hindquarters, which are marked (almost lasciviously) as desirable by Warhol with his scrawled stripes. And the mother's desire is figured in the drawing through other means as well: the strange, empty, almost deathly eyes; the lines of motion or emotion that flow from them toward the ears; the wide, unfinished nostril; and the marks across the cheek that might suggest an enormous tongue concealed within it.

Warhol's treatment of the neck and back is even stranger. Two lines, one fairly smooth, the other jagged, terminate horizontally at or near the mother's left ear. It is clear at first that the upper—smoother—line is meant to depict the mother's neck, and that the lower, jagged line depicts surface detail along that area. But, looked at a bit longer, the lower line can also easily be read as the silhouette of the neck, particularly since the upper line's left edge closely correlates with the upper edge of the mother's right ear, thus extending out beyond her head to form a massive and erect tail. A vulture's tail, or a kite's—ready, at least phantasmagorically, to tease, prod, and strike the beloved calf in expressions of the mother's desire and frustration. Viewed from this perspective, the mother becomes a far rougher, more aggressive creature. Once noticed, this ambiguity between aggression and vulnerability is difficult to unsee, and the mother's back takes on the strange doubling of Joseph Jastrow's rabbit/duck, here made not just visually reversible but emotionally and psychologically multiform as well.

Something similar happens along the mother's left foreleg, where Warhol's first attempt at a hoof was at some point judged to be too short, and was subsequently corrected with an extension that is also significantly wider than the hoof it replaces. By leaving the initial attempt intact in both the drawing and the prints based upon it, Warhol allows a second ambiguity to contaminate the mother's body, which here alternates between appearing weak and tentative (with the smaller leg) and strong and dominant (with the larger). And these two ambiguities are exacerbated by a third: the mother's left hind leg, which seems to have been added in quickly and belatedly. With its sharply pointed and blatantly bisected tip, it rhymes with the figure's ears and noses, and more closely resembles a tail than a hoof. Only its alignment with the other legs allows it to stand for one.

But perhaps the drawing's most engrossing feature is the silhouette that delimits the two creatures' bodies along its left half. Here two extraordinary contour lines trace a connection from the mother's mouth to the calf's striped haunches. In this respect, they are perhaps the drawing's most charged elements, since they connect the dam's fatal appetites—which are emblematized by the cavernous isosceles angle that delimits her throat—and the object desired: the crevices of her offspring's posterior. Or rather, they almost trace this connection, because at the point where they should meet, where our view of the mother's body is impeded by the calf's, the two lines break and are connected by a third: the calf's brow. The line of the mother's leg breaks the line of the brow, illogically traversing it. The result is a deathly "X" just below the drawing's center that becomes a ghostly and impossible triangle "within" the calf's brow, the third side of which, extending from the contour of the calf's back, seems always to be delayed in arriving. This transgressed and transgressive triangle, placed precisely at the site of cognition, is a striking figure for the ways in which, according to Freud, maternal oversexualization provoked a tragic, searching, homosexuality in the child, so that "the suppressed sexual activities of research return from the unconscious in the form of compulsive brooding, naturally in a distorted and unfree form, but sufficiently powerful to sexualize thinking itself and to colour intellectual operations with the pleasure and anxiety that belong to sexual processes proper."[116]

Almost all of these features of Warhol's drawing remain extant in the okapi prints he produced in collaboration with Rupert Jasen Smith. The only significant discrepancies are breaks and fading in the line that appear in the print but not in the drawing, and an overall generalizing of the line, which renders the delicacies of Warhol's drawing—its sharpness and roughness, wideness and thickness—invisible. In the prints, this line takes on an industrial, almost digital quality, as though it had been traced by a machine or computer rather than a human hand. But if anything, the "X" on the calf's brow grows even more prominent, as do the mother's ambiguous back and ear/tail, the calf's bound front legs, and the scrawling of the stripes more generally.

And yet, for all their fidelity to the drawing, the okapi prints nevertheless demonstrate a striking diversity of color, tone, affect, and construction. Here I will focus on four specific prints, including the two that were included in Benirschke's *Vanishing Animals* and two others that Warhol and Smith produced as variants. The variance among these prints suggests that Warhol and Smith could sense a range of possible implications for the okapi's unusual plight.

The least physically and formally complex of these prints is a two-color screen print on a single piece of light-rose-colored paper. (See figure 45.) An initial negative print of Warhol's drawing was laid down first in blood red, which recorded even the torn edges of the drawing's sheet. A positive image of the sheet in cinnabar was then printed. Had the two prints been perfectly aligned, they would have combined without remainder. Instead, they are slightly misaligned, so that the light-rose paper breaks through the two printed colors, providing a bright but inconsistent highlight to the blood-red contour lines. The result is an extremely vivid and gaudy image even by the standards of Warhol's late work. And nothing in the print is more garish than the

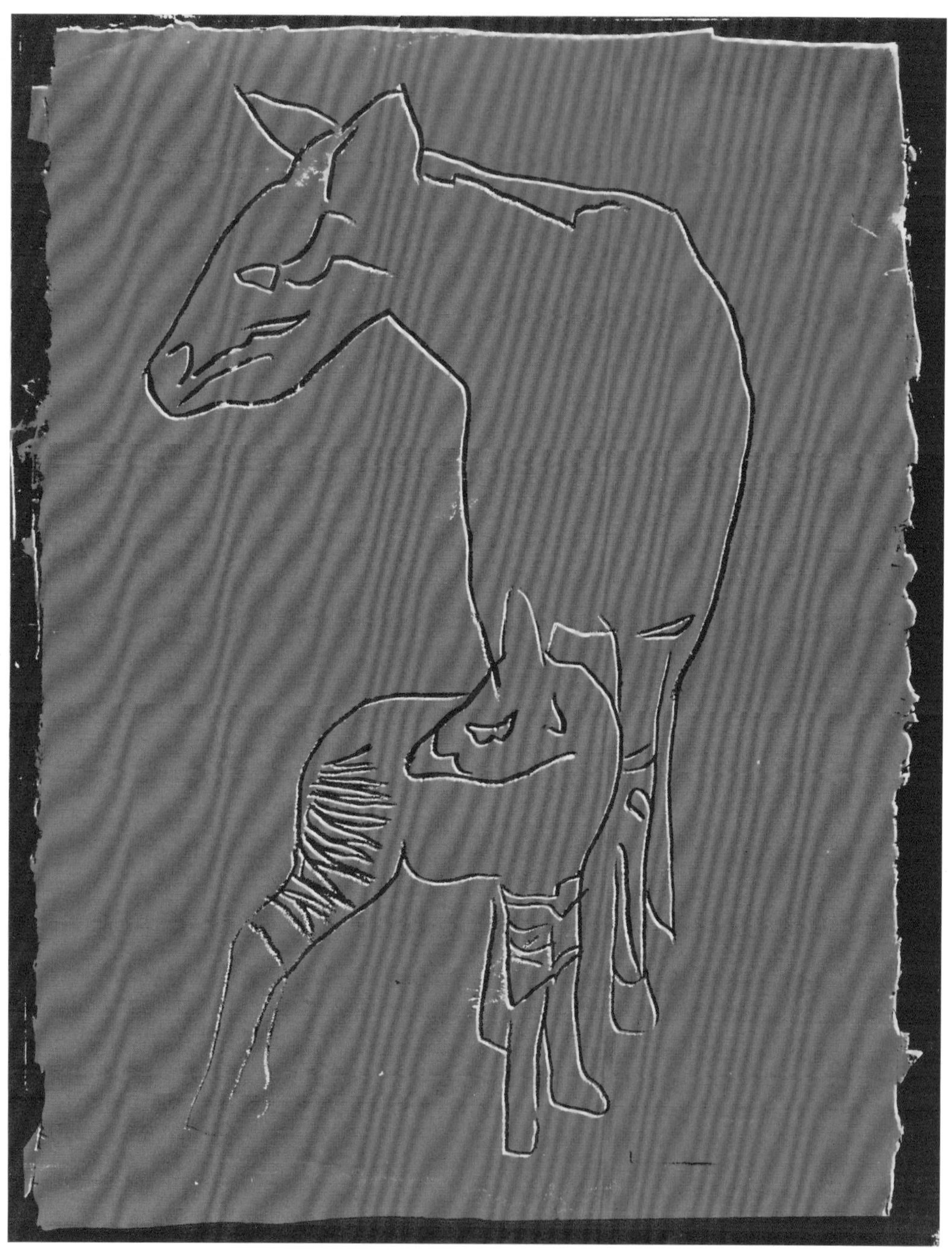

FIGURE 45
Andy Warhol, *Vanishing Animals (Okapi)*, 1986. Image and Artwork © The Andy Warhol Foundation for the Visual Arts, Inc./ Licensed by ARS.

stripes that adorn the calf's haunches, where rose and red alternate lasciviously across an expanse of hot orange. Here, with Smith's help, Warhol may have come as close as he ever did to celebrating Foucault's "zebra stripe" as heralding a new queer era where everything might be inflamed and transfigured by hitherto impossible forms of desire. The queer utopian narcissism—constituting "an interruption to the mandates to labor, toil, and sacrifice" remarked by José Esteban Muñoz in Warhol's *Silver Clouds*—might here have found another avatar.[117] Perhaps in this work Warhol was even able to prefigure what Rosi Braidotti calls "sexuality as a polymorphous and complex, visceral force" that can be "disengage[d] . . . from both identity issues and all dualistic oppositions"—beyond all categories of gender, ethnicity, species, and narcissism.[118]

In a second print, much more typical of the *Vanishing Animals* series, Warhol and Smith layered the positive drawing image in red ink over a collage of colored paper—a pink sheet with cut and torn rectangular scraps of yellow, cyan, and beige. (See figure 46.) At first glance, the brightness of these colors suggests a reiteration of the untamed utopianism that characterizes the first print. But the instability of the collaged material, which is imperfectly affixed to the base sheet, suggests a different range of connotations. As is the case in many of the *Vanishing Animals* prints, this instability effectively conveys precariousness: a species' potential inability to survive in a rapidly shifting environment. But in this instance, where it is paired with an image of potentially fatal desire, this precariousness calls to mind Lee Edelman's tragic Lacano-DeManian perspective, wherein "the sinthomosexual stands for the wholly impossible ethical act," "forsak[ing] all causes, all social action, all responsibility for a better tomorrow or for the perfection of social forms."[119]

This forsaking is often embodied, for Edelman, by moments of "unintelligibility."[120] In this collaged okapi print, intelligibility is fleetingly revealed as a precarious and ambiguous function of ground and matter. Edges—which typically work to frame and protect the work from its inartistic surroundings—here invade the work, disrupting the ground's ability to support the figures convincingly. What's more, Warhol and Smith layered the brighter colors beneath the dimmer ones (yellow beneath green beneath taupe), creating a disruptive effect whereby the "lower" scraps pop forward, counterfactually to their actual position. But in this print, "the wholly impossible ethical act" that Edelman describes is paired directly with this unintelligibility, since the print carefully isolates the dam's head and the calf's rear on the same scrap of bright but almost sickly cyan paper—a scrap that also seems to have disrupted the imprint of the calf's rear hooves. Its front hooves thus become the only parts of either figure that touch the bright yellow scrap that might almost be taken to connote a ground plane, were it not so conspicuously and incongruously artificial. We see the calf in this print performing a strange two-step, caught between its own historical memory and an unthinkable and perhaps impossible future. And this lost past, banished by the cyan scrap, is simultaneously linked by it to the moment of deadly maternal ennui and desire.

This ongoing ambivalence regarding the possible futures of queer desire is both suppressed and preserved in the print that was ultimately chosen for the okapi chapter

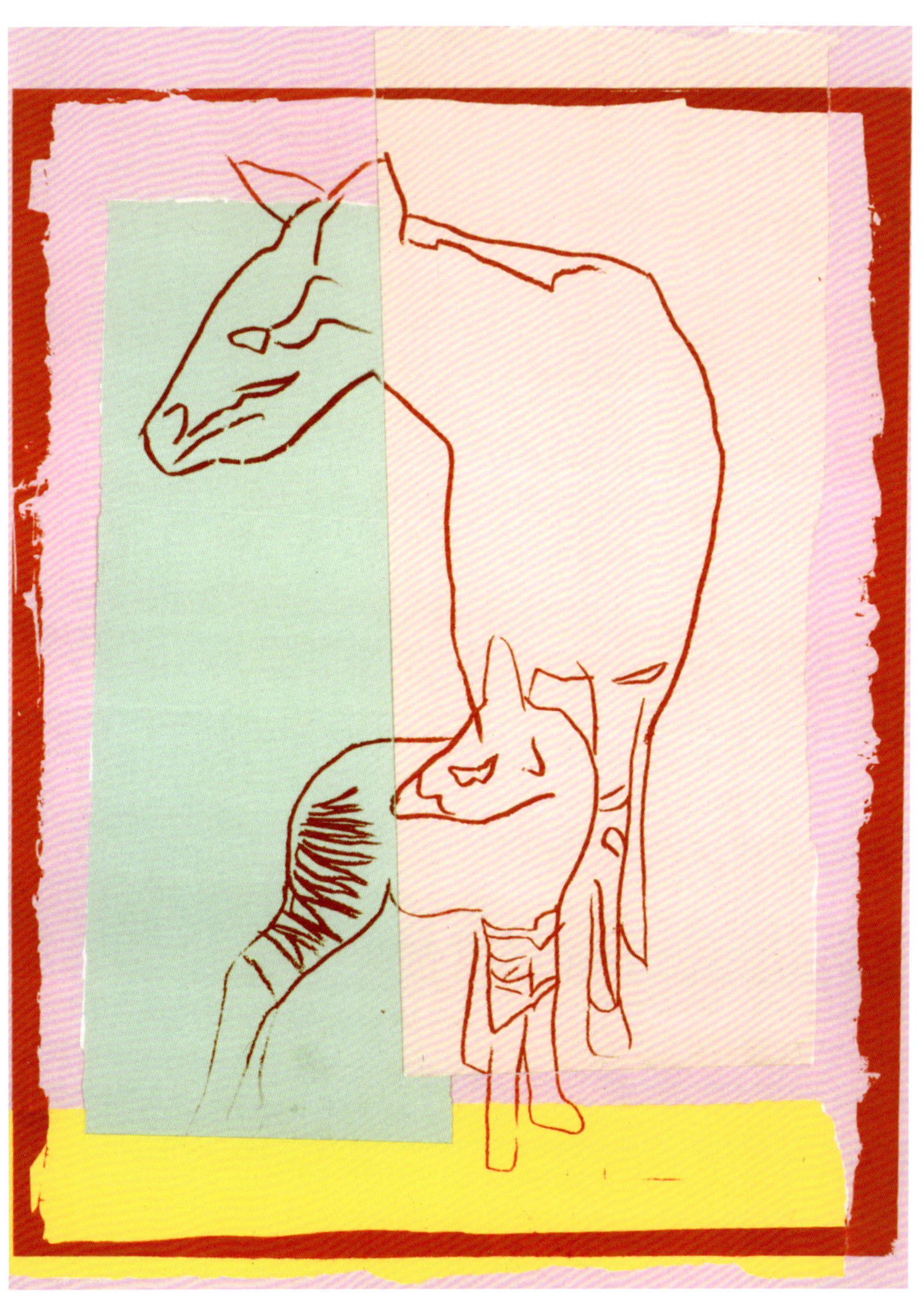

FIGURE 46

Andy Warhol, *Vanishing Animals (Okapi)*, 1986.

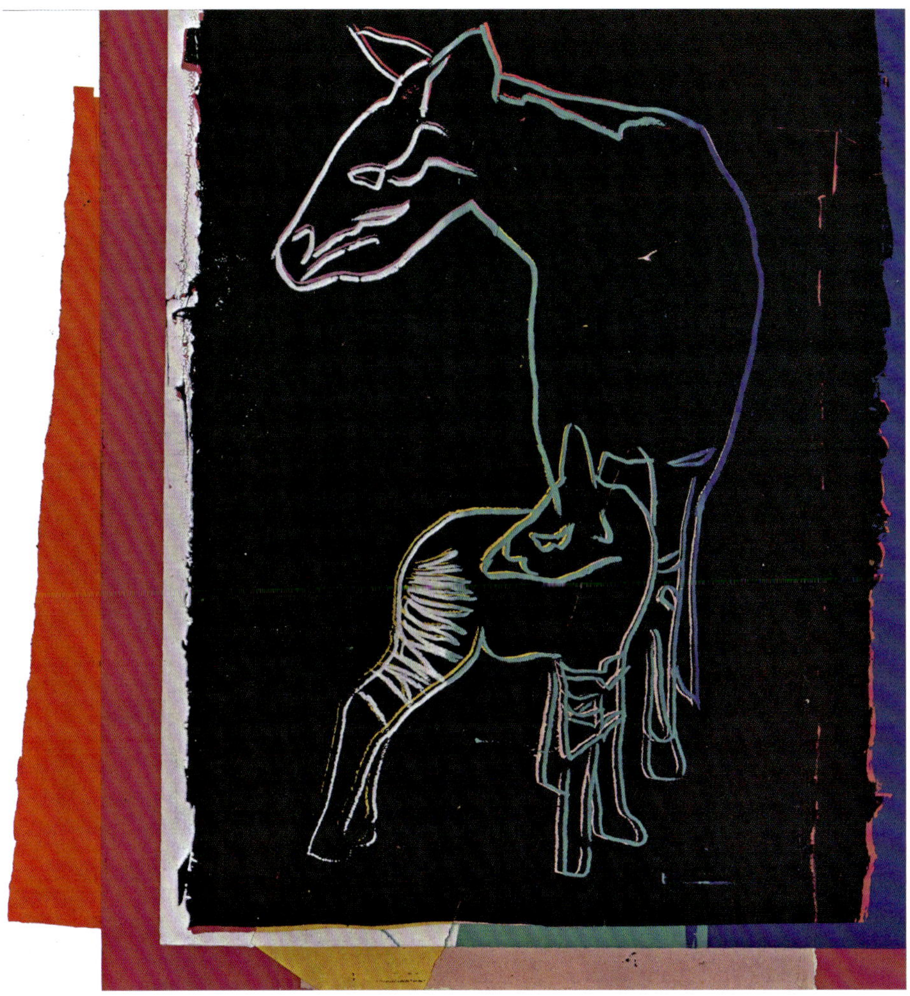

FIGURE 47
Andy Warhol, *Vanishing Animals (Okapi)*, 1986. © 2022 The Andy Warhol Foundation for the Visual Arts, Inc./ Licensed by Artists Rights Society (ARS), New York.

of *Vanishing Animals.* (See figure 47.) In this version, the layered colors of collage and print become almost impossible to read as a sequence of additions. Colors and layers overlap and coincide where they seemingly ought not to. The final printed layers of pink and then black obscure an entire history of prior scraps and layers that now appears forever unrecoverable. Given the color symbolism Warhol and Smith set up in this series—wherein the only other animal to be presented in a predominantly black print is the condor, a bird of prey long associated with death—and the ways in which bright color seems to have been associated with eroticism in other versions of the okapi print, it is difficult not to see this obscured history as signaling death's eventual shrouding and obstruction of the desires that preceded and produced it. Those pleasures remain somewhere underneath death, in this print, but their specific logic and progression are now no longer legible. In this image, arguably the most iconic of the series since it was selected for publication, the characteristic pessimism of the Freudian etiology of homosexuality seems to predominate. Finally, the exclusively black-and-white version selected for the book's cover, through its erasure of all chromatic layers, effectively consolidates this effacement of history and desire. But, by reversing the pair's horizontal orientation, it subtly allows them to anticipate a future beyond their threatened "vanishing."

The time Warhol and Smith spent producing the okapi prints seems to have allowed them to consider a range of resonances for this creature and its unusual circumstances. The plight of the captive okapi offered a fantastical naturalization of the traditional etiologies of male homosexuality that had dominated Western culture since Freud, including (through the prominence of the zoo) "the pervasive assumption that gay and lesbian communities are essentially urban."[121] But, by considering these etiologies as a factor in the development of nonhuman animals, Warhol and Smith also raised a strange challenge to the idea, later proposed by Leo Bersani, that desire is "distinctively human."[122] In this regard, they were straying into the conceptual territory of perspectivism described by Eduardo Viveiros de Castro, in which "[a]ll animals and cosmic constituents are intensively and virtually persons, because all of them, no matter which, can reveal themselves to be (transform into) a person."[123] By imagining the captive male okapi calf as a creature imbued by its mother with queer desire, Warhol and Smith's images produced the okapi as a person, in Viveiros de Castro's sense, endowed with "desire as [an] inhuman force."[124]

What's more, through their attention to Benirschke's description of the okapi's strange plight, Warhol and Smith also directly challenged conventional understandings of evolutionary selection, anticipating Elizabeth Grosz's observation that, even in nonhuman animals, "sexual selection is itself the bizarre and incalculable appeal of objects . . . that induce pleasure rather than progeny."[125] In the imperialist "Darwinist-Freudian" worldview critiqued by Lundblad, the captive okapi dam/calf relationship would seem fundamentally self-defeating and counter-evolutionary. As they are visualized by Warhol and Smith, however, these creatures strikingly illustrate Grosz's bold claim that "[s]exuality is not about the production of a norm but about the eruption of taste"—in this case, a taste that overwrote all concern for the survival of the species.[126] As Benirschke emphasized, the okapi mother apparently lavished attention on her infant out of boredom. She, too, for different reasons, might be considered a queer creature in the making.

Warhol knew that these "eruptions of taste" could ensnare human and nonhuman species; the bull-insemination narrative discussed in chapter 4 provides one such instance. His attitude toward interspecies eroticism was playful and suggestive: dropping innuendos about "sleeping with" his dachshunds, and how they "fool around";

laughing when a friend accused him of "raping her dog in a bathroom"; granting Truman Capote's bulldog permission to hump his leg: "It's all right, Maggie," he told the bulldog, "you can use my leg."[127] Warhol was well aware that erotic feelings could develop when animals and humans cohabited. He told Capote that he had "just got a dog and I think I'm falling in love with him. I think about him all the time, and I know he does, too. I was reading about the two Chinese pandas in Washington, and they won't let just one keeper take care of them because they might fall in love with him and then they wouldn't mate with each other . . . when they're supposed to mate."[128] He found the taboos around these relationships amusing, and seems to have wondered, with Alice Kuzniar, whether "trans-special love" produces a special type of "reassurance and calm . . . because [it] transcends the constrictions that gender and sexuality place upon the human body."[129] In 1977, Warhol and his Factory crew were kicked out of New York's gay BDSM sex club the Anvil when Archie licked the penis of a dancer, described by Bob Colacello as a "black hulk," doing "disco knee bends in front of Warhol's face." Colacello thought it was "the perfect Andy Warhol anecdote."[130] Warhol seems to have been aware that these cross-species attractions had a biochemical dimension as well. In April 1985, in his diaries, he speculated that his business partner Fred Hughes's mysterious trip to Zurich might be an opportunity for him to "[get] those sheep glands," a testicular xenotransplantation intended to boost libido.[131] As a connoisseur of perfume, Warhol likely would have been aware that castoreum—a key ingredient in many classic brands, producing scents similar to leather and vanilla—is harvested from the castor sacs of beavers, near their anal glands.[132]

But Warhol and Smith's okapi images pushed these eruptions of taste to their terminal limits. In these animals' strange jeopardy, the two artists found what seemed to be an instance of queer animal life in which sexuality was not only not reproductive but also often fatal. The okapi might thus have figured for Warhol and Smith a truly queer sexuality in Neel Ahuja's sense, in which "[a]t the heart of the body and the future lies the corpse."[133] Produced and distributed during the years in which both Smith and Warhol's boyfriend contracted and died of AIDS, along with at least 12,847 other people in the United States, these images could not have been more timely or ambivalent. They propose a form of eroticism that could look death squarely in the face.

In some prints, this queer deathliness veers toward the tragic and vindictive visions explored by Freud, Kristeva, Morrison, and Hitchcock; in others, it seems to anticipate the bold new world proposed by Foucault, Braidotti, and Butler: a "resignification of gay and lesbian sexuality through and against abjection" that constituted a "reformulation and proliferation of the symbolic itself."[134] Warhol, as much as any artist of this period, might be said to have contributed to this groundbreaking project. Taken together, the okapi prints demonstrate an important new dimension to Warhol's lifelong interest in nonhuman animals: an attention to forms of life that are themselves self-destructive, consumed by pleasures, unreproducible, etiologically or insurgently queer—and a tenacious effort to have these strange qualities resonate in the printed material. The okapi—this "cosmic misprint," born anal-retentive, flamboyant, and shy; delicious to eat; almost impossible to catch with its "queer rolling gallop"; prone, when bored, to inflict fatal rectal prolapse on its children with its blue eighteen-inch, dual-headed, snakelike tongue; abducted by the same ships that brought HIV to Europe and the Americas—what a bizarre and fitting emblem for the promises and challenges of Warhol's queer ecologies.

———

These queer ecological themes live on to the present day, intertwined and only slightly transfigured. In Luca Guadagnino's *We Are Who We Are* (HBO, 2020), a young soldier and the show's teenage protagonist recognize each other as queer through their shared eagerness for Ocean Vuong's new novel, *On Earth We're Briefly Gorgeous.* The book is written as a series of letters from a Vietnamese-American man to his illiterate mother, who has left her abusive husband, nicknamed her son "Little Dog," and raised him with her mother's help. The son realizes that his nickname is a form of protection that "both shield[s] him and turn[s] him into an animal at once," hiding someone frail and queer behind the name of something "worthless," to protect him from evil spirits. Little Dog's mother has told her young son that she delivered him rectally, and he proudly informs a store clerk that "I came out her asshole and I love her very much."[135] She teaches him to take pleasure in candy and find beauty in birds (29). Like Warhol, she is transfixed by the possibility of animal creativity, remembering her sole glimpse of magical possibility—a dog trained by its master to dance to Chopin on the streets of Saigon: "Even when the man stopped . . . and placed the treat in the dog's open mouth, proving again that it was hunger . . . not music that gave the dog its human skill, I still believed it. That anything could happen" (136). She wonders aloud to her Little Dog (whose aesthetic production is also fueled by appetite) whether she is a "monster" or a "mother," and he feels obligated to reassure her while wondering whether they are not both, in fact, monsters in the original sense: "animal[s] of myriad origins" (13). (Gould would sign letters to Warhol, "Monstrously XXX John [*sic*]."[136])

Despite blanching at his professor's claim that "gay men are inherently narcissistic" (136), Little Dog believes that "love, at its best, repeats itself" (34) and that "our being alive is beautiful enough to be worthy of replication" (138–39), and he finds another boy, Trevor, who has the "hurt expression of someone watching his favorite dog being put down too soon" (95). When they're kissing, Little Dog discovers that "Trevor speaks for [him]." These "dark words" are "[l]ike the calf waiting in its coffin house," being raised for veal—"inhaling . . . the earthly manure of his mother a field away" (157). The maternal, the animal, the lingual, and the abject/anal are closely tied together, a shared erotic and emotional language for the two queer boys.

Little Dog sucks Trevor's toes, "[t]he way [his] mother used to do when [he was] small and shivering" (158). When they fuck, Little Dog "didn't yet know how to prepare myself," and there is an unexpected mess: "A scent rose up to my head, strong and deep, like soil"—echoing the calf "inhaling" his mother's "earthly manure"—"but sharp with flaw" (203). Little Dog worries that "I had tainted him with my faggotry, the filthiness of our act exposed by my body's failure to contain itself" (203). He braces himself to be punished, beaten, abjected—as his father had beaten his mother, and as his mother had beaten him. Instead, in the novel's most remarkable moment, Trevor leads him to the river, bends him over, "kne[els] in the shallows, knees sunk in river mud," and eats him out (205). "I was devoured, it seemed, not by a person, a Trevor, so much as by desire itself. To be reclaimed by that want, to be baptized by its pure need. That's what I was" (205–6). Eating, desire, and dirt—"the unacknowledged vegetal background of human knowledge"—are reconciled in self-understanding and acceptance.[137] Finally, unexpectedly—five centuries after Leonardo's dream, but only a third of a century after Morrison's *Sula* and Warhol's okapi—a queer benediction for the shame and pain these works registered has been envisioned in popular fiction, and reproduced, obliquely, as a television dream.

CONCLUSION

The Python Priestess

THERE ARE CLEARLY MANY ANIMAL and vegetal Warhols—many ways in which Warhol was challenged by queer ecologies and nonhuman life-forms, in which he considered or embraced their perspectives and attempted to emulate or monetize their spirits, in himself and in those around him. His menagerie was eccentric: flowers and germs, dogs, cats, bees, bats, trees and clouds and cockroaches, cows, vultures, parrots, turtles, rabbits, and the okapi, which provided him with a late and fantastical glimpse of both "the eruption of taste" *and* the naturalization of traditional etiologies of the male homosexual. But no list of Warhol's favored life-forms could be complete without the snake. Snakes recurred frequently in his work, and throughout most of his life Warhol and those around him seem to have suspected that there was something serpentine about him.

During the early 1960s, Warhol was principle illustrator for the Fleming-Joffe leather company, which boasted an inventory of 2 million snakeskin leathers.[1] In 1963 he produced a series of prints entitled *Autobiography of a Snake,* chronicling the adventures of a creature whose skin serves various functions for the upper crust, becoming "Diana Vreeland's chicest shoe," "Liz Taylor's bracelet," and "Coco Chanel's shirt": "I am a snake . . . but I have the creative soul of an artist and an actor." On one level, this narrative neatly allegorized Warhol's contributions to the fashion industry, and his success in marketing his own eccentricities to a primarily wealthy and female audience. But the series carries other resonances as well. Each of snake-Warhol's contributions to fashion was, after all, something like a death: adult readers must have been aware that any actual snake would have had to be killed in order for its skin to become a commodity. Some might even have remarked that these mass killings funded Warhol's work for Fleming-Joffe. And, despite its ostensibly young readership, there are also sections of this series that emphasize an interspecies sexuality enjoyed by its hero and his human counterparts alike.

Throughout *Autobiography of a Snake,* as elsewhere in his life and work, Warhol drew heavily on a variety of serpentine connotations, including the five remarked by Aby Warburg in a note appended to his "Lecture on Serpent Ritual."[2]

1. Hibernation: Like a snake, Warhol seemed to have the uncanny ability to move back and forth between life and death, resurrecting himself after Solanas's failed assassination attempt, and perpetually skirting the line between the living and the dead in his work. Solanas's bullet had hit his lung, esophagus, intestines, liver, gallbladder, spleen, and stomach. A doctor massaged his heart by hand to revive it. Afterward Warhol claimed that he had "died"; he was left with "Frankenstein scars" across his torso.[3] His factory nickname, Drella, with its undertones of the immortal undead, attests to this quality, as does the recurrently gruesome subject matter (electric chairs, suicides, assassinations) rendered in DayGlo tones that populated his work, and the macabre leather S&M culture that fascinated him. And yet, despite his perceived invincibility, Warhol was notoriously terrified of hospitals, and obsessed with the threat of death.

2. Shedding skin: Like a snake, Warhol was known for his propensity for self-transformation, moving on from one skin to another almost effortlessly. From advertising to art, painting to film and music, film and music to media and modeling and publishing—always remaining "Warhol" despite these changes. His "mass produced" paintings, cranked out with only minor changes from one to the next, exemplify this adaptability. During the 1960s, for what he called "an experiment in mistaken identity," Warhol even hired an impersonator to deliver college lectures in his stead.[4] *Autobiography of a Snake* emphasizes this quality, melding it with the capacity for revivification to produce a snake/artist who can perpetually sell and regenerate his own skin for various commodities (shoes, luggage, clothing) without undermining his vitality. And yet snake-Warhol seems to have remained perpetually unsatisfied with the skins he had: "If someone asked me, 'What's your problem?' I'd have to say, 'Skin.'"[5]

3. Slithering but deadly: observers described Warhol as simultaneously elusive and dangerous—like something "you find under rocks."[6] As Stephen Koch remembered, "Evasion . . . played a large part in Warhol's physical presence. . . . One sensed a profound, very fearful removal from contact, which played into his charm."[7] Koch recounts a striking example. Confronted by "an old . . . associate" about "a pressing financial matter,"

> Warhol was recalcitrant, endlessly evasive, and kept edging away from his interlocutor. At last, in some irritation, the man said sharply, "Look at me when I talk to you," and briefly touched Warhol's shoulder to retrieve his attention. The response was electric: Warhol spun in terror and cowered. "The flunkies started coming out of the hills in horror. Horror of horrors—Andy had been touched." The meeting was instantly ended; some very extreme violation had occurred.[8]

Untouchable, but not meek: those who knew Warhol well attested to what one friend called "his vulgar peasant strength," and the viciousness of his tongue.[9] In *Autobiography of a Snake*, the hero's skin is used in various applications, but his actual body is rarely touched or caressed. (The only significant exception is a panel near the end, where a naked putto nuzzles against the snake's body, reiterating the prepubescent sexuality frequently emphasized in Warhol's early work.)

4. Camouflage: Like a snake, Warhol was known for being capable of blending into his environment, sinking into the background, becoming invisible. In *Autobiography of a Snake*, the hero's skin matches everything, and can be employed in the most delicate applications. Blake Gopnik rightly emphasizes that camouflage was central to Warhol's survival as a gay man in a deeply homophobic world.[10] Warhol thematized this ability in his late camouflage self-portraits, and camouflage is now widely (and paradoxically) recognized as one of his signature qualities.

5. Phallus: In *Autobiography of a Snake*, the hero takes pleasure from its proximity to human bodies, like a phallus. In one scene, its skin is used to cover the genitalia of the dancers at the Folies-Bergère: "Oh, what a job!" the snake exclaims. All the dancers on this page are female, but on the previous page, where snake-Warhol bragged about the use of his skin on the theater's curtains, the male dancers wear his skin as well, before it has been identified as such. It is unclear whether Warhol would have known that same-sex and group-sex relations are common in some species of snakes, and that, as Joan Roughgarden points out, "[a]ll male garter snakes wear female perfume and participate in same-sex copulation every year."[11]

These five serpentine connotations inform each other in interesting ways. Snake-Warhol is an odd phallus that, through his camouflageable, sheddable, shameful skin, can give of himself to anything, regardless of resemblance—with pleasure, but without attachment. Like the heteronormative phallus, he is generative, capable of reproduction, but unlike it he is sexually disinterested in the opposite sex. Near the series' conclusion, the smirking snake slithers behind the eroticized lower halves of four

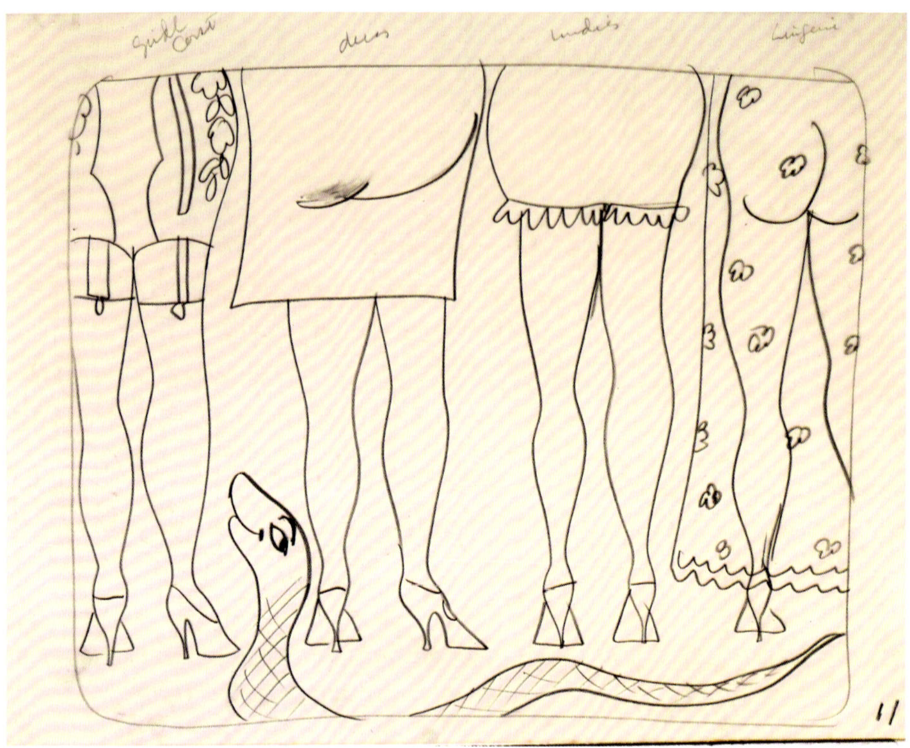

FIGURE 48
Andy Warhol, *Snake and Four Pairs of Female Legs*, 1963. The Andy Warhol Museum, Pittsburgh; Gift of Teddy and Arthur Edelman. © 2022 The Andy Warhol Foundation for the Visual Arts, Inc./Licensed by Artists Rights Society (ARS), New York.

women in lingerie, seen from behind: "I became the darling of women who needed me. I gave them chic." (See figure 48.) This sly but harmless snake might be said to conjure what Gopnik calls Warhol's paradoxically well-endowed "antivirility"—his restrained and unthreatening phallic presence, his becoming "somehow a being without needs."[12] Gary Indiana made the point clearly: "The Factory was a church. The Church of the Unimaginable Penis. Andy was the father confessor. The kids were the sinners."[13]

As a coy snake, Warhol could embody a powerful phallus without having to seem to *possess* one. As in his early drawing, snake-Warhol would be shaky, withdrawn, askew, coiled in upon himself but nevertheless alert and capable of action. (See figure 49.) In these respects, he adopted the strategy of male masquerade described by Joan Riviere, Judith Butler, and Cynthia Weber, which through "phallic disavowal . . . protects the male subject from the threat of castration . . . all the while underscoring that he is in possession of the penis and could possibly wield phallic power."[14] Snake-Warhol could maintain phallic power by having his penis be "unimaginable," abundant and powerful but always withheld.[15]

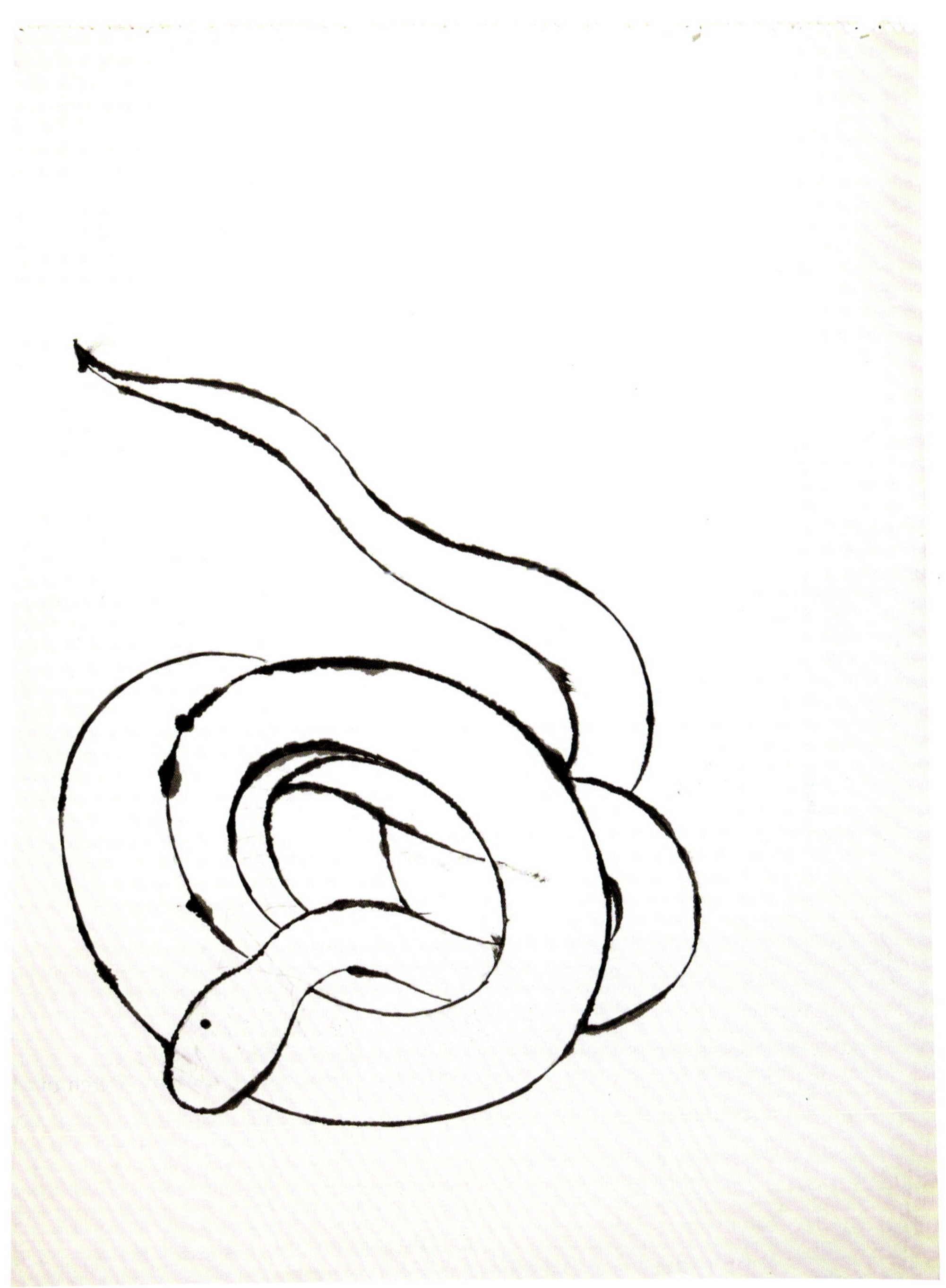

FIGURE 49
Andy Warhol, *Snake,* c. 1956. Image and Artwork © The Andy Warhol Foundation for the Visual Arts, Inc./Licensed by ARS.

Warhol's documented encounters with snakes, and with those who thought him serpentine, raise questions that touch on these concerns, as well as others that exceed their purview. In 1983, he recounted seeing the underground actor John Sex perform with his pet boa constrictor; he shot three rolls of photos, but was "scared of the snake" that Sex bragged of sleeping with. A year later, when Sex and Warhol made cameos in a music video for The Cars, Sex and his snake reminded Warhol of "the old Factory days," two decades after the fact.[16] Together, they took the eroto-serpentine possibilities that had long intrigued him and made them direct and explicit.

No such solution was available to Warhol, however. He could never actually dance with a snake, since he feared their touch, like that of other humans. The *Diaries* recount an incident in Colorado in 1981: "I was signing signing signing and then a guy came with a big fat yellow snake around his neck. He was so creepy, and he said, 'Sign my snake,' and Christopher [Makos] freaked out and said, 'No snakes!' So he said, 'Sign my forehead.' So here's this snake coming at me. So I put an 'X' on his forehead. Because I couldn't write, I was just too nervous with the snake."[17] It is an unusually anxious moment in Warhol's history with animals, particularly when one considers that he so often took pride in being comfortable with, and empathetic toward, creatures that other humans avoided. The "X"-marked forehead would return in Warhol's okapi prints.

Acquaintances sometimes wondered whether Warhol's aversion to touch signaled a serpentine or reptilian character. David Bowie remarked this quality immediately: "The guy doesn't like flesh, obviously he's reptilian."[18] *The Philosophy of Andy Warhol* recounts a conversation with a friend in Monaco, who teased Warhol about a recent review: "It said you were slightly repellent, like a reptile." Warhol expressed indifference: "She was testing me to see if it really didn't bother me when I heard things like that about myself. It really didn't. I didn't even know what it meant to be 'like a reptile.' 'Does that mean I'm slimy?' I asked her?" "'There's something about reptiles,' she said. 'Looks aside. They're the only animals who don't like to be touched.' As she said that she jumped out of the chair. 'You don't mind being touched, do you?' She was coming at me. 'Yes! Yes I do!'" Warhol exclaimed.[19]

Warhol's fear of human and serpentine touch pushes past Warburg's symbology and toward more contemporary readings. In a late essay, Deleuze proposed the snake as an exemplar for postwar "control societies": "If money's old moles are the animals you get in places of confinement, then control societies have their snakes. We've gone from . . . moles to snakes, not just in the system we live under but in the way we live and in our relations with other people too."[20] Where previous disciplinary regimes had exerted power primarily through physical institutions like factories, prisons, and schools, control societies deinstitutionalize and universalize this control through various "network controls," such as surveillance and passwords, but also, as William Bogard has shown, through haptic technologies that create "'immersive' environments . . . 'multi-media' interfaces that produce 'complete' sensory experiences."[21]

Warhol was, of course, a pioneer in all of these areas. His multimedia provocations like the *Exploding Plastic Inevitable* events helped to inaugurate the disciplinary changes that troubled Deleuze. Like many snakes, he managed to burrow, becoming partially subterranean, feeding on the cultural underground, harnessing its productive ecologies, and marketing the results to customers on the surface. What's more, Warhol hyperbolically embraced the individualism and grit that neoliberalism prescribed. His serpentine untouchability was a compelling instance of this market-fundamentalist ethos, as was his management style. As he put it in 1975, "Always when you're crying you could be laughing, you have the choice. . . . [T]ake the flexibility your mind is capable of and make it work for you."[22] Understanding himself from the neoliberal perspective of "a subject that must permanently struggle to accommodate itself to the world," Warhol had difficulty imagining himself as an agent of political change, someone who could propose and pursue transformations of power.[23] In a world where each of us is encouraged to fight only for ourselves and our interests, the flexible, resilient, untouchable, "unimaginable," serpentine artist strikes a resonant chord. By the mid-1970s, he was brokering art deals that resembled stock-market IPOs, anticipating Deleuze's observation that "[e]ven art has moved away from closed sites and into the open circuits of banking."[24]

There is one final serpentine quality in D.H. Lawrence's 1923 poem *Snake,* noted by Claire Colebrook, that I wonder whether Warhol ever sensed.[25] The poem's narrator recognizes a certain lordliness in a snake he encounters and attacks it with a log, but then immediately regrets this "paltry . . . vulgar . . . mean act," and offers the poem as a way "to expiate . . . / A pettiness." After the snake has retreated underground, "into that dreadful hole . . . that horrid black hole . . . the earth-lipped fissure"—more anxious figures for anal and oral desire—the narrator expresses what Derrida called "his love" for it: "my snake."[26] These figures resonate with Warhol's okapi, with Ocean Vuong's "earthly manure," and with what Michael Marder calls "the unacknowledged vegetal background of human knowledge."[27] The narrator's close, erotic attention to the snake allows him to see the otherwise reviled creature as "like a god, unseeing"—"a king in exile . . . one of the lords / Of life"—that models "another style of perception and duration."[28] There are moments when Warhol seems to have remarked and emulated this "liberation from mastery," this creaturely or vegetal power, "to live the earth not as one's own"—and perhaps even caught a glimpse of "the desire for communism" that Oxana Timofeeva posits in living creatures more generally.[29] His embrace of the animal-machine position—reacting rather than responding, tracing rather than drawing, grunting rather than speaking, moving at inhuman speeds—certainly suggested these tendencies, as did his long-standing interest in forms of ecological production, freed (if only in principle) from authorship, ownership, and shame, and in a "philosophy of the fragile" that might find common ground for all life-forms, even the most abject and unloved.

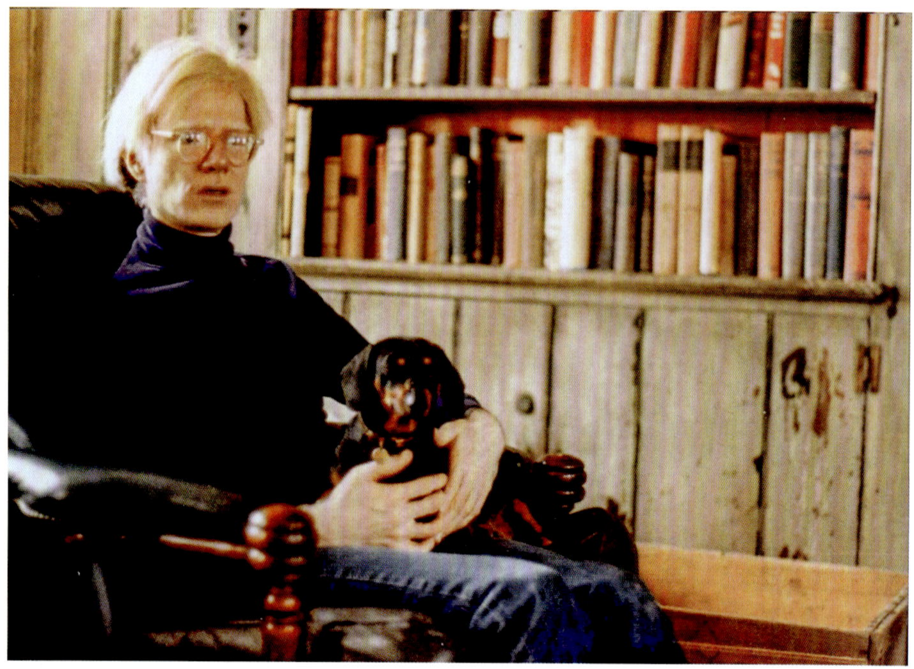

FIGURE 50
James Warhola, *Andy Holding Archie in Montauk, NY,* 1975. Paul Warhola Family Collection.

John Rublowsky noticed Warhol's reptilian qualities in 1965: "The skin is pallid, almost white, with a texture never coarsened by exposure to sun or wind. The eyes are soft, expressive. They are the eyes of a fragile night creature who discovers himself living in the blaze of an alien, but fascinating, world. . . . It could be the mask of a saint—or a satyr. . . . It is the python mask donned by the priestess when, drunk with visionary excess, she proclaims the future in rough hexameters."[30] Rublowsky's imagery undergoes a striking shift, from Warhol as subterranean creature to Warhol as priestess, wearing the snake's skin as her mask. Warhol's passions for leather and taxidermy buttress this latter image, as does his penchant for deploying an animal to shield him from the pressures of portraiture. (See figure 50.) Sometimes Warhol was like an animal or plant without trying to be so; sometimes he emulated the "spirits" of the life-forms around him; sometimes he took their lives and their skins and wore them as his own, converting them into animal and vegetal capital.[31] When he memorably imagined in his diaries that "the plants are screaming," he did so in the context of attempting to justify "killing animals to make coats." How could slaughter and pain be avoided, he wondered, when "cows are so big and beautiful and *everything's* alive"?[32]

Warhol as Pythia, then: parthenogenetic in origin, listening to snakes who slither underground, speaking "with words unwill'd, and wisdom not her own."[33] Able to summon an animal imagination that allowed him to foretell queer and unlikely futures, but for this very reason all too aware of his own "sheer animal vulnerability" in a world ruled by humans.[34] Spurning all principles of humanist aesthetics, and proposing not just appetite, but queer, earthy, beastly, transgressive appetites, as their replacements. Imagining the world from an organic, creaturely, unabjected perspective, but sometimes unable or reluctant to *face* these insights, and needing another living being—willing or unwilling, masks, dogs, factories, stables, archives, ecosystems, flowers, flaming creatures—to face them for him. Picking plants and animals up, dead or alive, to meet the camera, wearing their skin as a mask or garment, perhaps sometimes sympathizing with the life or lives this skin had cost, perhaps sometimes imagining that their skins belonged to him, as his had belonged for many years to his mother, Julia.

NOTES

A NOTE ON TERMINOLOGY

1. See Eva Meijer, *When Animals Speak: Toward an Interspecies Democracy* (New York: NYU Press, 2019), 154.
2. Christoph Cox, "Thinking like a Plant: Prolegomena to a Philosophy of Vegetables," *Cabinet*, no. 6 (Spring 2002), accessed November 15, 2020, https://www.cabinetmagazine.org/issues/6/cox.php.

INTRODUCTION

1. Quoted in Stephen Koch, *Stargazer: The Life, World and Films of Andy Warhol* (London: Marion Boyars, 2000), 23.
2. Wynn Chamberlain, quoted in Blake Gopnik, *Warhol* (New York: HarperCollins, 2020), 290; Andy Warhol, *The Philosophy of Andy Warhol (From A to B and Back Again)* (New York: Harcourt Brace Jovanovich, 1975), 92.
3. Linda Weintraub, *To Life!: Eco Art in Pursuit of a Sustainable Planet* (Berkeley: University of California Press, 2012), 11. Animals receive only passing mention in two recent exhibition catalogues of Warhol's work: Donna De Salvo, ed., *Andy Warhol: From A to B and Back Again* (New Haven, CT: Yale University Press, 2018); and Gregor Muir and Yilmaz Dziewior, eds., *Andy Warhol* (London: Tate Publishing, 2020). On the rare occasions when it has been addressed directly, nature in Warhol's work has been described as something that he felt "must be controlled,

manipulated, ultimately and finally fixed." Chad Alligood, "Warhol's Nature," in *Warhol's Nature,* ed. Linda DeBerry (New York: Scala Arts Publishers, 2015), 13.

4. Margot Norris, *Beasts of Modern Imagination: Darwin, Nietzsche, Kafka, Ernst, and Lawrence* (Baltimore: Johns Hopkins University Press, 1985), 5. For surveys of the use of animal themes and subjects in art, see Howard Morphy, ed., *Animals into Art* (London: Routledge, 2016); Petra Lange-Berndt, *Animal Art: Präparierte Tiere in der Kunst, 1850–2000* (Munich: Verlag Silke Schreiber, 2009); Steve Baker, *The Postmodern Animal* (London: Reaktion Books, 2000); and Ron Broglio, *Surface Encounters: Thinking with Animals and Art* (Minneapolis: University of Minnesota Press, 2011).
5. Norris, *Beasts of Modern Imagination,* 5.
6. Philip Low, "The Cambridge Declaration on Consciousness," declaration proclaimed at the Francis Crick Memorial Conference on Consciousness in Human and non-Human Animals, Churchill College, University of Cambridge, July 7, 2012. Accessed November 15, 2020. fcmconference.org/img/CambridgeDeclarationOnConsciousness.pdf. See also Cox, "Thinking like a Plant."
7. Warhol, *The Philosophy of Andy Warhol,* 48.
8. Wayne Koestenbaum, *Andy Warhol: A Biography* (New York: Open Road, 2001), 196; Nicole Shukin, *Animal Capital: Rendering Life in Biopolitical Times* (Minneapolis: University of Minnesota Press, 2009). For "vegetal life," see Michael Marder, *Plant-Thinking: A Philosophy of Vegetal Life* (New York: Columbia University Press, 2013).
9. Shukin, *Animal Capital,* 22; Nicole Shukin, "Capitalism," in *The Edinburgh Companion to Animal Studies,* ed. Lynn Turner, Undine Sellbach, and Ron Broglio (Edinburgh: Edinburgh University Press, 2018), 102.
10. Shukin, *Animal Capital,* 22.
11. Michael Lundblad, *The Birth of a Jungle: Animality in Progressive-Era U.S. Literature and Culture* (New York: Oxford University Press, 2013), 11.
12. Lundblad, 2.
13. In this respect, Warhol is deeply Nietzschean: "[A]dvanced physiology will comprehend the artistic powers already present in our development; and not only in human development, but in that of animals as well: it will claim that what is artistic has its inception in the organic." Friedrich Nietzsche, *Unpublished Writings from the Period of Unfashionable Observations,* trans. Richard T. Gray (Stanford, CA: Stanford University Press, 1995), 20.
14. Shukin, *Animal Capital,* 24. However, see Gopnik's *Warhol* for the myriad ways in which Warhol failed or refused to cash in on his fame to the degree that he might have.
15. Achille Mbembe, *Necropolitics,* trans. Steven Corcoran (Durham, NC: Duke University Press, 2019), 108.
16. Mbembe, 177.
17. Emile de Antonio, "Marx and Warhol," unpublished draft; cited in Branden W. Joseph, "1962," *October,* no. 132 (Spring 2010): 115.
18. Quoted in Otto Hahn, "Passport No. G255300," *Art and Artists* 1, no. 4 (July 1966): 7.
19. Quoted in Craig Copetas, "Beat Godfather Meets Glitter Mainman," *Rolling Stone,* February 28, 1974, 27.
20. Kennedy Fraser, "As Gorgeous As It Gets," *New Yorker,* September 7, 1986, 76.
21. Gary Comenas, "Andy Warhol: From Nowhere to Up There; An Oral History of Andy Warhol's Early Years," 18, accessed November 1, 2019, https://www.warholstars.org/nowhere/andy_warhol_pages.html; Gopnik, *Warhol,* 613.
22. Donald Newlove, "Prothalamion for Wet Harmonica and Johnny Stompanato," *The Realist,* no. 68 (August 1966): 19.

23. Andy Warhol, *America* (New York: Harper & Row, 1985), 191.
24. Victor Bockris, *Warhol: The Biography* (New York: Da Capo, 2003), 95; see Anthony E. Grudin, *Warhol's Working Class: Pop Art and Egalitarianism* (Chicago: University of Chicago Press, 2017).
25. Quoted in Bockris, *Warhol*, 64–65.
26. George Gruskin, "Who Is This Man, Andy Warhol?," in *I'll Be Your Mirror: The Selected Andy Warhol Interviews*, ed. Kenneth Goldsmith (New York: Carroll & Graf, 2004), 201.
27. Warhol, *America*, 11.
28. Rosi Braidotti, *The Posthuman* (Cambridge: Polity, 2013), 70; Michael Marder, *Grafts: Writings on Plants* (Minneapolis: Univocal, 2016), 47. See also Sarat Colling, *Animal Resistance in the Global Capitalist Era* (East Lansing: Michigan State University Press, 2021), xxix–xxx.
29. Bob Colacello, *Holy Terror: Andy Warhol Close Up* (New York: HarperCollins, 1990), 445–46. Warhol offered to contribute funding to Beuys's *7,000 Oaks* project (1988) in New York. Gopnik, *Warhol*, 859.
30. Colacello, *Holy Terror*, 438.
31. Kathryn Bond Stockton has observed that "Andy Warhol gathers nearly all queer children in himself. He is the ghostly gay, queerly colored, Freudian-fixated-on-his-mother, deceptively 'simple,' and grown homosexual child of postwar American art and culture." Stockton, *The Queer Child, or Growing Sideways in the Twentieth Century* (Durham, NC: Duke University Press, 2009), 219–20.
32. Ronald K. Siegel, *Intoxication: The Universal Drive for Mind-Altering Substances* (Rochester, VT: Park Street Press, 2005), 206.
33. Andy Warhol and Pat Hackett, *Popism: The Warhol Sixties* (New York: Mariner, 2006), 82.
34. Shukin, *Animal Capital*, 105.
35. "[A]s long as it is institutionally taken for granted that it is all right to systematically exploit and kill nonhuman animals simply because of their species," Cary Wolfe reminds us, "then the humanist discourse of species will always be available for use by some humans against other humans as well, to countenance violence against the social other of *whatever* species—or gender, or race, or class, or sexual difference." Wolfe, *Animal Rites: American Culture, the Discourse of Species, and Posthumanist Theory* (Chicago: University of Chicago Press, 2003), 8.
36. Warhol, *America*, 191.
37. Jacques Lacan, "The Mirror Stage as Formative of the *I* Function as Revealed in Psychoanalytic Experience," in *Écrits: The First Complete Edition in English*, trans. Bruce Fink (New York: Norton, 2006), 75–81.
38. Warhol, *America*, 188.
39. Warhol, 192.
40. Stockton, *The Queer Child*, 90.
41. Dominic Pettman, "Affection," in *The Edinburgh Companion to Animal Studies*, ed. Lynn Turner, Undine Sellbach, and Ron Broglio (Edinburgh: Edinburgh University Press, 2018), 32. Or, as Marc Shell more provocatively argues, they could provide a release valve for the pressures of normative family life, since in pet love, the bestiality taboo shields the human lover from the temptation to violate the incest taboo. Shell, "The Family Pet," *Representations*, no. 15 (Summer 1986): 141.
42. See Neil Printz and Sally King-Nero, *The Andy Warhol Catalogue Raisonné*, vol. 4, *Paintings and Sculpture, late 1974–1976* (New York: Phaidon, 2010), 372.
43. Shukin, "Capitalism," 99; ellipses in original. "At stake for critical thought, then," Shukin concludes, "are neoliberal forms of animal capital which are produced through liberating and loving relationships with certain elect creatures, fostering chances for (some) humans and

(some) animals to realise their specific potentials and *in this way redeeming value* for the system of capitalism" (102); emphasis in original.

44. Claire Colebrook, "How Queer Can You Go? Theory, Normality and Normativity," in *Queering the Non/Human*, ed. Noreen Giffney and Myra Hird (Burlington, VT: Ashgate, 2008), 30.
45. Koch, *Stargazer*, 29.
46. Gopnik, *Warhol*, 865.

1. "LIKE A LITTLE DOG"

1. Donna Haraway, *When Species Meet* (Minneapolis: University of Minnesota Press, 2008), 244.
2. For the double negative as an identity position, see Kathryn Bond Stockton, *Beautiful Bottom, Beautiful Shame: Where "Black" Meets "Queer"* (Durham, NC: Duke University Press, 2006), 91.
3. Warhol, *The Philosophy of Andy Warhol*, 63, 64.
4. Stockton, *Queer Child*, 90.
5. Matt Wrbican, "A View from the Archives: Nature as Culture in Warhol's Art," in *Warhol's Nature*, edited by Linda DeBerry (New York: Scala Arts Publishers, 2015), 52; Gopnik, *Warhol*, 21.
6. Gary Comenas, "Andy Warhol: From Nowhere to Up There; An Oral History of Andy Warhol's Early Years," 5, accessed November 1, 2019, https://warholstars.org/nowhere/andy_warhol_pages.html; Wrbican, "A View from the Archives," 21.
7. Bockris, *Warhol*, 75.
8. Bockris, 8.
9. Quoted in Bockris, 19.
10. Michael K. Rosenow, *Death and Dying in the Working Class, 1865–1920* (Urbana: University of Illinois Press, 2015), 30. Compare Frantz Fanon summarizing racist attitudes toward Black people: "To suffer from a phobia of Negroes is to be afraid of the biological. For the Negro is only biological. The Negroes are animals." Fanon, *Black Skin, White Masks*, trans. Charles Lam Markmann (London: Pluto, 2008), 127.
11. Rosenow, *Death and Dying in the Working Class*, 30.
12. Gopnik, *Warhol*, 10.
13. Tinka Preksta and John Elachko quoted in Bockris, *Warhol*, 35, 39.
14. Chester Stanek quoted in Colacello, *Holy Terror*, 20.
15. Quoted in Bockris, *Warhol*, 24.
16. D.W. Winnicott, "A Case Managed at Home," in *Through Paediatrics to Psycho-Analysis: Collected Papers* (London: Routledge, 2001), 120, 124.
17. Paul Warhola quoted in Bockris, *Warhol*, 24.
18. Bockris, 24.
19. American basements, as Kate Millett has argued, are "places of sexual experiment, the first exhibitionism, the showing of genitals." Basement play "was . . . directed by the boys, [and their] obsession with violence." See Millett, *The Basement: Meditations on a Human Sacrifice* (New York: Simon & Schuster, 1979), 19–20.
20. Victor Bockris, "Dinner with Andy and Bill" [1980], in Goldsmith, *I'll Be Your Mirror: The Selected Andy Warhol Interviews*, ed. Kenneth Goldsmith (New York: Carroll & Graf, 2004), 280. The expression calls to mind Warhol's reported response to the assassination of John F. Kennedy: "Andy kept saying, 'I don't know what it means!'" Gopnik, *Warhol*, 348.
21. Bockris, *Warhol*, 75.
22. Matt Wrbican, *A is for Archive: Warhol's World from A to Z* (New Haven, CT: Yale University Press, 2019), 40.
23. Bockris, *Warhol*, 75.

24. Bockris, 37.
25. Paul Warhola quoted in Bockris, *Warhol,* 37.
26. Bockris, 37, 38.
27. Bockris, 38. On the basis of these symptoms, Blake Gopnik has surmised that this disease might now be diagnosed as PANDAS, and that "Andrew Warhola started becoming the artist Andy Warhol, in a quite concrete and even neurological sense, in tandem with his childhood illness." Gopnik, *Warhol,* 23–24. From this perspective, the origins of Warhol's style become bacteriological.
28. See Gopnik, *Warhol,* 10n72; and Elaine Rusinko, "The Woman Behind the Artist: Andy Warhol's Mother," *Slovo,* Summer 2016, 28.
29. Bockris, *Warhol,* 38.
30. Gopnik, *Warhol,* 26.
31. Bockris, *Warhol,* 38; for the importance of popular culture for queer children, see Eve Kosofsky Sedgwick, "Queer and Now," in *Tendencies* (London: Routledge, 1994), 3.
32. Rusinko, "The Woman Behind the Artist," 27.
33. Rebecca Wanzo, "Precarious-Girl Comedy: Issa Rae, Lena Dunham, & Abjection Aesthetics," in *Abjection Incorporated: Mediating the Politics of Pleasure & Violence,* ed. Maggie Hennefeld and Nicholas Sammond (Cambridge: Cambridge University Press, 2020), 83.
34. Bockris, *Warhol,* 39, 40.
35. Cary Wolfe, "Exposures," in *Philosophy and Animal Life,* ed. Stanley Cavell, Cora Diamond, John McDowell, Ian Hacking, and Cary Wolfe (New York: Columbia University Press, 2008), 8.
36. Bockris, *Warhol,* 40.
37. Ann Elachko Madden quoted in Colacello, *Holy Terror,* 23.
38. Anna Lemak quoted in Gopnik, *Warhol,* 37.
39. Tony Scherman and David Dalton, *Pop: The Genius of Andy Warhol* (New York: Harper, 2009), 8.
40. Bill Shaffer quoted in Bockris, *Warhol,* 55–56. Gopnik has found evidence to dispute Shaffer's assumption; see *Warhol,* 334.
41. Winnicott, "A Case Managed at Home," 124.
42. Paul Warhola mentions this suspicion, without referencing the stereotypes, in Bockris, *Warhol,* 45.
43. John Warhola quoted in Bockris, 45.
44. Bockris, 46.
45. Jacques Derrida, *The Animal That Therefore I Am,* ed. Marie-Louise Mallet, trans. David Wills (New York: Fordham University Press, 2008), 129; I will return to this claim in chapter 3.
46. Sharon Patricia Holland, *The Erotic Life of Racism* (Durham, NC: Duke University Press, 2012), 110. For the "hybrid sexuality" of plants, see Prudence Gibson, *The Plant Contract: Art's Return to Vegetal Life* (Leiden: Brill Rodopi, 2018), 14.
47. Bockris, *Warhol,* 46.
48. Bockris, 47–48.
49. See Giorgio Agamben, *Homo Sacer: Sovereign Power and Bare Life,* trans. Daniel Heller-Roazen (Stanford, CA: Stanford University Press, 1998).
50. Julia Kristeva, *Powers of Horror: An Essay on Abjection,* trans. Leon S. Roudiez (New York: Columbia University Press, 1982), 12–13; emphasis in original; cited in Kelly Oliver, *Animal Lessons: How They Teach Us to Be Human* (New York: Columbia University Press, 2009), 281. Kristeva touched on Warhol briefly in a later work, placing his *Marilyn* paintings in a lineage of horrific images that she traced back through Picasso to Grünewald. Kristeva, *The Severed Head: Capital*

Visions, trans. Jody Gladding (New York: Columbia University Press, 2012), 103–4. For Warhol and the abject, see Christopher Schmidt, "From A to B and Back Again: Warhol, Recycling, Writing," *Interval(le)s* 2, no. 2; 3, no. 3 (Fall 2008/Winter 2008/9): 794–809; Gustavus Stadler, "'My Wife': The Tape Recorder and Warhol's Queer Ways of Listening," *Criticism* 56, no. 3 (Summer 2014): 425–56; and Bruce Hainley, "Urine Sample," in *Andy Warhol: Piss & Sex Paintings and Drawings* (New York: Gagosian Gallery, 2002), 4–9.

51. Oliver, *Animal Lessons*, 281; I am grateful to Wright Cronin for pointing out the importance of the semiotic/symbolic shift here.
52. Julia Kristeva, *Hatred and Forgiveness* (New York: Columbia University Press, 2010), 185.
53. Ruth Lipschitz, "Skin/ned Politics: Species Discourse and the Limits of 'The Human' in Nandipha Mntambo's Art," *Hypatia* 27, no. 3 (Summer 2012): 556.
54. See Judith Butler, *Bodies That Matter: On the Discursive Limits of "Sex"* (New York: Routledge, 1993); and Iris Marion Young, "Abjection and Oppression: Dynamics of Unconscious Racism, Sexism, and Homophobia," in *Crises in Continental Philosophy*, ed. Arleen B. Dallery and Charles E. Scott (Albany: SUNY Press, 1990) 201–13.
55. Imogen Tyler, *Revolting Subjects: Social Abjection and Resistance in Neoliberal Britain* (New York: Zed Books, 2013), 32–35. For Oliver, Kristeva's analysis is ultimately undermined by its anthropocentrism: it "constantly risks erasing animals by making them into nothing more than stand-ins for the maternal body." Oliver, *Animal Lessons*, 302.
56. Young, "Abjection and Oppression," 207.
57. Gopnik, *Warhol*, 24. Wayne Koestenbaum argues that the colostomy played a formative role in Warhol's artistic development. Koestenbaum, *Andy Warhol: A Biography*, 28. For the role of the father in Kristeva's theory, see Elaine P. Miller, *Head Cases: Julia Kristeva on Philosophy and Art in Depressed Times* (New York: Columbia University Press, 2014), 148–50.
58. Wanzo, "Precarious-Girl Comedy," 65.
59. Butler, *Bodies That Matter*, xxviii.
60. Stockton, *The Queer Child*, 91. See also Gustav Stadler, who argues that by focusing his artistic attention on childhood, "Warhol may have been resisting a kind of identity-politics logic, emergent in the homophile movement, that positioned self-realization—a form of coming into maturity—as a political goal." Stadler, "'My Wife,'" 441.
61. Max Nordau, *Degeneration* (New York: Appleton, 1895), 315; see Stockton, *The Queer Child*, 23.
62. Nordau, *Degeneration*, 10.
63. Gopnik, *Warhol*, 38.
64. Gopnik, 105.
65. Balcomb Greene, "Basic Concepts for Teaching Art," *College Art Journal* 8, no. 1 (Autumn 1948): 30; for Warhol's attendance, see Gopnik, *Warhol*, 44.
66. Greene, "Basic Concepts for Teaching Art," 33.
67. Nordau, *Degeneration*, 554; cited in Stockton, *The Queer Child*, 23.
68. Nordau, *Degeneration*, 555. David L. Eng points out that similar prejudices lie at the core of Freud's *Totem and Taboo*, which claims that "[p]rimitive men . . . are uninhibited: thought passes directly into action." Eng, *Racial Castration: Managing Masculinity in Asian America* (Durham, NC: Duke University Press, 2001), 9. See also Sigmund Freud, *Totem and Taboo: Some Points of Agreement between the Mental Lives of Savages and Neurotics*, trans. James Strachey (London: Routledge, 2001), 187.
69. Both quoted in Gopnik, *Warhol*, 45.
70. Sándor Ferenczi, "Embarrassed Hands" [1914], trans. John Rickman, *Further Contributions to the Theory and Technique of Psycho-Analysis* (London: Karnac Books, 2002), 316; D.W. Winnicott,

"A Note on Normality and Anxiety," in *Through Paediatrics to Psycho-Analysis: Collected Papers* (London: Routledge, 2001), 18.

71. Melanie Klein, *The Psychoanalysis of Children,* trans. Alix Strachey (New York: Grove Press, 1960), 144.
72. Gopnik, *Warhol,* 78.
73. Bockris, *Warhol,* 97.
74. Melanie Klein argued that "children often show a kind of over-liveliness which often goes along with an overbearing and defiant manner." Klein, *The Psychoanalysis of Children,* 144.
75. Peter Brook, "These Amazing Street Photos Show 20 Years of New York's Gritty Glam Era—Through One Woman's Eyes," *Timeline,* October 30, 2017, accessed November 1, 2019, https://timeline.com/new-york-photography-boretz-4bd72bbd202b.
76. Melanie Klein, "The Importance of Symbol-Formation in the Development of the Ego," in *Love, Guilt, and Reparation and Other Works 1921–1945*, vol. I of *The Writings of Melanie Klein* (New York: Free Press, 1984), 232.
77. Gopnik, *Warhol,* 30.
78. Quoted in Comenas, "Andy Warhol: From Nowhere to Up There," 17.
79. Eve Kosofsky Sedgwick, "Queer Performativity: Warhol's Shyness/Warhol's Whiteness," in *Pop Out: Queer Warhol,* ed. Jennifer Doyle, Jonathan Flatley, and José Esteban Muñoz (Durham, NC: Duke University Press, 1996), 141.
80. As Trevor Fairbrother would later put it, "[H]omosexuals were an invisible minority in the larger world, yet tolerated as a sub-group in a few professions—dance, theater, and the fine and applied arts." Quoted in Comenas, "Andy Warhol: From Nowhere to Up There," 13. Fairbrother also notes that Warhol "was attuned to the increasingly public debate about the status of gays in society," pointing out that a 1953 copy of "ONE, the first continuously published American gay magazine," was found in a box of 1950s ephemera in the Warhol archives. Quoted in Comenas, "Andy Warhol: From Nowhere to Up There," 17.
81. In the photograph, a male figure at the lower left almost approximates the checkered figure's posture; perhaps the gingham dress worn by the woman posed beside him inspired (or was inspired by) that figure's gridded skin.
82. Alice Kuzniar, "'I Married My Dog': On Queer Canine Literature," in *Queering the Non/Human,* ed. Noreen Giffney and Myra Hird (Hampshire, UK: Ashgate, 2008), 224.
83. Bockris, *Warhol,* 2; Freud, *Totem and Taboo,* 147; see the discussion of this passage in Oliver, *Animal Lessons,* 252–53.
84. Sigmund Freud, *Civilization and Its Discontents,* trans. James Strachey (New York: Norton, 1962), 47; cited in Kuzniar, "'I Married My Dog,'" 207.
85. Kristeva, *Powers of Horror,* 58.
86. Elissa Marder, *The Mother in the Age of Mechanical Reproduction: Psychoanalysis, Photography, Deconstruction* (New York: Fordham University Press, 2012), 2, 3.
87. Colacello, *Holy Terror,* 265.
88. Stadler, "My Wife," 426; Ellen Lupton and J. Abbott Miller, "Line Art: Andy Warhol and the Commercial Art World of the 1950s," in *"Success Is a Job in New York . . .": The Early Art and Business of Andy Warhol,* ed. Donna De Salvo (Pittsburgh: Carnegie Museum of Art, 1989), 32.
89. Schmidt, "From A to B and Back Again," 804.
90. Charles Giuliano, "Gerard Malanga on Andy Warhol's Mother Julia: Insights to Mother and Son Collaborations at WCMA," Berkshire Fine Arts, June 4, 2015, accessed November 1, 2019, https://www.berkshirefinearts.com/06-04-2015_gerard-malanga-on-andy-warhol-s-mother-julia.htm.
91. Albert Goldman quoted in Bockris, *Warhol,* 68.

92. Gopnik, *Warhol,* 55–57.
93. Quoted in Bockris, *Warhol,* 68; see Nicholas de Villiers, *Opacity and the Closet: Queer Tactics in Foucault, Barthes, and Warhol* (Minneapolis: University of Minnesota Press, 2012).
94. Perry Davis and Warhol quoted in Bockris, *Warhol,* 71.
95. Vollmer quoted in Gopnik, *Warhol,* 54.
96. Benjamin Fong, *Death and Mastery: Psychoanalytic Drive Theory and the Subject of Late Capitalism* (New York: Columbia University Press, 2016), 47.
97. Gopnik, *Warhol,* 79, 93, 94.
98. Gopnik, 99.
99. Catherine Johnson, *Thank You Andy Warhol* (New York: Glitterati, 2012), 38; Bockris, *Warhol,* 85.
100. See, for example, Chad Heap, *Slumming: Sexual and Racial Encounters in American Nightlife* (Chicago: University of Chicago Press, 2009); and George Chauncey, *Gay New York: Gender, Culture, and the Making of the Gay Male World, 1890–1940* (New York: Basic Books, 1994).
101. Gopnik, *Warhol,* 103.
102. Warhol quoted in Bockris, *Warhol,* 86.
103. Johnson, *Thank You Andy Warhol,* 18.
104. Charles Darwin, *The Formation of Vegetable Mould, through the Action of Worms, with Observations of Their Habits* (London: John Murray, 1881), 1; Jane Bennett, *Vibrant Matter: A Political Ecology of Things* (Durham, NC: Duke University Press, 2010), 21; see also Meijer, *When Animals Speak,* 153–56.
105. Johnson, *Thank You Andy Warhol,* 18.
106. Bockris, *Warhol,* 96.
107. Bockris, 97.
108. Quoted in Gopnik, *Warhol,* 136.
109. Bockris, *Warhol,* 96.
110. Quoted in Gopnik, *Warhol,* 121.
111. Gopnik, 121.
112. Bockris, *Warhol,* 24.
113. Steven Watson, *Factory Made: Warhol and the Sixties* (New York: Pantheon, 2003), 28.
114. Giuliano, "Gerard Malanga on Andy Warhol's Mother Julia."
115. Jordan Crandall, "Andy Warhol" [1986], in *I'll Be Your Mirror: The Selected Andy Warhol Interviews,* ed. Kenneth Goldsmith (New York: Carroll & Graf, 2004), 370–71.
116. Watson, *Factory Made,* 28.
117. Quoted in Bockris, *Warhol,* 361. Tennessee Williams described Warhol as "a lost little boy, lost in time." Quoted in Bockris, 362.
118. Gopnik, *Warhol,* 86–87.
119. Watson, *Factory Made,* 26.
120. Watson, 26.
121. Lucy Mulroney, *Andy Warhol, Publisher* (Chicago: University of Chicago Press, 2018), 9.
122. Koestenbaum, *Andy Warhol,* 42.
123. Quoted in Gopnik, *Warhol,* 59.
124. On snakes and homosexuality in Warhol's work, see Reva Wolf, *Andy Warhol, Poetry, and Gossip in the 1960s* (Chicago: University of Chicago Press, 1997), 69–70.
125. Sigmund Freud, *Three Essays on the Theory of Sexuality,* trans. James Strachey (New York: Basic Books, 2000), 88; quoted in Elizabeth Lunbeck, *The Americanization of Narcissism* (Cambridge, MA: Harvard University Press, 2014), 89.
126. Lunbeck, *The Americanization of Narcissism,* 89.

127. Bockris, *Warhol*, 29, 36. Colacello says Julia learned to speak English later in life. Colacello, *Holy Terror*, 73.
128. Comenas, "Andy Warhol: From Nowhere to Up There," 13.
129. Watson, *Factory Made*, 30.
130. Gopnik, *Warhol*, 136.
131. Warhol was attentive to animal smells. He would later describe the Stable Gallery as having been "an actual stable where rich people kept their horses, and in the spring when the wetness was in the air, you could still smell the horse piss, because that's a smell that never goes away." Warhol and Hackett, *Popism*, 30.
132. Matt Wrbican, "Meeooaaww-AW-AWW," in *Andy Warhol | Ai Weiwei*, ed. Max Delany and Eric C. Shiner (New Haven, CT: Yale University Press, 2016), 262; Mulroney, *Andy Warhol, Publisher*, 24.
133. Gopnik, *Warhol*, 183n94.
134. Wrbican, "Meeooaaww-AW-AWW," 263.
135. Gopnik, *Warhol*, 183n93.
136. Gopnik, 137.
137. Quoted in Wrbican, "Meeooaaww-AW-AWW," 263.
138. Robert Fleisher quoted in Gary Comenas, "Andy Warhol Pre-Pop," accessed November 11, 2020, https://warholstars.org/warhol1/4imperfection.html.
139. Wrbican, "Meeooaaww-AW-AWW," 265.
140. See discussion in Koestenbaum, *Andy Warhol*, 43.
141. Quoted in Mulroney, *Andy Warhol, Publisher*, 581.
142. Koestenbaum, *Andy Warhol*, 41.
143. Quoted in Scherman and Dalton, *Pop: The Genius of Andy Warhol*, 20.
144. See Richard Meyer, "Warhol's Clones," *Yale Journal of Criticism* 7, no. 1 (1994): 79–109.
145. Quoted in Gopnik, *Warhol*, 136.
146. Schmidt, "From A to B and Back Again," 803; Koestenbaum, *Andy Warhol*, 28–29.
147. Andy Warhol, *The Andy Warhol Diaries*, ed. Pat Hackett (New York: Warner Books, 1989), 325. Koestenbaum discusses this passage in his fascinating biography of Warhol (*Andy Warhol*, 35–38), but the book's anthropocentric emphasis on Warhol's "one conundrum: what does it mean to exist in a body, next to another person, who also exists in a body?" (11) seems to preclude any serious consideration of Warhol's relationships with nonhuman animals.
148. Quoted in Warhol and Hackett, *Popism*, 6.
149. See, for example, Arthur Danto, *Andy Warhol* (New Haven, CT: Yale University Press, 2010), 15–17, 33, 37, 131. For more on de Antonio, see Joseph, "1962." Hal Foster has pointed out that the de Antonio legend obscures the real complexities of Warhol's paintings; see Foster, "Andy Warhol, or the Distressed Image," in *The First Pop Age* (Princeton, NJ: Princeton University Press, 2012), 120–46.
150. Warhol and Hackett, *Popism*, 6.
151. Goldsmith, *I'll Be Your Mirror*, 96. Parts of this quote would also be reproduced in the catalogue for Warhol's 1968 retrospective.
152. Andy Warhol, *a: a novel* (New York: Grove Press, 1998), 344. In the words of Ondine, one of Warhol's central Superstars, "Andy was the queen of passivity . . . the absolute son of nonexistence. He was just divinely not there." Quoted in Jean Stein, *Edie: American Girl*, ed. with George Plimpton (New York: Grove Press, 1994), 214. This profound apathy forms the counterweight to what Jonathan Flatley describes as Warhol's propensity for "liking things"; see Flatley, *Like Andy Warhol* (Chicago: University of Chicago Press, 2017).
153. Derrida, *The Animal That Therefore I Am*, 15–21. See also Irus Braverman, who points out that, in zoos, "[n]aming . . . is an instance of caring for the animal and thus of exerting pastoral power

over it." Braverman, *Zooland: The Institution of Captivity* (Stanford, CA: Stanford Law Books, 2013), 98.

154. For the desexualizing consequences of pet "neutering," see Clare Palmer, "'Taming the Wild Profusion of Existing Things'? A Study of Foucault, Power, and Human/Animal Relationships," in *Foucault and Animals*, ed. Matthew Chrulew and Dinesh Joseph Wadiwel (Leiden: Brill, 2017), 127–28.
155. Hervé Guibert, *Ghost Image*, trans. Robert Bononno (Chicago: University of Chicago Press, 1996), 11.
156. Quoted in Bockris, *Warhol*, 361.
157. Glenn O'Brien, "Interview: Andy Warhol" [1977], in *I'll Be Your Mirror: The Selected Andy Warhol Interviews*, ed. Kenneth Goldsmith (New York: Carroll & Graf, 2004), 259.
158. Ann Curran, "CMU's Other Andy," *Carnegie-Mellon Magazine*, Spring 1985, 16.
159. Gopnik, *Warhol*, 199.
160. Comenas, "Andy Warhol: From Nowhere to Up There," 19.
161. Bockris, *Warhol*, 40; undertaker's apprentice quoted in Colacello, *Holy Terror*, 21.
162. Warhol, *The Philosophy of Andy Warhol*, 71.
163. Quoted in Bockris, *Warhol*, 133.
164. Quoted in Bockris, 133.
165. Koestenbaum argues that the fantasy of "having a pussy . . . impelled [Warhol's] gargantuan productivity." Koestenbaum, *Andy Warhol*, 41.
166. Bockris, *Warhol*, 133.
167. Martha C. Nussbaum, *Hiding from Humanity: Disgust, Shame, and the Law* (Princeton, NJ: Princeton University Press, 2004), 173.
168. Nussbaum, 14.
169. Sedgwick, "Queer Performativity," 135; this crucial essay does not explore the Kristevian links between shame, animality, and maternal abjection.
170. Rusinko, "The Woman behind the Artist," 30.
171. The first two elements of this combination—daughter and husband (but not animal)—are reminiscent of traditional etiologies of transsexuality and cross-dressing; see Robert J. Stoller, *Sex and Gender: The Development of Masculinity and Femininity* (London: Karnac Books, 1984), 264. For a thoughtful meditation on Warhol's interest in drag that does not touch on Stoller or animal life, see Hilton Als, "Mother," in *The Warhol Look: Glamour, Style, Fashion*, ed. Mark Francis (New York: Bulfinch, 1997), 212–17.
172. For a sophisticated analysis of this pursuit, see Robert E. Haywood, *Allan Kaprow and Claes Oldenburg: Art, Happenings, and Cultural Politics* (New Haven, CT: Yale University Press, 2017).

2. FACTORY BADLANDS

1. Danto, *Andy Warhol*, 77; Danto included *Empire* in this category as well.
2. Lester Bangs, "Of Pop and Pies and Fun," in *Psychotic Reactions and Carburetor Dung: The Work of a Legendary Critic: Rock 'N' Roll as Literature and Literature as Rock 'N' Roll*, ed. Greil Marcus (New York: Anchor, 1988), 48. For the Exploding Plastic Inevitable, see Branden W. Joseph, "'My Mind Split Open': Andy Warhol's Exploding Plastic Inevitable," *Grey Room*, no. 8 (Summer 2002): 80–107.
3. On this ambivalent egalitarianism, see Grudin, *Warhol's Working Class*.
4. Gopnik, *Warhol*, 355.
5. Quoted in Guy Trebay and Ruth La Ferla, "Tales from the Warhol Factory," *New York Times*, November 12, 2018, accessed November 1, 2019, www.nytimes.com/2018/11/12/style/andy-warhol-factory-history.html.

6. Ronald Tavel quoted in Bockris, *Warhol,* 214.
7. The first attempt to catalogue and analyze Warhol's relationship to drug use is Michael Angelo Tata's "Andy Warhol: When Junkies Ruled the World," *Nebula* 2, no. 2 (June 2005): 76–112. Unfortunately, it has remained almost completely uncited in subsequent criticism.
8. Quoted in Chelsea Weathers, "Drugtime," *Criticism* 56, no. 3 (Summer 2014): 664.
9. Colacello, *Holy Terror,* 66. As Bockris put it, "[W]hile everyone else mixed speed and grass and LSD, which made everything softer and more confused, Andy didn't give up the speed for a second." Bockris, *Warhol,* 207. A factory compatriot described Obetrols as "a good high, very gay, very lovely speed." Gopnik, *Warhol,* 310. Gopnik has unearthed a film from this period "that shows the impish poet Taylor Mead prancing around the Lexington town house as, butler-like, Warhol serves him a bottle of speed on a tray"—it is, Gopnik remarks, one of the rare times Warhol appears in his own films (310).
10. Quoted in Bockris, *Warhol,* 452.
11. For recent studies of animals and film, see Claire Molloy, *Popular Media and Animals* (Basingstoke, UK, and New York: Palgrave Macmillan, 2011); Adrian J. Ivakhiv, *Ecologies of the Moving Image: Cinema, Affect, Nature* (Waterloo, ON: Wilfred Laurier University Press, 2013); Anat Pick and Guinevere Narraway, eds., *Screening Nature: Cinema beyond the Human* (New York and Oxford: Berghahn, 2013); Adrienne L. McLean, ed., *Cinematic Canines: Dogs and Their Work in the Fiction Film* (New Brunswick, NJ, and London: Rutgers University Press, 2014); and Michael Lawrence and Karen Lury, eds., *The Zoo: Images of Exhibition and Encounter* (New York: Palgrave Macmillan, 2015).
12. Siegel, *Intoxication,* 206, 209.
13. Siegel, 13. See also Giorgio Samorini, *Animals and Psychedelics: The Natural World and the Instinct to Alter Consciousness,* trans. Tami Calliope (Rochester, VT: Park Street Press, 2002).
14. Gilles Deleuze and Félix Guattari, *A Thousand Plateaus: Capitalism and Schizophrenia,* trans. Brian Massumi (Minneapolis: University of Minnesota Press, 1987), 115.
15. Gopnik, *Warhol,* 357, 356.
16. Richard Hüelsenbeck quoted in Gopnik, 279.
17. Lester Bangs, "Kraftwerkfeature," in *Psychotic Reactions and Carburetor Dung: The Work of a Legendary Critic: Rock 'N' Roll as Literature and Literature as Rock 'N' Roll,* ed. Greil Marcus (New York: Anchor, 1988), 154–55.
18. Bangs, 155.
19. See Derrida, *The Animal That Therefore I Am,* 38–39, 74, 101, 119.
20. Lundblad, *The Birth of a Jungle,* 2. Drug use fits more plausibly within contemporary theories of evolution advanced by Manuel DeLanda and Richard Iveson, in which selection for mutation [is] necessarily nonlinear insofar as innovation depends upon strong mutual interactions (or feedback) between components," and therefore "[*b*]*eings can only* be *by being other than what they* are." Iveson, "Technology," *Edinburgh Companion to Animal Studies,* 509, 510; emphasis in original.
21. Theodor Adorno, *In Search of Wagner,* trans. Rodney Livingstone (London: Verso, 2005), 89.
22. Koch, *Stargazer,* 84.
23. Koch, 76.
24. Koch, 51.
25. Parker Tyler, "Drugtime and Dragtime or, Film a la Warhol," *Evergreen Review* 11, no. 46 (1967): 87.
26. Parker Tyler, "Warhol: Horrible or Beautiful Film Maker?" Harry Ransom Center, Parker Tyler Collection, uncatalogued box 2, n.d., 4–5; quoted in Weathers, "Drugtime," 666.
27. Juan A. Suárez, "Warhol's 1960s' Films, Amphetamine, and Queer Materiality," *Criticism* 56, no. 3 (Summer 2014): 633.

28. Suárez, 642.
29. Suárez, 639.
30. Weathers, "Drugtime," 665; emphasis in original; Elizabeth Freeman, *Time Binds: Queer Temporalities, Queer Histories* (Durham, NC: Duke University Press, 2010), 3. For Warhol's relationship to chrononormativity, see also Homay King, "Girl Interrupted: The Queer Time of Warhol's Cinema," *Discourse* 28, no. 1 (Winter 2006): 98–120; and Stadler, "'My Wife,'" 440-41.
31. Weathers, "Drugtime," 675, 676.
32. Warhol and Hackett, *Popism,* 197.
33. Pettman, "Affection," 35.
34. Louis Black, "On Ondine on Film: The Pope and the Artist, the Hotel and the Factory," *Austin Chronicle,* October 17, 2003, accessed November 1, 2019, www.austinchronicle.com/screens/2003-10-17/182197.
35. Warhol quoted in Callie Angell, "Batman and Dracula: The Collaborations of Jack Smith and Andy Warhol," *Criticism* 56, no. 2 (Spring 2014): 160. After their friendship disintegrated, Smith took to referring to Warhol as "Andy Panda," apparently because he "pandered to the art market." Constantine Verevis, *Flaming Creatures* (New York: Columbia University Press, 2020), 96.
36. Wolf, *Andy Warhol, Poetry, and Gossip,* 45.
37. Wolf, 45, 46.
38. Rick Setlove, *Variety,* quoted in "The Beard," Michael McClure website, accessed November 1, 2020, https://michael-mcclure.com/work/books/the-beard.
39. Gary Comenas, "Andy Warhol, Michael McClure and The Beard," accessed November 1, 2019, https://warholstars.org/michael_mcclure_beard.html.
40. Comenas.
41. Gopnik, *Warhol,* 421.
42. Quoted in Douglas Crimp, *"Our Kind of Movie": The Films of Andy Warhol* (Cambridge, MA: MIT Press, 2014),154n20. In his emphasis on the historical queerness of cowboys, Tavel anticipated Hiram Pérez's recent work on cowboys as "enduring objects of queer desire, prototypes for subcultures of gay clones," but also on their "unexpectedly queer, proletarian cosmopolitanism"—although bestiality does not figure in Pérez's analysis. Pérez, *A Taste for Brown Bodies: Gay Modernity and Cosmopolitan Desire* (New York: NYU Press, 2015), 9.
43. See J.J. Murphy, *The Black Hole of the Camera: The Films of Andy Warhol* (Berkeley: University of California Press, 2012), 67–73.
44. Patrick S. Smith, *Warhol: Conversations about the Artist* (Ann Arbor, MI: UMI Research Press, 1988), 309.
45. Tavel quoted in Crimp, *Our Kind of Movie,* 62.
46. Tavel quoted in Smith, *Warhol: Conversations about the Artist,* 310; emphasis in original.
47. Tavel quoted in Smith, 498.
48. Tavel quoted in Smith, 310.
49. Tavel quoted in Smith, 311.
50. Tavel quoted in Smith, 311.
51. Tavel quoted in Smith, 310. Tavel doesn't seem to have been aware that these musings on "racial memory" (310) had been inspired by a member of the Nazi party. He makes no mention of Lorenz's party membership, which hadn't been widely publicized at the time of his interview, in 1978. Bestiality, S&M, and Nazism would be explicitly connected in Warhol's *Bike Boy* (1967–68); see Murphy, *Black Hole of the Camera,* 200.
52. Crimp, *Our Kind of Movie,* 61.
53. Crimp, 61.
54. Neither Crimp nor Murphy addresses Warhol's interest in animals.

55. Jennifer Sichel, ed., "'What Is Pop Art?': A Revised Transcript of Gene Swenson's 1963 Interview with Andy Warhol," *Oxford Art Journal* 41, no. 1 (March 2018): 94.
56. Smith, *Warhol: Conversations about the Artist*, 312, 302.
57. See Murphy, *Black Hole of the Camera*, 39–40.
58. Angell, "Batman and Dracula," 176.
59. See Murphy, *Black Hole of the Camera*, 113–15.
60. Warhol and Hackett, *Popism*, 373–74.
61. Newlove, "Prothalamion for Wet Harmonica and Johnny Stompanato," 20.
62. Holland, *The Erotic Life of Racism*, 110. Warhol's interest in these themes may have been stimulated by his reverence for Luis Buñuel, whose films explored similar subjects, and whose "vast . . . talent" left him "practically speechless." Gopnik, *Warhol*, 695. See Jo Evans, "Luis Buñuel's Missing Dog and Other Animals: *Un Chien andalou* (1929), *L'Âge d'or* (1930) and *Las Hurdes: Tierra sin pan* (1933)," *Bulletin of Spanish Visual Studies* 1, no. 1 (2017): 117–37.
63. Kristeva, *Powers of Horror*, 12–13.
64. Whitney Davis, *Queer Beauty: Sexuality and Aesthetics from Winckelmann to Freud and Beyond* (New York: Columbia University Press, 2010), 226.
65. Shukin, *Animal Capital*, 84.
66. Newlove, "Prothalamion for Wet Harmonica and Johnny Stompanato," 23, 22.
67. See Chelsea Lea Weathers, "Andy Warhol's Cinema beyond the Lens" (PhD diss., University of Texas at Austin, 2013), for a thorough and sophisticated analysis of this film. Another character in the film declares, "You gotta have something . . . that just comes like animal. You know, uh, we're all animals."
68. Hunter Drohojowska-Philp, "A Chelsea Girl Still Bewitched by Warhol," *Los Angeles Times*, August 11, 2002, accessed November 15, 2020, www.latimes.com/archives/la-xpm-2002-aug-11-ca-hunter11-story.html.
69. Ronald Tavel, "Introduction," *Hanoi Hanna, Radio Star (Chelsea Girls)*, screenplay, 6.
70. Mary Woronov, *Swimming Underground: My Years in the Warhol Factory* (London: Serpent's Tail Press, 1995), 34.
71. MoMA, "Queen of China (Hanoi Hanna). 1966. Directed by Andy Warhol," accessed November 1, 2019, https://www.moma.org/calendar/events/4352.
72. Woronov, *Swimming Underground*, 40.
73. Koch, *Stargazer*, 91.
74. Woronov, *Swimming Underground*, 42.
75. Gilles Deleuze, *Coldness and Cruelty*, trans. Jean McNeil (New York: Zone Books, 1991), 40.
76. Anonymous Factory "newcomer" quoted in Bockris, *Warhol*, 206.
77. Stockton, *The Queer Child*, 4.
78. Marquis de Sade, *The Complete Justine Philosophy in the Bedroom & Other Writings*, trans. Richard Seaver and Austryn Wainhouse (New York: Grove Press, 1965), 253; Deleuze and Guattari, *A Thousand Plateaus*, 155–56.
79. Smith, *Warhol: Conversations about the Artist*, 303; Viva quoted in Gopnik, *Warhol*, 546. As Fong has shown, "children come to attempt to *engulf* others, to express an *omnipotence* over them, because they themselves have felt engulfed in the same way." Fong, *Death and Mastery*, 128; emphasis in original.
80. John Hallowell, *The Truth Game* (New York: Simon & Schuster, 1969), 251; quoted in Gopnik, *Warhol*, 637.
81. Quoted in Smith, *Warhol: Conversations about the Artist*, 185.
82. Georges Bataille, "Abjection and Miserable Forms," in *More & Less* 2, ed. Sylvère Lotringer, trans. Yvonne Shafir (Cambridge, MA: MIT Press, 1993), 13.

83. Maggie Hennefeld and Nicholas Sammond, "Not It, or, The Abject Objection," in *Abjection Incorporated: Mediating the Politics of Pleasure and Violence,* ed. Maggie Hennefeld and Nicholas Sammond (Durham, NC: Duke University Press), 4.
84. Quoted in Gopnik, *Warhol,* 549.
85. Taro Nettleton, "White-on-White: The Overbearing Whiteness of Warhol Being," in *Gay Shame,* ed. David M. Halperin and Valerie Traub (Chicago: University of Chicago Press, 2010), 77.
86. Gopnik, *Warhol,* 550.
87. Gopnik, 550.
88. Quoted in Bess Levin, "Trump's Toilet Obsession Just Took a Dark Turn," *Vanity Fair,* February 10, 2022, accessed February 11, 2022, https://www.vanityfair.com/news/2022/02/donald-trump-clogged-toilets.
89. Quoted in Bockris, *Warhol,* 205. Following Lucienne Frappier-Mazur, one might argue that, like Sade, Warhol "occupies both the place of the tyrant-father and that of the revolutionary parricide." Frappier-Mazur, "A Turning Point in the Sadean Novel: The Terror," in *Must We Burn Sade?,* ed. Frappier-Mazur (Amherst, MA: Humanity Books, 1999), 122.
90. Bockris, *Warhol,* 205.
91. Smith, *Warhol: Conversations about the Artist,* 268.
92. Smith, 183.
93. Weathers, "Drugtime," 662
94. Woronov, *Swimming Underground,* 39.
95. [Glenn O'Brien], "Factory Workers Warholites Remember: Billy Name," *Interview,* November 30, 2008, accessed November 1, 2019, http://www.interviewmagazine.com/culture/factory-workers-warholites-remember-billy-name/; [Glenn O'Brien], introduction to *Billy Name: The Silver Age* (London: Reel Art Press, 2014), xx.
96. Ondine quoted in Smith, *Warhol: Conversations about the Artist,* 268.
97. Smith, 243; [O'Brien], "Factory Workers Warholites Remember: Billy Name."
98. [O'Brien], "Factory Workers Warholites Remember: Billy Name."
99. Gopnik, *Warhol,* 350.
100. Soren Angenoux quoted in Watson, *Factory Made,* 59.
101. Quoted in Gopnik, *Warhol,* 700.
102. Gustavus Stadler, personal correspondence with author, 2013.
103. Warhol and Hackett, *Popism,* 80, 82. See the discussion between Warhol and Ondine in *a: a novel* regarding "get[ting] Billy back at the Factory" in order to "get rid of sloppiness." Warhol, *a: a novel,* 332.
104. Quoted in Smith, *Warhol: Conversations about the Artist,* 269.
105. Michel Auder, *Chelsea Girls with Andy Warhol,* black-and-white video, 1976.
106. Warhol, *The Philosophy of Andy Warhol,* 93. For an analysis of the repercussions of this approach on its participants, see Stefan Brecht, *Queer Theatre (Diaries, Letters, and Essays)* (Frankfurt am Main: Suhrkamp, 1978), 113–15; cited in Jon Davies, *Trash: A Queer Film Classic* (Vancouver, BC: Arsenal Pulp Press, 2009), 156.
107. "Glamour at Home: Cook with Cans," *Glamour,* May 1964, 169; cited in Scherman and Dalton, *Pop: The Genius of Andy Warhol,* 197.
108. Warhol, *The Philosophy of Andy Warhol,* 145.
109. [Michael Andre], "Andy Warhol's Interview," *Unmuzzled Ox* 4, no. 2 (1976): 44.
110. Richard Doyle, *Darwin's Pharmacy: Sex, Plants, and the Evolution of the Noösphere* (Seattle: University of Washington Press, 2011), 13.

111. Quoted in Stein, *Edie: American Girl,* 214. Warhol would later deny this story: "Someone thought they slipped [acid] to me once, but I wasn't eating." O'Brien, "Interview: Andy Warhol," 251.
112. Quoted in [O'Brien], "Factory Workers Warholites Remember: Billy Name,".
113. Valerie Solanas, *S.C.U.M.: Society for Cutting Up Men Manifesto* (New York: Olympia Press, 1968), 37.
114. Gopnik, *Warhol,* 613.
115. As reported in Tony Ortega, "Andy Warhol Shot by Factory Actress Valerie Solanas," *Village Voice* 13, no. 34 (June 6, 1968), accessed November 1, 2019, http://blogs.villagevoice.com/runninscared/2010/05/andy_warhol_sho.php.
116. Pat Hackett, introduction to Warhol, *The Andy Warhol Diaries,* xiii.
117. Koch, *Stargazer,* 15.
118. Quoted in John Leonard, "The Return of Andy Warhol," *New York Times,* November 10, 1968, 147. As Hal Foster has argued, "an intense imagining, via the creaturely, of new social links" can arise "whenever the symbolic order cracks under political pressure." Foster, "I Am the Decider," *London Review of Books* 33, no. 6 (March 17, 2011): 32, accessed July 7, 2019, https://www.lrb.co.uk/the-paper/v33/n06/hal-foster/i-am-the-decider.
119. Colacello, *Holy Terror,* 60.
120. Warhol, *The Philosophy of Andy Warhol,* 24.
121. Warhol, 24.
122. Warhol, 26.
123. Smith, *Warhol: Conversations about the Artist,* 303; Colacello, *Holy Terror,* 344.
124. Deleuze and Guattari, *A Thousand Plateaus,* 246.
125. Warhol, *The Andy Warhol Diaries,* 433.
126. Crandall, "Andy Warhol," 350–51.
127. Warhol, *The Andy Warhol Diaries,* 370.
128. Theodor Adorno, *Aesthetic Theory,* ed. Gretel Adorno and Rolf Tiedemann, trans. Robert Hullot-Kentor (New York: Continuum, 2002), 119.
129. Warhol, *The Andy Warhol Diaries,* 798.
130. Warhol, 405, 429, 582, 631.
131. Dawne McCance, *The Reproduction of Life Death: Derrida's La vie la mort* (New York: Fordham University Press, 2019), 95.
132. Mary Woronov, *Eyewitness to Warhol* (Los Angeles: Victoria Dailey Publisher, 2002), 8; cited in Murphy, *Black Hole of the Camera,* 2.
133. Warhol quoted in "Glamour at Home: Cook with Cans," *Glamour,* May 1964, 169; Jeffrey T. Nealon, "The Archaeology of Biopower: From Plant to Animal Life in *The Order of Things,*" in *Biopower: Foucault and Beyond,* ed. Vernon W. Cisney and Nicolae Morar (Chicago: University of Chicago Press, 2016), 139.
134. Warhol and Hackett, *Popism,* 186; see Thomas Morgan Evans, who argues that in works like the *Exploding Plastic Inevitable* and *Silver Clouds,* "one enters the Bakhtinian fray." Evans, *3D Warhol: Andy Warhol and Sculpture* (London: I.B. Tauris, 2017), 84.
135. Warhol and Hackett, *Popism,* 18.
136. Evans links these works together with Warhol's contemporaneous *Rain Machine* as evincing a "pastoral . . . quality of wistfulness . . . from the period surrounding Warhol's 'retirement.'" Evans, *3D Warhol,* 87.
137. Shukin, *Animal Capital,* 104–5. For a vivid firsthand account of the intra- and interspecies horrors of the slaughterhouse, see Charlie LeDuff, "At a Slaughterhouse, Some Things Never Die," in *Zoontologies: The Question of the Animal,* ed. Cary Wolfe (Minneapolis: University of Minnesota

Press, 2003), 183–97: "Kill-floor work is hot, quick, and bloody. The hog is herded in from the stockyard, then stunned with an electric gun. It is lifted onto a conveyor belt, dazed but not dead, and passed to a waiting group of men wearing bloodstained smocks and blank faces. They slit the neck, shackle the hind legs, and watch a machine lift the carcass into the air, letting its life flow out in a purple gush, into a steaming collection trough" (188).

138. Shukin, *Animal Capital*, 112.
139. Shukin, 104.
140. Shukin, 22. Compare Benjamin H.D. Buchloh, "Andy Warhol's One-Dimensional Art: 1956–1966," in *October Files: Andy Warhol*, ed. Annette Michelson (Cambridge, MA: MIT Press, 2001), which concludes that the *Clouds* and *Cows* represent "the farcical sacking" of "all the elements of modernism's most radical and utopian promises" (33).
141. See Mike Kelley, "Death and Transfiguration," in *Foul Perfection: Essays and Criticism*, ed. John C. Welchman (Cambridge, MA: MIT Press, 2003), 142.
142. Gopnik, *Warhol*, 537. In a recent essay, Michael Sanchez suggests that Warhol saw his Superstars as cows, and quotes him as describing the *Cows* as being "all of us." Sanchez, "Andy Warhol Inside Out," in *Andy Warhol—From A to B and Back Again*, ed. Donna De Salvo (New Haven, CT: Yale University Press, 2018), 61.
143. Quoted in William Wilson, "Warhol on L.A.: 'Everyone's Crazy,'" *Los Angeles Times*, May 11, 1970.
144. Quoted in Bockris, *Warhol*, 206.
145. Marjorie Baumgarten and Louis Black, "Ondine on Edie, on Warhol, on Ondine," *Austin Chronicle*, October 17, 2003, accessed November 1, 2019, www.austinchronicle.com/screens/2003-10-17/182251.
146. Quoted in Smith, *Warhol*, 298, 300.
147. Quoted in Bockris, *Warhol*, 214.
148. Leticia Kent, "Andy Warhol: 'I Thought Everyone Was Kidding,'" *Village Voice* 13, no. 48 (September 12, 1968): 37. Comments such as these make it difficult to fully accept Tata's defense of Warhol against the charge of being "a master manipulator," although I ultimately agree with his claim that "Warhol's affinity with [drug addicts] is the outgrowth of a deep and abiding infatuation with those individuals who actively seek out the limit situation and throw themselves into it without a care in the world." Tata, "Andy Warhol," 110.

3. MACHINES, ANIMAL AND VEGETAL

1. Quoted in Patrick S. Smith, *Andy Warhol's Art and Films* (Ann Arbor, MI: UMI Research Press, 1986), 141.
2. John Wilcock, *The Autobiography and Sex Life of Andy Warhol* (New York: Other Scenes, 1971), n.p.
3. Quoted in Wilcock, n.p.
4. Derrida, *The Animal That Therefore I Am*, 117; Michael Marder, "Seeking Refuge in the Vegetal World," in *Through Vegetal Being: Two Philosophical Perspectives*, by Luce Irigaray and Michael Marder (New York: Columbia University Press, 2018), 121. See also Marder, *Grafts*, 46.
5. Derrida, *The Animal That Therefore I Am*, 38–39.
6. As Marder points out, contemporary research on plants demonstrates that they "get involved with their environments and with one another in ways that are incredibly sophisticated, plastic and responsive—in a word, intelligent." Marder, *Grafts*, 46.
7. Warhol, *America*, 168; Warhol, *The Andy Warhol Diaries*, 279.
8. See Meijer, *When Animals Speak*, 36; and Monica Gagliano, John C. Ryan, and Patrícia Vieira, eds., *The Language of Plants: Science, Philosophy, Literature* (Minneapolis: University of Minnesota Press, 2017).

9. Warhol, *The Philosophy of Andy Warhol,* 147.
10. Warhol, 149–50.
11. Fanon, *Black Skin, White Masks,* 171; Derrida, *The Animal That Therefore I Am,* 76.
12. Koestenbaum, *Warhol,* 123; Koestenbaum clarifies that this last term, "now considered offensive, was widely used in [Warhol's] time, and . . . is an essential term in his lexicon, impossible to avoid" (123).
13. Quoted in Charlie Porter, "Andy Warhol through the Eyes of Bob Colacello," in *Andy Warhol,* ed. Gregor Muir and Yilmaz Dziewior (London: Tate Publishing, 2020),, 66.
14. Quoted in Calvin Tomkins, *The Scene: Reports on Post-Modern Art* (New York: Viking Press, 1976), 47.
15. Iveson, "Technology," 509.
16. Marder, *Plant-Thinking,* 112.
17. Jeffrey T. Nealon, *Plant Theory: Biopower & Vegetable Life* (Stanford, CA: Stanford University Press, 2016), 13.
18. Elaine P. Miller, *The Vegetative Soul: From Philosophy of Nature to Subjectivity in the Feminine* (New York: SUNY Press, 2002), 57.
19. Warhol, *The Philosophy of Andy Warhol,* 71; Warhol, *The Andy Warhol Diaries,* 279. See also Warhol, *America,* 168.
20. Andy Warhol and Pat Hackett, *Andy Warhol's Party Book* (New York: Crown, 1988), 25–26. A florist assured him that "they just keep breathing" (26).
21. Warhol, *The Philosophy of Andy Warhol,* 154.
22. Shukin, "Capitalism," 99.
23. Immanuel Kant, *Critique of the Power of Judgment,* trans. Paul Guyer and Eric Matthews (New York: Cambridge University Press, 2001), 198–99, cited in Jacques Derrida, "Economimesis," trans R. Klein, *Diacritics* 11, no. 2 (Summer 1981): 11. See Eugenie Brinkema, *The Forms of the Affects* (Durham, NC: Duke University Press, 2014), 126–29.
24. Derrida, "Economimesis," 6.
25. Quoted in Gopnik, *Warhol,* 509.
26. Kant, *Critique of the Power of Judgment,* 114.
27. Warhol, *Philosophy,* 48; Georges Bataille, "The Language of Flowers," in *Visions of Excess: Selected Writings, 1927–1939,* ed. Allan Stoekl (Minneapolis: University of Minnesota Press, 1985), 12.
28. Quoted in *Andy Warhol,* directed by Lana Jokel (1972).
29. Gerard Malanga, "Andy Warhol: Interviewed by Gerard Malanga," reprinted in Goldsmith, *I'll Be Your Mirror,* 49.
30. John Giorno, "Andy Warhol Interviewed by a Poet" [unpublished manuscript, 1963], reprinted in Goldsmith, *Mirror,* 25.
31. Jonathan Flatley has noted a dimension of Kantian disinterestedness in Warhol's collecting practices; see Flatley, "Liking Things," in *Possession Obsession: Andy Warhol and Collecting,* ed. Josh Smith (Pittsburgh: Andy Warhol Museum, 2002), 98.
32. Warhol quoted in Paul Carroll, "What's a Warhol?," *Playboy* 16, no. 9 (September 1969): 278.
33. "To relate to the thing such as it is in itself—supposing that it were possible—means apprehending it such as it is, such as it would be even if I weren't there. . . . That is why death is also such an important demarcation line." Derrida, *The Animal That Therefore I Am,* 160.
34. Quoted in Gopnik, *Warhol,* 17.
35. For a brilliant and nuanced discussion of the *Race Riot* paintings, see Flatley, *Like Andy Warhol,* 186–94.
36. Bénédicte Boisseron, *Afro-Dog: Blackness and the Animal Question* (New York: Columbia University Press, 2018), xxv–xxvi.

37. "Carnophallogocentrism" is Derrida's term; see Jean-Luc Nancy, "'Eating Well,' or the Calculation of the Subject: An Interview with Derrida," in *Who Comes after the Subject?*, ed. Eduardo Cadava, Peter Connor, and Jean-Luc Nancy (New York: Routledge, 1991), 96–119; cited in Boisseron, *Afro-Dog*, 54.
38. Boisseron, *Afro-Dog*, 71.
39. Beverley Skeggs has pointed out that a similar conceptual hierarchy has long been used to distinguish the working class from their wealthier contemporaries; see Skeggs, *Class, Self, Culture* (New York: Routledge, 2004), 38–39. See also Caroline A. Jones's discussion of Drella's functions and connotations in Jones, *Machine in the Studio: Constructing the Postwar American Artist* (Chicago: University of Chicago Press, 1998), 237–38.
40. G[ene] R. Swenson, "What Is Pop Art? Answers from 8 Painters, Part 1," *ARTnews* 62, no. 7 (1963): 27.
41. Copetas, "Beat Godfather Meets Glitter Mainman," 27.
42. Koch, *Stargazer*, 8.
43. Gopnik, *Warhol*, 860.
44. For the *Cock Book*, see Bockris, *Warhol*, 92; for the underwear store, see Emile de Antonio quoted in Stein, *Edie*, 196; for Ondine and the toilet, see Stadler, "'My Wife,'" 443–47; for the *Oxidation Paintings*, see Rosalind Krauss, "Horizontality," in Yves-Alain Bois and Rosalind Krauss, *Formless: A User's Guide* (New York: Zone Books, 2000), 102. See Bruce Hainley, "Urine Sample," in *Andy Warhol: Piss & Sex Paintings and Drawings* (New York: Gagosian Gallery, 2002), 6.
45. Warhol, *The Philosophy of Andy Warhol*, 48; Gopnik, *Warhol*, 813.
46. :Sichel, "'What Is Pop Art?'" 88.
47. Sichel, 88.
48. Gopnik has discovered that, in another 1963 interview, Warhol "insist[ed] that his talk about homosexuality be included in the printed version, only to see all such talk cut once the piece appeared." Gopnik, *Warhol*, 322.
49. Gopnik, 53.
50. Gopnik, 790; Georg Frei and Neil Printz, *The Andy Warhol Catalogue Raisonné*, vol. 2, *Paintings and Sculpture, 1964–1969* (New York: Phaidon, 2004), 8.
51. John Richardson, "The Secret Warhol: At Home with the Silver Shadow," *Vanity Fair*, July 1987, 68; later, the article mentions "a relationship with another young man," who "contracted AIDS and . . . died," and then remarks that "a girl—preferably bright, attractive, and well-born—was almost always on [Warhol's] arm" (124).
52. Quoted in Koch, *Stargazer*, 14.
53. Anonymous employee, circa 1974, quoted in Gopnik, *Warhol*, 789.
54. Gopnik recounts him looking down at commuters exiting a subway station: "Look at them, they're like ants. Oh, isn't it weird? It's like they're on wheels. Look at that one, he's out of step." Gopnik, *Warhol*, 675.
55. Warhol, *The Philosophy of Andy Warhol*, 146. The passage—easily dismissed as an indecent digression—has only occasionally been deemed worthy of scholarly discussion. When it has been engaged, its interpreters have chosen to excise the parenthetical comment on bees, and to focus instead on the passage's sexual or aesthetic implications. See Hainley, "Urine Sample," a refreshingly vivid account of the importance of sexual pleasure and experimentation in Warhol's work and life, which argues that the passage "proves [Warhol] recycling's most radical theorist" (8). See also Schmidt's crucial essay "From A to B and Back Again," 797; and Koestenbaum's *Andy Warhol*, which links the passage to Warhol's passion for creative recycling and his mother's colostomy (29).

56. See Kant, *Critique of the Power of Judgment*, 182; G.W.F. Hegel, *Aesthetics: Lectures on Fine Art*, vol. 2, trans. T.M. Knox (London: Oxford University Press, 1975), 646; and Karl Marx, *Capital: A Critique of Political Economy*, vol. 1, trans. Ben Fowkes (New York: Penguin Books, 1982), 283–84.
57. Derrida, "Economimesis," 5.
58. Quoted in Elmer A. Stephan, "Saturday Morning Art Classes," *Carnegie Magazine*, February 1932, 278; cited in Gopnik, *Warhol*, 29.
59. *Carnegie Magazine*, April 1940, 12.
60. Sigmund Freud, "The Excretory Functions in Psychoanalysis and Folklore," in *Character and Culture*, ed. Philip Rieff (New York: Collier Books, 1963), 220.
61. Jacques Derrida, *Acts of Religion*, ed. Gil Anidjar (New York: Routledge, 2002), 353; emphasis in original.
62. Derrida, 353; emphasis in original.
63. Derrida, 353; For bees and silkworms as "insects . . . bred for the benefit of man," see Craig McFarlane, "*Apum Ordines*: Of Bees and Government," in *Foucault and Animals*, ed. Matthew Chrulew and Dinesh Joseph Wadiwel (Leiden: Brill, 2017), 270.
64. Quoted in Scherman and Dalton, *The Genius of Andy Warhol*, 1. In this regard, Warhol's position resembles Kafka's mouse Josephine's; see Oxana Timofeeva, "Communism with a Nonhuman Face," *e-flux* 48 (October 2013), accessed November 1, 2019, http://www.e-flux.com/journal/communism-with-a-nonhuman-face/.
65. Marx, *Capital*, 1:484, emphasis in original.
66. Derrida, *Acts of Religion*, 354.
67. For "all woman" and "all witch," see Warhol, *a: a novel*, 38.
68. In 2007, scientists learned that honeybees also produce silk. CSIRO Australia, "Bees Are the New Silkworms," *ScienceDaily*, November 27, 2007, accessed November 20, 2019, www.sciencedaily.com/releases/2007/11/071126092140.htm.
69. Warhol, *The Philosophy of Andy Warhol*, 103. On the night before he died, facing surgery he was convinced would kill him, Warhol had an all-sweets dinner at the Serendipity III restaurant. Gopnik, *Warhol*, 906.
70. Stockton, *The Queer Child*, 238.
71. Kristeva, *Powers of Horror*, 147.
72. Derrida, "Economimesis," 25; see Eugenie Brinkema, "Laura Dern's Vomit, or, Kant and Derrida in Oz," *Film-Philosophy* 15, no. 2 (2011): 56–60; and Jan Zita Grover, *North Enough: AIDS and Other Clear-Cuts* (Minneapolis: Graywolf Press, 1997), which argues that "we have gone so far as to lose touch with what such substances as shit and vomit actually are" (116).
73. Sigmund Freud, "Notes upon a Case of Obsessional Neurosis," in *The Standard Edition of the Complete Psychological Works of Sigmund Freud*, vol. 10 (London: Hogarth Press, 1909), 214; cited in Lundblad, *Jungle*, 45.
74. Marder, *Grafts*, 123.
75. The results were not promising. See Carol Waslien, Doris Howes Calloway, and Sheldon Margen, "Human Intolerance to Bacteria as Food," *Nature* 221, no. 4 (January 1969): 84–85; cited in Mary Roach, *Gulp* (New York: Norton and Company, 2013), 13–14.
76. Warhol, *The Philosophy of Andy Warhol*, 155.
77. Warhol, *The Andy Warhol Diaries*, 506. This despite the fact that when Warhol had been hospitalized after his assassination attempt, "he was so impressed by the kindness of the Puerto Ricans among them that he came up with a new idea for a film about the work Puerto Ricans did in the city despite their reputation as 'the ones causing so much trouble.'" Warhol,

unpublished diary entry for October 25, 1972, Andy Warhol Museum Archives; cited in Gopnik, *Warhol,* 641–42. For recent discussions of racism in Warhol's work, see Ara Osterweil, "The Last Word: Dorothy Dean and Black Fugitivity in Andy Warhol's *My Hustler,*" *Art Journal* 78, no. 4 (2019): 58–75, and Glenn Ligon, "Pay It No Mind," in *Andy Warhol: A to B and Back Again,* ed. Donna De Salvo, *Andy Warhol: From A to B and Back Again* (New Haven, CT: Yale University Press, 2018), 60–65.

78. Timothy Morton, *Humankind: Solidarity with Nonhuman People* (New York: Verso, 2017), 95; see also Derrida, *The Animal That Therefore I Am,* 31.
79. Warhol, *The Andy Warhol Diaries,* 279.
80. Warhol, *America,* 14, 17. In her final book, Donna Haraway would propose a similar model in her notion of the Chthulucene; its denizens "are a buzzing, stinging, sucking swarm now, and human beings are not in a separate compost pile. We are humus, not Homo, not anthropos; we are compost." Haraway, *Staying with the Trouble: Making Kin in the Chthulucene* (Durham, NC: Duke University Press, 2016), 55.
81. Marder, *Plant-Thinking,* 173.
82. See Jacques Derrida and Bernard Stiegler, *Echographies of Television,* trans. Jennifer Bajorek (Cambridge, MA: Polity Press, 2002), 117.
83. John Coplans, *Warhol* (New York: New York Graphic Society, 1970), 52. See also the unreleased film *The Andy Warhol Story,* in which the actors were surrounded by orchids, described in Callie Angell, *The Films of Andy Warhol: Part II* (New York: Whitney Museum of Art, 1994), 25.
84. Marder, *Plant-Thinking,* 67.
85. Roger Vaughan, "Superpop or A Night at the Factory," *New York Herald-Tribune,* August 8, 1965, 7. The lead actor apparently threatened to sue, and the film was never released. See also Crimp, *"Our Kind of Movie,"* 154n19; and Christian Hite, "The Art of Suicide: Notes on Foucault and Warhol," *October,* no. 153 (Summer 2015): 65–95, which touches on the problem of the animal-machine in the context of suicide and homoeroticism (91–93).
86. Vaughan, "Superpop or A Night at the Factory," 7.
87. See José Esteban Muñoz, "A Jeté Out the Window: Fred Herko's Brilliant Illumination," in *Cruising Utopia: The Then and There of Queer Futurity* (New York: NYU Press, 2009), 147–67; and Paisid Aramphongphan, "Real Professionals?: Andy Warhol, Fred Herko, and Dance," *PAJ: A Journal of Performance and Art* 37, no. 2 (2015): 1–12, which compellingly argues that Warhol may have been envious of Herko's "resistance to the norms and progression of 'regular' modern life" (10).
88. Quoted in Leonard, "The Return of Andy Warhol," 143.
89. [Andre], "Andy Warhol's Interview," 47. Warhol was pronounced clinically dead on the operating table. Bockris, *Warhol,* 302.
90. Quoted in Leonard, "The Return," 32.
91. Billy Name, quoted in [O'Brien], "Factory Workers Warholites Remember: Billy Name."
92. Gopnik, *Warhol,* 883.
93. Jacques Derrida, *Aporias,* trans. Thomas Dutoit (Stanford, CA: Stanford University Press, 1993), 74; emphasis in original. See Haraway, *When Species Meet,* 77.
94. Derrida, *Aporias,* 76; emphasis added.
95. Lipschitz, "Skin/ned Politics," 556.
96. Warhol to Man Ray, November 30, 1973. © The Andy Warhol Foundation for the Visual Arts. Warhol quoted in Koestenbaum, *Warhol,* 173–74.
97. Quoted in Koestenbaum, *Warhol,* 174.
98. Andy Warhol, *Andy Warhol's Exposures,* ed. Bob Colacello (London: Arrow Books, 1980), 42; Gopnik, *Warhol,* 811.

99. Warhol quoted in Colacello, *Holy Terror,* 144.
100. Warhol quoted in Colacello, 361.
101. Gopnik, *Warhol,* 648.
102. Gopnik, 719.
103. Flatley, "Like: Collecting and Collectivity," *October,* no. 132 (Spring 2010): 83–88, 76; Walter Benjamin, "Doctrine of the Similar," trans. Michael Jennings, in *Walter Benjamin: Selected Writings,* vol. 2, ed. Michael W. Jennings, Howard Eiland, and Gary Smith (Cambridge, MA: Harvard University Press, 1999), 698; cited in Flatley, "Like," 83.
104. Walter Benjamin, "One-Way Street," trans. Edmund Jephcott, in *Walter Benjamin: Selected Writings,* 4 vols., edited by Michael W. Jennings, Howard Eiland, and Gary Smith (Cambridge, MA: Harvard University Press, 2004–2006), 451.
105. Benjamin, "Doctrine of the Similar," 695; Benjamin, "One-Way Street," 448.
106. Joyce Cheng, "Mask, Mimicry, Metamorphosis: Roger Caillois, Walter Benjamin and Surrealism in the 1930s," *Modernism/Modernity* 16, no. 1 (January 2009): 62.
107. See Martha J. Reineke, *Intimate Domain: Desire, Trauma, and Mimetic Theory* (East Lansing: Michigan State University Press, 2014), xvi–xvii, 196–97.
108. Julia Kristeva, "Motherhood Today," accessed November 15, 2019, http://www.kristeva.fr/motherhood.html; emphasis in original.
109. Kristeva, *Powers of Horror,* 72; Kelly Oliver, *Reading Kristeva: Unraveling the Double-Bind* (Bloomington: Indiana University Press, 1993), 72.
110. Kristeva, *Powers of Horror,* 58.
111. Gopnik, *Warhol,* 799.
112. Gopnik, 179.
113. Olivia Laing, "A La La La: An Andy Warhol Alphabet," in *Andy Warhol,* ed. Gregor Muir and Yilmaz Dziewior (London: Tate Publishing, 2020), 23.
114. Sichel, "'What Is Pop Art?,'" 91.
115. Sichel, 91.
116. Kristin Dombek, *The Selfishness of Others: An Essay on the Fear of Narcissism* (New York: Farrar, Straus, and Giroux, 2016), 135.

4. "PHILOSOPHY OF THE FRAGILE"

1. See, for example, Roberta Smith, "Andy Warhol: Outside His Comfort Zones," *New York Times,* June 17, 2010. For an exception, see Michael Jay McClure, "I Made It through the Wilderness," in *Warhol's Nature,* ed. Linda DeBerry, 16–23 (New York: Scala Arts Publishers, 2015), where McClure compellingly describes a "loss residing beneath the images" in *Endangered Species* and links this quality to the concurrent onset of the AIDS epidemic (20).
2. Danto, *Andy Warhol,* 134.
3. Keri Cronin, *Art for Animals: Visual Culture and Animal Advocacy* (University Park: Pennsylvania University Press, 2018), 6; see also Lauren Corman, "The Ventriloquist's Burden: Animal Advocacy and the Problem of Speaking for Others," in *Animal Subjects 2.0,* ed. Jodey Castricano and Lauren Corman (Waterloo, ON: Wilfrid Laurier University Press, 2016), 473–512.
4. See Julia Bryan-Wilson, "Simone Forti Goes to the Zoo," *October,* no. 152 (Spring 2015): 26–52; Elizabeth Sutton, *Art, Animals, and Experience: Relationships to Canines and the Natural World* (New York: Routledge, 2017); and Aloi Giovanni, *Art and Animals* (London: I.B. Tauris, 2012).
5. Bryan-Wilson, "Simone Forti Goes to the Zoo," 44. For more on how environmentalist sentiment in the United States built during the 1950s, see Adam Rome, *The Bulldozer in the Countryside: Suburban Sprawl and the Rise of American Environmentalism* (Cambridge: Cambridge

University Press, 2008); and Keith Makoto Woodhouse, *The Ecocentrists: A History of Radical Environmentalism* (New York: Columbia University Press, 2018).

6. Peggy Kamuf, *Book of Addresses* (Stanford, CA: Stanford University Press, 2005), 11–12.
7. Peter York quoted in Bockris, *Warhol,* 195.
8. Name quoted in Bockris, 196.
9. Warhol and Hackett, *Popism,* 134.
10. Warhol, *The Andy Warhol Diaries,* 451.
11. Gopnik, *Warhol,* 848.
12. Bockris, *Warhol,* 458.
13. Gopnik, *Warhol,* 847.
14. See Gopnik, 13, 14, 133, 187.
15. Weintraub, *To Life!,* 11.
16. Warhol, *The Andy Warhol Diaries,* 325.
17. Bockris, *Warhol,* 359.
18. Bockris, 362.
19. Quoted in Gopnik, *Warhol,* 742.
20. Derrida, *The Animal That Therefore I Am,* 117.
21. Gopnik, *Warhol,* 847.
22. Warhol, *The Andy Warhol Diaries,* 199.
23. Swenson, "What Is Pop Art?," 26. See discussions of this passage in Anne Middleton Wagner, "Andy Warhol's Patriotism," in *A House Divided: American Art since 1955* (Berkeley: University of California Press, 2012), 38–39; and Flatley, *Like Warhol,* 207–11.
24. Warhol, *The Andy Warhol Diaries,* 536.
25. Scott Cohen, "Andy Warhol Talks about Sex, Art, Fame and Money," *Forum: The International Journal of Human Relations,* January 1981, 20.
26. Warhol, *The Andy Warhol Diaries,* 683.
27. Warhol, 309.
28. Jacques Derrida, *The Beast and the Sovereign,* vol. 2, trans. Geoffrey Bennington (Chicago: University of Chicago Press, 2011), 340.
29. Quoted in Carroll, "What's a Warhol?," 278. Here, Warhol anticipated Leonard Lawlor's observation that "[t]here is finally, I think, no greater problem for thought today than the problem of how to conceive life in terms of powerlessness." Lawlor, *This Is Not Sufficient: An Essay on Animality and Human Nature in Derrida* (New York: Columbia University Press, 2007), 5.
30. Heinz Götze, *Springer-Verlag: History of a Scientific Publishing House: Part 2: 1945–1992,* trans. Mary Schäfer (New York: Springer-Verlag, 1996), 113.
31. David Sepkoski, *Catastrophic Thinking: Extinction and the Value of Diversity from Darwin to the Anthropocene* (Chicago: University of Chicago Press, 2020), 4.
32. Kurt Benirschke to Andy Warhol, February 13, 1986, Warhol archives.
33. Karel Havlíček to Andy Warhol, postcard, n.d., Warhol Museum Archives.
34. For the *Ladies and Gentlemen* series, see Flatley, *Like Andy Warhol,* 179–251; and Glenn Ligon, "Pay It No Mind," in *Andy Warhol: A to B and Back Again,* ed. Donna De Salvo (New Haven, CT: Yale University Press), 60–65.
35. Derrida, *The Animal That Therefore I Am,* 135.
36. Vanessa Lemm, *Nietzsche's Animal Philosophy: Culture, Politics, and the Animality of the Human Being* (New York: Fordham University Press, 2009), 152.
37. Gopnik, *Warhol,* 35–37.
38. In this respect, Benirschke's commentary partially falls prey to Matthew Chrulew and Rick De Vos's critique of conservation discourses: "their tendency to reduce animal life and behaviour

to genetic, biological and ecological mechanisms, to focus on sexual reproduction at the expense of . . . the meaning-making, world-forming cultural capabilities of animals." Chrulew and De Vos, "Extinction," in *The Edinburgh Companion to Animal Studies,* ed. Lynn Turner, Undine Sellbach, and Ron Broglio (Edinburgh: Edinburgh University Press, 2018), 192.

39. Joan Roughgarden, *Evolution's Rainbow: Diversity, Gender, and Sexuality in Nature and People* (Berkeley: University of California Press, 2004), 27.
40. Warhol, *The Philosophy of Andy Warhol,* 48.
41. Andy Warhol and Kurt Benirschke, *Vanishing Animals* (New York: Springer-Verlag, 1986), 97.
42. Warhol and Benirschke, *Vanishing Animals,* 97.
43. See Gopnik, *Warhol,* 193, 514, 740. Warhol would later tell a friend that this bird had been a parrot, and that it had died when he neglected to feed it in the aftermath of his mother's death. Bockris, *Warhol,* 362.
44. Warhol and Benirschke, *Vanishing Animals,* 97. Warhol would also have learned from Benirschke's essay that the habitat of the *Amazona vittata,* the Puerto Rican Amazon, was threatened because its "preferred nesting tree was considered to be a weed and was deliberately cut down until quite recently"—another example of arbitrary human value judgments regarding normative and nonnormative reproduction undermining the viability of vulnerable creatures.
45. Warhol and Benirschke, *Vanishing Animals,* 98.
46. Warhol and Benirschke, 98.
47. Roughgarden has suggested that the presence of monomorphism in animals poses interesting challenges to evolutionary theory, revealing genders "as occupational categories, with gendered symbolism to signal occupational roles in bringing about matings, raising young, or tending resources, much as a worker's uniform does in human society." Roughgarden, *Evolution's Rainbow,* 177.
48. As Jennifer Terry has pointed out, "almost all biological research on human sexual orientation based on animal behavior focuses on male homosexuality; little of it deals directly with female homosexuality." Terry, "'Unnatural Acts' in Nature: The Scientific Fascination with Queer Animals," *GLQ: A Journal of Lesbian and Gay Studies* 6, no. 2 (2000): 158. This bias characterizes *Vanishing Animals* as well.
49. Warhol and Benirschke, *Vanishing Animals,* 49.
50. Bruce Bagemihl, *Biological Exuberance: Animal Homosexuality and Natural Diversity* (New York: St. Martin's Press, 1999), 521. See also Volker Sommer and Paul L. Vasey, "Homosexual Behavior in Animals: Topics, Hypotheses, and Research Trajectories," in *Homosexual Behavior in Animals: An Evolutionary Perspective,* ed. Volker Sommer and Paul L. Vasey (Cambridge: Cambridge University Press, 2006), 3–44; and Lynda I.A. Birke, "Is Homosexuality Hormonally Determined?," *Journal of Homosexuality* 6, no. 4 (Summer 1981): 35–49.
51. Warhol and Benirschke, *Vanishing Animals,* 49.
52. Warhol and Benirschke, 50.
53. Warhol and Benirschke, 51. His concerns were justified: "the cross-fostering project lasted 15 years, cost millions of dollars, and used 289 endangered Whooping crane eggs," but it would ultimately be canceled because the whooping cranes failed to mate with each other due to imprinting from the sandhill cranes. Robert H. Horwich, "Developing a Migratory Whooping Crane Flock," *North American Crane Workshop Proceedings,* no. 86 (2001): 85.
54. Thom Van Dooren, *Flight Ways: Life and Death at the Edge of Extinction* (New York: Columbia University Press, 2014), 96.
55. Van Dooren, 97.
56. As Carolyn Merchant points out, the American Audubon Society had been an early voice in sounding the warning about the possible extinction of American species, including the

whooping crane, which was hunted for its feathers. Merchant, *Spare the Birds!: George Bird Grinnell and the First Audubon Society* (New Haven, CT: Yale University Press, 2016), 29–30.

57. Warhol and Benirschke, *Vanishing Animals,* 21.
58. Myra J. Hird, "Naturally Queer," *Feminist Theory* 5, no. 1 (2004): 85.
59. Warhol, *Philosophy of Andy Warhol,* 111; see Giovanna Di Chiro, "Polluted Politics?: Confronting Toxic Discourse, Sex Panic, and Eco-Normativity," in *Queer Ecologies: Sex, Nature, Politics, Desire,* ed. Catriona Mortimer-Sandilands and Bruce Erickson (Bloomington: Indiana University Press, 2010), 203–4.
60. Warhol and Benirschke, *Vanishing Animals,* 33.
61. Warhol and Benirschke, 33.
62. Warhol and Benirschke, 33.
63. Sigmund Freud, *The Interpretation of Dreams (II)* and *On Dreams,* in *The Standard Edition of the Complete Psychological Works of Sigmund Freud,* ed. and trans. James Strachey et al. (London: Hogarth Press, 1954–73), 5:560; cited in Silke-Maria Weineck, "Heteros Autos: Freud's Fatherhood," in *The Dreams of Interpretation,* 104–5. I have drawn on Freud, Kristeva, and psychoanalysis throughout this book not because I believe it can "diagnose" Warhol or his work, but instead because it constitutes one of the few "analytics of the human" that can grapple with the difficult sexual and cross-species issues raised by Warhol's work, and "that does not, a priori, assume the human as a given." Carla Freccero, "Queer Theory," *Edinburgh Companion to Animal Studies,* 433. Freud was unusually attuned to the intersection between sexuality and animality. As Dominic Pettman has argued, "Freud . . . use[d] the horse as his own symbol for the id itself: a powerful yet unruly animal, requiring the ever-straining harness of the superego to function with disciplined direction. For Freud, then, all humans are in some sense centaurs." Pettman, *Creaturely Love: How Desire Makes Us More and Less Than Human* (Minneapolis: University of Minnesota Press, 2017), 17.
64. Gopnik, *Warhol,* 855.
65. Warhol and Benirschke, *Vanishing Animals,* 56. For the reptilian qualities of Bram Stoker's *Dracula,* see Robert Azzarello, "Unnatural Predators: Queer Theory Meets Environmental Studies in Bram Stoker's *Dracula,*" in *Queering the Non/Human,* ed. Noreen Giffney and Myra J. Hird (Burlington, VT: Ashgate, 2008), 147. For Warhol's cinematic interest in the Dracula motif, see Angell, "Batman and Dracula," 159–86.
66. More recently, scientists have discovered antimicrobial peptides in Komodo saliva that may prove beneficial to humans; see Ezra M.C. Chung et al., "Komodo Dragon-Inspired Synthetic Peptide DRGN-1 Promotes Wound-Healing of a Mixed-Biofilm Infected Wound," *npj Biofilms Microbiomes* 3, no. 9 (2017), accessed July 17, 2019, https://doi.org/10.1038/s41522-017-0017-2.
67. Warhol and Benirschke, *Vanishing Animals,* 57.
68. This color scheme is almost exactly reversed in Warhol and Smith's douc-langur print, where the red background could be taken to stand for the monkey's war-ravaged habitat, and the pink scrap framing the mother and infant for a zone of maternal care.
69. Phillip C. Watts et al., "Parthenogenesis in Komodo Dragons, *Nature* no. 444, no. 7122 (2006): 1021–22, doi:10.1038/4441021a; see Greta Rensenbrink, "Parthenogenesis and Lesbian Separatism: Regenerating Women's Community through Virgin Birth in the United States in the 1970s and 1980s," *Journal of the History of Sexuality* 19, no. 2 (2010): 288–316. For incest and cannibalism as paired signs of monstrosity, see Michel Foucault, *Abnormal: Lectures at the Collège de France, 1974–1975,* trans. Graham Burchell (New York: Picador, 2003), 101.
70. Warhol and Benirschke, *Vanishing Animals,* 80; Haraway, *Staying with the Trouble,* 107.
71. Warhol and Benirschke, *Vanishing Animals,* 80.
72. Roughgarden, *Evolution's Rainbow,* 115.

73. Anne Faustosterling, *Sexing the Body: Gender Politics and the Construction of Sexuality* (New York: Basic Books, 2000), 181. As Beatriz Preciado points out, this research directly foreshadowed Nazi concentration camps, which would "reduce human bodies to biomaterial for research, revealing the inner links between the biopolitical apparatus and necropolitical techniques" Preciado, *Testo Junkie: Sex, Drugs, and Biopolitics in the Pharmacopornographic Era,* trans. Bruce Benderson (New York: Feminist Press, 2013), 164.
74. Faustosterling, *Sexing the Body,* 182–83; a similar biotechnological potential is emphasized in Benirschke's essay on the mouse armadillo, where he notes that armadillos ought to be protected because they can be "experimentally infected" with human leprosy bacilli, thus providing scientists with a living laboratory to explore the disease. Warhol and Benirschke, *Vanishing Animals,* 27.
75. Nubia Caballero-Mendieta and Carlos Cordero, "Enigmatic Liaisons in Lepidoptera: A Review of Same-Sex Courtship and Copulation in Butterflies and Moths," *Journal of Insect Science* 12, no. 1 (2012): 1–11.
76. For butterflies and homoeroticism, see Richard Meyer, *Outlaw Representation: Censorship and Homosexuality in Twentieth-Century American Art* (Oxford: Oxford University Press, 2002), 115–17.
77. Warhol, *Diaries,* 105. For more on "feminine male" animals, see Roughgarden, who argues that "Overlooking the positive value of feminine males is part of a larger problem of overlooking cooperation among animals" Roughgarden, *Evolution's Rainbow,* 98.
78. Compare with the account of a similar procedure given in Jane C. Desmond, *Displaying Death and Animating Life: Human-Animal Relations in Art, Science, and Everyday Life* (Chicago: University of Chicago Press, 2016), 1–4; and with Hervé Guibert's highly eroticized "Slaughter," the story of a boy visiting the slaughterhouse where his father works. Guibert, *Written in Invisible Ink: Selected Stories,* trans. Jeffrey Zuckerman (Los Angeles: Semiotext(e), 2020), 73–74. See also Gabriel Rosenberg, "How Meat Changed Sex: The Law of Interspecies Intimacy after Industrial Reproduction," *GLQ: A Journal of Lesbian and Gay Studies* 23, no. 4 (October 2017): 473–507, which concludes that "we must struggle with the interspecies entanglement that reproduces so much life, if only life to die" (499).
79. "New Hope is 90 percent gay. We went to a place called Ramona's and a drag queen served us and people were there drinking at 2 P.M. Gay old guys. It was too gay for me, it drove me crazy. Like a time warp." Warhol, *The Andy Warhol Diaries,* 718.
80. Warhol, 692.
81. Lemm, *Nietzsche's Animal Philosophy,* 152.
82. Bockris, *Warhol,* 75; Victor Bockris, "Dinner with Andy and Bill," in *I'll Be Your Mirror : The Selected Andy Warhol Interviews : 1962-1987,* ed. Kenneth Goldsmith (New York: Carroll & Graf, 2004),280.
83. For the Butterfly Brigade gay street patrol of the late 1970s, see Christina B. Hanhardt, "Butterflies, Whistles, and Fists: Gay Safe Streets Patrols and the New Gay Ghetto, 1976–1981," *Radical History Review,* no. 100 (Winter 2008): 65–74.
84. Warhol and Benirschke, *Vanishing Animals,* 73.
85. Warhol and Benirschke, 73.
86. Warhol and Benirschke, 74.
87. For Warhol as "a computer" see Ultra Violet quoted in Wilcock, *Autobiography and Sex Life,* n.p.
88. Michael Letko et al., "Bat-Borne Virus Diversity, Spillover and Emergence," *Nature Reviews Microbiology* 18, no. 8 (August 2020): 461–71, https://doi.org/10.1038/s41579-020-0394-z. For deforestation, see Mike Davis, *The Monster at Our Door: The Global Threat of Avian Flu* (New York: New Press, 2005), 58.

89. Gopnik, *Warhol,* 891–92.
90. Gopnik, 891.
91. For an important defense of Warhol's approach to AIDS, see Jessica Beck, "Love on the Margins: A Case for Andy Warhol and Jon Gould," in *Contact Warhol: Photography without End,* ed. Peggy Phelan and Richard Meyer (Cambridge, MA: MIT Press, 2018), 156-67.
92. Emily V. Driscoll, "Bisexual Species," *Scientific American Mind* 19, no. 3 (June/July 2008): 70.
93. Driscoll,70.
94. Vinciane Despret, *What Would Animals Say If We Asked the Right Questions,* trans. Brett Buchanan (Minneapolis: University of Minnesota Press, 2016), 132.
95. Gopnik, *Warhol,* 850.
96. Gopnik, 849.
97. Gopnik, 850.
98. Gopnik, 851, 267.
99. Gopnik, 849, 851, 6, 750.
100. Stacy Alaimo, "Eluding Capture: The Science, Culture, and Pleasure of 'Queer' Animals," in *Queer Ecologies: Sex, Nature, Politics, Desire,* ed. Catriona Mortimer-Sandilands and Bruce Erickson (Bloomington: Indiana University Press, 2010), 67.
101. Gopnik, *Warhol,* 775–76; Flatley, *Like Andy Warhol,* 242; Whitney Davis, "Queer Family Romance in Collecting Visual Culture," *GLQ: A Journal of Lesbian and Gay Studies* 17, nos. 2–3 (2011): 309–29.

5. QUEER BEAUTY AND EXTINCTION

1. Neel Ahuja, "Intimate Atmospheres: Queer Theory in a Time of Extinctions," *GLQ: A Journal of Lesbian and Gay Studies* 21, nos. 2–3 (June 2015): 367.
2. Warhol and Benirschke, *Vanishing Animals,* 66–67. For identification via striping, see Agatha Gijzen, "Studbook of the Okapi," *Acta Zoologica et Pathologica Antverpiensia,* no. 68 (August 1977): 1–47.
3. Cuthbert Christy, "Supposed Horn-Sheaths of an Okapi," *Nature* 95, no. 2378 (May 27, 1915): 343.
4. "Rare Okapi Group on Exhibition Soon: American Museum Announces the Mounting of Animals Which Formerly Mystified Scientists," *New York Times,* March 13, 1911, 3.
5. Eugenio Montale, *Farfalla di Dinard* (Milan: Arnoldo Mondadori Editore, 1960; expanded ed., 1973); cited in Montale, *Collected Poems: 1920–1954,* trans. Jonathan Galassi (New York: Farrar, Straus, and Giroux, 1998), 604.
6. Attilio Gatti, "A Strange Beast, the Okapi," *New York Times Magazine,* August 8, 1937, 11; accessed November 20, 2020, https://timesmachine.nytimes.com/timesmachine/1937/08/08/118984772.html?pageNumber = 113.
7. A photograph of a lone okapi is centrally placed in Hannah Höch's epochal 1919 collage *Cut with the Dada Kitchen Knife through the Last Weimar Beer-Belly Cultural Epoch in Germany,* alongside the faces of Johannes Baader, Karl Radek, and Vladimir Lenin, all overseen by "Die große" Karl Marx.
8. Warhol, *The Andy Warhol Diaries,* 495. The display, which had first been planned in 1911, was finally installed in 1938; it "was refurbished in the late 1960s/early 1970s," but has otherwise "remained largely unchanged since its opening." Mai Reitmeyer, Sr. Research Services Librarian, Department of Library Services, American Museum of Natural History, private correspondence with author, August 2020.
9. Ryuta Kawasaki and Tatsuhiro Suginaka, "Changes in the Milk Composition of Okapi (Okapia johnstoni) during the First 6 Months of Lactation," *Animal Science Journal* 83, no. 4 (April 2012): 349.

10. See S.L. Lindsey et al., "Functional Analysis of Infrasound in the Okapi (*Okapia johnstoni*): Mother–Infant Communication," *American Association of Zoological Parks and Aquariums Annual Conference Proceedings 1993*, 299–305.
11. Gatti, "A Strange Beast," 11.
12. Warhol and Benirschke, *Vanishing Animals,* 45. Zoos would eventually prevent this "abnormal" and "obsessive" behavior, which could also result in "tail sloughing" and "vaginal trauma," by devising various structures to separate dam and calf; see Terry DeRosa, Fran Lyon, and Ann Petric, eds., *Husbandry Guidelines for the Okapi SSP* (Chicago: Chicago Zoological Society Brookfield Zoo, 2004), 23.For "the poverty of the worlds often created for the animals purported to be rescued or resurrected," see Chrulew and De Vos, "Extinction," 193.
13. Douglas Quenqua, "For a Baby Okapi, Don't Push Too Hard," *New York Times,* November 7, 2011, accessed November 20, 2020, https://www.nytimes.com/2011/11/08/science/birth-of-bronx-zoos-mbura-overcomes-okapi-odds.html?searchResultPosition = 3.
14. Gatti, "A Strange Beast," 11.
15. Warhol and Benirschke, *Vanishing Animals,* 45.
16. Gatti, "A Strange Beast," 17.
17. Warhol and Benirschke, *Vanishing Animals,* 44. In 1965, Warhol had filmed a laxative advertisement in the style of a *Screen Test*: "New Cadence is the light laxative for constipation so often caused by tension, nerves or irregular living." Gopnik, *Warhol,* 501.
18. Bockris, *Warhol,* 38. Perhaps she subscribed to the tradition described by Laurinda S. Dixon, in which enemas were understood by "generations of philosophers and physicians" to treat "hypochondriacal melancholy." Dixon, "Some Penetrating Insights: The Imagery of Enemas in Art," *Art Journal* 52, no. 3 (Fall 1993): 28.
19. Gopnik, *Warhol,* 922, 173, 196.
20. Joseph Gelmis, "A Grotesque Prism," *Newsday,* May 6, 1977.
21. Stadler, "'My Wife,'" 445–56.
22. Gopnik, *Warhol,* 549.
23. Quoted in Bockris, *Warhol,* 333; Blake Gopnik tells me that he did not encounter any evidence of such an archive in his research. Gopnik, personal correspondence with author, August 11, 2020.
24. Gopnik, *Warhol,* 717.
25. Warhol and Benirschke, *Vanishing Animals,* 44.
26. Davis, *Queer Beauty,* 225.
27. Walter Pater, *The Renaissance: Studies in Art and Poetry* (London: Macmillan, 1901), 125; cited in Davis, *Queer Beauty,* 226. Pater expressly emphasized nonhuman-animal appetites in his description, singling the model out as a Leda, who embodies "the animalism of Greece, the lust of Rome." (125).
28. Davis, *Queer Beauty,* 226.
29. In a 1912 letter to Sigmund Freud, Sandor Ferenczi linked the condition to both homosexuality and hypochondria (widely reported as a tendency in Warhol's personality); see Eva Brabant, Ernst Falzeder, and Patrizia Giampieri-Deutsch, eds., *The Correspondence of Sigmund Freud and Sandor Ferenczi,* vol. 1, *1908–1914*, trans. Peter T. Hoffer (Cambridge, MA: Belknap Press, 1993), 358. Magnus Hirschfeld had included prolapse in his list of "physical signs of degeneration" in *The Homosexuality of Men and Women.* Hirschfeld, *The Homosexuality of Men and Women,* trans. Michael Lombardi-Nash (Amherst, NY: Prometheus Books, 2000), 442. See also S.H. Burges and J. E. Hilton, *The New Police Surgeon: A Practical Guide to Clinical Forensic Medicine* (London: Hutchinson Benham, 1978), 261.
30. Davis, *Queer Beauty,* 230; emphasis in original.

31. Judith Butler, "Political Philosophy in Freud: The Death Drive and the Critical Faculty," in *On Psychoanalysis and Violence: Contemporary Lacanian Perspectives,* ed. Vanessa Sinclair and Manya Steinkoler (New York: Routledge, 2019), 23.
32. Gabor Maté, *In the Realm of Hungry Ghosts: Close Encounters with Addiction* (Berkeley, CA: North Atlantic Books, 2010), 162.
33. Warhol, *The Philosophy of Andy Warhol,* 111.
34. Bagemihl, *Biological Exuberance,* 17–18; see also Aldo Poiani, *Animal Homosexuality: A Biosocial Perspective* (Cambridge: Cambridge University Press, 2010), 308.
35. Bagemihl, *Biological Exuberance,* 34–35; the cited studies were all by David M. Pratt and Virginia H. Anderson: "Giraffe Social Behavior," *Journal of Natural History* 19, no. 4 (1985): 771–81; "Population, Distribution, and Behaviour of Giraffe in the Arusha National Park, Tanzania," *Journal of Natural History* 16, no. 4 (1982): 481–89; and "Giraffe Cow–Calf Relationships and Social Development of the Calf in the Serengeti," *Zeitschrift für Tierpsychologie* 51, no. 3 (1979): 233–51.
36. Elizabeth Grosz, *Becoming Undone: Darwinian Reflections* (Durham, NC: Duke University Press, 2011), 130.
37. Despret, *What Would Animals Say,* 133; see Linda D. Wolfe, "Human Evolution and the Sexual Behavior of Female Primates," in *Understanding Behavior: What Primate Studies Tell Us about Human Behavior,* ed, James D. Loy and Calvin B. Peters (New York: Oxford University Press, 1991), 121–51; and Terry, "'Unnatural Acts' in Nature."
38. See Lundblad, *The Birth of a Jungle,* 2–11.
39. Sigmund Freud, "Leonardo da Vinci and a Memory of His Childhood," in *The Standard Edition of the Complete Psychological Works of Sigmund Freud,* ed. and trans. James Strachey et al. (London: Hogarth Press, 1954–73), 11:82; for a thorough review of Freud's argument and its limitations, see Raluca Soreanu, "Speaking of Leonardo Da Vinci's Mother: A Critique of Freud's Notion of Identification," *Studies in the Maternal* 10, no. 1 (August 2018): 1–22.
40. Freud to Lou Andreas-Salomé, February 9, 1919, in Ernst Pfeiffer, ed., *Sigmund Freud and Lou Andreas-Salomé: Letters,* trans. William and Elaine Robson-Scott (New York: Harcourt Brace Jovanovich, 1972), 90; quoted in Elizabeth Lunbeck, *The Americanization of Narcissism* (Cambridge, MA: Harvard University Press, 2014), 86.
41. Freud, "Leonardo da Vinci," 87, 98
42. Freud, 117; cited in Davis, *Queer Beauty,* 225.
43. Freud, "Leonardo da Vinci," 117; compare Hervé Guibert's mother's "imperceptible smile" in a "forbidden" photograph he attempts of her with his father absent. Guibert, *Ghost Image,* 13, 15.
44. Lunbeck, *The Americanization of Narcissism,* 86, 90.
45. Benirschke likely remarked this connection; he closed the condor essay by reminding his readers that the bird was "a symbol of immortality," emphasizing the Egyptian mythology that had been prominent in Freud's analysis. Warhol and Benirschke, *Vanishing Animals,* 15; Freud, "Leonardo da Vinci," 93–94.
46. Freud, "Leonardo da Vinci," 106n1.
47. Freud, 79n1.
48. "One writer who knew Warhol in the 1970s said that Warhol was always careful to hide the fact that he was 'exceptionally well and widely read: far more so than most visual artists, including many thought to be much brainier than he was.'" Gopnik, *Warhol,* 35–36; see also 239–46.
49. David Greven, *Intimate Violence: Hitchcock, Sex, and Queer Theory* (New York: Oxford University Press, 2017), 161.
50. Bruno's mother teases him for being "a naughty boy . . . who can always make me laugh." But when the name of the father is uttered, Bruno stiffens: "I am sick and tired of bowing and scrap-

ing to the king!" Like Freud, the mother proposes art and artmaking as forms of sublimation for these nonnormative and violent impulses: "Bruno, I do wish you'd take up painting! It's such a soothing pastime." When he sees the painting, Bruno bursts into hysterical laughter: "Oh, mother, you're wonderful! That's the old boy all right! That's father!" A jump cut reveals a garish, almost abstract-expressionist, portrait with large, haunted eyes, proffering a wedding band.

51. Jonathan Goldberg, *Strangers on a Train: A Queer Film Classic* (Vancouver, BC: Arsenal Pulp Press, 2012), 134–35; cited in Greven, *Intimate Violence*, 166.
52. Greven, *Intimate Violence*, 166–67.
53. Andy Warhol, "Hitchcock," redacted by Pat Hackett, in *Andy Warhol's Interview: The Crystal Ball of Pop Culture*, vol. 1, *Best of the First Decade, 1969–1979*, ed. Sandra J. Brant and Ingrid Sischy (Paris: Edition 7L, 2004), 94.
54. Warhol, "Hitchcock," 94; *Frenzy* centers on the police pursuit of a serial killer.
55. Warhol, 95.
56. Warhol, *The Andy Warhol Diaries*, 282.
57. Stockton, *Beautiful Bottom, Beautiful Shame*, 234n8. Freud's Leonardo essay does not appear in the otherwise comprehensive list of sources Stockton cites for this chapter (234n4). See also Darieck Scott, *Extravagant Abjection: Blackness, Power, and Sexuality in the African American Literary Imagination* (New York: NYU Press, 2010), 271–72n5.
58. Toni Morrison, *Sula* (New York: Vintage, 2004), 34.
59. See Leo Bersani, "Is the Rectum a Grave," in *Is the Rectum a Grave and Other Essays* (Chicago: University of Chicago Press, 2010), 24.
60. See Gopnik, *Warhol*, 248, 140.
61. See Gopnik, *Warhol*, 139–40.
62. See Maté, *Realm of Hungry Ghosts*, 162. One anonymous woman told Maté, "The first time I did heroin . . . it felt like a warm, soft hug" (165).
63. For "sacramental overtones" in Morrison's *Beloved*, see Erin Michael Salius, *Sacraments of Memory: Catholicism and Slavery in Contemporary African American Literature* (Gainesville: University Press of Florida, 2018), 13–66. The passage eerily echoes a pop song Warhol wrote in 1963: "Oh mommy, oh mommy, that's the bottle, yes. / So I took up an opener / And I drank up the bottle" (Gopnik, *Warhol*, 297).
64. Foucault, *Abnormal*, 101; see Margrit Shildrick, *Embodying the Monster: Encounters with the Vulnerable Self* (Thousand Oaks: Sage, 2002), 54.
65. The scene is reminiscent of "the dream of the burning child" analyzed by Freud in *The Interpretation of Dreams*, trans. James Strachey (New York: Basic Books, 2010), 550, 513–14. Here, a father dreams that his son is burning even as the child's actual corpse has been accidentally set aflame by a candle. Freud remarks that the most striking element of the dream is that it allows the father to imagine the dead child alive even at the expense of the corpse's actual safety. A similar, dreamlike, saving-through-burning logic characterizes Eva's attack on Plum.
66. Morrison, *Sula*, xvi–xvii.
67. Even Bruno's mother, Mrs. Anthony, who is wealthy, is shown to be neurotic and disconnected from the "normal" world of patriarchy: she is an aspiring artist.
68. Gopnik, *Warhol*, 776.
69. "Cooley" quoted in Bockris, *Warhol*, 140.
70. Stockton, *Beautiful Bottom*, 68. Unlike the Black citizens of the Bottom, one white policeman argues, "a decent white man" wouldn't "like to live in shit." Morrison, *Sula*, 133.
71. Morrison, *Sula*, 63. These connected themes are signaled perhaps most directly in *Sula* when Shadrack, a World War I veteran from the Bottom, experiences a transformative slumber, on

the eve of a psychotic break, that is described as "deeper than the hospital drugs; deeper than the pits of plums, steadier than the condor's wing; more tranquil than the curve of eggs"—foreshadowing avian-Eva; her son, Plum, and his addiction and demise; and the pleasures of anal eroticism (14).

72. See Stockton, *Beautiful Bottom,* 79–82, which summarizes Freud's views on this relationship and investigates its twists and turns in *Sula.* See also Karl Marx, who wrote that "capital comes dripping from head to toe, from every pore, with blood and dirt." Marx, *Capital,* 926.
73. Stockton, *Beautiful Bottom,* 82; Morrison, *Sula,* 70.
74. Oliver, *Reading Kristeva,* 57.
75. Kristeva, *Powers of Horror,* 53.
76. Julia Kristeva, *Revolution in Poetic Language,* trans. Margaret Waller (New York: Columbia University Press, 1984), 149.
77. Kristeva, 152.
78. Kristeva, 152.
79. Tyler, *Revolting Subjects,* 37–38.
80. Beck, "Warhol's Confession," 84–94.
81. Quoted in Gopnik, *Warhol,* 889.
82. Gopnik, 837–38.
83. Gopnik, 890.
84. Gopnik, 890.
85. Peter Wise quoted in Beck, "Love on the Margins," 157.
86. Colacello, *Holy Terror,* 585; cited in Beck, "Warhol's Confession," 89.
87. Beck, "Warhol's Confession," 89.
88. Warhol, *The Andy Warhol Diaries,* 372; cited in Beck, "Warhol's Confession," 85.
89. See, for instance, Hervé Guibert, who in his autobiographical novel quotes Muzil/Foucault as saying, "The damned thing [HIV] must have come from Africa" and "crossed over to us from the blood of green monkeys." Guibert, *To the Friend Who Did Not Save My Life,* trans. Linda Coverdale (New York: Atheneum, 1991)], 9.
90. See David Quammen, *Spillover: Animal Infections and the Next Human Pandemic* (New York: Norton, 2012), for an overview of competing theories for the origins of HIV; and Nuno R. Faria et al., "The Early Spread and Epidemic Ignition of HIV-1 in Human Populations," *Science* 346, no. 6205 (2014): 56, accessed November 28, 2020, doi:10.2307/24917739. I am grateful to Justin Underhill for directing me to this research.
91. Adam Hochschild, *King Leopold's Ghost* (New York: Houghton Mifflin, 1998), 244, 233, 4; see also Jules Marchal, *Lord Leverhulme's Ghosts: Colonial Exploitation in the Congo,* trans. Martin Thom (Brooklyn: Verso Books, 2017).
92. Warhol, *The Andy Warhol Diaries,* 172.
93. Warhol, 541.
94. Gopnik, *Warhol,* 892.
95. Beck, "Warhol's Confession," 85.
96. Morrison, *Sula,* 65.
97. Davis, *Queer Beauty,* 239.
98. Davis, 239, 238.
99. See Martin Meeker, *Contacts Desired: Gay and Lesbian Communications and Community, 1940s–1970s* (Chicago: University of Chicago Press, 2006).
100. Warhol and Hackett, *Popism,* 65.
101. Freud, "Leonardo da Vinci," 69.
102. Lunbeck, *The Americanization of Narcissism,* 101–3.

103. Michel Foucault, "Sexual Choice, Sexual Act," and "Sex, Power, and the Politics of Identity," in *Essential Works of Foucault: Ethics: Subjectivity and Truth,* ed. Paul Rabinow (New York: New Press, 1997), 151, 166; Davis, *Queer Beauty,* 255.
104. Michel Foucault, "Theatrum Philosophicum," in *Essential Works of Foucault: Aesthetics: Method and Epistemology,* ed. James D. Faubion (New York: New Press, 1997), 365, 367, 366.
105. Foucault, 361, 363.
106. Foucault, 362. Foucault would state the connection between Warhol and this new thought even more directly in 1973: "A day will come when, by means of similitude relayed indefinitely along the length of a series, the image itself, along with the name it bears, will lose its identity. Campbell, Campbell, Campbell, Campbell." Foucault, *This Is Not a Pipe,* trans. James Harkness (Berkeley: University of California Press, 1983), 54.
107. Foucault, "Theatrum Philosophicum," 362. For Foucault's thinking on animals and animality, see Chrulew and Wadiwel, *Foucault and Animals.*
108. Foucault, "Theatrum Philosophicum," 367; this expression is probably meant to recall the closing lines of Deleuze's *The Logic of Sense,* which propose that the function of the work of art is "to recover the independence of sounds and to fix the thunderbolt of the univocal." Deleuze, *The Logic of Sense,* ed. Constantin V. Boundas, trans. Mark Lester with Charles Stivale, rev. ed. (New York: Columbia University Press, 1990), 249.
109. Sichel, "'What Is Pop Art?,'" 88. See also Flatley, *Like Andy Warhol.*
110. See Rudolf Arnheim, *Art and Visual Perception: A Psychology of the Creative Eye,* rev. ed. (Berkeley: University of California Press, 1974), 33.
111. Cronin, *Art for Animals,* 120.
112. Warhol and Benirschke, *Vanishing Animals,* 44. For another scene linking HIV, snakelike tongues, and the figure of the mother, see Guibert: "With this white, raw wound festering on my throat, I'm haunted by the kiss I got in Mexico . . . from the old whore . . . who was the same age as my mother; the whore had suddenly shoved her tongue down my throat like a crazed snake." Guibert, *To the Friend,* 52.
113. Wilbur Schramm, Jack Lyle, and Edwin B. Parker, *Television in the Lives of Our Children* (Stanford, CA: Stanford University Press, 1961), 110; Pierre D. Martineau, "The Pattern of Social Classes," in *Marketing's Role in Scientific Management,* ed. Robert L. Clewett (Chicago: University of Chicago Press, 1957), 246.
114. Louis Schneider and Sverre Lysgaard, "The Deferred Gratification Pattern: A Preliminary Study," *American Sociological Review* 18, no. 2 (April 1953): 148.
115. Fanon, *Black Skin, White Masks,* 171.
116. Freud, "Leonardo da Vinci," 80.
117. José Esteban Muñoz, *Cruising Utopia: The Then and There of Queer Futurity* (New York: New York University Press, 2009), 136–37; the *Silver Clouds* were initially produced as a set design for Merce Cunningham's *RainForest* in 1968—another instance of post- or nonhuman imagining.
118. Braidotti, *The Posthuman,* 99; in this respect it would echo the spirit of its near contemporary, Mario Mieli's *Homosexuality and Liberation* (London: London Gay Male's Press, 1980).
119. Lee Edelman, *No Future: Queer Theory and the Death Drive* (Durham, NC: Duke University Press, 2004), 101.
120. Edelman, 107.
121. Catriona Mortimer-Sandilands and Bruce Erickson, "Introduction: A Genealogy of Queer Ecologies," in *Queer Ecologies: Sex, Nature, Politics, Desire,* ed. Catriona Mortimer-Sandilands and Bruce Erickson (Bloomington: Indiana University Press, 2010), 16.
122. Leo Bersani, *Homos* (Cambridge, MA: Harvard University Press, 1995), 60.

123. Eduardo Viveiros de Castro, *Cannibal Metaphysics*, trans. Peter Skafish (Minneapolis: Univocal, 2014), 57.
124. de Castro, 162.
125. Grosz, *Becoming Undone*, 130.
126. Grosz, 130. This eruption challenges Bersani's distinction between human and nonhuman sexuality: "If sexual selection imperils natural selection . . . this is because it also adds to natural selection the vagaries of individual (and species-specific) taste, an irreducible dimension of singularity" (131).
127. [O'Brien], "Interview: Andy Warhol," 256–57; Andy Warhol, "Sunday with Mister C.: An Audio-Documentary by Andy Warhol Starring Truman Capote," *Rolling Stone* 132 (1973): 28.
128. Warhol, "Sunday with Mister C.," 48.
129. Kuzniar, "'I Married My Dog,'" 208; for a more skeptical view, see Shell, "The Family Pet," 121–53.
130. Colacello, *Holy Terror*, 455–56.
131. Warhol, *The Andy Warhol Diaries*, 646; for the use of these glands, see *Key Issues in Plastic and Cosmetic Surgery*, vol. 16, ed. Mutaz B. Habal et. al. (New York: Karger, 1999), 9.
132. See Warhol, *Philosophy of Andy Warhol*, 150–52; and Fraser, "As Gorgeous As It Gets," 76.
133. Ahuja, "Intimate Atmospheres," 380; see also Tim Dean, who argues that, even in its riskiness, "erotic intimacy . . . can serve as a means for encountering something wonderfully strange to the self." Dean, *Unlimited Intimacy: Reflections on the Subculture of Barebacking* (Chicago: University of Chicago Press, 2009), 180.
134. Butler, *Bodies That Matter*, 73; the subsequent paragraph speaks urgently to the challenges this symbolic upheaval will face: "[T]he legitimation of homosexuality will have to resist the force of normalization for a queer resignification of the symbolic to expand and alter the normativity of its terms" (73).
135. Ocean Vuong, *On Earth We're Briefly Gorgeous* (New York: Penguin, 2019), 17, 18, 52.
136. Gopnik, *Warhol*, 889.
137. Marder, *Plant-Thinking*, 173.

CONCLUSION

1. Gopnik, *Warhol*, 257.
2. Aby M. Warburg, *Images from the Region of the Pueblo Indians of North America*, trans. Michael P. Steinberg (Ithaca, NY: Cornell University Press, 1995), 55n4.
3. [Andre], "Andy Warhol's Interview," 47; Gopnik, *Warhol*, 3.
4. Gopnik, *Warhol*, 578–80.
5. Warhol, *The Philosophy of Andy Warhol*, 8.
6. Quoted in Bockris, *Warhol*, 196.
7. Koch, *Stargazer*, 26.
8. Koch, 27.
9. Quoted in Gopnik, *Warhol*, 290.
10. Gopnik, 660.
11. Roughgarden, *Evolution's Rainbow*, 98.
12. Gopnik, *Warhol*, 127; Koch, *Stargazer*, 8.
13. Quoted in Bockris, *Warhol*, 206.
14. Cynthia Weber, *Faking It: U.S. Hegemony in a "Post-Phallic" Era* (Minneapolis: University of Minnesota Press, 1999), 110; see also Judith Butler, *Gender Trouble: Feminism and the Subversion of Identity* (New York: Routledge, 2006), 59–77.

15. Warhol's interest in other men's penises was widely known in the gay community but not widely publicized in official Warhol literature. "'He was interested in my dick, as he was in everyone's,' remembered Corey Tippin, echoing stories told by just about every pretty young man who found a place at Warhol's table. 'I wasn't sexually attracted to him,' said Tippin, 'but you knew you had the Power of the Penis around him.'" Gopnik, *Warhol,* 542.
16. Quoted in Warhol, *The Andy Warhol Diaries,* 560–61.
17. Warhol, 405.
18. Copetas, "Beat Godfather Meets Glitter Mainman," 27.
19. Warhol, *The Philosophy of Andy Warhol,* 180–81.
20. Deleuze, "Postscript on Control Societies," *Negotiations* (New York: Columbia University Press, 1995), 180.
21. William Bogard, "The Coils of a Serpent: Haptic Space and Control Societies," accessed November 11, 2021, https://journals.uvic.ca/index.php/ctheory/article/view/14513/5354.
22. Warhol, *The Philosophy of Andy Warhol,* 112.
23. David Chandler and Julian Reid, *The Neoliberal Subject: Resilience, Adaptation and Vulnerability* (New York: Rowman and Littlefield, 2016), 4.
24. Deleuze, "Postscript on Control Societies," 181.
25. Claire Colebrook, *Sex after Life,* vol. 2 of *Essays on Extinction* (Ann Arbor, MI: Open University Press, 2014), 98.
26. D.H. Lawrence, "Snake," in *Collected Poems,* vol 2, *Unrhyming Poems* (New York: Jonathan Cape and Harrison Smith, 1929), 217–19; Derrida, *The Beast and the Sovereign,* 325.
27. Marder, *Plant-Thinking,* 173.
28. Colebrook, *Sex after Life,* 98.
29. Colebrook, *Sex after Life,* 98; Oxana Timofeeva, *The History of Animals: A Philosophy* (New York: Bloomsbury Academic, 2018), 167. Homay King suggests a similar valence in Warhol's work when she describes his cinematic vision of "this ephemeral world of changing appearances." King, "Stroboscopic: Warhol and the Exploding Plastic Inevitable," *Criticism* 56, no. 3 (Summer 2014): 476.
30. John Rublowsky, *Pop Art* (New York: Basic Books, 1965), 111, 116.
31. Shukin, "Capitalism," 102; Shukin, *Animal Capital,* 22.
32. Warhol, *The Andy Warhol Diaries,* 279.
33. Erasmus Darwin, *The Botanic Garden,* vol. 2, *The Loves of the Plants* (New York: Garland, 1978), 101. See Marguerite Rigoglioso, *The Cult of Divine Birth in Ancient Greece* (New York: Palgrave Macmillan, 2009), 173.
34. J.M. Coetzee, *The Lives of Animals,* ed. Amy Gutmann (Princeton, NJ: Princeton University Press, 1999), 74; quoted in Cary Wolfe, *What Is Posthumanism?* (Minneapolis: University of Minnesota Press, 2010), 72.

SELECTED BIBLIOGRAPHY

Adorno, Theodor. *Aesthetic Theory.* Edited by Gretel Adorno and Rolf Tiedemann. Translated by Robert Hullot-Kentor. New York: Continuum, 2002.

———. *In Search of Wagner.* Translated by Rodney Livingstone. London: Verso, 2005.

Agamben, Giorgio. *Homo Sacer: Sovereign Power and Bare Life.* Translated by Daniel Heller-Roazen. Stanford, CA: Stanford University Press, 1998.

Ahuja, Neel. "Intimate Atmospheres: Queer Theory in a Time of Extinctions." *GLQ: A Journal of Lesbian and Gay Studies* 21, nos. 2–3 (June 2015): 365–85.

Alaimo, Stacy. "Eluding Capture: The Science, Culture, and Pleasure of 'Queer' Animals." In *Queer Ecologies: Sex, Nature, Politics, Desire,* edited by Catriona Mortimer-Sandilands and Bruce Erickson, 51–72. Bloomington: Indiana University Press, 2010.

Alligood, Chad. "Warhol's Nature." In *Warhol's Nature,* edited by Linda DeBerry, 8–15. New York: Scala Arts Publishers, 2015.

Als, Hilton. "Mother." In *The Warhol Look: Glamour, Style, Fashion,* edited by Mark Francis, 212–17. New York: Bulfinch, 1997.

Andre, Michael. "Andy Warhol's Interview." *Unmuzzled Ox* 4, no. 2 (1976): 40–47.

Angell, Callie. *Andy Warhol Screen Tests: The Films of Andy Warhol Catalogue Raisonné.* New York: Whitney Museum of American Art, 2006.

———. "Batman and Dracula: The Collaborations of Jack Smith and Andy Warhol." *Criticism* 56, no. 2 (Spring 2014): 159–86.

———. *The Films of Andy Warhol: Part II.* New York: Whitney Museum of American Art, 1994.

Aramphongphan, Paisid. "Real Professionals? Andy Warhol, Fred Herko, and Dance." *PAJ: A Journal of Performance and Art* 37, no. 2 (2015): 1–12.

Azzarello, Robert. "Unnatural Predators: Queer Theory Meets Environmental Studies in Bram Stoker's *Dracula.*" In *Queering the Non/Human,* edited by Noreen Giffney and Myra J. Hird, 137–58. Burlington, VT: Ashgate, 2008.

Bagemihl, Bruce. *Biological Exuberance: Animal Homosexuality and Natural Diversity.* New York: St. Martin's Press, 1999.

Baker, Steve. *The Postmodern Animal.* London: Reaktion Books, 2000.

Bangs, Lester. "Kraftwerkfeature." In *Psychotic Reactions and Carburetor Dung: The Work of a Legendary Critic: Rock 'N' Roll as Literature and Literature as Rock 'N' Roll,* edited by Greil Marcus, 154–60. New York: Anchor, 2013.

———. "Of Pop and Pies and Fun." In *Psychotic Reactions and Carburetor Dung: The Work of a Legendary Critic: Rock 'N' Roll as Literature and Literature as Rock 'N' Roll,* edited by Greil Marcus, 31–52. New York: Anchor, 2013.

Bataille, Georges. "Abjection and Miserable Forms." In *More and Less 2,* edited by Sylvère Lotringer, translated by Yvonne Shafir, 8–13. Cambridge, MA: MIT Press, 1993.

———."The Language of Flowers." In *Visions of Excess: Selected Writings, 1927–1939,* edited by Allan Stoekl, 10–14. Minneapolis: University of Minnesota Press, 1985.

Baumgarten, Marjorie, and Louis Black. "Ondine on Edie, on Warhol, on Ondine." *Austin Chronicle,* October 17, 2003. Accessed November 1, 2019. www.austinchronicle.com/screens/2003-10-17/182251.

Beck, Jessica. "Love on the Margins: A Case for Andy Warhol and Jon Gould." In *Contact Warhol: Photography without End,* edited by Peggy Phelan and Richard Meyer, 84–94. Cambridge, MA: MIT Press, 2018.

———. "Warhol's Confession: Love, Faith, and AIDS." In *Andy Warhol: From A to B and Back Again,* edited by Donna De Salvo, 84–94. New Haven, CT: Yale University Press, 2018.

Benjamin, Walter. "Doctrine of the Similar." Translated by Michael Jennings. In *Walter Benjamin: Selected Writings,* 4 vols., edited by Michael W. Jennings, Howard Eiland, and Gary Smith, 2: 694–98. Cambridge, MA: Harvard University Press, 2004–2006.

———. "One-Way Street." Translated by Edmund Jephcott. In *Walter Benjamin: Selected Writings,* 4 vols., edited by Michael W. Jennings, Howard Eiland, and Gary Smith, 1: 444–88. Cambridge, MA: Harvard University Press, 2004–2006.

Bennett, Jane. *Vibrant Matter: A Political Ecology of Things.* Durham, NC: Duke University Press, 2010.

Bersani, Leo. *Homos.* Cambridge, MA: Harvard University Press, 1995.

———. "Is the Rectum a Grave." In *Is the Rectum a Grave and Other Essays,* 3–30. Chicago: University of Chicago Press, 2010.

Birke, Lynda I.A. "Is Homosexuality Hormonally Determined?" *Journal of Homosexuality* 6, no. 4 (1981): 35–49.

Black, Louis. "On Ondine on Film: The Pope and the Artist, the Hotel and the Factory." *Austin Chronicle,* October 17, 2003. Accessed November 1, 2019. www.austinchronicle.com/screens/2003-10-17/182197.

Bockris, Victor. "Dinner with Andy and Bill." In *I'll Be Your Mirror: The Selected Andy Warhol Interviews: 1962-1987,* edited by Kenneth Goldsmith, 277–89. New York: Carroll & Graf, 2004.

———. *Warhol: The Biography.* New York: Da Capo, 2003.

Boisseron, Bénédicte. *Afro-Dog: Blackness and the Animal Question.* New York: Columbia University Press, 2018.

Brabant, Eva, Ernst Falzeder, and Patrizia Giampieri-Deutsch, eds. *The Correspondence of Sigmund Freud and Sándor Ferenczi.* Vol. 1, *1908–1914.* Translated by Peter T. Hoffer. Cambridge, MA: Belknap Press, 1993.

Braidotti, Rosi. *The Posthuman.* Cambridge: Polity, 2013.

Braverman, Irus. *Zooland: The Institution of Captivity.* Stanford, CA: Stanford Law Books, 2013.

Brinkema, Eugenia. *The Forms of the Affects.* Durham, NC: Duke University Press, 2014.

———. "Laura Dern's Vomit, or, Kant and Derrida in Oz." *Film-Philosophy* 15, no. 2 (2011): 56–60.

Broglio, Ron. *Beasts of Burden: Biopolitics, Labor, and Animal Life in British Romanticism.* Albany, NY: SUNY Press, 2017.

———. *Surface Encounters: Thinking with Animals and Art.* Minneapolis: University of Minnesota Press, 2011.

Bryan-Wilson, Julia. "Simone Forti Goes to the Zoo." *October*, no. 152 (2015): 26–52.

Buchloh, Benjamin H.D. "Andy Warhol's One-Dimensional Art: 1956–1966." In *October Files: Andy Warhol*, edited by Annette Michelson, 1-46. Cambridge, MA: MIT Press, 2001.

Butler, Judith. *Bodies That Matter: On the Discursive Limits of "Sex."* New York: Routledge, 1993.

———. *Gender Trouble: Feminism and the Subversion of Identity.* New York: Routledge, 2006.

———. "Political Philosophy in Freud: The Death Drive and the Critical Faculty." In *On Psychoanalysis and Violence: Contemporary Lacanian Perspectives*, edited by Vanessa Sinclair and Manya Steinkoler, 21–32. New York: Routledge, 2019.

Caballero-Mendieta, Nubia, and Carlos Cordero. "Enigmatic Liaisons in Lepidoptera: A Review of Same-Sex Courtship and Copulation in Butterflies and Moths." *Journal of Insect Science* 12, no. 1 (2012): 1–11.

Cadava, Eduardo, Peter Connor, and Jean-Luc Nancy, eds. *Who Comes after the Subject?* New York: Routledge, 1991.

Carroll, Paul. "What's a Warhol?" *Playboy* 16, no. 9 (September 1969): 132–34, 140, 278–82.

Castricano, Jodey, and Lauren Corman, eds. *Animal Subjects 2.0.* Waterloo, ON: Wilfred Laurier University Press, 2016.

Cavell, Stanley, Cora Diamond, John McDowell, Ian Hacking, and Cary Wolfe, eds. *Philosophy and Animal Life.* New York: Columbia University Press, 2008.

Chauncey, George. *Gay New York: Gender, Culture, and the Making of the Gay Male World, 1890–1940.* New York: Basic Books, 1994.

Cheng, Joyce. "Mask, Mimicry, Metamorphosis: Roger Caillois, Walter Benjamin and Surrealism in the 1930s," *Modernism/Modernity* 16, no. 1 (January 2009): 61–86.

Christy, Cuthbert. "Supposed Horn-Sheaths of an Okapi." *Nature* 95, no. 2378 (May 27, 1915): 342–43.

Chrulew, Matthew, and Rick De Vos. "Extinction." In *The Edinburgh Companion to Animal Studies*, edited by Lynn Turner, Undine Sellbach, and Ron Broglio, 181–97. Edinburgh: Edinburgh University Press, 2018.

Chrulew, Matthew, and Dinesh Joseph Wadiwel, eds. *Foucault and Animals.* Leiden: Brill, 2017.

Chung, Ezra M.C., Scott N. Dean, Crystal N. Propst, Barney M. Bishop, and Monique L. van Hoek. "Komodo Dragon-Inspired Synthetic Peptide DRGN-1 Promotes Wound-Healing of a Mixed-Biofilm Infected Wound." *npj Biofilms Microbiomes* 3, no. 9 (2017). Accessed November 15, 2019. https://doi.org/10.1038/s41522-017-0017-2.

Cohen, Scott. "Andy Warhol Talks about Sex, Art, Fame and Money." *Forum: The International Journal of Human Relations*, January 1981, 19–23.

Colacello, Bob. *Holy Terror: Andy Warhol Close Up.* New York: HarperCollins, 1990.

Colebrook, Claire. "How Queer Can You Go? Theory, Normality and Normativity." In *Queering the Non/Human*, edited by Noreen Giffney and Myra Hird, 17–34. Burlington, VT: Ashgate, 2008.

———. *Sex After Life.* Vol. 2 of *Essays on Extinction.* Ann Arbor, MI: Open Humanities Press, 2015.

Colling, Sarat. *Animal Resistance in the Global Capitalist Era.* East Lansing: Michigan State University Press, 2021.

Comenas, Gary. "Andy Warhol: From Nowhere to Up There; An Oral History of Andy Warhol's Early Years." Accessed November 1, 2019. https://warholstars.org/nowhere/andy_warhol_pages.html.

———. "Andy Warhol, Michael McClure and The Beard." Accessed November 1, 2019. https://warholstars.org/michael_mcclure_beard.html.

———. "Andy Warhol Pre-Pop," accessed November 11, 2020, https://warholstars.org/warhol1/4imperfection.html.

Copetas, Craig. "Beat Godfather Meets Glitter Mainman." *Rolling Stone*, February 28, 1974, 25–27.

Coplans, John. *Warhol.* New York: New York Graphic Society, 1970.

Corman, Lauren. "The Ventriloquist's Burden: Animal Advocacy and the Problem of Speaking for Others." In *Animal Subjects 2.0*, edited by Jodey Castricano and Lauren Corman, 473–512. Waterloo, ON: Wilfred Laurier University Press, 2016.

Cox, Christoph. "Thinking like a Plant: Prolegomena to a Philosophy of Vegetables." *Cabinet*, no. 6 (Spring 2002). Accessed November 15, 2020. https://www.cabinetmagazine.org/issues/6/cox.php.

Crandall, Jordan. "Andy Warhol." In *I'll Be Your Mirror: The Selected Andy Warhol Interviews, 1962–1987*, edited by Goldsmith, Kenneth, 348–81. New York: Carroll & Graf, 2004.

Crimp, Douglas. *"Our Kind of Movie": The Films of Andy Warhol*. Cambridge, MA: MIT Press, 2014.

Cronin, Keri. *Art for Animals: Visual Culture and Animal Advocacy*. University Park: Pennsylvania University Press, 2018.

Curran, Ann. "CMU's Other Andy." *Carnegie-Mellon Magazine*, Spring 1985, 16–17.

Danto, Arthur. *Andy Warhol*. New Haven, CT: Yale University Press, 2010.

Davies, Jon. *Trash: A Queer Film Classic*. Vancouver, BC: Arsenal Pulp Press, 2009.

Davis, Mike. *The Monster at Our Door: The Global Threat of Avian Flu*. New York: New Press, 2005.

Davis, Whitney. *Queer Beauty: Sexuality and Aesthetics from Winckelmann to Freud and Beyond*. New York: Columbia University Press, 2010.

———. "Queer Family Romance in Collecting Visual Culture." *GLQ: A Journal of Lesbian and Gay Studies* 17, nos. 2–3 (2011): 309–29.

de Castro, Eduardo Viveiros. *Cannibal Metaphysics*. Translated by Peter Skafish. Minneapolis: Univocal, 2014.

De Salvo, Donna, ed. *Andy Warhol: From A to B and Back Again*. New Haven, CT: Yale University Press, 2018.

———, ed. *Success Is a Job in New York: The Early Art and Business of Andy Warhol*. Pittsburgh: Carnegie Museum of Art, 1989.

de Villiers, Nicholas. *Opacity and the Closet: Queer Tactics in Foucault, Barthes, and Warhol*. Minneapolis: University of Minnesota Press, 2012.

Dean, Tim. *Unlimited Intimacy: Reflections on the Subculture of Barebacking*. Chicago: University of Chicago Press, 2009.

Delany, Max, and Eric C. Shiner, eds., *Andy Warhol | Ai Weiwei*. New Haven, CT: Yale University Press, 2016.

Deleuze, Gilles. *Coldness and Cruelty*. Translated by Jean McNeil. New York: Zone Books, 1991.

———. *The Logic of Sense*. Edited by Constantin V. Boundas. Translated by Mark Lester with Charles Stivale. Rev. ed. New York: Columbia University Press, 1990.

———. "Postscript on Control Societies." In *Negotiations, 1972–1990*, trans. Martin Joughin, 177–82. Rev. ed. New York: Columbia University Press, 1997.

Deleuze, Gilles, and Félix Guattari. *A Thousand Plateaus: Capitalism and Schizophrenia*. Translated by Brian Massumi. Minneapolis: University of Minnesota Press, 1987.

DeRosa, Terry, Fran Lyon, and Ann Petric, eds. *Husbandry Guidelines for the Okapi SSP*. Chicago: Chicago Zoological Society Brookfield Zoo, 2004.

Derrida, Jacques. *Acts of Religion*. Edited by Gil Anidjar. New York: Routledge, 2002.

———. *The Animal That Therefore I Am*. Edited by Marie-Louise Mallet. Translated by David Wills. New York: Fordham University Press, 2008.

———. *Aporias*. Translated by Thomas Dutoit. Stanford, CA: Stanford University Press, 1993.

———. *The Beast and the Sovereign*. 2 vols. Translated by Geoffrey Bennington. Chicago and London: University of Chicago Press, 2009, 2011.

———. "Economimesis." Translated by R. Klein. *Diacritics* 11, no. 2 (Summer 1981): 2–25.

Desmond, Jane C. *Displaying Death and Animating Life: Human-Animal Relations in Art, Science, and Everyday Life*. Chicago: University of Chicago Press, 2016.

Despret, Vinciane. *What Would Animals Say If We Asked the Right Questions*. Translated by Brett Buchanan. Minneapolis: University of Minnesota Press, 2016.

Di Chiro, Giovanna. "Polluted Politics?: Confronting Toxic Discourse, Sex Panic, and Eco-Normativity." In *Queer Ecologies: Sex, Nature, Politics, Desire*, edited by Catriona Mortimer-Sandilands and Bruce Erickson, 199–230. Bloomington: Indiana University Press, 2010.

Dixon, Laurinda S. "Some Penetrating Insights: The Imagery of Enemas in Art." *Art Journal* 52, no. 3 (Fall 1993): 28–35.

Dombek, Kristin. *The Selfishness of Others: An Essay on the Fear of Narcissism.* New York: Farrar, Straus, and Giroux, 2016.

Dooren, Thom Van. *Flight Ways: Life and Death at the Edge of Extinction.* New York: Columbia University Press, 2014.

Doyle, Jennifer, Jonathan Flatley, and José Esteban Muñoz, eds. *Pop Out: Queer Warhol.* Durham, NC: Duke University Press Books, 1996.

Doyle, Richard, *Darwin's Pharmacy: Sex, Plants, and the Evolution of the Noösphere.* Seattle: University of Washington Press, 2011.

Driscoll, Emily V. "Bisexual Species." *Scientific American Mind* 19, no. 3 (June/July 2008): 68–73.

Drohojowska-Philp, Hunter. "A Chelsea Girl Still Bewitched by Warhol." *Los Angeles Times,* August 11, 2002. Accessed November 15, 2020. www.latimes.com/archives/la-xpm-2002-aug-11-ca-hunter11-story.html.

Edelman, Lee. *No Future: Queer Theory and the Death Drive.* Durham, NC: Duke University Press, 2004.

Eng, David L. *Racial Castration: Managing Masculinity in Asian America.* Durham, NC: Duke University Press, 2001.

Evans, Jo. "Luis Buñuel's Missing Dog and Other Animals: *Un Chien andalou* (1929), *L'Âge d'or* (1930) and *Las Hurdes: Tierra sin pan* (1933)." *Bulletin of Spanish Visual Studies* 1, no. 1 (2017): 117–37.

Evans, Thomas Morgan. *3D Warhol: Andy Warhol and Sculpture.* London: I.B. Tauris, 2017.

Fanon, Frantz. *Black Skin, White Masks.* Translated by Charles Lam Markmann. London: Pluto, 2008.

Faria, Nuno R., Andrew Rambaut, Marc A. Suchard, Guy Baele, Trevor Bedford, Melissa J. Ward, Andrew J. Tatem, et al. "The Early Spread and Epidemic Ignition of HIV-1 in Human Populations." *Science* 346, no. 6205 (2014): 56–61.

Faustosterling, Anne. *Sexing the Body: Gender Politics and the Construction of Sexuality.* New York: Basic Books, 2000.

Ferenczi, Sándor. "Embarrassed Hands." Translated by John Rickman. In *Further Contributions to the Theory and Technique of Psycho-Analysis,* 315–16. London: Karnac Books, 2002.

Flatley, Jonathan. *Like Andy Warhol.* Chicago: University of Chicago Press, 2017.

———. "Like: Collecting and Collectivity." *October,* no. 132 (2010): 71–98.

Fong, Benjamin. *Death and Mastery: Psychoanalytic Drive Theory and the Subject of Late Capitalism.* New York: Columbia University Press, 2016.

Foster, Hal. "Andy Warhol, or the Distressed Image." In *The First Pop Age,* 120–46. Princeton, NJ: Princeton University Press, 2012.

———. "I Am the Decider." *London Review of Books* 33, no. 6 (March 17, 2011): 31–32. Accessed November 15, 2019. https://www.lrb.co.uk/the-paper/v33/n06/hal-foster/i-am-the-decider.

Foucault, Michel. *Abnormal: Lectures at the Collège de France, 1974–1975.* Translated by Graham Burchell. New York: Picador, 2003.

———. *Essential Works of Foucault: Aesthetics: Method and Epistemology.* Edited by James D. Faubion. New York: New Press, 1998.

———. *Essential Works of Foucault: Ethics: Subjectivity and Truth.* Edited by Paul Rabinow. New York: New Press, 1997.

———. *Security, Territory, Population: Lectures at the Collège de France, 1977–78.* Edited by Michel Senellart. New York: Palgrave Macmillan, 2009.

———. *This Is Not a Pipe.* Translated by James Harkness. Berkeley: University of California Press, 1983.

Fraser, Kennedy. "As Gorgeous As It Gets." *New Yorker,* September 15, 1986, 42–77.

Freeman, Elizabeth. *Time Binds: Queer Temporalities, Queer Histories.* Durham, NC: Duke University Press, 2010.

Frei, Georg, and Neil Printz, eds. *The Andy Warhol Catalogue Raisonné*. Vol. 1, *Paintings and Sculpture, 1961–1963*. New York: Phaidon, 2002.

———. *The Andy Warhol Catalogue Raisonné*. Vol. 2, *Paintings and Sculpture, 1964–1969*. New York: Phaidon, 2004.

Freud, Sigmund. *Civilization and Its Discontents*. Translated by James Strachey. New York: Norton, 1962.

———. "The Excretory Functions in Psychoanalysis and Folklore." In *Character and Culture*, edited by Philip Rieff. New York: Collier Books, 1963.

———. *The Interpretation of Dreams*. Translated by James Strachey. New York: Basic Books, 2010.

———. "Leonardo da Vinci and a Memory of His Childhood." In *The Standard Edition of the Complete Psychological Works of Sigmund Freud*, edited and translated by James Strachey et al., 11: 63–137. London: Hogarth Press, 1954–73.

———. "Notes upon a Case of Obsessional Neurosis." In *The Standard Edition of the Complete Psychological Works of Sigmund Freud*, edited and translated by James Strachey et al., 10: 151–318. London: Hogarth Press, 1954–73.

———. *Three Essays on the Theory of Sexuality*. Translated by James Strachey. New York: Basic Books, 2000.

———. *Totem and Taboo: Some Points of Agreement between the Mental Lives of Savages and Neurotics*. Translated by James Strachey. London: Routledge, 2001.

Gagliano, Monica, John C. Ryan, and Patrícia Vieira, eds. *The Language of Plants: Science, Philosophy, Literature*. Minneapolis: University of Minnesota Press, 2017.

Gatti, Attilio. "A Strange Beast, the Okapi." *New York Times Magazine*, August 8, 1937, 11, 17. Accessed November 20, 2020. https://timesmachine.nytimes.com/timesmachine/1937/08/08/118984772.html?pageNumber = 113.

Gelmis, Joseph. "A Grotesque Prism." *Newsday*, May 6, 1977.

Gibson, Prudence. *The Plant Contract: Art's Return to Vegetal Life*. Leiden: Brill Rodopi, 2018.

Gijzen, Agatha. "Studbook of the Okapi." *Acta Zoologica et Pathologica Antverpiensia*, no. 68 (August 1977): 1–47.

Giovanni, Aloi. *Art and Animals*. London: I. B. Tauris, 2012.

Giuliano, Charles. "Gerard Malanga on Andy Warhol's Mother Julia: Insights to Mother and Son Collaborations at WCMA." Berkshire Fine Arts, June 4, 2015. Accessed November 1, 2019. https://www.berkshirefinearts.com/06-04-2015_gerard-malanga-on-andy-warhol-s-mother-julia.htm.

Goldberg, Jonathan. *Strangers on a Train: A Queer Film Classic*. Vancouver, BC: Arsenal Pulp Press, 2012.

Gopnik, Blake. *Warhol*. New York: HarperCollins, 2020.

Greene, Balcomb. "Basic Concepts for Teaching Art." *College Art Journal* 8, no. 1 (1948): 21–34.

Greven, David. *Intimate Violence: Hitchcock, Sex, and Queer Theory*. New York: Oxford University Press, 2017.

Grosz, Elizabeth. *Becoming Undone: Darwinian Reflections*. Durham, NC: Duke University Press, 2011.

Grover, Jan Zita. *North Enough: AIDS and Other Clear-Cuts*. Minneapolis: Graywolf Press, 1997.

Grudin, Anthony E. *Warhol's Working Class: Pop Art and Egalitarianism*. Chicago: University of Chicago Press, 2017.

Gruskin, George. "Who Is This Man, Andy Warhol?" In *I'll Be Your Mirror: The Selected Andy Warhol Interviews*, edited by Kenneth Goldsmith, 200–220. New York: Carroll & Graf, 2004.

Guibert, Hervé. *Ghost Image*. Translated by Robert Bononno. Chicago: University of Chicago Press, 1996.

———. *To the Friend Who Did Not Save My Life*. Translated by Linda Coverdale. New York: Atheneum, 1991.

———. *Written in Invisible Ink: Selected Stories*. Translated by Jeffrey Zuckerman. Los Angeles: Semiotext(e), 2020.

Hahn, Otto. "Passport No. G255300." *Art and Artists* 1, no. 4 (July 1966): 6–11.

Hainley, Bruce. "Urine Sample." In *Andy Warhol: Piss and Sex Paintings and Drawings*, 4–9. New York: Gagosian Gallery, 2002.

Halperin, David M., and Valerie Traub, eds. *Gay Shame*. Chicago: University of Chicago Press, 2010.

Hanhardt, Christina B. "Butterflies, Whistles, and Fists: Gay Safe Streets Patrols and the New Gay Ghetto, 1976–1981." *Radical History Review*, no. 100 (2008): 65–74.

Haraway, Donna. *Staying with the Trouble: Making Kin in the Chthulucene.* Durham, NC: Duke University Press, 2016.

———. *When Species Meet.* Minneapolis: University of Minnesota Press, 2008.

Haywood, Robert E. *Allan Kaprow and Claes Oldenburg: Art, Happenings, and Cultural Politics.* New Haven, CT: Yale University Press, 2017.

Heap, Chad. *Slumming: Sexual and Racial Encounters in American Nightlife.* Chicago: University of Chicago Press, 2009.

Hegel, G.W.F. *Aesthetics: Lectures on Fine Art.* Vol. 2. Translated by T.M. Knox London: Oxford University Press, 1975.

Hennefeld, Maggie, and Nicholas Sammond, "Not It, or, The Abject Objection." In *Abjection Incorporated: Mediating the Politics of Pleasure and Violence,* edited by Maggie Hennefeld and Nicholas Sammond, 1–31. Durham, NC: Duke University Press, 2020.

Hird, Myra J. "Naturally Queer." *Feminist Theory* 5, no. 1 (2004): 85–89.

Hite, Christian. "The Art of Suicide: Notes on Foucault and Warhol." *October,* no. 153 (2015): 65–95.

Hochschild, Adam. *King Leopold's Ghost: A Story of Greed, Terror, and Heroism in Colonial Africa.* New York: Houghton Mifflin, 1998.

Holland, Sharon Patricia. *The Erotic Life of Racism.* Durham, NC: Duke University Press, 2012.

Irigaray, Luce, and Michael Marder, eds. *Through Vegetal Being: Two Philosophical Perspectives.* New York: Columbia University Press, 2016.

Iveson, Richard. "Technology," in *The Edinburgh Companion to Animal Studies,* edited by Lynn Turner, Undine Sellbach, and Ron Broglio, 504–17. Edinburgh: Edinburgh University Press, 2018.

Johnson, Catherine. *Thank You Andy Warhol.* New York: Glitterati, 2012.

Jones, Caroline A. *Machine in the Studio: Constructing the Postwar American Artist.* Chicago: University of Chicago Press, 1998.

Joseph, Branden W. "1962." *October,* no. 132 (2010): 114–34.

———. "'My Mind Split Open': Andy Warhol's Exploding Plastic Inevitable." *Grey Room,* no. 8 (Summer 2002): 80–107.

Kamuf, Peggy. *Book of Addresses.* Stanford, CA: Stanford University Press, 2005.

Kant, Immanuel. *Critique of the Power of Judgment.* Translated by Paul Guyer and Eric Matthews. New York: Cambridge University Press, 2001.

Kawasaki, Ryuta, and Tatsuhiro Suginaka. "Changes in the Milk Composition of Okapi (*Okapia Johnstoni*) during the First 6 Months of Lactation." *Animal Science Journal* 83, no. 4 (April 2012): 344–49.

Kelley, Mike. "Death and Transfiguration." In *Foul Perfection: Essays and Criticism,* edited by John C. Welchman, 138–49. Cambridge, MA: MIT Press, 2003.

Kent, Leticia. "Andy Warhol: 'I Thought Everyone Was Kidding.'" *Village Voice* 13, no. 48 (September 12, 1968): 1, 37–38.

King, Homay. "Girl Interrupted: The Queer Time of Warhol's Cinema." *Discourse* 28, no. 1 (2006): 98–120.

———. "Stroboscopic: Warhol and the Exploding Plastic Inevitable." *Criticism* 56, no. 3 (Summer 2014): 457–79.

Klein, Melanie. "The Importance of Symbol-Formation in the Development of the Ego." In *Love, Guilt, and Reparation and Other Works, 1921–1945,* vol. 1 of *The Writings of Melanie Klein,* 219–32. New York: Free Press, 1984.

———. *The Psychoanalysis of Children.* Translated by Alix Strachey. New York: Grove Press, 1960.

Koch, Stephen. *Stargazer: The Life, World and Films of Andy Warhol.* London: Marion Boyars, 2000.

Koestenbaum, Wayne. *Andy Warhol: A Biography.* New York: Open Road, 2001.

Kristeva, Julia. *Hatred and Forgiveness.* Translated by Jeanine Herman. New York: Columbia University Press, 2012.

———."Motherhood Today." Accessed July 15, 2019. http://www.kristeva.fr/motherhood.html.

———. *Powers of Horror: An Essay on Abjection.* Translated by Leon S. Roudiez. New York: Columbia University Press, 1982.

———. *Revolution in Poetic Language.* Translated by Margaret Waller. New York: Columbia University Press, 1984.

———. *The Severed Head: Capital Visions.* Translated by Jody Gladding. New York: Columbia University Press, 2012.

Kuzniar, Alice. "'I Married My Dog': On Queer Canine Literature." In *Queering the Non/Human,* edited by Noreen Giffney and Myra Hird, 205–26. Hampshire, UK: Ashgate, 2008.

Laing, Olivia. "A La La La: An Andy Warhol Alphabet." In *Andy Warhol,* ed. Gregor Muir and Yilmaz Dziewior, 20–25. London: Tate Publishing, 2020.

Lange-Berndt, Petra. *Animal Art: Präparierte Tiere in der Kunst, 1850–2000.* Munich: Verlag Silke Schreiber, 2009.

Lawlor, Leonard. *This Is Not Sufficient: An Essay on Animality and Human Nature in Derrida.* New York: Columbia University Press, 2007.

Lawrence, Michael, and Karen Lury, eds. *The Zoo: Images of Exhibition and Encounter.* New York: Palgrave Macmillan, 2015.

Lemm, Vanessa. *Nietzsche's Animal Philosophy: Culture, Politics, and the Animality of the Human Being.* New York: Fordham University Press, 2009.

Leonard, John. "The Return of Andy Warhol." *New York Times,* November 10, 1968.

Letko, Michael, Stephanie N. Seifert, Kevin J. Olival, Raina K. Plowright, and Vincent J. Munster. "Bat-Borne Virus Diversity, Spillover and Emergence." *Nature Reviews Microbiology,* 18, no. 8 (August 2020): 461–71. https://doi.org/10.1038/s41579-020-0394-z.

Ligon, Glenn. "Pay It No Mind." In *Andy Warhol: A to B and Back Again,* ed. Donna De Salvo, 60–65. New Haven, CT: Yale University Press.

Lindsey, S.L., C.L. Bennett, J.J. Fried, and J.K. Prichard. "Functional Analysis of Infrasound in the Okapi (Okapia Johnstoni): Mother–Infant Communication." *American Association of Zoological Parks and Aquariums Annual Conference Proceedings* 1993, 299–305.

Lipschitz, Ruth. "Skin/Ned Politics: Species Discourse and the Limits of 'The Human' in Nandipha Mntambo's Art." *Hypatia* 27, no. 3 (2012): 546–56.

Lunbeck, Elizabeth. *The Americanization of Narcissism.* Cambridge, MA: Harvard University Press, 2014.

Lundblad, Michael. *The Birth of a Jungle: Animality in Progressive-Era U.S. Literature and Culture.* New York: Oxford University Press, 2013.

Lupton, Ellen, and J. Abbott Miller. "Line Art: Andy Warhol and the Commercial Art World of the 1950s." In "*Success Is a Job in New York . . .": The Early Art and Business of Andy Warhol,* edited by Donna De Salvo, 29–41. Pittsburgh: Carnegie Museum of Art, 1989.

Marchal, Jules. *Lord Leverhulme's Ghosts: Colonial Exploitation in the Congo.* Translated by Martin Thom. Brooklyn: Verso Books, 2017.

Marder, Elissa. *The Mother in the Age of Mechanical Reproduction: Psychoanalysis, Photography, Deconstruction.* New York: Fordham University Press, 2012.

Marder, Michael. *Grafts: Writings on Plants.* Minneapolis: Univocal, 2016.

———. *Plant-Thinking: A Philosophy of Vegetal Life.* New York: Columbia University Press, 2013.

———. "Seeking Refuge in the Vegetal World." In *Through Vegetal Being: Two Philosophical Perspectives,* edited by Luce Irigaray and Michael Marder, 117–21. New York: Columbia University Press, 2018.

Marx, Karl. *Capital: A Critique of Political Economy.* Vol. 1. Translated by Ben Fowkes. New York: Penguin Books, 1982.

Maté, Gabor. *In the Realm of Hungry Ghosts: Close Encounters with Addiction.* Berkeley, CA: North Atlantic Books, 2010.

Mbembe, Achille. *Necropolitics.* Translated by Steven Corcoran. Durham, NC: Duke University Press, 2019.

McCance, Dawne. *The Reproduction of Life Death: Derrida's La vie la mort.* New York: Fordham University Press, 2019.

McClure, Michael Jay. "I Made It through the Wilderness." In *Warhol's Nature,* edited by Linda DeBerry, 16–23. New York: Scala Arts Publishers, 2015.

McFarlane, Craig. "*Apum Ordines*: Of Bees and Government." In *Foucault and Animals,* edited by Matthew Chrulew and Dinesh Joseph Wadiwel, 263–85. Leiden: Brill, 2017.

Meeker, Martin. *Contacts Desired: Gay and Lesbian Communications and Community, 1940s–1970s.* Chicago: University of Chicago Press, 2006.

Meijer, Eva. *When Animals Speak: Toward an Interspecies Democracy.* New York: NYU Press, 2019.

Merchant, Carolyn. *Spare the Birds! George Bird Grinnell and the First Audubon Society.* New Haven, CT: Yale University Press, 2016.

Meyer, Richard. *Outlaw Representation: Censorship and Homosexuality in Twentieth-Century American Art.* Oxford: Oxford University Press, 2002.

———. "Warhol's Clones." *Yale Journal of Criticism* 7, no. 1 (1994): 79–109.

Mieli, Mario. *Homosexuality and Liberation.* London: London Gay Male's Press, 1980.

Miller, Elaine P. *Head Cases: Julia Kristeva on Philosophy and Art in Depressed Times.* New York: Columbia University Press, 2014.

———. *The Vegetative Soul: From Philosophy of Nature to Subjectivity in the Feminine.* New York: SUNY Press, 2002.

Millett, Kate. *The Basement: Meditations on a Human Sacrifice.* New York: Simon & Schuster, 1979.

Moon, Michael. *A Small Boy and Others: Imitation and Initiation in American Culture from Henry James to Andy Warhol.* Durham, NC: Duke University Press, 1998.

Morphy, Howard, ed. *Animals Into Art.* London: Routledge, 2016.

Morrison, Toni. *Sula.* New York: Vintage, 2004.

Mortimer-Sandilands, Catriona, and Bruce Erickson. "Introduction: A Genealogy of Queer Ecologies." In *Queer Ecologies: Sex, Nature, Politics, Desire,* edited by Catriona Mortimer-Sandilands and Bruce Erickson, 1–50. Bloomington: Indiana University Press, 2010.

Morton, Timothy. *Humankind: Solidarity with Nonhuman People.* New York: Verso, 2017.

Mulroney, Lucy. *Andy Warhol, Publisher.* Chicago: University of Chicago Press, 2018.

Muñoz, José Esteban. "A Jeté Out the Window: Fred Herko's Brilliant Illumination." In *Cruising Utopia: The Then and There of Queer Futurity,* 147–67. New York: NYU Press, 2009.

Murphy, J.J. *The Black Hole of the Camera: The Films of Andy Warhol.* Berkeley: University of California Press, 2012.

Nancy, Jean-Luc. "'Eating Well,' or the Calculation of the Subject: An Interview with Derrida." In *Who Comes after the Subject?,* edited by Eduardo Cadava, Peter Connor, and Jean-Luc Nancy, 96–119. New York: Routledge, 1991.

Nealon, Jeffrey T. "The Archaeology of Biopower: From Plant to Animal Life in *The Order of Things.*" In *Biopower: Foucault and Beyond,* edited by Vernon W. Cisney and Nicolae Morar, 138–57. Chicago: University of Chicago Press, 2016.

———. *Plant Theory: Biopower & Vegetable Life.* Stanford, CA: Stanford University Press, 2016.

Nettleton, Taro. "White-on-White: The Overbearing Whiteness of Warhol Being." In *Gay Shame,* edited by David M. Halperin and Valerie Traub, 76–87. Chicago: University of Chicago Press, 2010.

Newlove, Donald. "Prothalamion for Wet Harmonica and Johnny Stompanato." *The Realist,* no. 68 (August 1966): 1, 17–23.

Nietzsche, Friedrich. *Unpublished Writings from the Period of Unfashionable Observations.* Translated by Richard T. Gray. Stanford, CA: Stanford University Press, 1995.

Nordau, Max. *Degeneration.* New York: Appleton, 1895.

Norris, Margot. *Beasts of Modern Imagination: Darwin, Nietzsche, Kafka, Ernst, and Lawrence.* Baltimore: Johns Hopkins University Press, 1985.

Nussbaum, Martha C. *Hiding from Humanity: Disgust, Shame, and the Law.* Princeton, NJ: Princeton University Press, 2004.

[O'Brien, Glenn]. "Factory Workers Warholites Remember: Billy Name." *Interview,* November 30, 2008. Accessed November 1, 2019. http://www.interviewmagazine.com/culture/factory-workers-warholites-remember-billy-name/.

O'Brien, Glenn. "Interview: Andy Warhol." In *I'll Be Your Mirror: The Selected Andy Warhol Interviews, 1962–1987,* edited by Goldsmith, Kenneth, 233–64. New York: Carroll & Graf, 2004.

[O'Brien, Glenn]. Introduction to *Billy Name: The Silver Age,* xv–xxii. London: Reel Art Press, 2014.

Oliver, Kelly. *Animal Lessons: How They Teach Us to Be Human.* New York: Columbia University Press, 2009.

———. *Reading Kristeva: Unraveling the Double-Bind.* Bloomington: Indiana University Press, 1993.

Osterweil, Ara. "The Last Word: Dorothy Dean and Black Fugitivity in Andy Warhol's *My Hustler.*" *Art Journal* 78, no. 4 (2019): 58–75.

Palmer, Clare. "'Taming the Wild Profusion of Existing Things'? A Study of Foucault, Power, and Human/Animal Relationships." In *Foucault and Animals,* edited by Matthew Chrulew and Dinesh Joseph Wadiwel, 105–131. Leiden: Brill, 2017.

Pérez, Hiram. *A Taste for Brown Bodies: Gay Modernity and Cosmopolitan Desire.* New York: NYU Press, 2015.

Pettman, Dominic. "Affection." In *The Edinburgh Companion to Animal Studies,* edited by Lynn Turner, Undine Sellbach, and Ron Broglio, 30–41. Edinburgh: Edinburgh University Press, 2018.

———. *Creaturely Love: How Desire Makes Us More and Less Than Human.* Minneapolis: University of Minnesota Press, 2017.

Pfeiffer, Ernst, ed. *Sigmund Freud and Lou Andreas-Salomé: Letters.* Translated by William and Elaine Robson-Scott. New York: Harcourt Brace Jovanovich, 1972.

Phelan, Peggy, and Richard Meyer, eds. *Contact Warhol: Photography without End.* Cambridge, MA: MIT Press, 2018.

Poiani, Aldo. *Animal Homosexuality A Biosocial Perspective.* Cambridge: Cambridge University Press, 2010.

Porter, Charlie. "Andy Warhol through the Eyes of Bob Colacello." In *Andy Warhol,* edited by Gregor Muir and Yilmaz Dziewior, 64–69. London: Tate Publishing, 2020.

Preciado, Beatriz. *Testo Junkie: Sex, Drugs, and Biopolitics in the Pharmacopornographic Era.* Translated by Bruce Benderson. New York: Feminist Press, 2013.

Printz, Neil, and Sally King-Nero. *The Andy Warhol Catalogue Raisonné.* Vol. 3, *Paintings and Sculpture, 1970–1974.* New York: Phaidon, 2010.

———. *The Andy Warhol Catalogue Raisonné.* Vol. 4, *Paintings and Sculpture, 1976–1987.* New York: Phaidon, 2014.

Quammen, David. *Spillover: Animal Infections and the Next Human Pandemic.* New York: Norton, 2012.

Reineke, Martha J. *Intimate Domain: Desire, Trauma, and Mimetic Theory.* East Lansing: Michigan State University Press, 2014.

Rensenbrink, Greta. "Parthenogenesis and Lesbian Separatism: Regenerating Women's Community through Virgin Birth in the United States in the 1970s and 1980s." *Journal of the History of Sexuality* 19, no. 2 (2010): 288–316.

Richardson, John. "The Secret Warhol: At Home with the Silver Shadow." *Vanity Fair,* July 1987, 66–74, 124–27.

Rome, Adam. *The Bulldozer in the Countryside: Suburban Sprawl and the Rise of American Environmentalism.* Cambridge: Cambridge University Press, 2008.

Rosenberg, Gabriel. "How Meat Changed Sex: The Law of Interspecies Intimacy after Industrial Reproduction." *GLQ: A Journal of Lesbian and Gay Studies* 23, no. 4 (October 2017): 473–507.

Rosenow, Michael K. *Death and Dying in the Working Class, 1865–1920.* Urbana: University of Illinois Press, 2015.

Roughgarden, Joan. *Evolution's Rainbow: Diversity, Gender, and Sexuality in Nature and People.* Berkeley: University of California Press, 2004.

Rusinko, Elaine. "The Woman Behind the Artist: Andy Warhol's Mother." *Slovo* (Summer 2016): 26–31.
Sade, Marquis de. *The Complete Justine Philosophy in the Bedroom & Other Writings.* Translated by Richard Seaver and Austryn Wainhouse. New York: Grove Press, 1965.
Salius, Erin Michael. *Sacraments of Memory: Catholicism and Slavery in Contemporary African American Literature.* Gainesville: University Press of Florida, 2018.
Samorini, Giorgio. *Animals and Psychedelics: The Natural World and the Instinct to Alter Consciousness.* Translated by Tami Calliope. Rochester, VT: Park Street Press, 2002.
Sanchez, Michael. "Andy Warhol Inside Out." In *Andy Warhol—From A to B and Back Again,* edited by Donna De Salvo, 60–65. New Haven, CT: Yale University Press, 2018.
Scherman, Tony, and David Dalton. *Pop: The Genius of Andy Warhol.* New York: Harper, 2009.
Schmidt, Christopher. "From A to B and Back Again: Warhol, Recycling, Writing." *Interval(le)s* 2, no. 2; 3, no. 1 (Fall 2008/Winter 2008/9): 794–809.
Scott, Darieck. *Extravagant Abjection: Blackness, Power, and Sexuality in the African American Literary Imagination.* New York: NYU Press, 2010.
Sedgwick, Eve Kosofsky. "Queer and Now." In *Tendencies,* 1–8. London: Routledge, 1994.
———. "Queer Performativity: Warhol's Shyness/Warhol's Whiteness." In *Pop Out: Queer Warhol,* edited by Jennifer Doyle, Jonathan Flatley, and José Esteban Muñoz, 134–43. Durham, NC: Duke University Press, 1996.
Sepkoski, David. *Catastrophic Thinking: Extinction and the Value of Diversity from Darwin to the Anthropocene.* Chicago: University of Chicago Press, 2020.
Shell, Marc. "The Family Pet." *Representations,* no. 15 (Summer 1986): 121–53.
Shildrick, Margrit. *Embodying the Monster: Encounters with the Vulnerable Self.* Thousand Oaks, CA: Sage, 2002.
Shukin, Nicole. *Animal Capital: Rendering Life in Biopolitical Times.* Minneapolis: University of Minnesota Press, 2009.
———. "Capitalism." In *The Edinburgh Companion to Animal Studies,* edited by Lynn Turner, Undine Sellbach, and Ron Broglio, 94–114. Edinburgh: Edinburgh University Press, 2018.
Sichel, Jennifer, ed. "'What Is Pop Art?': A Revised Transcript of Gene Swenson's 1963 Interview with Andy Warhol." *Oxford Art Journal* 41, no. 1 (March 2018): 85–100.
Siegel, Ronald K. *Intoxication: The Universal Drive for Mind-Altering Substances.* Rochester, VT: Park Street Press, 2005.
Skeggs, Beverley. *Class, Self, Culture.* New York: Routledge, 2004.
Smith, Patrick S. *Andy Warhol's Art and Films.* Ann Arbor, MI: UMI Research Press, 1986.
———. *Warhol: Conversations about the Artist.* Ann Arbor, MI: UMI Research Press, 1988.
Sommer, Volker, and Paul L. Vasey. "Homosexual Behavior in Animals: Topics, Hypotheses, and Research Trajectories." In *Homosexual Behavior in Animals: An Evolutionary Perspective,* edited by Volker Sommer and Paul L. Vasey, 3–44. Cambridge: Cambridge University Press, 2006.
Soreanu, Raluca. "Speaking of Leonardo Da Vinci's Mother: A Critique of Freud's Notion of Identification." *Studies in the Maternal* 10, no. 1 (August 2018): 1–22.
Stadler, Gustavus. "'My Wife': The Tape Recorder and Warhol's Queer Ways of Listening." *Criticism* 56, no. 3 (Summer 2014): 425–56.
Stein, Jean. *Edie: American Girl.* Edited with George Plimpton. New York: Grove Press, 1994.
Stockton, Kathryn Bond. *Beautiful Bottom, Beautiful Shame: Where "Black" Meets "Queer.* Durham, NC: Duke University Press, 2006.
———. *The Queer Child, or Growing Sideways in the Twentieth Century.* Durham, NC: Duke University Press, 2009.
Stoller, Robert J. *Sex and Gender: The Development of Masculinity and Femininity.* London: Karnac Books, 1984.
Suárez, Juan A. *Bike Boys, Drag Queens, and Superstars: Avant-Garde, Mass Culture, and Gay Identities in the 1960s Underground Cinema.* Bloomington and Indianapolis: Indiana University Press, 1996.

———. "Warhol's 1960s' Films, Amphetamine, and Queer Materiality." *Criticism* 56, no. 3 (Summer 2014): 623–52.

Sutton, Elizabeth. *Art, Animals, and Experience: Relationships to Canines and the Natural World.* New York: Routledge, 2017.

Tata, Michael Angelo. "Andy Warhol: When Junkies Ruled the World." *Nebula* 2, no. 2 (June 2005): 76–112.

Terry, Jennifer. "'Unnatural Acts' in Nature: The Scientific Fascination with Queer Animals." *GLQ: A Journal of Lesbian and Gay Studies* 6, no. 2 (2000): 151–93.

Timofeeva, Oxana. *The History of Animals: A Philosophy.* New York: Bloomsbury Academic, 2018.

Tomkins, Calvin. *The Scene: Reports on Post-Modern Art.* New York: Viking Press, 1976.

Tyler, Imogen. *Revolting Subjects: Social Abjection and Resistance in Neoliberal Britain.* New York: Zed Books, 2013.

Tyler, Parker. "Drugtime and Dragtime or, Film a la Warhol." *Evergreen Review* 11, no. 46 (1967): 28–31, 87–88.

Verevis, Constantine. *Flaming Creatures.* New York: Columbia University Press, 2020.

Vuong, Ocean. *On Earth We're Briefly Gorgeous.* New York: Penguin, 2019.

Wagner, Anne Middleton. "Andy Warhol's Patriotism." In *A House Divided,* 25–45. Berkeley: University of California Press, 2012.

Wanzo, Rebecca. "Precarious-Girl Comedy: Issa Rae, Lena Dunham, & Abjection Aesthetics." In *Abjection Incorporated: Mediating the Politics of Pleasure & Violence,* edited by Maggie Hennefeld and Nicholas Sammond, 64–85. Cambridge: Cambridge University Press, 2020.

Warburg, Aby M. *Images from the Region of the Pueblo Indians of North America.* Translated by Michael P. Steinberg. Ithaca, NY: Cornell University Press, 1995.

Warhol, Andy. *a: a novel.* New York: Grove Press, 1998.

———. *America.* New York: Harper & Row, 1985.

———. *The Andy Warhol Diaries.* Edited by Pat Hackett. New York: Warner Books, 1989.

———. *Andy Warhol's Exposures.* Edited by Bob Colacello. London: Arrow Books, 1980.

———. *The Philosophy of Andy Warhol (From A to B and Back Again).* New York: Harcourt Brace Jovanovich, 1975.

———. "Sunday with Mister C.: An Audio-Documentary by Andy Warhol Starring Truman Capote." *Rolling Stone,* no. 132 (1973): 28–54.

Warhol, Andy, and Kurt Benirschke. *Vanishing Animals.* New York: Springer-Verlag, 1986.

Warhol, Andy, and Pat Hackett. *Andy Warhol's Party Book.* New York: Crown, 1988.

———. *Popism: The Warhol Sixties.* New York: Mariner, 2006.

Watson, Steven. *Factory Made: Warhol and the Sixties.* New York: Pantheon, 2003.

Watts, Phillip C., Kevin R. Buley, Stephanie Sanderson, Wayne Boardman, Claudio Ciofi, and Richard Gibson. "Parthenogenesis in Komodo Dragons." *Nature* 444, no. 7122 (2006): 1021–22. doi:10.1038/4441021a.

Weathers, Chelsea. "Andy Warhol's Cinema beyond the Lens." PhD diss., University of Texas at Austin, 2013.

———. "Drugtime." *Criticism* 56, no. 3 (Summer 2014): 652–85.

Weber, Cynthia. *Faking It: U.S. Hegemony in a "Post-Phallic" Era.* Minneapolis: University of Minnesota Press, 1999.

Weineck, Silke-Maria. "Heteros Autos: Freud's Fatherhood." In *The Dreams of Interpretation: A Century down the Royal Road,* edited by Catherine Liu, John Mowitt, Thomas Pepper, and Jakki Spicer, 97–114. Minneapolis: University of Minnesota Press, 2007.

Weintraub, Linda. *To Life!: Eco Art in Pursuit of a Sustainable Planet.* Berkeley: University of California Press, 2012.

Wilcock, John. *The Autobiography and Sex Life of Andy Warhol.* New York: Other Scenes, 1971.

Wilson, William. "Warhol on L.A.: 'Everyone's Crazy.'" *Los Angeles Times,* May 11, 1970.

Winnicott, D.W. "A Case Managed at Home." In *Through Paediatrics to Psycho-Analysis: Collected Papers,* 118–26. London: Routledge, 2001.

———. "A Note on Normality and Anxiety." In *Through Paediatrics to Psycho-Analysis: Collected Papers*, 3–21. London: Routledge, 2001.

Wolf, Reva. *Andy Warhol, Poetry, and Gossip in the 1960s.* Chicago: University of Chicago Press, 1997.

Wolfe, Cary. *Animal Rites: American Culture, the Discourse of Species, and Posthumanist Theory.* Chicago: University of Chicago Press, 2003.

———. "Exposures." In *Philosophy and Animal Life*, edited by Stanley Cavell, Cora Diamond, John McDowell, Ian Hacking, and Cary Wolfe, 1–41. New York: Columbia University Press, 2008.

———. *What Is Posthumanism?* Minneapolis: University of Minnesota Press, 2010.

———, ed. *Zoontologies: The Question of the Animal.* Minneapolis: University of Minnesota Press, 2003.

Woodhouse, Keith Makoto. *The Ecocentrists: A History of Radical Environmentalism.* New York: Columbia University Press, 2018.

Woronov, Mary. *Eyewitness to Warhol.* Los Angeles: Victoria Dailey Publisher, 2002.

———. *Swimming Underground: My Years in the Warhol Factory.* London: Serpent's Tail Press, 1995.

Wrbican, Matt. *A Is for Archive: Warhol's World from A to Z.* New Haven, CT: Yale University Press, 2019.

———. "Meeooaaww-AW-AWW." In *Andy Warhol | Ai Weiwei*, edited by Max Delany and Eric C. Shiner, 256–85. New Haven, CT: Yale University Press, 2016. 262.

———. "A View from the Archives: Nature as Culture in Warhol's Art." In *Warhol's Nature*, edited by Linda DeBerry, 52–55. New York: Scala Arts Publishers, 2015.

Young, Iris Marion. "Abjection and Oppression: Dynamics of Unconscious Racism, Sexism, and Homophobia." In *Crises in Continental Philosophy*, edited by Arleen B. Dallery and Charles E. Scott, 201–13. Albany, NY: SUNY Press, 1990.

ILLUSTRATIONS

INDEX

Page numbers in italics refer to illustrations.

Founded in 1893,
UNIVERSITY OF CALIFORNIA PRESS
publishes bold, progressive books and journals on topics in the arts, humanities, social sciences, and natural sciences—with a focus on social justice issues—that inspire thought and action among readers worldwide.

The UC PRESS FOUNDATION
raises funds to uphold the press's vital role as an independent, nonprofit publisher, and receives philanthropic support from a wide range of individuals and institutions—and from committed readers like you. To learn more, visit ucpress.edu/supportus.